IN LOVE AND WAR

IN LOVE AND WAR

----

*The Story of a Family's Ordeal
and Sacrifice During the Vietnam Years*

Jim & Sybil Stockdale

HARPER & ROW, PUBLISHERS, New York
*Cambridge, Philadelphia, San Francisco, London
Mexico City, São Paulo, Singapore, Sydney*

1817

James B. Stockdale is a Senior Research Fellow at the Hoover Institution on War, Revolution and Peace, Stanford University.

Grateful acknowledgment is made for permission to reprint:

The editorial entitled "Hanoi and the American Prisoners" which appeared in *The Washington Post*, May 23, 1969. Copyright © 1969 by *The Washington Post*. Reprinted by permission of *The Washington Post*.

Excerpt from Jack Anderson's column on August 8, 1967, entitled "Disturbing Reports on U.S. Prisoners." Reprinted by permission of United Media Enterprises.

The article "POW Wife Vacationing Here, Thinks Nixon Will Bring Mate Home Soon" which appeared in the *New Haven Register* on July 25, 1972. Reprinted from the *New Haven Register*, New Haven, Connecticut, by permission of the Jackson Newspapers.

Illustration from page 89 of *Prisoner of War: Six Years in Hanoi* by LCDR John M. McGrath, USN. Copyright © 1975, U.S. Naval Institute, Annapolis, Maryland. Reprinted by permission of Naval Institute Press.

Epigraph from *Letters to His Son W. B. Yeats and Others* by J. B. Yeats (E. P. Dutton, 1956). Reprinted by permission.

FIRST EDITION

Designer: Sidney Feinberg

Maps and plans by George Colbert

Library of Congress Cataloging in Publication Data
Stockdale, James B.
  In love and war.
  Includes index.
  1. Stockdale, James B.   2. Stockdale, Sybil.
3. Air pilots, Military—United States—Biography.
4. United States.   Navy—Aviation—Biography.
5. Prisoners of war—United States—Biography.
6. Prisoners of war—Vietnam—Biography.   7. Vietnamese
Conflict, 1961–1975—Personal narratives, American.
I. Stockdale, Sybil.   II. Title.
V63.S78A35   1984   358.4'14'0924 [B]   84–47600
ISBN 0–06–015318–0

---

84 85 86 87 88 10 9 8 7 6 5 4 3 2 1

Dedicated to
all those who went to Vietnam
but never came home

Contents

ILLUSTRATIONS

Prologue

This is the true story of Jim Stockdale, a navy fighter pilot shot down and taken prisoner during the Vietnam War; and his wife, Sybil, who, back home in California, carried on a valiant fight on behalf of her husband and all other POWs during the eight years of his imprisonment.

Vice Admiral Stockdale entered the fray as a commander in 1964, when the American commitment totaled about 16,000 men, and left it in 1973, when the number was about the same. In between, however, our commitment had shot up to over thirty times that number. The truth about the Tonkin Gulf incidents—and how they precipitated our huge investment of treasure and blood—is a story Jim Stockdale has protected for twenty years, almost eight of them at great risk in a Communist prison.

Sybil and Jim tell their story in alternating chapters—Jim recounting his experiences in prison during those years; Sybil telling of her struggle to get the U.S. government to acknowledge the inhumane treatment of POWs in North Vietnam and to enforce the terms of the Geneva Convention—all the while raising four sons on her own.

In Love and War is about a couple's deep commitment to each other and to the values of their society. It will likely contain some surprises for American readers, but nothing is revealed here that is not already known by the North Vietnamese government.

Chapter 1

Three Days in August

> Only for his dreams is a man responsible—his actions
> are what he must do.
>
> —J. B. Yeats, in *Letters to His Son
> W. B. Yeats and Others*

Sunday, August 2, 1964

My stateroom aboard the USS *Ticonderoga* was located three decks
below the flight deck, starboard side, just forward of the island
structure. It was relatively large, as officers' quarters go on an aircraft carrier. I enjoyed relaxing there on that Sunday morning,
August 2, partaking of rare leisure at sea, reading the fresh wire-
service news stories radioed from New York and Washington way
out there to Vietnamese waters every night. I was bone-tired. I had
been continuously at sea, flying fighter planes off this carrier and
the USS *Constellation* every day since leaving the Philippine Islands
in May 1964.

At that time, I was a forty-year-old naval officer, the squadron
commander of Fighter Squadron Fifty-one, VF 51. I had gone to
Annapolis when I was nineteen, had been in the navy ever since,
and for the past two and a half years had held the rank of full
commander. My squadron flew the single-seat, supersonic Crusader, just about the fastest and best all-around airplane in the navy
in those days. In fact it was our versatility that had kept us at sea.
We were the only squadron in the navy with the speed and air-to-
ground rocket capability required for some Washington-controlled
secret missions we had been flying deep into Laos since early June.

VF 51 had been summoned from the *Ticonderoga* to join the *Constellation* off Vietnam, and from the latter we had flown those secret missions until mid-July. By then, the secret missions and the stationing of an aircraft carrier just southeast of the Tonkin Gulf had become more or less institutionalized. As the *Constellation* left "Yankee Station" for port, the *Ticonderoga* replaced her, and we moved back and flew the missions from our old ship. In a few days, the *Constellation* was due to leave Hong Kong to come down and take over the station and missions again, and we were scheduled to fly back to her.

This was becoming the best flying summer of my life. And it was my squadron command tour. I loved it. The Laos missions could be flown properly only if we operated our airplanes well outside their normal range and speed envelopes, and I was just the guy who knew how to shave the corners on that.

We knew we were making history, yet sometimes my pilots and I sensed that the people around us—particularly the intelligence officers whose job it was to make sure that the story of our flights was recorded accurately—were not conscious of the import of what was going on. They seemed continually to miss the point in the official documents; to fill in gaps in the record, we adopted the habit of writing up the details of all we had seen and done on historically significant flights right after landing. We always stashed these personal accounts in my stateroom strongbox for safekeeping.

We were not scheduled to fly till after noon on that Sunday, and there were to be only a dozen sorties—just for pilot training right around the ship. Four Crusaders and eight little Skyhawk jets would do formation and target practice on a big wooden spar towed astern the ship. This would be a good opportunity for me to size up the progress in the flying skills and marksmanship of one of our new pilots, Lieutenant junior grade Dick Hastings. Therefore I had asked that our Crusaders be loaded with full 20mm ammunition for each of our four fuselage-mounted cannons, and that a big, six-foot-long, five-inch-diameter Zuni rocket be hung on each side of our fuselages.

At a surprise intelligence briefing that morning, our air-group pilots had been told that the USS *Maddox*, an old destroyer identical to one I had served in eighteen years before, was steaming up the nearby North Vietnam coast, reaffirming our navy's right to passage in international waters. That was the whole message, except we were told that the code name for the *Maddox*'s operation was "De Soto Patrol." Unscheduled intelligence briefings were very unusual on Sunday mornings, but this seemed a reasonable thing to know about, and, so far as I knew, none of my pilots thought more of it.

At least I didn't hear the name *Maddox* again until I was forty minutes into my afternoon hop. Then, at 2:55 on my cockpit clock, while doing formation loops with Hastings over the ship, I was told to switch all four Crusaders to strike control for a message: The *Maddox* had notified the *Ticonderoga* that she was being menaced by some distant shadowing torpedo boats; I was to take the Crusaders and head out to her location. The Skyhawks were told to jettison their bombs and land back aboard.

The *Ticonderoga* was operating about a hundred miles south of Red China's Hainan Island and about a hundred miles east of the South Vietnam port and airfield complex of Danang. We were given a course and distance to go—just over 300 nautical miles.

It was just 3:00 P.M. when four Crusaders spread out as a tactical unit and climbed on a northwesterly heading, scrambling for thinner air and more fuel-efficient cruising. Hastings was number two, on my right wing, and Commander Robair Mohrhardt and Lieutenant Commander Ev Southwick, both very experienced fighter pilots, the number three and number four spots on my left. We all instinctively knew to keep radio silence while climbing. We could almost see the Red Chinese fighter bases of Hainan Island off to our right as Robair and Ev automatically fanned well out to the left and up abeam of me, leaving a couple of miles between each of us in a defensive "combat spread." Hastings followed suit to the right without signal.

I felt really good having Southwick out there constantly scanning the rear for distant moving specks, those Russian-built MIGs we occasionally saw flicking through the air around Hainan. I had flown Crusaders with Ev Southwick for eight years and knew him to be one of the best fighter pilots in all the Pacific Fleet. He had superb visual acuity and unusually keen instincts for air-combat maneuvering; he would tell us when to break right or left if any of those MIGs tried to sneak up behind us for a missile shot.

My nose was just poking through 33,000 feet when I heard a familiar tick-tick in my headset. That was Ev, of course, flicking the mike button on his throttle to prevent being homed in on, but thereby telling me that I was just starting to penetrate the bottom of the telltale condensation-trail level. I throttled back slowly to best cruise power and eased us all down to 32,000 feet, where to distant scanning eyes we would be no more than fleeting specks if we could be seen at all. Thus, effortlessly and almost unconsciously, with practiced teamwork, our flight had set itself up at the best airspeed for range, and at an altitude that offered the best combination of stealth and fuel efficiency. Each of us, in our long, flexing, limber Crusaders, bobbed along just short of the speed of sound, in slightly bumpy air; way out in front of wings we could see only through rearview mirrors, suspended at the end of what felt like long aluminum vaulters' poles.

About 130 miles from the *Ticonderoga,* our radio reception of her strike control began fading out. They had just told us the *Maddox* was definitely being threatened by surface vessels which had emerged from behind the little offshore island of Hon Me. I acknowledged and said we were switching to the *Maddox's* radio frequency.

We picked up the voice of that destroyer's air controller faintly at first, but within five minutes, when we were within eighty-or-so miles of him, his words were coming in clear as bells, capturing our total attention. It sounded like we had just tuned in to World War III. "Under attack by three PT boats . . . Torpedoes in the water . . . I am engaging the enemy with my main battery."

In a couple of minutes, I started us downhill at about Mach 1, saving fuel rather than using afterburner for a supersonic dash. We had been airborne for about an hour and fifteen minutes, and our high-power acrobatics in the first forty minutes of flight had used up a lot of fuel. Even by approaching the *Maddox* subsonically, we would be arriving on the battle scene with only an hour's fuel before flameout, and we were 300 miles from home.

As we started our descent, the *Maddox's* controller continued to bombard us with battle accounts. He had an unforgettable rapid-fire delivery and excited manner of speaking that reminded me of Clem McCarthy, the famous radio boxing announcer of the 1930s. As a boy back in my little hometown of Abingdon, Illinois, I had sat at the family radio and hung on every word of Clem's blow-by-blow calls of Joe Louis's championship fights. Now, squinting through my narrow, bulletproof windshield in search of the *Maddox* as my flight glided toward the sea through wispy clouds, that Clem Mc-Carthy voice made my hair stand up on the back of my neck.

The radio had become quiet by the time the ship came into view about fifteen miles dead ahead. We were descending through 15,000 feet; I throttled back to hold us at an indicated airspeed of about 400 knots as we continued in, aiming to pass over the destroyer at about 8,000 feet in descent, toward the PT boats we could now make out beyond her. For the past few minutes, my wingmen had been moving in, closing up the flight to where there were now perhaps only a hundred feet between airplanes. We were on a northerly course, paralleling the North Vietnamese coastline, which we could make out in the haze, twenty or thirty miles to our left. As soon as I told Clem we had the *Maddox* in sight, he said, "Your mission is now to attack and destroy the PT boats."[1]

At just 3:30 P.M., as we roared over the *Maddox* in descent, all four of us noticed a peculiar long "cloud," probably smoke, about two miles north of the destroyer, low on the water, extending east and west for perhaps a half-mile. The *Maddox* was heading south. The PT boats were about three miles north of the smoke cloud, just turning northwest for home. From their long, foamy wakes, much more pronounced than the wake of a destroyer at full speed, it was clear that all three were making speeds of at least forty knots. Two of the boats were out ahead, shoulder to shoulder, and the third was about a mile behind but catching up. Their attack on the *Maddox* had clearly come to an end minutes before we arrived.*

I told Robair and Ev to attack the trailing boat, and I called "In" on a diving, leftward-arcing 400-knot run on the lead boat to the left. I instructed Hastings to spread out to the right and follow me around in my turn until he could get his sights on the lead boat to the right, and then to maneuver so he could attack it simultaneously with my run on its mate.

I selected a single Zuni rocket on my armament panel, aimed, and fired as I passed through about a thousand feet. I could clearly see the crew of the antiaircraft gun on the stern firing up at me. I was flying through tracers, pulling out left, disappointed to see my rocket splash close to the port beam, when I heard Hastings yell on

*See Appendix 1.

the radio, "I've been hit! My port wing is shot up!"

I jammed my throttle forward, and immediately picked him up in my right-hand rearview mirror. He was at my altitude, on a parallel track, and, like me, in a left climbing turn, black smoke pouring from his tailpipe as it always did at full power at sea level with the Pratt Whitney J-57 engine model then installed in our airplanes. I told him to cut back toward the *Maddox*, and, as we both turned left, I joined up with him and moved in close to have a look at his damaged wing. There was no scorched paint, no fire, just a peeled-back and torn leading edge. I was almost positive that he had simply overstressed his airplane with an abrupt, excited jerk of the stick. By this time, the *Maddox* was at least ten miles south of the PT boats, and the distance between them was opening at about a mile a minute. Telling Hastings to set up a comfortable orbit over the destroyer, I continued to examine his plane. Once he verified that he could control the plane satisfactorily at low speed, and that his gauges showed him losing no plane fluids, I left him orbiting the *Maddox*. "You wait here," I said. "I'm going back to the war."

Meanwhile, Mohrhardt and Southwick had been raking all three boats with cannon fire at close range. As I raced back north to catch up with the fleeing PT boats, I saw Southwick decisively hose down the trailing boat with his four 20mm cannons. Smoke burst from the various openings in the hull, and the boat suddenly stopped dead in the water. The crew threw a smoke-generating device into the water in a futile effort to conceal themselves.

With Southwick's last victim clearly sinking, I proceeded on to the two lead boats, both of which had been hit and slowed, and one of which was now lagging behind the other. I joined Mohrhardt and Southwick in making firing runs on them, first with my remaining Zuni rocket (I again missed, by about thirty feet), and then getting in close and hosing them down with my 20mm cannon. As I pulled off that first strafing run, Mohrhardt and Southwick called "Bingo" on the radio—they had hit their minimum fuel reserve and were heading back to the *Ticonderoga*. Before I ran out of ammunition, I made three more strafing runs—good ones. I had the hang of it now, and as I pulled off the lead boats to return to the *Maddox*, I imagined they had about a fifty-fifty chance of making it to port.

Climbing out, I marveled at how much more visual perception I'd had as I relaxed on those last few passes. I could clearly see not only the flashes of boats' guns but sparks of my projectiles striking their hulls. And all of that in bright sunlight.

As I sighted the *Maddox*, I realized that Hastings was gone! Continuing south, I soon heard radio conversations between my planes up ahead, and pieced the story together. Dick Hastings had become alarmed when his fuel dropped below "bingo." No longer able to see me or the distant boats to the north, he had tried to join Mohrhardt and Southwick as they flew over him toward home, but Dick had been unable to match their speed with his damaged wing. By the time I got to the *Maddox*, he was calling for me on the radio. I picked him up on my air-intercept radar and told him to continue on course toward the *Ticonderoga*. As I started to overtake him, I checked out with the *Maddox*: "All boats hit, two still under way toward the coast, one dead in the water and burning."

The rest of the flight was routine. I fell in behind Hastings to stay with him. When I saw that his impaired speed was going to run us out of fuel short of the carrier, I called ahead to the *Ticonderoga* for a tanker plane and we both took on fuel about eighty miles short of the carrier. I decided to escort him to the landing strip at the U.S. air base at Danang, where landing a crippled plane would be much less dangerous than on a carrier deck. I watched him land safely from above, then lit out for my *Ticonderoga* home.

I caught her cross-deck pennant at 5:45, three and a half hours after I had been catapulted for that "routine training flight." It happened to be my four-hundredth carrier-arrested landing in a Crusader.

I immediately went down to the intelligence spaces to see what sense could be made of that crazy PT-boat attack against our destroyer. Nobody seemed to know what the motive was. I learned that the *Maddox* had had some warning of the attack not only from observing the boats, but from intercepted radio transmissions. They were carrying an intelligence-communication van between their stacks; in it, a small navy and marine Vietnamese-language-trained crew could listen in on the chatter of some North Vietnamese military command circuits on the beach. From such intercepts during the morning and early afternoon hours, the *Maddox* had figured out that something was up. Moreover, I learned that the PT boats had fired a couple of torpedoes at the *Maddox*, both of which missed, and had also fired at her with those big machine guns down whose barrels I had just been looking. The only hit the destroyer took was from one small machine-gun round, which punctured the pedestal of a gun director and fell harmlessly into a compartment below.

It had been a memorable day, and we pilots decided we would write and stash personal accounts after Hastings got back to the ship the next morning. I went to bed that night more tired than usual, thinking of and missing the love of my life, Sybil, and our four sweet boys. It would be a Sunday morning back there in Connecticut, where they were spending the summer. I thought about the day Syb and I were married there seventeen years, one month, and a week ago. I fell asleep wondering what they would all think when they heard the national news talking about the Tonkin Gulf, North Vietnam, and Fighter Squadron Fifty-one.

Tuesday, August 4, 1964

There was a sense of urgency, a change of emphasis, about the ship during the hours and days immediately following the PT-boat incident. Now it was all "ship defense." On Monday, August 3, I had flown two "combat air patrol" hops up into the Gulf, on guard against a Communist answer to our PT-boat sinking of Sunday. On Tuesday I was scheduled to lead two more such flights.

I lay in bed awhile that morning, relishing my life of change and flexibility, thanking Providence for the totally unexpected joy of having command during a period of such instability that I could do damned near anything I wanted to—provided the squadron delivered under pressure. I hated the "by-the-numbers" rules of the navy. On this cruise we were anything but "by the numbers"; we were completely off the page. It seemed to me imperative that we have the independence to act on our feet, by instinct, when defending our ships from the North Vietnamese or Red Chinese forces.

Time to get up. I rushed for a shower, then down to the wardroom for a nice breakfast. There I seized the morning press clips at the table and frantically looked for Washington's reactions to Sunday's events. (We were eleven hours ahead of Washington, so Atlantic Seaboard Monday morning news would have been transmitted to the ship during our Monday night—last night.) There it was. The president had met with State and Defense Department officials about five hours after the PT-boat attack. They had issued a warning, but decided not to follow up on the incident, to consider the attack merely the impulsive act of a trigger-happy PT-boat commander. It sounded like Johnson's inner circle had burned their bridges, eliminating their chance to rebut Goldwater's "soft on defense issues" charges. This struck me as odd, given the tenor of the current presidential-election campaign.

My first flight that Tuesday, August 4, 1964, was uneventful. My wingman and I took a good look at the De Soto patrol up in the Gulf. The destroyer *Turner Joy*, fifteen years newer than the *Maddox*, had joined her the day before with orders to stay with her throughout. The military commander of the two ships, Captain John J. Herrick, was still in the *Maddox*. His job was that of a destroyer division commander, and he was senior to the captain of either ship. Herrick spoke for the destroyer unit just as Rear Admiral R. B. Moore, a carrier division commander aboard the *Ticonderoga*, spoke for our carrier unit.

My second flight that Tuesday took place late in the afternoon, and I spent most of my time up in the Gulf in the vicinity of our destroyers. They were heading east toward the center of the Gulf, and the cloud cover was steadily getting lower, the sea becoming choppy with whitecaps, when I left them about 6:00 P.M.

The *Ticonderoga* was as usual operating outside the Gulf, south of Hainan Island, east of Danang, and west of the tiny Paracel Islands. At about sunset when I landed back aboard, she was again right at 300 nautical miles southeast of the De Soto patrol. The skies outside the Gulf were overcast, but less ominous. Walking down the deck after parking my plane at about 6:30, I watched occasional lightning flashes far to the northwest, in the Gulf.

I went directly to the wardroom and ate dinner in my flight gear. Casual table talk there included mention of a little afternoon intercept activity up in the Gulf. The *Maddox*'s intelligence van had picked up Vietnamese chitchat about the destroyers' geographic position. That bit of news hardly seemed odd to me; through most of the daylight hours, the destroyers were in plain sight of land, to

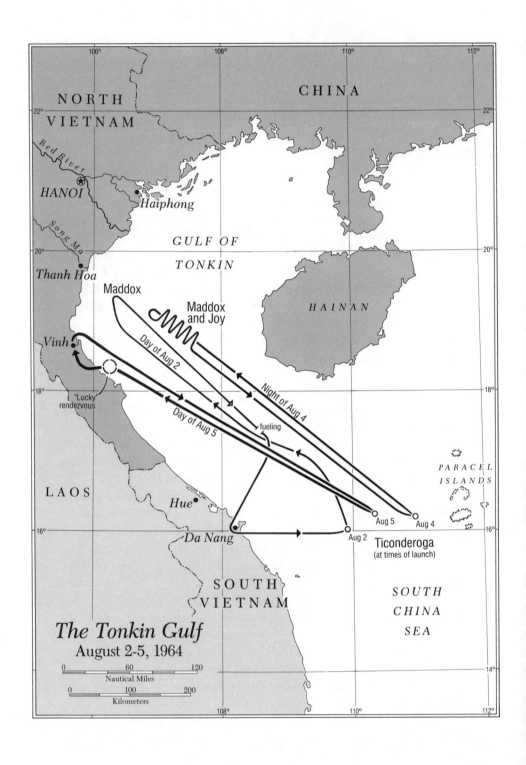

106°   108°   110°   112°

CHINA

NORTH
VIETNAM

22°

Red River

HANOI ✪
Haiphong

Song Ma

GULF OF
20°
TONKIN

Thanh Hoa
HAINAN

Maddox

Maddox
and Joy

Vinh
Day of Aug 2
Night of Aug 4
18°
"Lucky"
rendezvous
Day of Aug 5
fueling

LAOS

PARACEL
ISLANDS

Hue

Aug 5   Aug 4

Da Nang   Aug 2

Ticonderoga
(at times of launch)

16°

SOUTH
VIETNAM
SOUTH
CHINA
SEA

The Tonkin Gulf
August 2-5, 1964

0   60   120
Nautical Miles

0   100   200
Kilometers

108°   110°   112°

14°

say nothing of being in sight of the many North Vietnamese coastal fishing boats thereabouts. The very purpose of the De Soto patrol, as I understood it, was to be seen, and the destroyers' location was a perfectly ordinary thing for the North Vietnamese to be talking about.

After dinner, still in my flight suit, I paid a routine visit to my squadron maintenance officer. We chatted about the problems of keeping ten or more of our fifteen Crusaders in commission and available for flight at sea. I then wandered into our squadron pilots' preflight briefing room to chat with my pilots. We had no flying scheduled that night, but two of our planes were to remain in "Condition CAP," standing by for prompt takeoff should a need arise. These two Crusaders were parked on the ship's catapults above us, fully fueled and armed, engines not running but with electrical starting cords plugged in, pilots in the cockpits.

Given the North Vietnamese PT-boat action the previous Sunday, and the fact that the De Soto patrol was up in the Gulf, maintaining an alert readiness posture was routine. In fact, those years we spent half our nights in the Western Pacific on such standby. Perhaps we had grown too casual about it: As I checked the status board, I noticed with some misgivings that for this particular watch, my scheduling officer had put two "first cruise" pilots up there, rather than one junior man and one old hand as I preferred.

The red lights were on in our ready room to protect the night vision of the relief pilots who were set to go up and man backup planes if need be. It was so muggy aboard ship that night that the air-conditioner was huffing and puffing. It was very rare to have that degree of humidity so far from land. Atmospheric conditions such as those in the lightning-charged air up in the Gulf tonight could be expected to "duct" or play tricks on old-fashioned radar.

I was in the middle of an animated conversation with my pilots when I became conscious of the fact that a couple of our air group's old workhorse A-1 Skyraiders, affectionately called "Spads," were being turned up on the flight deck above. At first I thought they were probably just being given engine-maintenance checks, but when they went to high power, I realized they were about to be launched off the angled deck. A friend of mine from the ship's

Combat Information Center across the passageway stuck his head in our door, looking harassed. He saw me, motioned me out into the passageway, and asked guardedly, "Are they ready to go?"

I was confused. "What's going on?" I asked. My friend said that, based on another intercept they'd picked up from the beach in North Vietnam, the destroyers suspected they were about to be attacked. Rear Admiral Moore's staff had ordered the Spads to head out toward the De Soto patrol. Two of my Crusaders were to follow as soon as the flight-deck crew could get them turned up and ready.

I ran back to the ready room, where my flight gear was stowed, ripped my flight helmet out of its bag, grabbed my torso harness off the hook, and slithered into it. I could already hear a Crusader engine winding up. Would I have the guts to stop all the count-down action up there just to get myself into an airplane? *Yes!* The dark night, the bad weather, the Crusader's nighttime-carrier-landing accident rate, and Dick Hastings's having nearly pulled the wings off his airplane on Sunday—all made me realize I had to go. Moreover, just two days ago I'd received a very expensive lesson in exactly how to sink North Vietnamese PT boats. I now knew what they looked like close up, how they maneuvered, and how to hose them down. No use starting over with somebody else!

The key was getting a fast airplane up there quickly. I could go up at sonic speed and beat the prop-driven Spads by a full hour! I ran up the ladder and onto the blacked-out flight deck chanting to myself, "Get there quick, get low, get close, get lined up, and hose 'em down. No misses this time!"

The Crusader on the starboard catapult was all started and being given preflight checks when I sprinted out into the crowd of maintenance and catapult personnel around the planes. I could feel the ship leaning as she was turned into the wind. I grabbed Petty Officer Third Class Charles Pattin, my plane captain, and yelled into his ear to lower the steps of the plane on the port catapult and get its canopy open. As soon as he climbed down, I climbed up and screamed above the engine noise into the ear of my startled junior pilot, "Unstrap and get out—I'm getting in!"

I jumped in and strapped on my parachute in a flash. With 2,000 hours of flight time in that cockpit, I could do it all in the dark; in a few seconds, a dozen or more switches were set and I gave my "thumbs up" signal. Pattin gave me the "external power" signal and I felt the jolt of electrical power flooding into the plane.

In the plane to my right, young Lieutenant (jg) Roy Miller, my wingman for the night, was answering the catapult officer's illuminated-wand signal to shove his throttle all the way forward for the shot down the track into the black void ahead. Miller and I had had no radio communication, but he knew he had to wait for me over the ship before we headed out together.

Wham—down the track he went, hot, straight, and normal—from a dead stop to 170 miles an hour within hardly more than three or four plane lengths. As soon as he entered that black void right off the bow, out went all his lights! My God! That was the first time I'd ever seen *that* happen! Roy's electrical generator had dropped off the line just as he took the shot. Right then he was suspended in midair, just above stall speed, with a tricky combination wheels-up/wing-down transition to make in a totally black cockpit—no instrument lights, no time to fool with a flashlight, and, on this particularly humid night, absolutely no natural horizon to give him a level reference through his windshield.

I held my breath, praying that he would not fly into the water, praying we'd see no telltale flash of flame—when suddenly his lights came on! There he was, at 300 feet, climbing out! He'd found the emergency windmill-generator air bottle handle, popped it out, and would have enough equipment going to enable him to jettison fuel and land right back aboard. The land/launch radio frequency was full of chatter about courses and altitudes that Roy Miller could fly to get safely back aboard. I broke in and told them I wanted to be launched immediately, without a wingman. Up on the bridge, the *Ticonderoga*'s commanding officer, Captain Hutch Cooper, sticking his neck out to back me to the hilt as always, gave his okay to this unorthodox request. Combat Information Center radioed me my course and I inched the plane forward until she was brought up short, locked in catapult position.

Full power, lights on, I felt that familiar kick as I was plastered to the back of my seat by the catapult's accelerating force. And then for the hundredth-plus time, I endured that moment of terror and ecstasy of a night "cat" shot in a powerful jet, gasping for breath while my field of vision narrowed and narrowed like a focusing telescope as the longitudinal pull sucked the blood from my head. That is the time in the shot when the simple physics of blood circulation prevents the pilot from seeing anything to the side; he must make his eyes focus like a camera, like a flashlight beam, on the most important thing in his life at that instant—that jittering gyro horizon instrument in the middle of his dashboard. I skimmed down the track, felt that wonderful *thump* telling me I was free of the catapult bridle, and was up and away.

I had cleared the deck at 8:46, only three minutes behind Miller—not enough time lost to worry about. I prayed that Roy was now getting safely back aboard. I felt all would go well—and in truth, I was even a little relieved at the thought of being able to gyrate at will on this important flight and not have to make maneuvering allowances for a wingman, even a good stick-and-throttle wingman like Roy Miller.

I thanked my lucky stars for the chance to be the man on the spot at the very eye of the storm. This would be a night I would tell my grandchildren about! In that private world, arcing through a stormy sky, I felt that no amount of future promotions or high-sounding peacetime duties would ever count for so much as what was to happen in the next couple of hours.

As I passed through 15,000 feet, I recognized the voice of my old pal, fellow squadron commander, and Naval Academy classmate Wes McDonald, checking in with strike control. Wes had just been catapulted off the *Ticonderoga* with a wingman. They were flying little A-4 Skyhawk jets from Wes's Attack Squadron Fifty-six. Wes was about thirty miles behind me. I calculated that he would reach the destroyers about fifteen minutes after me.

I leveled off between cloud layers at about 25,000 feet. Farther up into the Gulf, things were looking more and more spooky. There were lightning flashes all around. I called Wes, using that name rather than his official squadron voice call. We knew each other so well that we really didn't need any call; five words into oxygen-mask microphones from either of us to the other told the complete story of identity, mood, and purpose. Wes understood that I was without a wingman, about 150 miles from the *Ticonderoga*, and preparing to shift to the destroyers' radio frequency. As I reached over to change my radio channel, I noticed that I was just a hundred miles short of the De Soto patrol and that my cockpit clock said exactly 9:00 P.M. I felt like I was poised on a diving tower, ready to make the leap. I wondered if Syb and the boys were getting any telepathic signals of my situation.

My reverie was broken by Clem McCarthy's voice in my earphones. He was reporting multiple radar contacts with a vengeance and it sounded like we were in for one hell of a sea battle down there tonight.

I gave Clem my position and started down in a fast descent. Passing 10,000 feet, about forty miles from my objective, I charged my four 20mm cannons. The compressed air blew the gun bolts home with a satisfying thump, and I fired a short burst from each barrel into the night just to make sure they all worked. It was eerie to see the tracers skip off into the black distance through the cloud puffs ahead.

About that time Wes McDonald and his wingman came up on the destroyers' radio circuit. Clem's reports of the melee ahead, plus my years-ago experience with radar air control aboard my old *Maddox*-like destroyer, convinced me that it was just not going to make sense for me to relinquish my aircraft's freedom of movement: Those destroyers just didn't have the capability or equipment to keep Crusaders under positive radar control and even halfway exploit their true boat-killing ability; I had to have freedom to zig and zag and change my mind faster than I could talk on the radio.

I was positive they were not going to be able to keep track of me as I maneuvered close in, very low, darting like a waterbug. I was just going to have to try to see what the destroyers were shooting at, then aim and shoot at whatever it was from close range if I could see it, or just shoot where they shot if I couldn't see it. Knowing the destroyers would never agree to this on the radio, I doused my lights so they wouldn't know where I was and get all excited. I advised Wes that all my external lights would be off for the duration, that I would stay below 2,000 feet, and asked him to stay above that level unless he called and told me otherwise.

I throttled way back and kept my nose down just enough to hold about 300 knots as I flew in and out of clouds and occasional rain squalls, feeling my way toward the water. It must have been about eight minutes after nine when I leveled off at about a thousand feet, just below and sometimes in the clouds, and picked up two very luminous wakes several miles ahead. I told Clem, and he said he would have the ships flash their red masthead "truck" lights for a check. The red lights popped on, confirming that the only wakes in sight—the ones I was looking at—were the two wakes of the De Soto patrol. I told Clem I had positive identification and the destroyers doused their lights right away.

For the next hour and a half, I hovered around those two ships at a thousand feet maximum and usually below that altitude, always within two or three miles of the destroyers and never outside the range at which I could keep their vivid, highly luminescent wakes in sight.

By 9:35 P.M., the almost constant radio conversation between the destroyers seemed to concentrate on some radar contacts closing from the east, maybe five miles out. Then they opened fire for the first time that night—star shells to port as the destroyers plowed through choppy seas at about thirty knots, heading southeast. The star-shell illumination was not good because the projectiles were bursting in the clouds and the flares were just about burned out by the time their little parachutes got below them. By twenty minutes of ten, this spate of American shelling had stopped; the radar indications had disappeared from destroyer scopes.

Then almost immediately there was talk of a torpedo in the water and for about an hour there were torpedo calls and torpedo calls and destroyers turning and turning, with at least two and probably three intervals of frantic-to-sporadic destroyer gunfire, one siege lasting nearly ten minutes. The *Joy* was firing at "targets" the *Maddox* couldn't track on radar, and the *Maddox* was dodging "torpedoes" the *Joy* couldn't hear on their sonar, and neither ship was detecting any electromagnetic emissions (enemy radio or radar) in the area.

I talked to Clem frequently, though sometimes it was hard to break in. By gleaning what he could from the shouts I could hear in the background, he kept giving rapid-fire, blow-by-blow descriptions of ongoing sea battles that for the life of me I couldn't find on my horizons. I was frustrated, and I frequently heard an equally frustrated Wes and his wingman up above talking about dropping flares in an effort to find out what was going on down there.

It was totally appropriate for all those planes to stay up above me and try to get the big picture so they could fire some rockets at a target. However, I had assigned myself the job of being the pouncer, of staying right over the *Maddox* and the *Joy*, of leaving the big picture to somebody else while I maneuvered close to the water, unencumbered by a wingman, lights off, trying to find whatever boat the destroyers were talking about and blast it immediately.

I had the best seat in the house from which to detect boats—if there were any. I didn't have to look through surface haze and spray like the destroyers did, and yet I could see the destroyers' every move vividly. Time and again I flew right over the *Maddox* and the *Joy*, throttled back, lights out, like a near-silent stalking owl, conserving fuel at a 250-knot loiter speed. I could roll over and look right up the two churning phosphorescent destroyer wakes and see their decks heaving in choppy seas, spray coming over their bows on easterly headings as they maneuvered and kept the airwaves full of course-change signals. There must have been twenty knots of surface wind down there.

When the destroyers were convinced they had some battle action going, I zigged and zagged and fired where they fired unless it looked like I might get caught in their shot patterns or unless they had told me to fire somewhere else. The edges of the black hole I was flying in were still periodically lit by flashes of lightning—but no wakes or dark shapes other than those of the destroyers were ever visible to me.

"Batterup one-O-one [my voice call], we are taking a boat under fire abeam to port, two thousand yards."

"Rog, I see your fire; when you lift it, I'll go in and have a look and hose the area down."

"Batterup, we are in a hard port turn; we think there is a boat closing us from astern."

"Rog, I see your port turn; I can always see your wakes; I will fire astern of you."

And so on into the night. I was sweating like a pig, and periodically scaring myself to death. I shouted to myself as I brought years and years of day, night, extra cruise, extra weekend, seat-of-the-pants, stick-and-throttle experience into full play at last: "I have to press in, I have to press in, I've got to see him, I've got to see him!"

It was on that "boat closing from astern" that I remember wheeling around behind the ships on a wide, fast, very low, leftward-arcing turn, ever-closing on the big, sparkling, foamy destroyer wakes well out in front and going from ten o'clock to eleven to dead ahead as I squinted through my dimmed gunsight into the dark void of swirling sea. By that time I was about an hour into this frantic maneuvering, and with an eye on the fuel gauge, I decided that this was a good place to invest those big Zuni rockets. I was right on the water and flipping switches on my armament selector panel down between my knees by finger touch, talking to myself all the way.

"Rocket selected . . . Now close one eye to keep it night-adapted through the flash and *squeeze* the trigger button on the joy stick . . . *Kawhoosh!* Feel that jolt! There she goes! Hike up your head—can you see anything like a hit? . . . Nothing . . . Again quickly, one eye closed, another rocket selected, squeeze . . . *Ka-whoosh!* What's that torch flying out in front of me? . . . My God— one switch detent too far! It's a sidewinder! Oh, hit the water, hit the water, you zooming roman candle! . . . If your seeker head picks up that hot destroyer stack up ahead, we'll finally see some *real* metal-to-metal contact and some *real* fireworks!

"All black; thank goodness—it must have splashed . . . Pull up, pull up, Jim, don't *you* fly into the water. God Almighty, you've got saltwater spray on your windshield . . . That's *too* close![2]

"Now calm down and think, Jim. You're getting caught up in this thing. Watch that altimeter. There's something wrong out here. Those destroyers are talkin' about hits, but where are the metal-to-metal sparks? And the boat wakes—where are they? And boat gun flashes? The day before yesterday, I saw all of those signs of small-boat combat in broad daylight! Any of those telltale indicators would stand out like beacons in this black hole we're operating in."

Now the *Turner Joy's* guns were firing astern as she took a sinuating evasive course generally southward. Even figuring that. we had been working generally south for the hour and a half that I'd been right over the destroyers, and thus a little closer to the *Ticonderoga* than when I had first flown up here, I was by then right down to what I considered a minimum-level, straight-in approach, steady deck bingo. The *Joy* ceased fire and I took a couple of minutes to shoot my other Zuni rocket and the dregs of my 20mm magazines into that general area astern of her, then added full throttle, picked up the nose, and started climbing out to the southeast toward the *Ticonderoga*.

I checked out with Wes and then with Clem, and finally with

my old shipmates from the *Constellation*, who were just joining this fiasco from a launch point far out to the east on their ship's track into this area from Hong Kong. As I broke out on top of the clouds and throttled way back to get maximum range, bleeding off altitude slowly in a gentle descent, my adrenaline pump slowed down after its wild gyrations of the past couple of hours. I enjoyed the quiet intimacy of the *Ticonderoga*'s strike control frequency: Nobody was talking on the circuit but myself and the ship's air controller; there was not another airplane in the sky within a hundred miles of us and we needed to say very little. My electronic navigation equipment had picked up the carrier's homer, and my tacan distance indicator was clicking off the miles as I approached the dear old boat. As I continued my gentle glide, it was clear to the radar controller that I was setting myself up for a short straight-in and an easterly recovery course. We had worked together too much to require snappy orders and replies back and forth. What a joy to be alive and to perform so effortlessly the arabesques of maneuver I'd worked so long and hard to perfect. It was no longer a matter of memorized procedures and geometric designs; it was free-form art, intuition over reason, with only the utilitarian aim of getting to that carrier's ramp, lined up, on speed, ready to go into the arresting wires with as much fuel remaining as I could keep in the tanks. And that was not going to be very much fuel tonight.

"Switch to land/launch frequency," the controller said gently. Two clicks on my throttle mike button told him all he needed to know.

"Hello, Panther, this is Batterup one-O-one, fifteen miles out for a straight-in. Low state. Four hundred pounds. I have two Skyhawks about seventy miles behind me."

"Roger, Jim. We have you on radar. Landing course zero-eight-zero degrees. Cleared straight in. We're just about out of sea room, and to stay off the rocks we'll have to come out of the wind and tank you if you miss the wires and bolt. I'm launching a tanker now; we'll have to top off the Skyhawks for sure before they land."

"Okay, smart guy," I say aloud to myself. "If you bolt, as soon as you add power, you'll have only about two minutes to find that tanker plane and get plugged in before you flame out. So slow this baby down and work! work! work! There's the meatball coming right up to the center of the lens—now lock on and hold it there!

Just goose the power up a shade." On the radio, I say softly, nonchalantly, "One-O-one; meatball; fuel remaining three hundred pounds" [three minutes].

Then the familiar voice of my squadron's maverick landing-signal officer, cool Tim Hubbard, came up—but that voice of his was a bit tight that night, a little anxious for old Ice Water. "Roger, skipper, I've got you at three hundred pounds. No sweat—we've got a nice steady deck; we'll trap you; just bring her right on down."

Lieutenant Tim Hubbard was one guy I really liked to work with in a pinch—he was always steady and relaxed, and I could depend on him to call 'em like they were and never get destabilized by the urge to butter me up. Tim's voice on the radio was saying, "Ease it down, ease it down, take off a little power, skipper; you're light as a feather and ballooning." I could see the old meatball starting up toward the top of the lens.

I gritted my teeth and crammed the stick forward and jammed that old bird onto the deck. *Wham! Screech!*—and then I felt that lovely sensation of being snubbed up short by the wire. I parked forward, folded the wings, and shut the engine down.

Wheeling into the ready room I had hurriedly left three hours before, I came face-to-face with about ten assorted ship's company, air group, and staff intelligence officers—all with sheepish grins on their faces. The mood of the group was informal and mirthful; obviously they had some big joke to tell me. "What in hell has been going on out there?" they laughingly asked.

"Damned if I know," I said. "It's really a flap. The guy on the *Maddox* Air Control radio was giving blow-by-blow accounts just like he did on Sunday. Turning left, turning right, torpedoes to the right of us, torpedoes to the left of us—boom, boom, boom! I got right down there and shot at whatever they were shooting at. I came around toward the destroyers once, right on the deck, chasing some imaginary PT boat they said was running up behind them, and fired every type of weapon I had—including a *sidewinder!* I thought for a second that its heat-seeker head had picked the *Turner Joy*'s hot stack, but luckily I had let it go when I was so low it hit the water. A little higher and wow!"

I was rather giddy by this time, and delivered this "debriefing" with elaborate gestures as a kind of catch-on hilarity enveloped the room.

"Did you see any boats?"

"Not a one. No boats, no boat wakes, no ricochets off boats, no boat gunfire, no torpedo wakes—nothing but black sea and American firepower. But for goodness' sake, I must be going crazy. How could all of that commotion have built up out there without *something* being behind it?"

"Have a look at this. This is what Herrick, the commodore on the *Maddox,* has been putting out, flash precedence, plain language to Washington and the world in general tonight." [3]

I was handed a few sheets of a rough communication log—on which were transcribed all the messages from the *Maddox* since I had left the ship. Alongside each message was the time of its receipt. For most of the two and a half hours, there had been a message every few minutes—except they had come more frequently near the end. At first glance it looked like the same stuff I had been hearing on my cockpit radio all night—"Taking boat to port under fire with main battery . . . Torpedo bearing zero-eight-zero degrees," etc. But as I studied the document, I realized that this was not the record of Clem's blow-by-blow; there were also things in it that I wasn't getting on the air, the sort of stuff the commodore was probably shouting to his radioman inside the pilothouse.

The document as a whole read like a monologue of a man turning himself inside out. For the first hour or so, it was all assertive, all Clem McCarthy-type stuff. Then every so often a message of doubt, a message expressing reservations, would pop up—about sonars not operating properly, about radars not locking on targets, about probable false targets, about false perceptions due to lack of visibility. But still, it mainly reflected the tone of victimized vessels being attacked—that is, until I got to the last page and a half; then, as I read down them, everything seemed to flip around. There was denial of the correctness of immediately preceding messages, doubt about the validity of whole blocks of messages, ever more skeptical appraisal of detection equipment's performance, the mention of overeager sonar operators, the lack of any visual sightings of boats by the destroyers, and finally there were lines expressing doubt that there had been *any boats out there that night at all.* The commodore urged a complete evaluation of the mixup before any further action be taken.

"My God," I exclaimed, tossing my helmet toward the low ceiling, "three hours of terror, almost busting my ass, nearly flying into the water, shooting rockets at nothing, sidewinders at destroyers, all brought about by spooked operators and spooked equipment! It was all a Chinese fire drill! I'm pooped; I'll see you guys tomorrow."

I wound my way up forward to my stateroom, put my flight gear in my locker, and washed my hands and face in my stateroom sink. I looked at myself in the mirror. Boy, you look tired, I thought. But it's good to feel good. At least you didn't fly into that water; and at least there's a commodore up there in the Gulf who has the guts to blow the whistle on a screw-up, and take the heat to set the record straight.

As I lay down and turned out the bed lamp, musing on the levity of the late-night session in the ready room and the absurdity of the goings-on up in the Gulf, I would never have guessed that commodores in charge on the scene of action are sometimes not allowed to blow the whistle on a screw-up or set records straight themselves.

Wednesday, August 5, 1964

After what seemed like a very short night, I felt myself being shaken. Somewhere in the distance I could hear a pleading voice calling me "commander." That was odd; my men would call me "skipper." I groggily opened my eyes and in the dim light coming through my open stateroom door I could make out the single bars of an ensign's or junior-grade lieutenant's rank insignia on the collar of the man hovering over me. What's going on? Who would send an officer to wake a person up?

"Who are you?" I asked.

"I'm the junior officer of the deck, sir. The captain sent me down to wake you. We just got a message from Washington telling us to prepare to launch strikes against the beach, sir. Both the 'Connie' and we are to launch strikes. The 'Tico' has a six-plane strike against a PT-boat base, sir, and a big strike against the oil-storage facilities in the city of Vinh. The captain wants you to start getting ready to lead the big one, sir. It's now a quarter of five, sir; we set our clocks ahead one hour in the night. Please get up, sir; your target is Washington's priority number one."

"What's the idea of the strikes?"

"Reprisal, sir."

"Reprisal for what?"

"For last night's attack on the destroyers, sir."

I flipped on my bed lamp and the young officer left.

I felt like I had been doused with ice water. How do I get in touch with the president? He's going off half-cocked.

As I spattered my face with cold water and pulled on my khaki trousers, I felt like I was one of the few men in the world who really understood the enormity of what was going to happen. The bad portents of the moment were suffocating. We were about to launch a war under false pretenses, in the face of the on-scene military commander's advice to the contrary. This decision had to be driven from way up at the top. After all, I'd spent the summer reading messages setting up our Laos operations and I had grown familiar with the linkages. It was all straight shot: Washington, Saigon, Ambassador Vientiane. On-scene naval officers couldn't turn that on or off any more than they could this thing now. There is no question of coming up with the truth from out here. The truth is out. Even a small potato like me is on the wire with a straight report of "no boats."[4]

The fact that a war was being conceived out here in the humid muck of the Tonkin Gulf didn't bother me so much; it seemed obvious that a tinderbox situation prevailed here and that there would be war in due course anyway. But for the long pull it seemed to me important that the grounds for entering war be legitimate. I felt it was a bad portent that we seemed to be under the control of a mindless Washington bureaucracy, vain enough to pick their own legitimacies regardless of evidence.* On second thought, this had after all been a night I would surely tell my grandchildren about.

It was 5:00 A.M. by the new time when I walked out on deck. I had grown used to early dawn light at this time, but now it was pitch-black. This "daylight saving" switch had moved us from North Vietnam time to Saigon time. We probably moved up an hour to be an even twelve hours ahead of Washington, an easy conversion factor they liked. As my eyes adapted, I became con-

*See Appendix 2.

scious of working parties in action at the ammunition hoists and behind the ship's island structure. I could hear sounds of clanging metal, the noises and grinding gears of forklifts and jeeps down on the hangar deck, and excited muffled voices coming from various quadrants. The *Ticonderoga* was alive with bustling action. Heavy ordnance was being broken out from the magazines where it had long been in repose in peacetime storage.

The center of attraction of this ammunition breakout was a long row of big thousand-pound bombs laid out on deck ready for immediate fusing and loading. Apparently the big wallop for my priority strike against the Vinh oil-storage tanks was to be those big TNT bombs, hung on the only airplane we had aboard capable of carrying a truly blockbusting conventional load: our prop-driven Spads.

That struck me as wise. Although the Spads were much slower than the jets, and thus quite vulnerable in heavy antiaircraft fire, they not only could carry a much heavier and diverse bomb load than our light jets, but by having more time to track, more time to aim in a slower dive, and being able to pull out lower, they were much more accurate bombers. We would need the factor of surprise to get them by without heavy losses, but this day of all would be our best chance for it.

"What do you want on the Crusaders?" asked Commander Hap Chandler, approaching me in the dim light. Hap was the *Ticonderoga*'s executive officer, second-in-command of the ship. He and I had been neighbors and test pilots together ten years before at Patuxent River, Maryland. He was a highly experienced fighter pilot who was winning air-combat medals in World War II as a veritable kid aviator while I was still studying books as a midshipman at Annapolis.

"Eight Zuni rockets and full ammo, each airplane," I replied.

"No sidewinders? What if you meet some enemy fighters up there?"

"There won't be any air opposition today; we might as well load every rack with air-to-ground stuff. We'll take sidewinders tomorrow; they'll be bringing MIGs down from China after today."

I remember that prophetic, rather casual early-morning conversation as though it happened yesterday. I spoke almost without thinking; the essence of the total mixup was so clearly etched in my mind, it was not necessary for me to reason consciously in order to answer Hap's question. The North Vietnamese wouldn't be expecting a strike today.

In hindsight, one of the most interesting things about that brief conversation was the fact that my word was final: Hap called down and told the ordnancemen to load what I wanted and that was it. Almost ever after—from that August 5, 1964, forward—such decisions were taken out of the hands of the on-scene operators and made in McNamara's Pentagon by his systems analysts. Civilian override of recommendations of on-scene military commanders became a major theme of the Vietnam War, and ironically it came into full sway just after its pitfalls were most dramatically demonstrated on August 4, 1964.

As the sky lightened in the east, I caught sight of Commander Lee McAdams, executive officer of the Spad squadron, on the hangar deck. Without asking, I knew that Lee must have been called to lead the Spad element against Vinh. Together we went down to the wardroom to have a bite of breakfast and get started on planning the jet-prop coordination for this long strike against a highly visible target.

In the midst of our conversation, we heard aircraft being turned up on the *Ticonderoga* flight deck above us. One of the ship's operations officers came into the wardroom breakfast scene at about 6:15. "What's the story?" I asked.

"They're launching several jets and a few props to go out and look for battle debris in the water from last night. *Constellation* airplanes spent most of the early-morning hours trying to locate retreating torpedo boats, with no luck, and now the big deal is to find the wreckage up there where you were last night."

"Don't hold your breath," I muttered. Lee and I got up and headed for the Air Intelligence Office to get a map of Vinh. The best one we could find was a little wilted, faded thing at least ten years out of date. The fenced-in compound in which the oil-storage tanks were located was less than an inch on a side. A tiny speck was meant to represent each multithousand-gallon tank, and we counted fourteen of them. One look at this miserable map would invalidate any argument that the screwed-up mess in the western Pacific was part of any planned conspiracy.

Lee and I stayed in the Air Intelligence Office and bore down on figuring out the best approach plan to provide the necessary element of surprise for his slow, vulnerable, heavily armed planes. That meant we had to study the area charts for probable locations of antiaircraft guns. There were hills just to the south of the city of Vinh. We decided to have the Spads approach from behind them, just high enough to build up 400 or so knots of speed in a near-vertical dive so that they could release their bombs, pull out, wheel around, and still have maybe 300 or so knots of escape speed to get back over the hills before they got plastered with flak.

We agreed that with this flight profile, the Spads' chances were good unless our jet "flak suppressors" and rocket-armed tank busters got in a few seconds ahead of them and alerted the gunners. We picked an advantageous jet-prop rendezvous location a few miles offshore and behind the hills shielding the city, in what we figured had to be a Vinh radar blind spot. It was there that the overtaking jets would pick up the Spads and carry out timing-coordination maneuvering to ensure simultaneous attack. We figured transit times and I called the ship's operations officer and told him I didn't want the jets to start their engines on the flight deck till the Spads were half an hour down the road toward our rendezvous circle. I then called all the ready rooms and told them to have their assigned pilots meet me in the wardroom at 7:00 A.M. for a final briefing.

I called ready room 1 and assigned Crusader pilots over the phone, speaking almost without conscious thought as I had to Hap Chandler earlier. I didn't want anybody with me on this flight unless he was, first, emotionally stable and, second, very good on the stick and throttle. Squadron maverick Tim Hubbard was among the men I chose.

At the briefing, I assigned each of the six Crusaders and four of the Skyhawks a specific antiaircraft-gun emplacement for flak suppression. Wes McDonald, my partner of the night before, would be second-in-command of the raid and the lead Skyhawk pilot. He and his wingman would not be on flak suppression but would be overtaking and bracketing the Spads as the latter were in their bombing dives so that his rockets and the Spad big bombs would hit the tanks simultaneously. To preclude early detection, Wes would take all six Skyhawks up a narrow valley from the south, right on the deck. These heavily laden Skyhawks going up that steep-sided gulch would be the first planes irrevocably committed to the target area. Accordingly, we agreed that it would be Wes who would give the "go" signal that committed us all. He would call out "This is Champion lead" (his squadron call). And then his words "Play ball" from down in that valley behind the town, two minutes before the bombs and rockets were to hit, would be the kickoff.

The plan made, a mood of relaxation came over us. The original idea had been for us and the *Constellation* to launch coordinated strikes at eight o'clock. The whole operation now seemed sidetracked by some high official's order to keep planes from both carriers searching for battle debris. Pilots who had been out on that wild-goose chase would stroll into the wardroom to hear what was new about Vinh. I don't remember anyone even asking them if they'd seen any evidence of debris out there. Nevertheless, it was understood that the search flights would continue.

It was after noon when we manned our planes. As we left the ready room, we were told that half an hour before, the president had announced on national television that we would be striking North Vietnam targets. That struck fear in my heart because surprise was so important to the Spads' safety on this maneuver.

Mine was the first plane down the catapult tracks of the *Ticonderoga*. My cockpit dashboard clock said 12:16 that Wednesday afternoon, August 5, 1964, as I flipped the handle to "wheels up." Now it was up to me to get thirteen heavily loaded jets through 300 miles of sticky weather, picking up four Spads along the way, to go and obliterate that fuel farm on the Asian mainland.

About forty minutes after the last jet had been catapulted, we were descending in formation in radio silence, cutting in and out of cloud layers and intermittent rain into our rendezvous area southeast of Vinh. I was growing apprehensive because it was looking more and more like our rendezvous was going to be touch and go. I thought of those Japs going into Pearl Harbor; I had to do this one right the first time. If I didn't find those Spads and get this flight together and coordinated, they were going to get their asses shot off. This flight was a history maker and I felt like the load of the world was on my shoulders.

It was about 1:12 P.M. on my clock when I spied those big,

beautiful, prop-driven babies. They were camouflaged to the exact color of the clouds we were flitting through. Hallelujah! How lucky can you get! We left the starting gate at 8,000 feet in a ripple motion just after 1:15 P.M.

Suddenly the hills just south of Vinh came into sight as we broke out into clear air over the coast. The Spads started climbing and angling for their roll-in spot. Wes McDonald and his six Sky-hawks swooped down over the lush green countryside, first edging under and then scooting west of the climbing Spads. Wes was look-ing for that narrow little one-way gulch up which he would sweep to converge with the Spads at the bottom of their dive.

I circled the Crusaders in hard *g* for one 360-degree turn to avoid getting too far out ahead, then started up the coast. I waved "bye bye" to our single post-strike photography Crusader; he would do his work alone. I then took my gunsight camera from my helmet bag on the console and snapped it into its latch in front of my face as I goosed up the throttle to set us up in a gentle climb. Soon I could peek around the hills and I started to see parts of Vinh, a city of 44,000 people, at eleven o'clock low. Looking at nine o'clock and level, maybe four miles out, I could see the Spads, hanging on their props and groaning upward with all those bombs, trying to climb a little more to get that needed evasion speed at the bottom of their dive. And several miles farther out to my left, way down on the deck, were the six little Skyhawks, heading for the gulch.

Now we six Crusaders were high and out in front, the city spread out in bright sunshine in clear view down and to our left as we passed the harbor mouth. And then, at 1:28 on my cockpit clock, Wes McDonald broke the radio silence with a piercing, con-fident blast: "*Panther lead, this is Champion lead. Play ball, play ball.*" I answered for radio backup, "Panther lead, roger roger, Wes, *play ball,*" as I reached down and turned on my master armament switch, charged my four cannons, and then set my armament selector to the upper right-hand rocket pair. That was it—we were committed. Wes McDonald would be coming out of that little valley I could now see. I turned my Crusaders in a big left-hand arc to the south. Those fourteen beautiful, tall, fat, silver tanks were now clearly visible.

I nodded my head to tell my wingmen I was still going up with

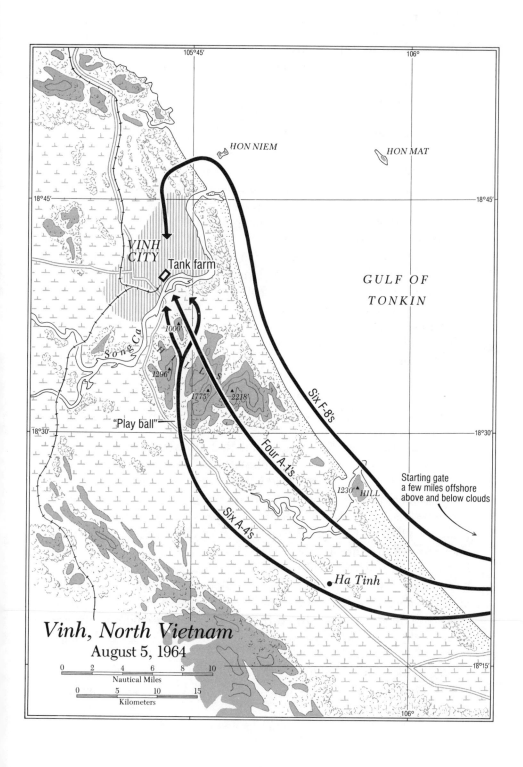

HON NIEM

HON MAT

18°45'   18°45'

VINH
CITY

Tank farm

GULF OF

TONKIN

*1000'

Song Ca

*1296'

H I L L S

*1775'   *2218'

Six F-8's

"Play ball"

18°30'   18°30'

Four A-1's

*1230' HILL

Starting gate
a few miles offshore
above and below clouds

Six A-4's

• Ha Tinh

18°15'

Vinh, North Vietnam
August 5, 1964

| 0 | 2 | 4 | 6 | 8 | 10 |
Nautical Miles

| 0 | 5 | 10 | 15 |
Kilometers

105°45'   106°

106°

more power, and then down we Crusaders started from about 15,000 feet. Once we were established in our dive, I glanced up toward my southern horizon; there in plan view were four old-fashioned, straight-winged, big, stubby, workhorse Spads, all going what looked to be straight down, one behind another, just like four silver bags of cement dropped at about five-second intervals.

Time stopped for an instant before our aircraft noise reached the streets below. I brought my gunsight pipper onto the cluster of guns encircled by a big tublike abutment down there in the city, which appeared to be made mostly of red tiled roofs. It was then exactly 1:30 P.M. on my instrument-panel clock, a sultry, silent 12:30 noonhour below.

I was just outside my open-firing range, going north to south, head-to-head with the first Spad pulling out from his northward dive at what looked like barely 200 feet of altitude. I had already squeezed the stick trigger down to the first notch and felt the tiny vibrations of the gunsight movie camera grinding. "The red tile roofs! It's like looking down on the Stanford Quad from the top of the Hoover Tower! I'm too low already!" *Kawhoosh!* (Upper-right rocket pair gone.) *Kawhoosh!* (Lower rights gone.) "Now! Flip the armament panel to cannon!" *Burrrrrrrrrup!* and off, the old bird careening leftward and upward. "Reset the panel to upper-left rockets."

I can't say I saw any people on that run, but I did see those Zunis tear into the abutment (each with the impact of a 500-pound bomb), and I could see dust and tile flying everywhere.

I sashayed right with a quick deep wing dip for a peek toward the tanks and—my God!—I couldn't believe the fire! It was so red. It almost filled that three- or four-square-city-block Cyclone-fenced enclosure where the tanks were (or had been?). In that split second, a great truth was revealed to me: In the last ten seconds, America had just been locked into the Vietnam War. No question about it; as of *right now*, all other options were now closed. And the rest of those big Spad TNT bombs were still falling in a column, 28,000 pounds of them, and all going right down inside that fenced enclosure.

I climbed and wheeled to the left, and was instantly scooting across a featherbed of puffy black clouds. Flak! It was coming from everywhere.

I reeved that old Crusader down through those black puffs like a toy in abrupt and hard rolls right and left as I searched for and finally spotted my "gun tub" target again. Now I could see soldiers scrambling around inside that circular abutment—and I could see the orange flashes coming out of their guns' muzzles. First trigger notch—one potato, two potato, upper-left pair *whoosh*, lower-left pair *whoosh*, now guns, trigger down and hold! *Burrrrrrrrrup!* and off again. Then another sashay right and peek at the fire. Flames to 5,000 feet—red flames—black smoke billowing on up past 10,000 feet and still puffing up and up. Right wing dipped to see down— last Spad off and up over the hills! Home free!

Out over the water and at high altitude, after radio check-ins had been completed with all sixteen of the planes with me, I called the *Ticonderoga:* "Panther, this is double-O-seven in the blind. Clear of Vinh with seventeen airplanes. All bombs within the fence. All tanks hit and exploding. Fuel spraying from rocket holes. Smoke passing fourteen thousand feet and still climbing. Attacking PT boats now. Out."

My clock said 1:32. It had all taken only a minute and a half.

During the week or two following those three days of August 1964, the carriers *Constellation* and *Ticonderoga* and assorted destroyers and auxiliaries conducted exercises at sea in the area outside the Tonkin Gulf from which the strikes of August 5 had been launched. Our ships and airplanes all remained well outside North Vietnam's territorial waters, but we were ready to defend ourselves should attacks against our units come by air or sea from North Vietnam or Red China. My days were spent flying Combat Air Patrol hops, attending meetings about Fleet defense, analyzing our tactics during all the Tonkin Gulf events with my pilots, and reading and digesting the voluminous messages that flooded in from Hawaii and Washington.

Also I had time to digest American wire-service stories that arrived by radio each night and the periodicals which came in the daily mail deliveries from the Philippines.

The news-magazine stories of "the great sea battle of the night of August 4, 1964," were read with interest. *Time* magazine said on August 14:

. . . Through the darkness, from the west and south, the intruders boldly sped. There were at least six of them, Russian-designed "Swatow" gunboats armed with 37mm and 28mm guns, and P-4's. At 9:52 they opened fire on the destroyers with automatic weapons, this time from as close as 2,000 yards. The night glowed eerily with the nightmarish glare of air-dropped flares and boats' searchlights . . . Two of the enemy boats went down.

On the same date, *Life* said the following:

. . . In 20 more minutes, the *Joy* and the *Maddox* were under continuous torpedo attack and were engaging in defensive counterfire. There was now plenty for the radar-directed guns to shoot at. The *Maddox* and the *Joy* were throwing everything they had. By 10:15 the *Maddox* had avoided several torpedoes and had sunk one of the attacking craft. For the next half hour the *Maddox* and the *Joy* weaved through the night seas, evading more torpedoes and sinking another of the attackers.

The August 17 issue of *Newsweek* had this to say:

At 9:30 P.M. the *Maddox* reported that enemy craft, identified as Soviet-built 50 and 100 ton PT boats, were closing in. By 9:52, both destroyers were under continuous torpedo attack. In the mountainous sea and swirling rain, no one knew how many PT boats were involved as they rose and fell in the wave troughs. The U.S. ships blazed out salvo after salvo of shells. Torpedoes whipped by, some only 100 feet from the destroyers' beams. A PT boat burst into flames and sank. More U.S. jets swooped in, diving, strafing, flattening out at 500 feet, climbing, turning 90 degrees at 8,000 feet, and diving again . . . The battle was won. Now it was time for American might to strike back.

Wire-service stories during the first week after the raids of August 5 included both the good news and the bad. The Vinh oil tanks were described as 90-percent destroyed; but two of my old *Constellation* shipmates had been shot down on their raid up northeast of Haiphong a little over two hours after ours. A Spad pilot by the name of Sather was presumed dead; but a Skyhawk jock named Alvarez, whom I had grown very fond of as we shared his squadron's ready room, was reported captured by the North Vietnamese in a story dated August 7. McNamara had announced the movement of lots more American hardware and manpower into Southeast Asia. The Tonkin Gulf Resolution passed both House and Senate on August 7 on the coattails of the "second" Tonkin Gulf incident, the fiasco of August 4. And on the morning of August 11, we read in the wire-service stories at the breakfast table that, following our raids of August 5, a Harris poll showed that LBJ's national popularity rating jumped fourteen percentage points. Said Lou Harris in the *Washington Post* on August 10:

> In ordering an air strike on North Vietnam PT boat bases, according to a just completed survey of a cross-section of the public, in a single stroke Mr. Johnson has, at least temporarily, turned his greatest political vulnerability in foreign policy into one of his strongest assets.

Just before noon on that same day, August 11, 1964, I was sitting at my desk doing squadron paper work when suddenly the ship's yodel horn on the flight deck blared the welcome-aboard honors appropriate for a vice admiral. I remember wondering how that could happen out there in the middle of the ocean, and I decided I must have missed the noise of a helicopter landing. Just then the phone rang. It was Captain Hutch Cooper.

"Jim, a couple of guys just came aboard and they say they want to talk to you. You go up to my in-port cabin and answer their questions. I'll send them down with an escort."

I threw on a clean shirt, thinking it was odd that the captain had said "guys." If it were an admiral, he would have said "admiral." I decided that it must be some defense official who ranked with a vice admiral. I bolted up the ladder and down the passageway. Yes, they were two guys all right: Both were in sport shirts and slacks, one about my age and the other at least five years younger. The young one was introduced as Alvin Friedman, deputy assistant secretary of defense for international security affairs. I decided the honors must have been rendered for him. He was clearly uncomfortable in the surroundings; in fact I distinctly remember thinking that he acted like he was trapped in enemy territory and scared to death. I don't remember his saying a word after "hello." The other man had obviously been around. He introduced himself as Jack Stempler, special assistant to Secretary McNamara.

We stepped into the vacant cabin and closed the door. Stempler was affable and offhand as he spoke: ". . . I knew damned well something was up. Day before yesterday, Sunday, I was down with my family at the cottage at Nag's Head. About four in the afternoon, I was walking back from the beach and what do I see but a government staff car in the driveway. I was to go right to Washington; so I packed a bag and away we went. We were sent out here just to find out one thing: Were there any fuckin' boats out there the other night or not?"

That said it all—I could stand right there in the cabin and write the script of what was to come: Washington's second thoughts, the guilt, the remorse, the tentativeness, the changes of heart, the backout.

And a generation of young Americans would get left holding the bag.

Chapter 2

The Navy Wife

Some of my earliest memories are of spinning tales of romantic fantasy about my present and future life as I whiled away the hours tossing a tennis ball against the side of our white clapboard house, high on a Connecticut hillside. My favorite fantasy was that I was really a royal princess, and that a handsome prince had already been chosen as my future husband. I would dream about his looks and where he might be at this very moment.

Actually, I often spent summer afternoons with my father, feeding the chickens and cleaning their coops, spraying apple trees for bugs and tent caterpillars—jobs I didn't like at all. My dad was proud of the family dairy business—started in 1884—in which he and his brother had worked with their dad since their early teens, and he lamented the fact that I'd probably never learn to milk. The tremendous pride he took in everything he did made me less inclined to complain about learning the things he felt I should know. I'll never forget his admonition to me about my future life: I was to be sure to leave my cellar door open during warm summer days!

He took me to visit the only navy ship I was ever aboard in my life before I met Midshipman Stockdale. One of my dad's dairy workers was in the naval reserve. He urged us to visit a small vessel that tied up in New Haven Harbor during one Memorial Day weekend in about 1935. I went aboard with my mother, father, and brother during the ship's holiday open house. I was impressed by the strength of the heavy gray metal and the power of the huge guns. I'd never dreamed navy ships would be so strong and powerful. This was a world I knew nothing about—nor did I care to know

more. I was eager to get back to shore. Memorial Day weekend was
the time each year when all the families who spent the summer at
Sunset Beach would be down for the first time since winter.

I'd been spending my summers at Sunset Beach since I was five
years old. My parents had bought our fully furnished Victorian cottage in 1929; it was only ten miles from our winter house, so my
father could drive back and forth to his dairy business. I learned to
swim our first summer there, and began to row a small boat early
the next year.

At Sunset Beach I had playmates for the first time, too. At low
tide we sailed mussel-shell boats in the nearby tide pools and threw
rocks to make the clams squirt so our big brothers would know
where to dig for them. At high tide, wearing our round tubes, we'd
swim out to the raft offshore. When I was nine, I learned to dive
headfirst from that raft. As we grew older, we played dress-up using
an empty garage as our headquarters. To this day I remember my
exotic suitcase—a patent-leather hatbox. The climax of a dress-up
session was always a mock wedding. We'd drape ourselves elabo-
rately in lace curtains, taking turns being the bride, and promenade
in solemn procession up and down the seawall, humming the wedding march and tossing rose petals in the bride's path. Each year I
learned new ways to fill the long, carefree summer days. My dad
had bought a fourteen-foot rowboat with a nine-horsepower outboard motor. He'd often let me steer and he taught me where all
the rocks and sandbars were located. I learned to mix the proper
amounts of oil and gasoline to operate the motor. When I was
strong enough to pull the cord to start the motor, I occasionally was
allowed to take the boat out alone. When I was eleven, I asked my
dad for a boat of my own.

"You'll enjoy it more if you earn the money to buy it yourself,
Sybil," he told me. "This winter you can take complete charge of
the chickens and I'll sell the eggs on the milk route. I'm sure that by
spring you'll have made enough profit to buy a small rowboat."

He was right, and after countless days of watering, feeding,
buying supplies, and collecting eggs as well as cleaning the coop by
myself, I bought my very own lightweight, square-ended rowboat. I
even had enough money left over to buy a secondhand bicycle.
Hard work produced handsome rewards. I was heartbroken when
the hurricane of 1938 swept my little boat out to sea. The following

summer, my brother, Merwin, had an eighteen-foot sailboat called a "knockabout." When I helped him with his chores, he'd give me a sailing lesson. He and I were never close, probably because he was so much older.

The one wintertime activity I absolutely adored was my dancing class. I had started taking ballet and tap in the third grade and loved every minute of it. I'd practice by the hour on our big front porch, and if I'd had long legs and a liberated mother, I think I might have become a Rockette. Shortly after I started the seventh grade, my feet began to hurt in toe shoes. By November, walking on the frozen ground brought tears to my eyes. In December, a bone specialist diagnosed excessive scaffoid bones—an extra bone in each foot. As I matured, it would become increasingly difficult for me to walk. The remedy was to remove the extra bones surgically. The operation took place at Grace–New Haven Hospital, and afterward my legs were encased in plaster casts from my toes to my knees for six weeks. But two years later, I was back in my toe shoes and thankful indeed for my recovery.

I had my first date at the shore the summer I was fourteen. It was with the brother of one of my childhood friends, and she and his friend went with us. Her father drove us to the big white wooden summer hotel called the Montowese House. Each evening as soon as the orchestra started to play, all the visitors in residence would turn their rocking chairs around to face the dance floor so they could enjoy watching the young people dance. For years afterward, with numerous boyfriends, I danced for hours at that summer hotel. Between dances we'd saunter out onto the boardwalk and exchange romantic kisses under a mellow moon and shining stars.

By the summer I was sixteen, I was sailing or canoeing or swimming almost every waking hour of those summer days with one or another of my high-school pals. I had a portable windup Victrola, and four of us would dance on our front porch until well after midnight to our favorites, the "Dipsy Doodle" and "Who."

One Friday night, three weeks into my high-school junior year, my mother announced that she had made arrangements for me to charge to a private girls' day school starting Monday morning. She was dissatisfied with the quality of the public high school, but I was devastated at the idea of being separated from all my friends, both male and female. I bawled and screeched, and declared I was not going to go. She calmly told me she'd do anything she could to help me with the adjustment but she wanted me to understand clearly that I was going to go.

The next day we bought the required blue serge uniform with white blouse and white socks, and on Monday morning, with every trace of makeup scrubbed from my face, I took my place in the room with my class of eighteen other girls. Some were from the other New Haven suburbs, but the majority were from the more affluent west side of the city. The headmistress looked as if she'd stepped right out of a Victorian novel. She always wore black and sent chills of terror through my heart. On my first day, she removed her pince-nez from her beaklike nose and coldly told me I was fortunate to be at the school and would have to work extremely hard to keep up with the others, most of whom had been in private schools all their lives. She'd be watching me closely.

She frightened me, but I decided I'd show her that this hick kid from the country on the east side of town could do just as well as the others. In retrospect, probably some of the stern lessons I learned from that headmistress helped toughen me up for some of my future ordeals with my own teenagers. She was right about my having to work hard. She announced that during the spring vacation I'd have to increase my vocabulary greatly to qualify for Mount Holyoke on the College Board exams. She handed me a copy of the *Johnson O'Connor Vocabulary Builder,* saying she doubted I'd have enough time to study it thoroughly before the exam. I spent the entire vacation memorizing that book. When I came to the vocabulary section of the exam, I whizzed through with ease. I'm sure that was the reason I was accepted at Mount Holyoke.

My mother was more thrilled than I. She had always wanted to go there but because of the expense had to settle for Normal School, the local teachers' college. She and I spent the summer of 1942 preparing my wardrobe for college. For the first time, I had the thrill of selecting store-bought clothes; always before, we'd look in the stores and then my mother would do her best to make reasonable facsimiles on her Singer. I was completely absorbed in packing my trunk and matched suitcases imprinted with my initials in gold.

I had never seen the college before the September day when I arrived as a freshman. Indeed, World War II gas rationing precluded my parents' driving me to South Hadley even on this day. We said goodbye at the New Haven Railroad Station. I was a little too warm in my black-and-white herringbone suit, but I felt I looked so voguish, I wouldn't even take off the jacket. I did take off my red-and-black pillbox hat, however, after waving my mother and dad out of sight.

"Just be yourself, Sybil" had been my mother's parting advice. "That way you'll be just fine." And "just fine" I was during my years at college. By sophomore year, I'd found the perfect college roommate—a tall, blond Southerner from Richmond, Virginia, named Bebe Woolfolk. Her stunning good looks attracted young men from far and wide despite the wartime gas shortage. I happily shared double dates and did my best to improve the morale of our young men in the services. My special heartthrob was in the Army Air Corps. My letters followed him from camp to camp, and for a long time I wore his fraternity pin. But when he was home on leave during the fall of my senior year, we decided to break it off.

I had accelerated my academic program so I could graduate early and help the war effort. But the war had ended by the time I graduated in January 1946. Bebe had also graduated early, and we wanted to share an apartment, so I accepted a job teaching medieval history and modern dance at St. Catherine's School in Richmond. As a new teacher, I also drove day students to and from school, monitored a study hall two nights a week, ate my meals at an assigned table in the dining room, and chaperoned boarding students on shopping trips. None of this slowed down my social life in the least. Richmond is a social city, and Bebe introduced me to most of the young men returning home from World War II.

Another young teacher, Anne Rogers, became a close friend. She was engaged to a midshipman at the U.S. Naval Academy and visited him there as often as she could. She was anxious to have Bebe and me share the fun of dating at the academy, so she had her fiancé, Joe Cofer, arrange blind dates for us for Easter weekend in the spring of 1946. We three girls stayed at a guesthouse in Annapolis and were waiting there in the living room when the three midshipmen came through the door. They looked stunning in their dark blue uniforms, gold buttons sparkling, white gloves gleaming, and black shoes shimmering. Joe introduced Bebe and me to the other two young men—one a tall blond fellow named Marvin Scoggins; the other a shorter, dark-haired fellow named Jim Stockdale. It was not at all clear whose date was whose, but as we all left the house to walk through the grounds, we naturally paired off according to height. Bebe was taller than Jim, so it was more logical for Jim to walk with me.

In answer to my queries, Jim explained that he was from a small town in Illinois called Abingdon, near Galesburg, about fifty miles from Peoria and about 200 miles southwest of Chicago. He'd been to Monmouth College in Illinois for one year after graduating from Abingdon High School. His dad was in the pottery business in Abingdon. He was in charge of the artware division, but the Abingdon Potteries also made sanitary ware, Jim said, adding that the next time I rode a Pullman train, if I looked at the label on the toilet, I'd probably see it said "Abingdon Potteries."

I thought we were getting into a really personal subject pretty quickly, but I admired his no-nonsense forthrightness, though I had to concentrate hard to understand his rapid speech and midwestern accent. I had on flat heels for this walk, but I estimated his height at about five foot nine, so the heels I would wear with my evening dress would be just fine. He had a square, powerful-looking build; dark brown wavy hair; and the biggest, most incredibly blue eyes I'd ever seen in my life. I asked about the three narrow gold stripes on the sleeves of his uniform, which the other fellows didn't have. He explained that he and Joe and Marvin were all midshipmen first class, which meant they'd graduate as ensigns in June. His gold stripes meant that he was a midshipman officer and a member of the brigade staff. The "brigade" was the student body—all 4,000 midshipmen in all four classes at the academy; the brigade staff were the seven midshipmen appointed as leaders of the brigade. He said that when I watched the parade to evening meal formation, I'd see him march out in a separate group with the brigade staff. He'd worked hard and was glad to have the recognition. The competition was fierce because some fellows had had two or three years of civilian college before coming to the academy.

✧

Before I knew it, we were back at the guesthouse making arrangements to meet for the evening. Jim took charge, naming times and places to meet and outlining the schedule for the evening. I was impressed with the way he got everyone to cooperate with his ideas. He had a wonderful sense of humor and we were all laughing as we parted to get dressed for the evening. While Anne was zipping up my long black velvet gown, I babbled on about how much I liked my blind date. She told me quietly that there had been all that confusion about who would escort whom because Jim had made a deal with Joe before they met us. Jim had a real bomb-out of a blind date the weekend before and he would agree to go along on Joe's date only if he was given first choice of the two girls after he'd had a look at them. Joe had agreed, but little did Jim know that Bebe would tower over him in height. Fate can be a powerful force.

By the time I left Annapolis that weekend, Jim and I had made plans to meet again in three weeks, as well as spend June Week together when he graduated. His parents would come east for that, and there would be a full week of parties and dancing. I knew very well that a midshipman invited only a special girl for those festivities, and I was thrilled at the prospect. I told Bebe's sister about Jim the day after we returned to school, and she was aghast when I said, "I think I've found the man I want to marry."

When I met Jim's parents during June Week, I was immediately taken with his dad's friendliness and good humor. His mother was much more reserved; it was hard to figure out whether she liked me or not. She had Jim's huge blue eyes, and she was a very portly, dignified lady. She reminded me just a little bit of the headmistress at the girls' school I'd attended before college. She had an exquisite peaches-and-cream complexion and almost always wore shades of blue to match her eyes. She was having a painful bout with arthritis, so was using a cane for walking. Jim's dad was infinitely patient with her slow gait and obviously adored her. His widowed sister, Hazel, was with them also. She often visited them and was especially fond of Jim.

I was proud to be Jim's date—he was both popular and intelligent. It felt good to watch him salute Admiral Nimitz and, as the man in his company with the highest academic standing, accept the diplomas for the whole company. Jim's dad was so thrilled, he'd hired a professional photographer to take pictures of Jim during the ceremony.

Right after June Week, Jim and I, along with Anne and Joe and another couple, had a post-June Week house party in Anne and Joe's hometown in West Virginia. We were so reluctant to be apart before the brand-new ensigns had to depart for a month of special training at Jacksonville, Florida, that the last night of our house party we just stayed up all night. Afterward I slept thirty-six hours straight. As I drove home to Connecticut for the summer, the world seemed a forlorn and lonely place apart from Jim.

A week later, however, Jim telephoned and asked me to come to Florida so we could continue our celebrations. Anne and our other house-party pal would be there, and he hoped I'd come as soon as I could. I was on the train within twenty-four hours. From Jacksonville, Jim was going home to Illinois on leave before reporting to his destroyer in the Pacific. He decided to come with me to Connecticut to meet my parents before going home. Later he described his tremendous relief at finding my parents similar to his in many ways. The Protestant work ethic was the center post of their lives and they never drank alcohol.

Each time we met, it became more and more difficult to say goodbye. The summer stretched ahead with little to look forward to after he left for Illinois. Three days later, he called and asked if I could come out the following week and visit his hometown. I'd never been west of the Allegheny Mountains, and as I rode west on the train, I marveled at the stretches of flat open country with no trees. At first I caught myself searching for the sea in the distance; the only flat open land I'd ever seen was salt meadows bordering the seashore.

During my visit, Jim's mother questioned me pretty carefully about my family background, college studies, and plans for the future. I still didn't feel any sense of real warmth or approval. One morning, when I emerged from my bedroom in a modest housecoat, I was stunned to have Jim tell me his mother preferred I be fully dressed before coming to breakfast. Embarrassed and puzzled, I quickly complied.

When I left for home this time, Jim and I knew we were saying goodbye for a long time. We agreed to concentrate on the good times we'd had together and write to each other often. I waved and watched out the train window until he disappeared from sight.

In mid-November of that fall of 1946, Jim called me at St. Catherine's School saying he had leave to come east; would I go to the Army-Navy game with him and get him a room in Richmond for the following week? It was heavenly to be back with him again, sharing his humor and his sea stories. The day after the Army-Navy game, he asked me if I'd like to go to Annapolis the following week to look at miniatures. Breathlessly, I said, "Do you mean what I think you mean?" He said he did, and I told him I thought it was a grand idea. Most Naval Academy graduates give miniatures of their class rings as engagement rings. Thus, Jim had just asked me to marry him, and I had accepted.

I was ecstatic. We decided not to announce it until spring. Meanwhile I had to finish my year of teaching and he would try to get transferred to an East Coast ship. We would be married in Connecticut in June.

I think my principal despaired at my dreamy behavior in the next months. More than once she found me in the library gazing into the distance. Sharply she would remind me that my class was waiting.

I continued to be impressed with Jim's ability to get things done. Early in 1947 he called and said that in the spring he'd be transferred to the USS *Charles H. Roan*, DD853, home-ported in Newport, Rhode Island. My mother and dad announced our engagement at a big family party at home on March 29, 1947. After that, my principal's despair grew more complete: I forgot not only classes but chapel services I was supposed to conduct and faculty meetings I was required to attend. I read *The Navy Wife* numerous times and was thrilled at the future it portrayed for me. My mother came to Richmond, where we shopped for my wedding dress and trousseau. She was delighted to have a free hand planning the wedding. Our own church was too tiny to hold the 250 people we planned to invite; instead, we reserved the picturesque Congregational church in nearby North Branford, which my mother and her parents had always attended. Jim would be sent to Sonar School in Key West for our first eight weeks of marriage. This was a lucky break because it eliminated his being at sea or having the duty aboard ship every third night. We were married on June 28, 1947, and flew to Key West the next day. School would start for Jim on Monday morning.

I couldn't believe the wall of wet, sticky heat that smacked me in the face when we changed planes in Miami. It was a long way from the cool summer breezes at Sunset Beach, but *The Navy Wife* had prepared me for some unpleasant living conditions. I was going to make the best of everything. We rented a tiny furnished house next to the southernmost house in the United States. Tour buses came by regularly and announced this fact loudly while the tourists stared at me hanging my laundry. My mother had valiantly tried to teach me to cook when I was a young girl, but I was stubborn and insisted I never planned to be without servants.

Jim was patient with me that summer and fortunately was not a fussy eater. Unfortunately my best dish was broiled steak and I soon learned that his take-home pay of $280 a month wouldn't support my talent. I was good at American goulash, too, and little by little I added to my repertoire. I spent most of the day at the pool, where other young navy wives chattered away about every aspect of married life. I listened carefully. I loved the camaraderie and easy friendliness among them. We were all a long way from home, which made us even friendlier. In the evening Jim and I would often go to the open-air ten-cent movie with another couple, stopping at the patio bar for a drink afterward. I reveled in my freedom to be with Jim during all his free time. Often before bed we'd walk down to the seawall in our pajamas and sit with arms entwined watching the Southern Cross hanging over the tropical sea, counting our blessings.

By the time we left Key West in early September, the ship was in the yard for overhaul in Boston. We found a third-floor apartment with a hot plate for cooking and space to share in the first-floor refrigerator. It cost $100 a month, so I found a job as a typist to supplement our income.

While living there, we paid our first formal twenty-minute call—as described in *The Navy Wife*—on Jim's commanding officer and his wife. The actual doing didn't seem quite as glamorous as I had envisioned from reading about it. It seemed foolish to me to drive an hour to get there and an hour to get home, just to stay only twenty minutes, but I certainly had no intention of criticizing the system; I was sure they had good reasons for all their customs and traditions. Jim, however, coached and played on the destroyer squadron football team that fall, and I was dismayed at his audacity when he refused to let his team stay in some filthy quarters aboard a ship when playing in Newport; instead, he took the team to the YMCA. When I asked if he didn't think he'd get into trouble doing that, he said he knew he was right and was going to take care of his men first. I never would have dared such defiance.

Shortly after the beginning of the new year, 1948, Jim left with the ship for a six-month deployment to the Mediterranean. This was my first big test as a navy wife. I moved home and got a job as a Dictaphone typist with Dun & Bradstreet in New Haven. I'd go to the movies or visit old friends occasionally, but I was glad to have parents for company. I wrote to Jim almost every day, and he was always good about writing long, loving, descriptive letters. I really lived for the mail.

Finally in June came the glorious day of the ship's return to Newport. Through my binoculars, I could see Jim waving wildly from the radio mast as the squadron of ships steamed past Castle Hill at the entrance to Newport Harbor. I'd been in town a week and had settled into a small furnished apartment, but hadn't liked staying in that strange apartment alone. I barricaded the bedroom door each night and stayed awake until almost dawn. For more than one reason, I was glad to have Jim home again.

He announced immediately that he wanted us to go to Washington to try to get his orders changed so he could be on a ship that would spend more nights in port. Sure enough, two weeks later he was ordered to a small submarine chaser in Key West. We packed the car with all our worldly possessions and headed south. Somewhere between Georgia and Florida, I mentioned I might want to buy a vacuum cleaner someday. That brought on our first real disagreement. He did not intend to become encumbered with a load of material possessions that would slow him down. He planned to travel fast and light, and he felt it important that I agree. I did not agree, nor did I see how a vacuum cleaner was going to cause him that much trouble. He would understand if he were the one who had to do the cleaning. I sniffled awhile and silence prevailed as we made our way south.

✦

We found a furnished efficiency apartment our first day in town. The management provided a vacuum cleaner, so that subject was put on the back burner. As soon as we were settled, I heard they needed teachers at the high school. The following week I was presiding over a class of eighth-graders studying general science. It wasn't my area, but they were hard up for teachers. I learned twice as much as the students, with Jim helping me through some of my shakier spots.

Jim liked his smaller ship. There were only two officers aboard, so he was the executive officer even though still an ensign. We laughed about the speedy progress of his career. In the middle of that year, we moved to a cheap, substandard navy-housing apartment, which I painted before we moved in. Both sets of parents visited us that winter, along with almost everyone else from our hometowns. We were busy acting as tour guides around our tiny island.

Jim's mother was upset because he'd applied for flight training at Pensacola. She talked him into applying for a Rhodes Scholarship where he'd be safer. She wasn't too happy with me for not opposing the flight-training idea; she wanted me to help her influence him to become a lawyer. Jim applied for the Rhodes Scholarship, but a civilian was selected.

We left Key West for flight training in Pensacola in June 1949. We rented our first real house in Pensacola. It was fully furnished but had only throw rugs, so I didn't mention a vacuum cleaner. Frustrated in our efforts so far to start a family, we bought a boxer dog instead. Jim played football with the Pensacola Navy team and would sometimes be away on weekend trips. The dog helped calm some of my night terrors, but I still barricaded the bedroom door. I hated being alone all night in that house, but didn't dare tell Jim. Part of my job as a navy wife was to make the best of my situation. I didn't want to fail him in any way.

✧

Late in the spring of 1950, I knew we'd have our first child in December. I was thrilled at the prospect, but felt dreadful most of the day. Jim would leave about four in the morning to drive out to Whiting Field with a lunch I'd packed. As soon as he left, I'd flop onto the sofa and doze and groan my way through the day. I felt somewhat better by June, when we left for another phase of flight training in Corpus Christi. We rented a brand-new furnished apartment there, surrounded by unplanted dusty fields. The dirt would blow in and literally drift on the windowsills. After the first week, we bought a vacuum cleaner.

✧

By the time our first son, James—Jimmy—was born in December 1950, we were living in Norfolk, Virginia, in yet another furnished house. Jim was in an antisubmarine squadron flying TBMs. In the fall of 1951 he was sent to Landing Signal Officer School back in Pensacola. I particularly disliked the tacky furniture in that Florida house and was glad to return to Norfolk and a nicely furnished house in Virginia Beach.

At a wedding reception we attended early in 1952, someone raved about the good buy they'd gotten on a house in a Norfolk suburb. Jim and I decided to look at the same development on the way home. Relaxed by the wedding champagne, before we knew it we'd signed up to buy a three-bedroom brick house for $10,200. On the way home, as I sobered up, I suddenly remembered we didn't have any furniture. To my surprise, Jim said, "We've got a room full of baby furniture and so much other stuff now, we might as well buy the rest." I began haunting the unclaimed-freight warehouse and we asked our parents for anything they could spare from their attics. I felt very much the complete navy wife when we moved our own furniture into our own house at 6432 Otis Circle.

The moves were getting harder, though, with a baby and so many more possessions, and Jim was beside himself with frustration because the navy wouldn't send him to the Korean War. I was astounded that he wanted to go. He even offered to pay his own way to California to board an aircraft carrier if they would let him go. "You have to understand," he insisted, "fighting is my profession. When my country's at war, I want to be part of it. That's what I'm trained to do." I tried to understand, but was secretly glad he couldn't go.

I was pregnant again early in 1953. But while Jim was at sea, I realized I might lose the baby. A neighbor called an ambulance, which took me to the navy hospital. I'd had Jimmy in a civilian hospital so I could use natural childbirth to avoid anesthesia. I'd heard frightening stories about the horrors of navy hospitals—they were the one part of the system in which I did not have complete faith.

I miscarried during the night and had the minor routine operation that follows in the morning. I woke up in a room by myself, overwhelmed with grief and feelings of failure. I cried so steadily that the captain of the hospital came to my room to try to console me. I was inconsolable and just had to cry until I didn't have any more tears. A friend sent Jim a message through navy channels. By mail, and in person when he returned, he reassured me over and over again that he did not consider me a failure in any way. It was the first major storm I'd weathered alone as a navy wife and it left me shaken and uncertain.

In January Jim was thrilled to be ordered to test-pilot training at Patuxent River, Maryland—and I was expecting once more. Because the doctor admonished me to walk fifteen minutes out of every hour during the trip, Jim would drop me off and drive way ahead, where he'd park and read *Time* until I caught up with him.

In Patuxent, we moved into an apartment on the base in a big cinder-block building. It was hideous. Big pipes ran across the ceilings of all the rooms, and the plasterboard walls were dented and scarred. In the spring we bought a house out in the country near Chesapeake Bay. For the first time we had our own fireplace. Jim could pick up oysters at low tide in the bay, and Jimmy had some nice playmates nearby. We bought an Oldsmobile for $125 for Jim to drive to work. He had started flying jets for the first time and was completely absorbed and happy with his work. I felt better carrying this baby and even dared to go to a navy doctor and navy hospital.

There was no other hospital for miles around anyway. Sidney, named after my father, was born on August 3, 1954.

Although I knew very well that life as a test pilot was extremely risky, I was sharply reminded of this one day in 1955 when Jim announced that a close friend had been killed. Several of us drove to Washington together for his funeral at Arlington, and I was shocked at all the laughing and joking that went on among the men on the ride up and back. Later I told Jim I thought they could at least have shut down flight operations on the day the fellow was buried. Jim explained that would be the worst thing they could do; it would destroy morale and depress everybody; you had to accept death as a natural part of the business. I felt sure the navy had thought the whole thing through, but more than once my heart almost stopped when I looked out the window of our country house and saw a black sedan approaching. The navy chaplain always came to tell you about death in a black sedan.

In January 1957 Jim received his orders to Fighter Squadron 211 at Moffett Field in California. I was delighted to finally be going to the West Coast, but I cried when I left my pretty little house in Patuxent.

My first days in California were a nightmare. We were in a rented furnished house again, and it rained steadily. I caught a cold that turned into an ear infection, and both children had dreadful colds too. Jim was nervous as a cat. He was waiting for the squadron to return from a deployment and suffered from fears that he might not measure up; he'd never been in a fighter squadron before. He stood and played solitaire on the kitchen counter until I thought I'd scream.

When I began to feel better, we went house-hunting and finally found one in Los Altos we could afford. This one was $21,500 and I painted it both inside and out. I'd painted all our other houses inside, but this was my first outside job. Fortunately it was a one-story house. Jim rototilled the yard and planted new grass. The sun came out that spring and Jim was getting along fine at the squadron. I miscarried again but was much better able to handle the disappointment. It led me to a civilian doctor I adored. When I miscarried a third time a few months later, he told me to come see him the minute I thought I might be pregnant. By the time that happened, I was enrolled in a master's program in education at Stanford University. The doctor prescribed thyroid medication and on December 6, 1959, six months after I was awarded my master's from Stanford University, our own baby Stanford was born. My mother and father were there for the event and stayed for the winter. Jim was in the Western Pacific with his fighter squadron on his second nine-month deployment of this California stint.

Back home again in the spring of 1960, Jim received orders to report to Stanford University in September. The navy was sponsoring him to a two-year master's degree program there. We rented out our house downtown and moved to a house in the nearby hills that had a separate study for Jim. The house was surrounded by twenty-five acres of pastureland, and came with an old horse. Jim taught eleven-year-old Jimmy to drive the car up and down the long driveway, and Sid became an expert at swinging across the nearby canyon on a rope. Our fourth son, Taylor, was born on April 3, 1962.

While at Stanford, Jim took some courses in philosophy and fell in love with the subject. He read philosophy books in his spare time, and I was pleased he'd found a diversion from his technical world. When he completed his degree, he was assigned to a fighter squadron in San Diego. At last I was going to see what was described as the best duty station in the navy. We sold our house in Los Altos and each drove a car with two sons in it south to Coronado, where we'd already rented a house. Coronado calls itself an island but is connected to the mainland by a narrow strip of land called the "silver strand." Most people went to and from San Diego on the auto ferry across San Diego Bay.

By the time Jim was deployed in April 1964 as commanding officer of Fighter Squadron Fifty-one aboard the aircraft carrier USS *Ticonderoga*, we were living in a big old shingled house at 547 "A" Avenue on the island of Coronado. I had bought the house while he was away, perhaps partly because it reminded me of the white clapboard house where I was born in the Connecticut countryside. The front door and double french doors on either side of it, as well as the windows in both the spacious living room and dining room, contained rows of tiny square panes of glass. I'd once had a book about Peter Pan that showed him looking through old English windows like these, watching the loving family life within. The living room of our new house had a heavy-beamed ceiling, bookcases framing a huge brick fireplace, and highly polished maple floors that sparkled in the late afternoon sunshine. One wall of the dining room consisted of a built-in buffet and china closet. A swinging door led into a butler's pantry, and there was a porch across the back. Another, smaller back porch had been glassed in and converted to a dinette; a second pantry, lined with shelves and cupboards, was home for the refrigerator. An old-fashioned water cooler had bubbled and blupped as the former owner drew me a drink of mineral water into a paper cup. Stairs from the kitchen led down to a two-bedroom apartment and up to four bedrooms, two bathrooms, and a long sleeping porch.

My best friend, Doyen Salsig, lived only a block away. Her husband, Budd, a navy captain, was aboard the *Ticonderoga* with Jim at that point. Doyen was a couple of years older than I and her dad was a retired admiral, so she knew all the ins and outs of navy life. Like me, she was raising four children—in her case, two boys and two girls. We'd play tennis together while our husbands were away on cruise.

Navy tradition dictated that, as the wife of the commanding officer of a fighter squadron, I should guide and help the younger wives. There were about twenty-five of them, and my role increased in importance when the squadron was away at sea. Usually the commanding officer's wife accompanied the chaplain when he had to give someone news about her husband's death. I shuddered at the thought and fervently hoped I'd never have to get that close to raw grief. Otherwise, I relished my role and felt well prepared for it. I'd been a Navy Relief volunteer for years and an officer in numerous wives' organizations. I liked being president best because it seemed easier to me just to be in charge of everything while others did the hard jobs.

During the summers, however, when Jim was at sea, I left my navy life behind and went to Sunset Beach with my boys. Coronado was the perfect navy town to live in during the school year—small enough so the boys could ride their bikes to all their activities and only a ten-minute ferry ride from San Diego. Not so good for teenagers without enough to do in the summertime, however. Along with a beautiful beach and ideal conditions for surfing came a beach-bum psychology this New England-trained mother found frightening. One day, by chance, I discovered Jimmy, our eldest, surfing in the forbidden North Beach area. I was almost as sad as Jimmy when I told him he'd have to sell his beloved board. From my own experiences and as a teacher, I knew only too well that rules were worthless without penalties for violation. I also knew Jimmy had to be an example for his three younger brothers.

In 1964, before Jim left in April, we'd agreed I'd have our nine-year-old station wagon overhauled for me to drive across the country with the boys that summer. Jimmy was thirteen and graduating from eighth grade; Sid was nine; Stanford four; and Taylor two. I rented a luggage carrier for the top of the car and a desert evaporator cooler for the front door window, bought sunscreens for the other windows, and plotted a northern route to avoid as much heat as possible. Since I'd have to do all the driving, I planned to cover only 350 miles a day. Some people from Arizona had rented our Coronado house for $700, which I figured would pay for the trip both ways. Jimmy was in charge of the maps, and Sid was in charge of his younger brothers. On our journey we let Stanford and Taylor play in the first snow they'd ever seen, in the Rocky Mountains, and marveled at the McDonald's signs proclaiming over one million hamburgers sold. We also stopped in Omaha to visit Jim's aunt Hazel, a great favorite of mine. A closet smoker myself, I was awed by Hazel's audacity to smoke wherever she pleased, even in the face of Jim's mother's disapproval. When Jim would light up his pipe, I'd smoke with him in the evening, and I smoked with Hazel. This shared flaw was a bond between us. I also shared with Hazel some of my apprehensions about our next stop, in Abingdon, to visit Jim's parents. Jim's mother had written to me in May outlining her plans for me and the boys while in Abingdon. Hazel brought me up to date on Jim's dad's health. He'd had a heart attack the year before and hadn't made a satisfactory recovery.

When I arrived in Abingdon a couple of days later, Jim's dad's labored breathing, gray pallor, and slow responses shocked me—he was in much worse shape than I had imagined. When in top form, he was the life of the party, regaling us all with laughter. In both winter and summer, he made numerous trips to the furnace room, where he enjoyed a bit of toddy in private so as not to alarm his beloved "Meb." In years past when he'd visited us alone while on business trips, we'd all drunk openly together. While in Abingdon, however, he and I both obeyed the rules of the household—publicly anyway. But he was unusually quiet and thoughtful during these steaming June days of 1964.

In spite of Jim's heavy flying schedule, he had written me some wonderfully long letters since his departure in April. I could tell from his letter dated June 7 that he was greatly excited. He said not to talk to anybody about its contents unless it became common knowledge. He'd been awakened by a phone call from the carrier air-group commander (CAG) about five that morning, summoning him at once. A secret message had just been received from Vice Admiral Moorer, commander of the Seventh Fleet, requesting that eight F-8 airplanes with air-to-ground capability be sent to the USS *Constellation* off Vietnam. It was clear that it would be Jim's squadron, since his was the only squadron with such a capability—the only airplanes in the fleet that could follow photo planes through the mountains at more than 600 miles an hour carrying the firepower of a destroyer. Jim's squadron had this capability only because they had taken the initiative to experiment, bypassing some of the navy's bureaucratic directives.

Ten minutes after Jim and his CAG concluded that VF 51 was being called for, Jim and his superb maintenance officer, Russ Baker, were in the ship's Operations Office compiling lists of men and supplies needed. Shortly, a second message arrived telling them to land aboard the USS *Constellation*, 100 miles east of Danang, South Vietnam, at 1630 hours. Jim would be aboard the "Connie" for dinner that evening. He asked me not to change the address on his mail as he would change locations by secret movement report.

The next day he wrote from the *Constellation* that the war in Vietnam was apparently at a turning point. The decision had been made to send F-8 fighter escorts with the photo planes when they flew over the Plain of Jars in Laos. The USS *Kitty Hawk* had had the duty the last two days; one photo F-8 had been shot down Saturday and one F-8 escort shot down Sunday. The pilot of the latter plane, a friend of ours named Bud Lynn, had been lifted out of the Laos jungle by helicopter.

In a later letter, he told me two more young pilots had been brought over from the "Tico" (USS *Ticonderoga*). He said their eyes almost fell out when he gave them their cloth maps, Laotian "pointee talkies" (sheets of paper with English phrases and Laotian dialect alongside), malaria pills, water-purifying pills, pep pills, and morphine (for pain, if you've got to make it up the hill anyway).

Jim and I had agreed we'd be honest with each other in our letters and not try to frost the truth. In one letter he explained carefully and mathematically that his chances of being killed were only one in 10,000. I thought those were pretty good odds.

In a letter written on June 12, he told me how the regular hierarchy was being bypassed as the war accelerated. He said General Harkins, who spoke for Henry Cabot Lodge in Vietnam, and the State Department were running things. He said a message from the Seventh Fleet was about as valuable a guide as a Christmas card, and that all the important events were run from the White House—the State Department and the Pacific military hierarchy just concentrated on the details.

I could tell he felt tremendously proud of VF 51's self-made attack capability. Every night, targets were assigned for the next day, and about 2:00 A.M. messages started coming in from Washington not to go. Jim's frustration with this sort of equivocating was clearly evident in his letters. On the Fourth of July, he reported that no one there knew a thing about what they were doing or when they might leave the area off Vietnam. He said that even rushing into port for a couple of days was out of the admiral's control. He thought maybe the whole thing was starting to fizzle out. Once he thought a "strike" really was on: At noon that day, Jim was to lead his F-8s into a place called Tha Thom and shoot at some military installations; a photo F-8 would take pictures afterward. But at 7:00 A.M. a "no execute" had come down the chain of command. The American ambassador to Laos hadn't liked the sound of it.

On the Connecticut shore, there was much for children of all ages to do. On the incoming tide there was fishing both from the rocky points and from boats. I wrote Jim about how the older boys rigged up a line with a fish on it so four-year-old Stan would think he'd made a catch. A couple of weeks later, the glee was shared by all when Stan really did catch a fish and I found it in his bureau drawer, where he was saving it until we returned to California! At low tide there was clamming for both steamers and quahogs. High tide was good for swimming, and both Taylor and Stanford, wearing their big orange "life deceivers"—as Stan called them—could safely pull themselves out on the pulley line to the pulley pole. I could sunbathe on the seawall reading a book, close at hand while seeming not to hover. Between tides this summer, Jimmy took his fourteen-year-old "girlfriend" from a nearby cottage riding on the Sailfish.

Meanwhile, letter after letter from Jim described his roller-coaster existence between frustration and exhilaration. I first heard the news about the initial Tonkin Gulf attack when I came in from sailing the first Sunday in August, and I felt sure Jim was involved.

On August 1, for the first time, I'd written Jim of my feelings of despair about his dangerous flying conditions. I was counting the days until the ship reached Hong Kong so the men could have some rest. I said my prayers with extra fervor every night and my heart seemed to stop every time the telephone rang. I watched every news broadcast. Being a navy wife was a hell of a way to live; every night I dropped into bed exhausted from tension. Even in a crowd, I felt lonely and different.

On Monday, August 3, 1964, the day after I heard the news about the Tonkin Gulf attack, my dad and I took all the boys sight-seeing in New York City to celebrate Sid's tenth birthday. All day I wondered if Jim felt satisfaction at having heard his first shots fired in anger. He'd often despaired of ever being given the opportunity to apply his accumulated knowledge. Nevertheless, it worried me that he was entering a time of crisis in such an exhausted physical condition.

A week later a young lieutenant from Jim's squadron telephoned me from the Philippines. The connection was bad, but I could make out enough to know that Jim was fine; he hadn't had time to write and had asked the first man ashore to let me know he was okay, that everyone on the "strike" he had led had done a good job, and that there might be some TV news coverage in the coming week. It was like Jim to be thoughtful enough to have someone call me when he didn't have time to write.

That week the *New York Times* carried a story entitled "Navy Pilots Tell of Vietnam Raid—Describe Attack at PT Base and Setting Oil Ablaze." In it, "Commander James B. Stockdale, leader of an F-8 squadron," was quoted. A reporter and photographer from the *New Haven Register* came for an interview, which appeared in the paper on Sunday, August 23. I was fascinated to read about my life and family in such detail in the press. I was pleased with their accuracy and especially happy for my parents' sake to have their friends know more about my life and Jim's.

Two days later, on August 25, the boys and I began our drive west to California. When we stopped in Abingdon again for another short visit, I was aghast to find Jim's dad in terrible shape. He'd been having injections every day for some time and needed an oxygen tank right beside his bed. He was pitifully weak and frail. We had arrived on a Thursday evening and by Saturday morning he agreed we should call an ambulance to transfer him to the hospital. That night in my letter to Jim, I told him not to be overly alarmed but to be prepared for a future emergency call.

I continued my drive west, telephoning Jim's mother every evening along the way. When I reached Salt Lake City, I cabled Jim that his dad was in a coma at St. Mary's Hospital (in Galesburg) and was not expected to live. As I drove on, I kept my fingers crossed that the navy's communication system would get the message to him swiftly.

We arrived back in Coronado on Saturday night, September 5. By Labor Day I was all unpacked and was relaxing on the beach when suddenly Doyen appeared. Jim had just called from March Air Force Base at Riverside. He was on emergency leave on his way to Illinois and wanted me to drive up there and pick him up so he could spend the night in Coronado. Doyen said her daughter, Fay, would take care of the children.

I was on the road to Riverside within an hour. I felt guilty about being so excited at the prospect of seeing Jim, with his dad's illness the cause. But a visit seemed like a gift from God—we'd been separated for more than four months.

Chapter 3

Growing Up in Illinois

In late August 1964, we were still at Yankee Station, just outside the Gulf of Tonkin, where we had been all summer. We had not moved back to the *Constellation* as planned, but were still at home on the *Ticonderoga*. Lots had changed since that first Sunday of this month when the *Ticonderoga* had been all alone and my four planes had gone up to help the *Maddox*. Now four aircraft carriers, and scores of surface ships of every sort maneuvered about this point. We carrier pilots no longer flew over the beach; we just circled the Seventh Fleet below us in a defensive crouch, ready to ward off Communist bombers should they attempt to retaliate for our "re-taliation" of the fifth.

Our Laos mission, way around North Vietnam and up into the Plain of Jars, had evaporated, boiled off. I sensed a total change of mood and posture in the whole operation. What had been, for this cruise and the one I had made just before it in 1963, a series of ad hoc special assignments around Vietnam now seemed congealed into a single permanent mission. Those three days in August had changed the situation: We were here to stay.

Certainly *I* was here to stay, at least for another year and a half. I'd had a letter from a friend in officer assignments in Washington giving me the momentous news that I had been selected for air-group commander. I was to stay out here in command of VF 51 until November, and then take command of the air group of the carrier *Oriskany* in February 1965. I would do that in San Diego, but we would head over here to Yankee Station six weeks later, about the first of April.

Of the carriers at Yankee Station that August, the *Ticonde-roga*—the first in—was the first to be replaced. On Thursday, September 3, we headed for Japan for eleven days of rest and recreation in Yokosuka. As we left Vietnam behind us and steamed off for what would be my squadron's first rest ashore since May, I relaxed and reflected in my stateroom: What about those orders to take over the *Oriskany* air group? What about Syb and Jimmy and Sid and Stan and Taylor? I was being offered a space on the very peak of the fighter pilots' pyramid just as they were finishing their second year of my almost continual absence from home.

Our last days of normal home life had ended in September 1962 when we finished our wonderful two-year sabbatical at Stanford. I had been given the time off to study history, political science, philosophy, and economics, in preparation for eventual assignments in strategy, plans, and policy in the Navy Department. I had felt very much at home and was motivated to try for a Ph.D. I wrote to my admiral to ask if the navy would give me two more years. I was told that I could go up the operational aviation command chain or go for a Ph.D. and become a specialist, but not both.

I wrestled with that decision, but Syb read through me. I loved to fly and had a feel for the sea, and Syb knew that and loved me and made my decision easy. "Do what you do best: Take the command route and go to sea."

So I took the master's degree in June 1962, and accepted the old admiral's "oversight" of not ordering me back to a squadron until after I had finished a special philosophy program he knew I particularly wanted to continue in summer school. In September the six of us headed for Coronado, near San Diego, where my fighter squadron was waiting.

Syb had been right. Now that the war was starting, I could never have lived with myself knowing that I had dodged the ultimate challenges of what I had spent my life preparing for: I had to take command of that air group.

After leaving for Japan on the first Thursday of September, the *Ticonderoga* conducted regular flight-training operations while we steadily eased northward. As we recovered the last airplanes in midafternoon on that Sunday, September 6, we also recovered a

plane from Cubi Point that had flown up with a load of newly arrived mail for the ship, bringing a letter from Syb. Her words about
my dad's health were ominous.

I bolted up the ladders to see Captain Hutch Cooper on the
bridge, and he got the picture immediately: I wanted to fly home
while the ship was in Japan, with the understanding that I would be
back before she sailed again. Within an hour, Hutch had launched a
special plane taking me on ahead to the overseas military air transport terminal at Tachikawa, Japan.

By dinnertime Monday, September 7, Syb and I were at our
home in Coronado with our four boys, I with a reservation on a
military plane to Omaha, Nebraska, early the next morning. A
phone call to mother had revealed that dad was still alive, but still
in a coma.

Even after a seeming lifetime of eight-month cruises, a reunion
with the family is an unusual and emotion-packed experience.
There at the dinner table was Jimmy, a fast-growing high-school
freshman, trying to summarize for me the high points of the last
months, including his first-ever regular football workouts the previous week. Sid, just starting the fifth grade, was full of tales of a
summer of fishing with his grandfather on Long Island Sound.
There was Stan, my four-year-old sand-castle builder, and sweet
little two-year-old Taylor, who was trying hard not to look at me as
if I were a total stranger.

My mind was spinning with pride in our sons' handsome and
wholesome development, and with thankfulness for our great good
fortune of having Syb to set the tone and act as head of the family.
Of course, the scene also stirred within me an occasional jolting
guilt pang. The whole family was sacrificing a great deal so that I'd
be free to satisfy my drives to fly and fight. But after seventeen
years of marriage, I had learned that Syb would never waver in her
insistence that I follow the career that suited me best, and the boys
understood that and never questioned it.

It was a heady time. I felt the precious nearness of Syb, who
had been in my dreams for the past five months. But I felt a muted
sadness, too, that in only a few hours I would be catching a plane to
see my dying father—and in less than a week I would fly back to
my squadron in the Western Pacific and leave them all on their own
again.

At that moment, too, I was harboring a gnawing sense of anxiousness to pass on the truth of the Tonkin Gulf to a few reliable friends just in case I didn't come home in November. Syb and the Salsigs, our neighbors and best friends, seemed the best choice. Budd was now on shore duty in San Diego and had been my pal on the *Ticonderoga* cruise the year before. He'd been three years ahead of me at the Naval Academy, was also a fighter pilot, had a graduate engineering degree, and had been included in the top 3 percent of his class selected for promotion to captain a year ahead of the rest. I asked Syb to have Budd and Doyen over at ten o'clock when the boys were already in bed, and the four of us talked late into the night. My description of the August 4 debacle took the cake. When they had it all straight, we opened a couple of bottles of champagne. Budd and Doyen left about midnight, just before Syb and I teetered up the stairs to celebrate our very brief time together.

By eight the next morning, the landing gear had been retracted on a rattletrap, prop-driven transport plane that was taking a dozen or more of us itinerant military hitchhikers east from California to Omaha. From there, I planned to board the Denver Zephyr, the overnight train to Galesburg, Illinois, where dad was hospitalized. The trip would be slow and tedious, but already I was becoming conscious of the fact that I needed these twenty-four hours alone. I saw this voyage home as more than just the duty of a loving son. I had taken my upbringing a lot more seriously than most, and to me this trip marked the end of an era in my life, a pilgrimage to my birthplace. It was there that I had taken on a driving sense of obligation, and become permanently encumbered with all that valuable emotional baggage that made me a conscientious but self-governing fighter pilot. I figured it was healthy to be reminded of my upbringing and who I was from time to time; I would take all those qualities I acquired in my boyhood home with me to the grave.

My father, Vernon Stockdale, was born in Mount Pleasant, Iowa, in 1888. By the time he was sixteen, his father had become an invalid and he had to quit school and work full-time to support his parents and sister, Hazel. His mother had been born in Abingdon, Illinois, had lived the first thirty-four years of her life there as a spinster, and owned property there. When my dad was nineteen, he moved his mother and father and fifteen-year-old sister back to his mother's house in that little town of 3,000 people and took a job in a brass-fixture factory.

Within a few months, dad met an Englishman who liked his manner and offered him a better job in the new vitreous-china (bathroom-fixture) factory he was about to start in the town. Vernon Stockdale would be the new company's timekeeper, setting up the payroll for the local men hiring on and for the immigrant Italian ceramic artisans. Twenty-year-old, good-natured "Stock," as the townspeople were starting to know him, unfamiliar with the Italian language and its proper names, assigned each of these immigrants an Anglo-Saxon name that went on his payroll: Angelo Ippolito became Andy Martin; Angelo Mangieri became Charley Morey; and so on. This was accepted by all parties as a humorous and practical solution to a problem Abingdon was not yet ready to cope with, and many of the "borrowed" names stayed with these Italian men for the rest of their lives.

My mother, Mabel Bond, was born in 1889 on a farm called Rolling View, owned by her father and mother, located four miles from Abingdon. She was their eighth child, but since the first five had died in a diphtheria epidemic in 1879, she became the third in a "second family" of four. She loved the farm and her home there, but when she was nine the family moved to town so that all four children would be near Abingdon's Hedding College.

Mabel finished Hedding with the class of 1910 at age twenty-one, with a B.A. in English and history. Her hometown beau was Vernon Beard Stockdale, but marriage was not yet on the horizon; they both had careers to develop. That fall "Meb," as "Stock" called her, went off to graduate school in Chicago for a year, and then started work as a high-school English teacher, public-speaking teacher, and drama coach. For six years she taught in New Mexico and Montana, but she returned to her alma mater, Abingdon High School, to start the fall term in 1917.

By that time Meb was twenty-eight and Stock twenty-nine. They had seen each other summers and corresponded throughout. Marriage was on their minds—but there was a problem: Her father didn't consider Stock good enough for his well-educated daughter.

That put their romance in limbo. With the United States then mobilizing for World War I, Stock obtained his employer's okay for a leave of absence from the pottery and joined the navy.

Dad was in the navy for only a couple of years, but it had a profoundly beneficial effect on him. He was thirty years old, and for half of his life had worked in Mount Pleasant and Abingdon as the sole source of financial support for a family of four. His mother and father were not used to poverty, and he had felt himself under the gun. For him, the navy was freedom, it was his first look at the big wide world, it was his "college."

Of course, he didn't have the education required for Officer Candidate School, but he went up through the enlisted ranks like a skyrocket and made chief petty officer within a year. He was kept right there where he joined, at Great Lakes Naval Training Station, near Chicago, and worked in parts procurement for the airplanes in brand-new Naval Aviation.

Meb's father died in his sleep the first winter Stock was gone, freeing Meb and Stock to marry in 1919, as soon as he got out of the navy. She was thirty and he thirty-one. She wrote a check for what became my boyhood home, the red brick house at 609 West Meek Street. Four years later, pregnant Meb resigned her teaching post, and I was born two days before Christmas, 1923, in the Cottage Hospital in Galesburg. My dad was in the delivery room at the time. I was named for his employer and mentor, Jim Simpson. I was an only child.

My alarm went off in my roomette on the Denver Zephyr at 5:00 A.M. The train was due to arrive in Galesburg in about an hour and a half, but we would be passing through dad's Mount Pleasant, Iowa, shortly before sunrise and I wanted to see if I could recognize anything as we whizzed through.

Dad had given me one of my earliest naval experiences in Mount Pleasant. He had taken me to an Iowa Wesleyan Commencement there in 1935, when I was only eleven, and I'd gone right up to Admiral Byrd and gotten his autograph on my program. He had just finished the address at that little college, and I still remember the stories he told about his recent South Pole expedition of 1933–34. I'll never forget how I, a somewhat overweight kid just out of the fifth grade, dreamed of doing something as extraordinary some-day. And the admiral—how splendid he was in his white service uniform with gold shoulder boards!

In hindsight it does not seem odd that dad picked that one as the only graduation we ever attended at Mount Pleasant. Nor does it seem strange that four years before, when I was seven and just out of the first grade, we drove to Annapolis, well out of our way, on my first summer vacation trip to see New York. There I stood by the Tecumseh figurehead in front of Bancroft Hall as the drums rolled and the bugles blared and the midshipmen marched back into their giant dormitory for their evening meal. From the time of my first memories, there had been no question about it: I would be going to Annapolis to make a career in the navy dad loved so much.

He had insisted on having his way on very few issues in his lifetime, but this was the big one, and even stubborn mom knew there was no arguing with it. I wasn't about to argue about it—I loved the idea throughout. But why did I believe it would really happen? Driving to Annapolis, driving to see Admiral Byrd, we were at the bottom of the Great Depression with no particular po-litical influence, no means of getting a service-academy appoint-ment, and I was a fat primary-school kid, unproved academically or physically. Moreover, there had been only one other boy who had ever left Abingdon for Annapolis; he had been from a wealthy fam-ily, a good athlete, a good student, and he had flunked out his second year. My dad's commitment to a pipe dream was not at all like him, but this was to be the exception that proved the rule. He was making a big statement to himself, to me: You do your part, I'll do mine, and it *will* happen.

In retrospect, I realize that dad didn't just survive the depres-sion, he prevailed in the face of it—and it nearly cost him his life. I remember that fall of 1929, soon after the bottom dropped out of the stock market, and afterward how he seemed to spend all of his time down at the plant, day and night. He came home with chills about the first of February 1930 and fell into bed with bronchial pneumonia. Hazel came and moved in with us, and so did a full-time nurse. It was a close thing. The word spread that he was on his deathbed, and mom had to lay down the law to debtors and credi-tors alike: No visitors/no deals in the sickroom. In April, when he started to be up and around, more than one of the Italian women—

wives of his original crew—came to the door and in halting English presented mom with big baskets of rich food and bottles of home-made wine for "Mr. Dale." Mom was never much at ease in these circumstances: Prohibition was on, she didn't approve of drinking, and she didn't know the women or they her. They all knew dad; he had helped them get jobs for their kids, and he had helped more than one of them get out of scrapes with the local police when they bent fenders driving cars without licenses. He liked them, and spoke up in calm but serious disapproval when mom referred to them as "dagos."

In the remaining depression years, the pottery not only lived, it grew, and dad gained in relative financial position. Dad bought out mom's brothers and sister and presented her with the deed to the property she cherished, Rolling View Farm. He also gained in rela-tive political position. By the time I entered high school, he and our congressman had agreed that if I met the physical and academic standards, an Annapolis appointment would be mine.

The Denver Zephyr was east of the Mississippi River now and the sun was coming up into clear skies. We were speeding along at seventy-five miles an hour, Galesburg only a few minutes up ahead. By the time the train began slowing, I was dressed in my navy commander's khaki uniform, my small handbag packed, and was ambling toward the door. It was about 6:30 in the morning and I was the only passenger who got off.

I stepped into familiar territory, familiar air that still had sum-mer heat in it; only the clear azure sky, unique to Midwest Indian summers, betrayed an approaching autumn. The platform was de-serted. I crossed behind the departing train and walked through the deserted big old depot, listening to my footsteps echo off its high arched ceiling.

I walked a few blocks west, past one of Galesburg's more fash-ionable cocktail bars (which had been in my orbit long before mom ever suspected), and turned left. In a couple of minutes, I was at the courthouse corner with Mother Bickerdyke, in bronze, treating a wounded Civil War soldier to my right, and St. Mary's hospital to my left.

It was now just before 7:00; mom and Hazel weren't due till 8:30. But I wanted to see dad. I was able to get his room number without arousing suspicion, climbed the stairs, and stealthily walked in, no nurses in sight. He lay curled in a fetal position, his back to me, in a bed with high guardrails. There were hanging bottles with hoses attached to him and an oxygen mask over his mouth and nose through which I could hear irregular panting. I touched his hand and kissed his cheek. He was hot as fire, and so tiny and weak that there was no question of his being awakened or recognizing anybody—he was in another world. Draped over the chair beside his bed, looking like new, was the Naval Academy bathrobe I had bought him when I graduated, my Junior Varsity football numerals sewn on the back of it. He had brought that with him on his last trip to the hospital. I walked out and down the stairs, still unnoticed. Dad was all but dead and I had to have some air.

I cut across the courthouse yard in front of Mother Bickerdyke and down the walk in front of Whiting Hall, the women's dormitory of Knox College. I aimlessly turned right at the corner—and saw Beecher Chapel. In the morning sunlight, I walked up to the chapel door and took a good look inside. Twenty-five years ago I had really rung the bell with mom by winning an important piano competition here. There was the stage, the grand piano, the seat where mom had sat. I turned on the heel of my navy shoes and automatically started retracing my steps of twenty-five years before across the Knox campus toward Willard Field. My watch, a beautiful Abercrombie & Fitch model named "Shipmate," which dad had given me when I graduated from high school, showed about ten minutes of eight. I was to meet mom and Hazel on the steps of the hospital in forty minutes. I walked by Knox's Old Main, past its side doorway where Abraham Lincoln had stood and debated while Grandma Bond and her father stood on this very lawn and listened, and out onto the running track.

Twenty-five years ago, I had come running out here in my track shorts and spikes after hurriedly changing clothes. I had been just in time for my race, the 120-yard high hurdles, but I finished next to last in my heat. No surprise—a short guy like me wasn't built for high hurdles, but there was nobody else to run them. I was filling a vacuum, but I was also following the advice of the wonderful freshman football coach I had played for the previous fall. He had told me that high-hurdle races were excellent developers of leg muscles for football.

That coach was an inspiration to me. He had me believing that if I conditioned myself and kept trying, I might even aspire to be captain of the varsity team when I was a senior; he made me feel I could do anything I set my mind to. Unlike me, he was a natural athlete; he had just finished college and was starting a teaching career in American history. His name was Sam Mangieri. He was the son of the immigrant potter my Dad had named Charley Morey in 1908.

Conditioning, conditioning, conditioning—that was one of the big things on my mind in those days. My work on the farm fit this pattern—lifting, straining, making myself keep going in the awful summer heat. That summer of '39, I begged dad to give me a job right alongside the biggest and toughest guys in the pottery, the saggar-shop division of the kiln gang. He checked with the foreman, Henry Way, and with Henry's okay I went to work at forty cents an hour. We were all stripped to the waist to stand the 130-degree heat by the kiln fires. We wore work caps with a doughnut-shaped pad inside them, right on the forecrown of our heads. It was on these pads that we carried the ninety-pound damp clay saggars from the big hydraulic press that punched them out, across to the drying racks in the reflected heat of the tunnel kilns. Back and forth we went, beasts of burden, supporting the wooden saggar slab with our extended arms until we slid it off onto the rack. I really felt I was one of the men, and more important, they were starting to treat me like one of them.

My dad would walk by once in a while on a tour of the plant, never letting on that he noticed me. At dinner one night, he did let the hint drop that there was talk down at Tony Faralli's pool hall (Abingdon's sports-information center) that I might make the varsity starting lineup as a guard that fall.

I thought about that a lot in the privacy of my swing in the backyard—one of my favorite thinking spots. And it happened. I knew the very instant the varsity coach made up his mind to give me the nod. It was a Wednesday afternoon scrimmage, the week between our second and third games. As a substitute, I had made my share of tackles in those first games, but I could tell that the coach still considered me too small for a regular berth—a "watch-fob guard," in the jargon of the sports pages of those days.

The best athlete in the school, and the nicest guy on the squad, was a senior named Bill Stanforth. Bill was built like a Greek god, was hands-down a faster runner than I was, and outweighed me by twenty pounds. He was a tailback, and as part of the scrimmage that afternoon he was returning kickoffs with the starting eleven against the second-team defensive unit on which I was taking my hits. Those hits are bad on open-field kickoff drills, and I suddenly looked up to see yet another one coming. Stanforth had caught the ball on his ten-yard line, had cut to his right, and was coming up the sideline full speed right toward where it looked like I was going to have a clear shot to intersect his path. As I ran toward my cutoff point, I secretly hoped that some varsity lineman would come out of nowhere and block me down, but no such luck. Finally, I could see what had to be done. Bill Stanforth's eyes showed a glint of surprise when I swung out from behind a pile of blocked bodies and dived headfirst right into his churning knees. I have never forgotten the loud cracking sound of my helmet and shoulder pads hitting those pounding knees. Bill bounced into the air, fell flat to his left, then sprang right up and ran over to where I was trying to get up off my back by the sideline. He stuck his big grinning face right down in mine, popped me on the shoulder with his hand, and yelled, "Way to go, Jim, way to go! You'll be on the starting team this weekend!"

I was really dizzy but trying not to show it as I got up and spun around, striving to collect my wits enough to remember where to line up for the next play, when I came face-to-face with my dad. He gave me a look of love, pride, and approval that I'll never forget. He never missed any of my scrimmages or games.

Dad never missed *any* turning points in my life. When it came time to get on the train for Annapolis, he was with me. The night before I was to be sworn in, we stood by the Tecumseh statue and watched the evening parade into huge Bancroft Hall just as we had twelve years before. "I want you to try your best to be the best man in that hall," he said.

And I did try. The academics frightened me a little that first fall. I wrote home every Sunday, and my anxieties showed through and alarmed my mom. "You must not humiliate us," she wrote back. I was a little disappointed in that reply, but she was right, I must not. And I did not. I went out for football every year and never missed a practice, but never made the varsity team. Nevertheless, to decide rationally that I would be better off in some other sport would have been beyond my comprehension. The best man in that hall would play football like a man. I had debts to pay, and I paid them on Wednesday afternoons when we "JVs" would scrimmage against the varsity. That team had eleven players who hit at least as hard as Bill Stanforth. On those cold, rainy scrimmage afternoons, I would try to get out on the field early and pump up my courage for what was coming. One of my most vivid memories is of a warm-up drill we used to run that always ended with our diving on our bellies and sliding through the icy puddles. *That* woke you up.

I finally did make a navy football team, and it was a good one. After graduation and three years of sea duty, I finally got to flight training at Pensacola. The Naval Air Training Command had an athletic department that functioned like one in a college. Their varsity football team was called the Goslings, and every member of the squad of fifty or sixty had played football in college, half of them at the Naval Academy. We had a coaching staff of five professionals, practiced every afternoon, and played a regular schedule against southern colleges. I was a late bloomer in physical things: I was a starter on this team, a 170-pound guard, and had my twenty-sixth birthday just as the season ended.

Most of us on the team were married; Syb learned fast how to care for charley horses and cut lips. Our wives would sit in the cheering section for home games, and get together to share pot-luck meals and listen to the game on the radio when we were away. We had good friends there, many with kids. Syb and I were having a wonderful married life and hoped she would get pregnant soon.

Some of the Goslings players were flight instructors, but most, like me, were in the process of getting their wings. One of the fringe benefits of varsity football was having a flight instructor who was also a teammate. You got personalized attention that way. Learning to fly was a dangerous business; Syb and I got used to going to the funeral services of my classmates.

I got my wings in the summer of 1950, and I was so proud when Syb pinned them on me, looking beautiful, and great with child. I was assigned to a squadron of propeller-driven planes flying off East Coast carriers. I loved the culture of the carrier pilots, the "tail-hookers," and their constant drill at perfecting the art of flying on and off ships. As soon as I had the minimum required carrier landing experience, I pressed for and got to Landing Signal Officers' school back in Pensacola. In our four months there I learned how to wave the flags to get the planes aboard, and how to land aboard myself in about six more kinds of airplanes.

I was back with my squadron on a cruise in the Mediterranean when I got the word that when my LSO tour was finished, I was scheduled to go to Test Pilot School. That was good; the news helped me get over the frustration of not having been able to get into the now-ended Korean War. But missing that war left me with more debts to pay.

Patuxent River Maryland's Test Pilot School was my kind of place! There was no "book" to follow; you set and passed or failed your own challenges at your own risk. No formal airplane checkouts, no forms to sign, no bureaucratic Mickey Mouse. "Cover-your-ass" documentation didn't go with being a test pilot. Test pilots had to improvise on their feet and know their own limitations. If pilots assigned couldn't do that, the sooner the top test pilots at Patuxent River knew that, the better. I had never flown a jet! "So read the manual and come down Saturday afternoon and I will have told the sailors on the flight line to have a plane ready for you."

Cold sweat. Syb brings Jimmy, three years old, and drives me out to the field. Snowdrifts all along the runways. Clouds above. I kiss Syb and Jimmy goodbye and approach the machine, trying not to let the enlisted plane captain know how nervous I am. The engine starts just like the book says! I call the tower and learn mine is the only plane at Patuxent scheduled to fly that afternoon. Next I learn that these stovepipes taxi funny; you have to add a lot of power to get them rolling. But you can sure see where you're going better than when that big prop is up front. Learn as you go. Here I am at the end of the runway; there's no place to hide. Take a deep breath. "Patuxent River tower, this is Teakettle zero-four-seven, ready for takeoff, one hour local."

"Roger, zero-four-seven, cleared to roll. Winds are light and variable."

Hold the brakes. Run that engine up all the way. God, please be with me. Release!

It starts slow, slow—but, my God, once it gets going, it really goes! It's wonderful! Just like they say! It seems like a bird, climbing up and up. Even my landing is passable. Taxi back, into the chocks, shut down. There's our car right by the line shack on that desolate, dingy winter afternoon—Syb and little Jimmy sitting there with the engine running to keep warm. Clutching embrace. A little tear of thankfulness escapes from Syb's eye. I can do it! I'm going to make the first team!

And first team it was. I finished the seven-month school as number three of seventeen great pilots enrolled. After a while in a test unit, I was invited to join the Test Pilot School faculty. I loved the classroom teaching every morning and the flying every afternoon. Through my ex-students, I got to fly everything on the field—forty-one different kinds of airplanes! After nearly three years of this, the Crusaders came, right out of the factory, ready for flight tests. I was an old hand by then, one of the first to fly them. When they'd passed their tests and were certified ready for the fleet, I got orders from Patuxent River to California to join the first squadron of Crusaders scheduled for carrier deployment to the Western Pacific.

But first, Survival School, up in the mountains behind San Diego. This was prescribed now; all first-line carrier pilots had to undergo instruction in the American Fighting Man's Code of Conduct, which President Eisenhower had just signed. The Korean War reminded our nation that not all governments considered the prisoners they took in war to be just liabilities that must be guarded and fed and treated in accordance with international law. With a little ingenuity, like torture, they could be turned into captors' assets—propaganda assets. So the Code of Conduct reminded us that, if captured, our American chain of command remained in effect behind the prison walls: "If senior, I will take command." It reminded us that all Americans were obliged to physically resist being used: "If I am captured, I will continue to resist by all means available." And it reminded us that the highest form of resistance was escape: "I will make every effort to escape and aid others to escape."

For training, we spent a week in the wilds learning how to evade and avoid capture, and a week in a mock prison compound learning how to resist, how to escape, and how to set up and maintain an American chain of command in the face of opposition. It was realistic training. Enlisted instructors in mock Chinese uniforms were authorized to slap us officers around, at least to the point where we saw stars. We all got some claustrophobia experience in a tiny black box. I panicked, but remembered a lesson I'd learned when I was about eight years old.

My dad always encouraged me to become a good swimmer; he drove me to a pond on most summer afternoons and sat on the nearby bank as my sole supervisor. After repeated dives off a raft one day, I finally got disoriented under water and came up under the flotation drums by mistake. I picked a direction to swim, but it turned out to be the long way. I changed my mind once, twice, and finally panicked. Then I felt his arms around me and he led me out. He had dived in, pants, shirt, and all. We had a very serious talk about staying cool under pressure, keeping your imagination under control.

This navy survival school had a good way of expressing how you ward off claustrophobia: "Get your head out of the box. There's plenty of air in there, even if you are scrunched down by the lid. Trace your route to your old grade school; concentrate on how many blocks between each turn, which way you turned; take yourself all the way to the schoolhouse door." Good stuff. I asked to go through that training again six years later, just before this sea tour. The navy let me.

From Willard Field, I could see mom parking her big Buick by the courthouse, Hazel beside her in the front seat. After the embraces of greeting, I told them I had seen dad. Funny thing about mom—she was so flighty at times, over-reacting to minor annoyances, but when real crises struck, she was as cool as a cucumber. So it was now. We said nothing about dad's life expectancy, but with our eyes we agreed it was all over. We went up and sat in his room while nurses came and went, checking his many connections to life-support systems.

At about nine, dad's doctor, John Bowman, arrived. He felt dad's pulse, touched his forehead, and asked me if I'd had any breakfast. I had not, and the two of us headed for the hospital coffee shop. John Bowman and I knew each other well. Maybe eight years older than I, he had been an army medical officer before setting up a general practice in Abingdon. Dad had suffered from emphysema for several years and had had several heart attacks, all of which had been treated by Bowman. During the last five years, each time I'd flown back to see my parents I had made it a point to get a face-to-face read-out on dad's prognosis from Dr. Bowman.

Our breakfast conversation was remarkable for what was *not* said. John told me that dad had been very normal a month before. He brought up the fact that the Tonkin Gulf raids had been in all the local papers and that dad had been quite proud of my name being prominent in the accounts. A *Peoria Journal Star* reporter had even driven the fifty miles to Abingdon for an interview with mom and dad in their living room. The article, with their pictures, had come out well and they had both been pleased with it. But dad's problems were cyclic ones that John had warned me about; the last couple of times I had seen him, he had stressed that dad could have a relapse and die at any time.

"How much time have you got before you have to fly back to Japan?"

"Five or six days at most. I suppose you can keep a person alive indefinitely with chemicals."

"More or less. Your dad now has a very bad case of uremic poisoning and his fever has been running very very high for several days. I think his brain is probably seriously damaged by now."

"When that happens, there's not much point in living, is there?"

A little small talk followed, and then Hazel appeared at the door. I excused myself and took her for a walk. When we got back, I noticed that there was no more life-support equipment plugged into dad. Mom made no comment.

That evening we drove the ten miles down to Hillcrest, mom and dad's big white house in the country. I wandered into dad's bedroom and stopped, seeing newspapers, even the *New York Times*, all folded out with the Tonkin Gulf articles showing. Many local papers had my name in their headlines: "Abingdon Man Leads Reprisal Air Raid Against North Vietnam." I opened the little drawer in dad's dresser that I used to love going through as a tiny kid. He had all his pins and mementos in there. I smiled as I picked up his policeman's star that said "Deputy Sheriff" on it. Often he would get calls to go down to the plant at night; on rare occasions he would pin that to his vest under his coat. I asked him questions about it, but never got any real answers.

Dad was pronounced dead in his hospital bed late the next afternoon, Thursday, September 10, 1964. Mother, Hazel, and I were at his side when he drew his last breath. I called Syb. She had already checked on the plane schedules; she would leave for St. Louis the next morning and arrive in Galesburg on a little commuter plane in midafternoon. Our four sons, who had just visited their grandfather Stockdale while coming across country, would not come back for his funeral but would stay in Coronado and go to school.

Dad's funeral was set for Sunday the thirteenth. How I wish *he* could have heard all the things I was told on the streets of Abingdon Friday and Saturday. His old friends all had good stories to get off their chests. The local newspaper publisher told of dad's generosity toward his parents: "I'll never forget asking your dad to join me for a trip to Galesburg and a night on the town in about 1915. He said, 'Fred, I'd really like to go, but to tell you the truth I can't afford it; my mother needs a new hat.' " One of the older members of the kiln gang wanted to talk about dad's loyalty to his men. "Your dad really liked a fellow named Bob Doss, a good-looking young single man who worked at the plant. It was during the depression. We always thought Bob was having some trouble with Chicago bootleggers; underworld characters were often down here buying homemade whiskey. You probably don't remember it, but a dead man was found down by the railroad tracks one night; the case was never solved, but Bob Doss disappeared for good the next day. I always figured your dad had gotten him out of town."

The original Italians were more emotional about dad's death than any other group. I'd had no idea how involved he had been in getting their citizenship papers through with minimum trouble and in helping them get bank loans to buy houses. Dominic Fiacco sought me out and expressed his sorrow. He was a favorite of dad's and the only man at the groundbreaking ceremony of 1908 who was still on the payroll when dad retired forty-five years later.

The funeral on Sunday was magnificent. The American Legion ceremonial squad mustered at the plaza on Main Street by the artillery piece that dad had acquired for the city years before, and marched to the church with a drum-and-bugle corps. The church was packed with people, many standing in back and outside. There was a sermon by the regular minister and a Masonic rite, then the procession started to the cemetery behind the marching units.

Mom started to fail visibly as soon as dad died. The change in her was more than just the onset of depression. My mom and dad were hardly the typical old arm-in-arm couple; they were quite different from one another—in temperament, in background, in likes and dislikes, in education—and yet, they seemed to have an almost inexplicable attraction for each other. There was a kind of dynamic tension between them. I don't mean friction; I mean a permanence through stabilized stress, almost like the old Greek concept of unity through opposing forces.

For the trip to the cemetery, she took her cane for support for her suddenly weakened arthritic knees. I sat with her before dad's casket as we observed the firing squad volleys and heard the nearby taps. After a short wait, she whispered to me, "Aren't they going to answer the taps?" Her hearing was failing; a sweet, distant echo had in fact just been played. I replied in a soft voice, "They've already answered it, mom." Just then a uniformed Legionnaire put the folded flag on her lap. "It's time to go," she said. As she got up with her cane and turned to leave, I had a hunch she would cry a little, but not a tear appeared on her sad face.

It was a beautiful day, with the blue sky of autumn and a hint of coolness in the breeze. Just before we got to the waiting car, mom stopped unexpectedly and turned almost in an about-face maneuver, handling her cane well. She looked toward the grave, her head tilted back slightly, her breathing controlled, taking a mental snapshot of the scene, the crowd, nodding slightly as though to say, "This he would have approved of." She did another about-face, got into the back seat with me, and we had a pleasant conversation on the way back to the big white house on the hill. We agreed that she would arrange to have her cleaning woman spend nights with her, and that she would come to California for a stay about Christmastime.

Chapter 4

Japan Reprieve

In mid-June 1965, nine months after Jim's dad's death, I once again rented out the Coronado house for the summer. Having been home for four months between November 1964 and April 1965, Jim was once again on a nine-month deployment in WestPac (the Western Pacific)—this time aboard the USS *Oriskany*, sometimes referred to as the "Big Risk." This summer the boys and I were flying to Connecticut rather than going by car. On the plane going east, I thought back over the events of the past year.

The most memorable day for me had been Jim's change of command when he took over as carrier air-group commander 16. On that February day, he became the "CAG" of the air group aboard the aircraft carrier *Oriskany*. That made him the senior aviator aboard ship who still flew from the carrier. He was in charge of six squadrons flying five different kinds of airplanes. He flew all of them himself as he felt required to do in his leadership position.

We were thrilled when he got his orders for this job. CAG was the apex of every naval aviator's flying career, and only a few ever attained the position. We accepted the loneliness of another nine-month separation without complaint; we knew a hundred others would jump at the chance. Anyway, this would be the last cruise before shore duty; then we'd probably go to Washington, where Jim would do a payback tour at the Pentagon, applying his Stanford University education. We'd even planned to send Jimmy to Mercersburg Academy in Pennsylvania for his last two years of high school so he wouldn't be too far from Washington.

The colorful change-of-command ceremony took place on the

flight deck of the USS *Oriskany* on a brilliant blue morning in San Diego. Tied up alongside the pier at the North Island Naval Air Station in Coronado, the carrier was fully dressed with brightly colored flags and the Navy Band played as the guests filed aboard. I wore a new shocking-pink suit and hat on which I'd spent more than for any outfit I'd ever had, but the occasion warranted it.

After the shipboard ceremony and reception for everyone, we entertained the squadron commanding officers and their wives along with the air-group staff at our home with a champagne brunch. The highlight was that the ship's commanding officer, Captain Bart Connolly, and his wife, Marj, attended. Bart Connolly's easygoing personality and quick sense of humor made him a great favorite with the men. I was relieved that Jim had a commanding officer he liked and admired for this tour of duty. On more than one occasion in the past, Jim had been at odds with his CO much of the time. In those circumstances he'd had to suppress his feelings, and this time he was going to need all his energy for the job ahead. Things in Vietnam were heating up. It made life much easier to have a CO with whom he got along well. That change-of-command day was a happy memory.

The day the ship departed, the fifth of April, was a lot less joyful. No matter how many times I endured that tearing away from my beloved, it never got any easier. The first three weeks were always the worst; then I began to get used to being without him.

An unusual event occurred after he'd been gone about a month. A commander from Naval Air Pacific Headquarters, speaking at a wives' meeting, gave guidelines about how to conduct yourself if your husband was shot down and taken prisoner in Vietnam. He said the "next of kin" (as he called us) would be notified as soon as possible, not to talk to any strangers on the telephone, not to talk to anyone in the news media, and not to acknowledge to anyone but family that your husband was a prisoner. Eventually, the Communists would probably announce he'd made some confession and next of kin shouldn't comment about this in any way. When given an address to write to the prisoner, the next of kin should write only in general terms, leaving out all forms of endearment. Under no circumstances should next of kin intercede on behalf of the prisoner in any way. The State Department believed the few Americans now being held were well treated, and any interference by an individual could jeopardize State Department negotiations.

As a senior aviator's wife, I felt sad for the young wives present; I thought their chances of being in such a situation were much greater than mine. I took notes for those unable to attend. I was impressed that the government seemed so well informed and so well prepared. Things were getting rough in Vietnam. One of Jim's letters, written in late May, had said the pace was tough but invigorating and that lots of self-discipline was involved. He said he felt good at night but knew that the next day, when he crossed the North Vietnam beach and saw the antiaircraft bursts coming his way, he'd be choked up as usual.

I rented a separate cottage at Sunset Beach for our visit that summer. We were only two doors from my parents and could enjoy more freedom with separate cottages. Early in July, Jim began to ask in his letters if I thought I might be able to come to Japan at the end of the month when the ship would go in for two weeks' rest and recreation. We had enough money saved for a ticket—about $1,000—and when both my mother and father urged me to go, I knew I would be foolish not to. I made a reservation on Northwest Airlines for July 24 and cabled Jim.

It was early evening when my plane glided into the terminal at Tokyo's Haneda Airport. I hoped against hope that Jim had made it in from the ship in time to meet me. Masses of Oriental faces peered at me from behind a barricade as I approached the customs inspectors. I searched the faces in the crowd. It wasn't like Jim not to be up in front if he was here. I was beginning to have a sinking sensation when—oh, blessed relief—I saw him. Near the back. Waving and smiling. But he looked so tired! The wear and tear of everyday combat flying showed in his eyes. This vacation was coming at just the right time. In minutes I was in his arms, loving the feel once again of his kissing and the familiar aroma of his pipe tobacco.

When we got to our room at the Hilton, I was momentarily disappointed to see that the decor was completely American rather than Japanese. I'd hoped we might sleep on the floor on the native beds I'd heard about. All such thoughts vanished, however, as Jim pulled me close to him, telling me how much he'd missed me. All our cares and responsibilities dissolved and we lost ourselves in the joy of being together after so many months.

Toward midnight, we walked to the Sanno Hotel next door to have a nightcap and see who might be there. What a great treat it was to see the familiar face of a close friend, Gloria Netherland! Her husband was stationed on the staff in Yokosuka and they lived on the base there. She was in Tokyo doing some shopping and would go back to Yokosuka in the morning. That was a break for us because she could show us the right train to board. She took us to their favorite bar in the Sanno, called the Frontier. There we caught up on each other's news over pastrami sandwiches and beer. I smiled to myself, thinking how little I had expected to be sitting in a bar named the Frontier drinking beer and eating pastrami sandwiches my first night in Tokyo.

Jim knew lots of the fellows we saw at the Sanno. There was a large cocktail lounge filled with tables occupied by Americans in uniform. Orchestra music drifted up from the dance floor below. Jovial voices rang out above the music as men called out to greet friends from other ships they hadn't seen in some time. A TV mounted above the bar showed Mickey Rooney in a film speaking Japanese that had been dubbed in. Every so often a small cheer would go up from one of the tables as the men toasted each other's activities. Everyone was here to forget his cares and responsibilities, and the holiday atmosphere was infectious. I squeezed Jim's hand, feeling so lucky to be here with him.

The next morning, after breakfast at the Sanno, we took a cab to Tokyo Central to catch the train for Yokosuka, where the ship was to tie up and there was to be a change of command of one of Jim's squadrons. On each side of the taxi, next to the rear window, there was a flower holder, and in each holder a few fresh flowers. I marveled at that touch of the aesthetic in this shabby vehicle speeding through a maze of city traffic.

The train departed precisely on schedule. As we glided through the countryside, I watched the industrious workers tilling their small, immaculate gardens and made a mental note to describe this scene in particular to my farm-loving father when I got home. I felt a twinge of conscience because I hadn't thought of the boys once since leaving them. As if reading my thoughts, Jim leaned toward me and kissed me lightly on the cheek. How I loved this man, and how glad I was to be here with him now.

At the dock in Yokosuka, as always when I approached an aircraft carrier, I was overwhelmed at the size and sight. Almost 5,000 men worked and lived aboard this man-made giant, more than the population of Jim's hometown. Leaning forward to climb the steep gangplank, I never failed to feel a thrill of pride at being a small part of this life-and-death world. The pungent smell of aviation engine oil stung my nostrils at first; then I inhaled deeply, glad to be immersed in these sounds and smells. During the change of command, I couldn't help wondering how many in this squadron might never make the return trip on this ship. Better not to dwell on such things now. That was in God's hands.

As Jim's flying had become more and more dangerous through the years, I'd developed a strong personal relationship with God. I'd majored in religion at college, but the faith I'd worked out since was more closely related to sermons I'd heard as a girl in the little white Congregational church in Connecticut. One particular sermon stood out in my mind: It had pointed out that there came a time when you could proceed only by having total faith in God's existence and love. My faith was simple but strong. I believed it was my responsibility to help myself in every way I could, and having done that, I'd have to rely on God for the rest. I'd had a difficult time resolving the coexistence of free will and determinism, but I felt comfortable with my resolution of the problem. I often talked to God in a very personal way. I asked God to take special care of the men involved in this ceremony. Their love of flying was so strong, it overcame their fears. I marveled at their faith in themselves and their aircraft.

A huge ice sculpture of a navy plane was the centerpiece for the buffet table at the Officers' Club reception after the ceremony on the ship. Halfway through this champagne celebration, Jim and I had a quick conference about where we would stay that night in Yokosuka. Jim had discovered that all the rooms at the Officers'

Club were reserved by more-senior officers and the only space available was at something on the base called the "J." We decided it was as good as we could do and made the best of it.

After Sunday brunch aboard the ship the next morning, in accordance with my wish to see everything, we walked through an area called Thieves Alley. Jim warned me it wasn't a pretty part of town. Heavily made-up prostitutes lounged in the doorways as we strolled by. Despite Jim's warning, I was somewhat shocked by this blatant display in the early-morning sunshine, but hoped my attempt at nonchalance hid my dismay. I'd heard numerous stories about this side of life when the ships were in foreign ports, but never envisioned this sidewalk advertising.

We later decided to take the train to Atsugi. For years I'd heard about the air station there, and it was one of the places I didn't want to miss. We arrived at the train station just in time to buy our tickets with the unfamiliar money and get aboard. As we picked up speed, Jim located the conductor and tried to find out where we'd have to change trains. I saw the man shaking his head—he didn't understand. By the time Jim returned, we were whizzing along at a furious rate. The sea was on our left, and the countryside on our right was becoming less and less populated. With no timetable and no idea where we'd make our next stop, we decided to let the mixup become an adventure. We'd get off and spend the night wherever the train stopped first.

It was the seaside town of Atami. Looking around the station, we saw a big sign advertising a hotel. It looked inviting, so we pointed it out to our cabdriver. We drove down a hill on a narrow, winding street lined with Japanese lanterns. The ladies along the way all wore kimonos and carried parasols.

At the hotel, only one employee spoke English. He led us to a large, airy room looking out over the hills at the back. When we explained that we wanted a native dinner, he had a young boy guide us to the second floor of an old woman's home. In her tidy apartment, we all sat cross-legged on the floor while she cooked sukiyaki over a charcoal burner. As she braised the thin slices of beef and vegetables, she told us in halting English that her husband had been killed by a bomb in World War II. She seemed to feel no animosity toward us, and I marveled at my past fears and apprehensions about the Japanese people.

Back in the hotel that night before bed, I had my first Japanese hot bath. An attendant showed me into a large room where, mimicking the Japanese ladies in the room, I knelt before a faucet, soaped myself thoroughly, and then rinsed by pouring water over my body from a wooden bucket. I felt self-conscious as they peered at my white and suntanned skin, so unlike their smooth olive complexions. When I submerged myself in the pool afterward, it was so hot it took my breath away. Jim reassured me later, as we lay snuggled in each other's arms, that all hot baths weren't that hot; I'd like my next one better.

The next morning when we were dressing and looking out over the hills, Jim said rather thoughtfully, "You know, that fellow who speaks English told me there was a Japanese prison camp right there in those hills during the war."

"Where they held Americans?" I asked.

"Yes. Kind of gives you an eerie feeling, doesn't it?" he said.

That afternoon we arrived at the station early and made sure we boarded the right train. When we gathered in Yokosuka for a party we were giving at sunset, I noted that another spectacular ice carving dominated the table. This was the easy way to be a host and hostess, I thought as I looked around me. A friend had loaned us the Japanese garden of his quarters there on the base and had arranged to have the Officers' Club cater the drinks and the food. All we had to do was pay the bill. The summer twilight was soft and warm. Everyone was relaxed. I felt the depth of the closeness among these men. I wished life could drift along forever this way. I was jolted back into reality when Jim told me we were all going to a restaurant in Thieves Alley for dinner. Before I had a chance to reply, the Catholic chaplain said, "It's okay, Sybil. Don't panic—I'm going, too. This is a nice place called the Black Rose. It just happens to be in a seedy part of town. We'll have a great time."

He was right. We had a grand time. Dinner was served on a big low table. We sat around it cross-legged, Japanese-style. Afterward we played a game called "rock, paper, and scissors," and I came out a winner every time. Maybe the others were being kind to "the old man's" wife, a Navy expression for the boss, but I decided it was beginner's luck and a good omen. The whole journey seemed blessed with good fortune. It had been a lucky day for both of us when I decided to come.

That night in Yokosuka, we had a handsome room at the Officers' Club. We slept late into Tuesday morning, which was a day to do errands. Jim had messages to read aboard ship as well as paper work to finish. We also planned to take advantage of some of the bargains at the big Navy Exchange there.

Making our way to Jim's room down the narrow passageway aboard ship, we passed a heavily bolted door marked "Restricted."

"What's in there?" I asked.

"Intelligence stuff," Jim answered briefly.

"Can you go in there?" I inquired.

"If I want to," he replied. "I don't, though, because I'd rather not know that stuff."

I was silent while I thought about his answer. He doesn't want to know any more than he has to, I realized, in case he's taken prisoner by the enemy. We proceeded the rest of the way in silence.

Later, at the Navy Exchange, we went to the men's underwear department first and searched in vain for the plain white boxer shorts Jim preferred. There were only polka dots, checks, and stripes on blues, greens, and reds. We laughed as we paid for them, and Jim quipped, "They'll add a cheery note in my lonely gray room when I'm dressing and undressing, anyway."

We found everything else he needed, including a couple of dark-colored lightweight suits, and congratulated ourselves for having outfitted him completely at such a reasonable cost. He'd need these extra civilian clothes when he was in Washington on shore duty next summer.

The next morning we packed our bags for a sojourn into the mountains near Hakone—a trip we made in style in the captain's navy car with a marine driver at the wheel. We were with Captain Bart Connolly—whom Jim admired tremendously—and his wife. As we started to climb out of the humid lowland heat, leaving the clogged roads behind, the cool mountain air washed over us. Marj explained that the old Fujiya hotel we were going to was as lovely as any in the Orient, famous for its accommodations and service.

Our spacious room looked out over a rock-garden pool where huge goldfish swam lazily back and forth. Jim and I studied the names of the hot bath pools at the hotel. We needed to make a reservation so we could bathe together in privacy before dinner. Laughing and feeling a little foolish, we decided on the "Dream Pool." Wearing kimonos—a gift from the hotel—we made our way there at the appointed time. The temperature was perfect and we reveled in our long soak in this greenery-encircled paradise.

Back in our room afterward, two lovely young ladies presented themselves to administer our massages. Such luxury seemed almost indecent. Feeling rested and refreshed, we met Bart and Marj in the dining room. Never had I tasted a more delicious chicken curry; and later, out on the stone patio, the Hawaiian music seemed sweeter than any I'd ever heard. Jim and I held each other with extra gentleness and closeness as we danced to the haunting strains of "Beyond the Reef." If life could stand still forever, I thought, I'd have it do so now.

After breakfast the next morning, we took a bus higher into the mountains, then boarded a glassed-in cable car for the ride up the steep mountain incline. At the summit we transferred to a huge basket that carried us swinging from an overhead wire high above the rolling green hills toward Lake Hakone in the distance. A storybook steamboat took us across the lake as we admired the Japanese country homes along the shores. At a hotel dining room there, we enjoyed a long and leisurely wine-accompanied lunch. We returned to our hotel in a rattletrap bus that raced around each curve like a rocket plunging through space. Safely back in our lovely old Fujiya room, we made love as the sun set behind the mountains.

Later, dressing for dinner, I called Jim to the window. Down the hillside, we were looking directly into the kitchen of a Japanese home where the family was gathered for the evening meal. The center of love and attention was the baby in the high chair.

After dinner that night, as we sat on the patio listening to the mellow music, there was an unusual quietness among us. We all sensed that this might be a memory that would have to last forever.

The next day, after some local shopping and a swim, Bart and

Marj took a taxi with us to Yumoto, where Jim and I would catch the train back to Tokyo. Bart and Marj were staying at the Fujiya one more night, so we said farewell at the station.

Back at the Sanno in Tokyo that evening, the years fell away as Jim and I held each other close and danced to "Sentimental Journey."

We spent the next day shopping on the Ginza, and saw a stage show at the Nichigeki Music Hall. *Hello, Dolly!* was the popular show in New York and we laughed at the Japanese pronunciation, "Herro Dorry," as they sang the song at the Music Hall.

On Sunday morning we enjoyed reading the few newspapers available in English, as well as *Stars and Stripes.* That afternoon we went to a John Wayne movie, *In Harm's Way.* It was a real war picture, parts of which proved to be prophetic. At one point John Wayne woke up on a hospital ship with one leg amputated.

When we arrived back at the Sanno, a young American officer with only one leg was waiting for a taxi. I could see Jim studying him carefully. I leaned closer to Jim and whispered, "I just know God will bring you back to me."

We had only three days left. Jim wanted to see me off safely before the ship left Thursday morning, so my departure was scheduled for Wednesday evening. Our time together would end all too soon and we spent a deliciously indecent amount of time making love. On Monday we took the train back to Yokosuka so Jim could check the message traffic aboard ship. After lunch, a senior officer made a navy car available to him and we were driven to Atsugi. There at last I had a chance to sleep on the floor Japanese-style. During a gathering at the club that night, Jim heard that a Naval Academy classmate of his, Jerry Denton, had been shot down and captured in Vietnam. It was a sober moment for all of us, and it shattered my idea that only younger pilots could be shot down. For some time Jim was lost in his own thoughts.

We spent most of Tuesday around the swimming pool after an absolutely perfect hot bath and massage, then drove back to the Sanno that night.

On Wednesday, our last day together, we made my customs list for the gifts I was taking back to the boys: a portable radio for Jimmy, a walkie-talkie for Sid, a toy telephone for Stanford, and a stuffed dog for Taylor. Together at the jewelry counter in the hotel's shopping arcade, we selected a lovely strand of pale blue baroque pearls as Jim's Christmas gift to me. We agreed he would keep them with him and bring them home when the ship returned to San Diego just before Christmas. That afternoon we went to a movie appropriately entitled *Love in the Afternoon*. During the film we sat snuggled close together like two teen-agers, holding hands and exchanging kisses in the dark.

Later, I smiled wistfully at the fresh flowers on either side of the back window of our taxi to the airport. There was plenty of time, so Jim left his suit coat with me on the open-air balcony and went inside to get us each a drink. I found a scrap of paper in my handbag, hastily wrote a love note, and tucked it into his coat pocket. We quietly reminisced about the perfection of these days together. Then it was time to go. I tried hard not to cry. One last embrace. The tears were beginning to spill over and Jim felt their wetness on my face. One final "I love you" and I turned away and walked toward the plane. He was walking the other way. We'd agreed not to look back.

Chapter 5

Shootdown

By ten o'clock on Thursday August 5th, 1965, I had finished my breakfast aboard the carrier *Oriskany*, read war messages for a couple of hours, and ventured out onto the flight deck to watch the ship get under way and move out from Yokosuka into Tokyo Bay, and head south for open sea. My heart grew heavy in spite of the nice sunshine and breeze as I pulled out and re-read the love note from Syb I'd found in my coat pocket on the train back from the airport the night before. She had now been gone for just over twelve hours and I missed her terribly as we started the familiar trip back down to Yankee Station and the firing line.

My mind scanned the events and trends in this Air War in North Vietnam over the months it had been going on since I led the strike that started it. It was one year ago right now, on August 5th, 1964, that we were manning planes to go over and blow up the Vinh oil storage tanks. While Washington had chosen to hide its head in the sand during that August of 1964, it was now suddenly hovering over me as the final authority on the most minute details of air tactics. A year ago I'd seen myself as a shield of protection between my pilots and the North Vietnamese; now I saw myself as a shield of protection between my pilots and McNamara's Pentagon whiz kids.

All targets were selected in Washington on the basis of a naïve idea that delicate, tacit peacemaking signals could be transmitted by military action: My pilots saw it as taking very expensive and highly capable airplanes right by the power plant to bomb the privy—which the Vietnamese had of course figured out was the place to put their guns. More encroachments were being made daily on my authority as a combat air commander; we found ourselves foolishly risking airplanes and pilots' lives on meaningless targets, on specified flight paths with specified ordnance loads that were frequently dangerous or incorrect or both.

Captain Bart Connolly, skipper of the *Oriskany* and a living jewel in the combat environment, was very tolerant of my ever-more-flagrant rule-bending in my attempt to maintain tactical autonomy for the sake of effectiveness and safety. Bart watched me like a hawk, and as long as I met his standards, all the pilots aboard—those regularly assigned to my air group and the many that were being sent out from shore bases to temporarily reinforce us—were mine to work with as I saw fit.

Bart and I had long talks on the few lazy days at sea enroute to Yankee Station for our upcoming line period. This, like our others before it since we had arrived in May, was to be a solid month of combat. But not only the number of rules but the frequency of casualties had been steadily increasing, and I had premonitions of this August 10th to September 10th siege being brutal. We talked about a plan that had been advanced by my Marine Corps fighter squadron to hang two 2,000-pound bombs on their Crusaders to hit the best-defended bridges and get their spans dropped quickly without so much pilot exposure to flak. (Crusaders with this non-regulation ordnance load would be overweight for takeoff with their fuel tanks full, so we planned to catapult them with half-empty tanks and top them off with tankers while inbound toward the targets.)

We talked about the gut-wrenching problem of whether to declare pilots dead or missing when their wingmen were not sure whether they survived or not. We agreed to continue our policy of declaring them "missing" if it was a true toss-up, but KIA or "killed in action" if we really thought they were dead, with or without positive proof. In the latter case Bart and I thought it was better not to drag it out, but to give the widow freedom to re-marry even though the pay to her would stop.

And we talked about who would take over the air group if I wound up missing or KIA. We decided that the senior Squadron Commander, Lieutenant Colonel Chuck Ludden, should take over my job. This flouted a little bit of tradition, since Chuck was of course a marine officer and carrier air groups were normally the province of naval officers. But Chuck was our kind of guy and knew the job inside out.

There wasn't much talk in the air group about "the war" as an international event. I knew of nobody who thought of himself as primarily an agent of national policy. Most of my sailors wanted to be "the best plane captain on the ship," my pilots "the best wingman in the squadron," and I wanted to be "the best CAG in the navy." I liked it that way. Nobody sat around deep into the night talking about American foreign policy; nobody felt the obligation to address the air group extolling the virtues of our government. Things like that just aren't done in elite fighting groups. It would be a very odd speech that would extol an obstructionist bureaucracy, and that's what *government* was beginning to mean to me.

Personally, in that midsummer of 1965, I wouldn't have given a nickel for America's chances to get out of Vietnam, win or lose, in less than five years. The forward air controllers, USAF pilots who flew light planes out of the little fields deep in South Vietnam, would come out to the ship for visits and tell us how in the countryside "the Viet Cong owned that place at night."

Of course, my own pessimism was deepened by a rather thorough knowledge of modern Southeast Asian history; scarcely three years earlier, I had spent a year in the Hoover Library at Stanford writing a master's thesis on it. And then there was the Tonkin mess of the previous summer. I kept that Tonkin stuff a secret as long as I was a group commander; it would never do to disillusion those wonderful young men of mine with the real truth of that story.

We flew a couple of days of practice missions, and spirit started to pick up as we neared Yankee Station on August 9th. A lot of pilots had their own projects they wanted to work on as a part of the coming combat stint. Commander Jack Shaw, skipper of one of my Skyhawk squadrons, was an electronics engineer with a very interesting mind and a great sense of humor. He carried his own camera in the cockpit and took pictures of targets we *should* have been hitting as we flew by them; he would dutifully submit them to Washington and receive no reply. Jack had been the navy project officer on an antiradar homing missile, the Shrike, and with my okay set up a system of running his own research project on the accuracy of those Shrikes he chose to fire.

Marine Corps Major Jerry Mitchell had come whistling out to

the *Oriskany* in his Crusader photo plane from the marines' Composite Photo Squadron up at Iwakuni, Japan. He had a fleet-wide reputation for taking terrific low-level pictures of the roadways and prospective targets way up north of Hanoi. He did it like an artist, picking his routes on airborne impulse on the basis of local weather, MIG activity, and so on. He did not want to be hindered by the Mickey Mouse rule to submit proposed tracks a day in advance. He also asked not to be required to take a wingman; he considered one an unnecessary impediment. After I had a look at some of his vivid strip maps of what had been virgin photographic territory, I gave him an okay on both requests.

At my instigation, Commander Harry Jenkins, skipper of "the Saints," Attack Squadron 163, was busy making up creative strike plans. He was a genius in the sneak use of air power. A month before, he had laid out a scenario for wiping out the fuel storage in Nam Dinh that could have come right out of a cowboy film. All targeted tanks were wiped out, none of our planes hit. And Harry and his wingman Bill Smith were the two braves in first. I needed more of his ideas to spice up the canned stew from Washington.

Harry was a great man to go to sea with. Morale soared around him, and keeping morale soaring was my primary job. High-spirited pilots are more effective pilots and safer pilots. And they like to see their boss in the cockpit. I gave all major strike briefings myself and always flew in these missions, but not always as strike leader; as often as not, I would give strike lead to a squadron commander and I would fly back in the pack. Every one of my 120 pilots knew my voice, however, and knew that I maintained override authority over any airborne action taken or order given. They seemed to like my personalized James Bond voice call, which I always took the liberty to use: "Double-O-Seven." The sailors liked it, too. They painted "007" on "my" plane in every squadron, and on all of their tow tractors, starting jeeps, forklifts, and crash cranes.

By early morning of August 10, we were back on Yankee Station and had resumed combat flying with a major strike against the Son La army barracks. That target was a long way inland; and with the routing I chose, the distance we had to cover from catapult to arrested landing was just over a thousand nautical miles. I flew a little Skyhawk and brought back considerable antiaircraft lead in my starboard wing—a bad omen for starters.

A week later we made a series of daily strikes against the Ham Rong (Dragon's Jaw) Bridge. This was a big, tough old rail-and-highway span that crossed the wide Song Ma River just northwest of the coastal town of Thanh Hoa. We had bombed this old structure before and it seemed to be our nemesis. We hit both the bridge decks and superstructure with bullpup guided bombs, 500-pound bombs, and even a few 1,000-pound bombs, but to no permanent avail. From the air, one could look down and see its structural members broken and bent, but the bridge continued to stand there week after week, deck planking replaced during the nights and truckloads of imported munitions from the seaport of Haiphong streaming across it heading west and south for delivery to the Viet Cong. Next time I would instruct the marine Crusaders to carry our new 2,000-pound bomb load.

On Monday, August 23, four more of our Skyhawks were badly hit but luckily made it back aboard. Then things started turning worse. On August 26 we lost young Ed Davis, just three years out of Annapolis; Ed had been married only a few weeks before we left San Diego. He was on a near-vertical bombing run on a dark night in a Spad, was hit by flak as he passed through two thousand feet, and was last heard from as he passed a thousand feet calling "Mayday," struggling to get out of his burning airplane. Ed's flight leader saw the fireball when his plane hit the ground; we sent search planes back to the scene at first light the next morning and all that could be seen was a scorched place on the earth where the plane was consumed by fire. (The North Vietnamese had already removed whatever remained.) I sent the first **KIA** message of this line period, and Ed's wife became a legal widow.

Sunday, August 29, was another bad day—two pilots killed in action. Hank McWhorter, Crusader photo pilot, was shot down and killed on a strike near Vinh, and Ed Taylor was booby-trapped and killed in one of our Spads on temporary duty with the U.S. Air Force in far western North Vietnam near Dien Bien Phu. When I went up that night to assist the search, I got a new appreciation for the Spad's rescue capabilities. I took my sector and matched the others' treetop altitudes while patrolling those spooky valleys, not at my usual 600 miles an hour but loafing along at a mere 150 knots like sitting ducks, never knowing when we would fly into a wall of fire. The word finally came over the air to cease the search, and I rendezvoused my navy planes and headed back across backwoods North Vietnam for the carrier. I felt like I'd had a reprieve from certain death.

Death was becoming a familiar subject of discussion aboard the *Oriskany*. The senior chaplain and I worked closely together in scheduling individual memorial services on the flight deck as one airman after another became a victim of North Vietnamese gunfire.

On Sunday morning, September 5, we inaugurated a new Washington-planned target package called Rolling Thunder #30 with a thirty-aircraft strike against the Ha Tinh army barracks. Harry Jenkins was strike lead, and he took a bad hit in the cockpit; luckily he got the plane back aboard. It was his one-hundredth combat mission on this cruise. Hearing this, I looked at my logbook and saw that, counting the *Ticonderoga* combat cruise, I was edging up toward my two-hundredth mission. This was our twenty-seventh day of thirty-one scheduled days on the firing line for this period at sea; in those twenty-seven days, I had flown thirty-three combat missions: six in Crusaders, five in Spads, and twenty-two in the little Skyhawk dive bombers.

The next afternoon, Monday, just before sunset, I was bringing a flight of four airplanes back to the ship. We were heading south, paralleling the North Vietnamese coast about ten miles offshore, when we heard a "Mayday" call from a stricken shipmate in another flight over the beach. Then he flew right out in front of us, a little Skyhawk streaming fire. When he was about twelve miles out to sea, he advised us who he was and that he was losing his flight-control system and preparing to eject. Out he went, chute okay. We called for a helicopter, the plane crashed well clear, and all signs were good in what was becoming a familiar scene. As the pilot was picked up and pronounced okay over the radio by the *Oriskany's* helo pilot, I found myself musing about the rescued officer's case. He was Jim Burton, a lieutenant from Attack Squadron 164.

Jim Burton had started the cruise with a peculiar restriction: He was not to fly over North Vietnam until September 1, 1965. The reason for his restriction was that people from certain types of intelligence duty were not to be exposed to possible capture until the secret material had been rendered essentially useless to an enemy because it was out-of-date.

I remember contemplating the irony of Jim Burton's case as I gave my wingmen the head nod, letting them know that I was about to throttle back and pop open my speed brakes to start a descent into the *Oriskany*'s landing pattern. Here I was, flying every day and bringing back flak holes in my airplane occasionally, all the while with knowledge of something that had to be a lot more sensitive than anything Burton had held. I was in possession of the most damaging information a North Vietnamese torturer could possibly extract from an American prisoner in that war. If I were captured, and if my captors had read my name in most any American newspaper of a year ago after the Tonkin Gulf episodes, the simple confession they might be able to torture out of me would be the biggest Communist propaganda scoop of the decade: "American Congress Commits to War in Vietnam on the Basis of an Event that Did Not Happen." In this war it was already becoming clear that it was the propaganda bombs, not the TNT bombs, that were going to make the difference.

Two days later, Wednesday, September 8, young "Rudy" Rudolph, another Crusader photo pilot, was hit by a big flak site about thirty miles inland from Thanh Hoa. We all heard a "Mayday" and his wingman reported he had seen Rudy go in with the plane with no chance of survival. The day was altogether another sad one—yet another memorial service was planned, for Friday the tenth, the day the ship would be heading for Hong Kong for a rest.

Our last day on the line, Thursday, September 9, was one we had been waiting for. Our target was the Dragon's Jaw Bridge again. Our marine squadron was holding me to my word—the main effort would be their Crusaders, each to drop two 2,000-pounders into that rugged old structure. With any luck, we would head for

Hong Kong having severed the main north-south rail and truck route between South Vietnam and the seaport of Haiphong. Poor Rudolph; a week before he was killed, he had brought in very clear photos of the docks at Haiphong just after a Soviet merchantman had been unloaded. It had shown piles of guns and ammunition, and not a few Russian-built SAMs, which would be coming up to meet American pilots in the skies over the beach soon enough. What a way to fight a war! Give Communist merchantmen free access to the Haiphong docks and watch them peaceably wave to you as they pass your flight deck returning south while you hold a memorial service for a pilot killed by the missiles they delivered.

This total picture was very disturbing to our recently embarked flag officer, Rear Admiral Ralph Cousins. That night of September 8, he gave me a call and invited me up to his cabin for a visit. We had been friends for half a dozen years, ever since I had flown off the carrier *Midway* when he commanded that ship. His chief of staff, Captain Willy House, joined us. Willy had preceded Bart Connolly as captain of the *Oriskany*. We talked seriously about how Rudolph had been killed that day and about the air war in North Vietnam in general. Here we were, wasting good lives on targets that often weren't worth it while we flew right by prohibited targets that were crucial to North Vietnam's war machine. At about 10:30, I excused myself to go down and see how many changes the Teletype would impose on me in tomorrow's raid on the Dragon's Jaw Bridge.

Relieved to find that there were no significant changes yet, I looked up the aircraft handling officer and talked over the aircraft pre-launch parking plan (deck spot). Every night before a major strike, we talked over the deck spot in order to make a plan that would get the planes off in the best order to fit my tactical plan. I had learned in the navy to proceed from the general viewpoint that "the system does not work." If I left the deck spot up to someone who just read the flight schedule, we would be twice as long in getting rendezvoused after tomorrow's launch and would be short just that much fuel over the beach where we needed it. I had the game plan all in my head and there was no use trying to go through intermediaries. For tomorrow's flight, we had to configure a whole bunch of Skyhawks with tanker in-flight refueling pods and launch them first with the marine Crusaders right behind them. That way, they could be going through the fuel-topping-off operation while the rest of the planes were overtaking them on their way to the beach.

The squadron's night maintenance crews would work from now until thirty minutes before launch to get as many airplanes as possible "up" to go, which meant there would be unknowns on the board right up to the wire. My last-minute memo to all "go" pilots—giving the side numbers of airplanes in commission, target times, and so forth—would be on a handwritten briefing sheet that I would produce and xerox about ten minutes before the pilots assembled in the intelligence center for my last preflight instructions in the morning. My last act before retiring at midnight was to see the weatherman; he estimated conditions to be generally favorable at the bridge, although at that time there were rain squalls here and there.

Just after midnight I got back to my stateroom. I got into my pajamas, set my alarm for 5:00 A.M., and started a concentrated second reading of my mail that had come aboard that day. There was a letter from son Jimmy with a Chicago newspaper clipping with his picture in it. He had been enroute from his summer camp in Michigan back to Connecticut and looked strong for fourteen and very tan in the big picture in the July 29 *Daily News*. He was shown staring soulfully at a television screen in a Michigan Avenue shop at noontime while President Johnson delivered his Vietnam escalation speech doubling the draft call to 35,000 a month and adding another 50,000 troop increment in the South. Jimmy's enclosed note to me said, "A lot of people in that place were griping and moaning as the speech was going on. They didn't realize that there was a guy there whose dad was over there."

The editorial in the *Life* magazine that had arrived that day opened its comments on that same speech as follows: "'This is really war,' said President Johnson. But not a 'national emergency'; that he refused to declare. A similar ambivalence marked his whole report to the people on his much-publicized full-dress review of our Vietnam policy last week."

I tossed and turned for a long time before I got to sleep that night.

And I awoke from that troubled sleep before my bedside alarm went off—so much to think about. In just a few hours, if the weather held, I would be rolling in on the Dragon's Jaw Bridge with about thirty-seven airplanes—with that overload of bombs on the Marine Corps Crusaders. I could hear the sea rushing by in the darkness outside my open porthole as I switched on the bedlamp and blinked at my clock on the desk. Ten of five. I sat up and swiveled around, planted my feet on the soft rug Syb had bought and put there six weeks ago, and stared at my familiar surroundings.

The closets and drawers were full of books, papers, and clothes, including my voluminous hoard of flight suits, crash helmets, and boots, plus pistols, knives, miniature two-way radios for calling in rescue helicopters, and morphine Syrettes for pain-killing in case of crash. But they were also full of memories, the stuff Syb and I bought in Japan—like the Japanese baroque pearls for her Christmas which I would put under the tree in Coronado.

In many ways, thought I, this old ship and I were at the same point in our careers. We were both commissioned just too late for WWII, but we had stayed at sea and grown salty ever since; and now our cruising days were about over. I was soon to be forty-two, and this was to be my last cruise as a fighter pilot, as a carrier aviator. I couldn't have a better way to end those many flying years—as an air-group commander, the boss of all the pilots and aircrews aboard. Disillusionment with officialdom could never detract from the deep joy of flying and working with courageous men.

I got up, took a shower, and dressed for the flight. My regular laundry was a day late being returned and I was short of underwear. I opened the package Syb and I had brought back from the Yokosuka Navy Exchange men's shop and thought of her as I put on a pair of the red polka-dot boxer shorts. I put my Naval Academy class ring in my safe, as always before I flew combat; my twenty-two-year-old Abercrombie & Fitch "Shipmate" wristwatch with "JBS, 1942, Love Dad" on the back stayed with me. The fact that it was a year ago today that I'd been at dear old dad's hospital bedside flicked through my mind.

I had a quick breakfast and then went up to the flight deck, where, in the dim light of dawn, the maintenance crews were preparing the planes for launch. The thirty-seven airplanes I had asked for were ready. I picked out mine, the lead Skyhawk in the flak-suppression group, one of Harry's "Saints" airplanes. I was irritated to find that my plane had been loaded with snake-eye-configured bombs for flat, low-level runs; this flight's flak suppression had to be done in a steep-angle dive delivery. I called for Harry's ordnance chief and started to read him off when he patiently showed me a new switch that had just been installed in the cockpit; it allowed me to select either the dive-bomb mode (fins stay in) or snake-eye mode (fins pop out to ensure that the dropping plane is far enough ahead to avoid blast damage when the low-drop bombs hit the earth). This brought lots of good-natured snickers from the crew. I usually posed as a sort of absent-minded professor and made a joke about my not being able to keep up with all the changes that were being installed out there on the ship by the week. I knew I had my men behind me and that there was no need to put on airs.

The weatherman met me in the Intelligence Center, where I was about to brief the flight crews. Conditions were somewhat more iffy than they'd been last night, but the chances were still better than even that we would have acceptable visibility at the bridge. At the general briefing, I designated one of the big A-3 electronic "jamming" airplanes to streak on ahead and give us a weather report over the bridge at about the time we were to cross the coastline.

When the order came in to "man planes," on the way to the flight deck I walked by Admiral Cousins's morning meeting in complete flight regalia—pistol, radios, and all—stuck my head in and waved, and said I would see them in the afternoon. The weather was good at the ship and I felt good as the plane captain helped me strap in. "Stand by to start engines," said the flight-deck bullhorn. As we swung into the wind, the flight-deck scene took on the look of a ballet stage as dozens of sailor-technicians in blue or brown or red or green shirts, their planes checked, ducked for the catwalks as the yellow-shirted plane directors deftly signaled pilots to swing their jets around in those close quarters and move them in their predetermined order toward the catapults. The big A-3 electronic jammer and weather scout launched with the Skyhawk tankers; then came the Crusaders, looking incongruous with those massive bombs on each side; then we flak suppressors, and so on.

The fueling of the Crusaders worked perfectly, and the big flight was pressing on to the beach in good order in record time. Our spirit was up; this was the last day of a grueling period and was to be our day of triumph against that tough old bridge. I had briefed the flight to cross the coast about sixty miles to the south of the city of Vinh to make a subtle feint inland for the benefit of enemy radar, and gradually bend around to make a run-in to the bridge on a northeast heading. We were at 32,000 feet, above a broken cloud deck and just catching glimpses of the beach directly below us, when my weather scout ahead called in, "Heavy rain at the bridge, ceiling and visibility zero zero."

Dismayed, I came up on the radio and did what I had to do: "This is Double-0-Seven. Break up into sections and proceed to secondary targets as briefed; see you all back aboard ship in an hour and a half."

What a letdown! With a wave to my wingman of the day, Commander Wynne Foster, Harry Jenkins's second-in-command, we roll our little Skyhawks sharply left and start winding our way down through breaks in the clouds. It is 11:30 A.M., September 9, 1965. My plan is to get under these clouds and proceed up the coast about sixty miles to a railroad siding where trains are usually parked. On four or five past occasions, I have been able to make good use of bomb loads there when assigned targets have been weathered in. Flak has never been a problem up there; I relax totally, note that my cockpit pressure is increasing normally as we descend, unsnap my oxygen mask to give my pinched face a rest, and let it dangle.

As we pass through about 15,000 feet, I start seeing enough flashes of the ground to make out where we are. We're over the river just west of the city of Vinh, working east toward the Gulf. Then I catch sight of a familiar view that always brings me up short: fourteen burned-out black spots on the north bank of that Song Ca River where it forms the southern boundary of Vinh City proper. Wouldn't you know that today we would pop out of the clouds directly above those charred holes? It was exactly 400 days ago this noon that we were blowing up the tanks that stood over those holes.

We tool along northward up the coast for a distance I could cover in five minutes in that Crusader I was flying 400 days ago, skirting just outboard of Hon Me Island; it had been from behind this island's rocks that the PT boats came out to attack the *Maddox* a year ago last August 2. Exactly two minutes after we pass Hon Me, I bend my little Skyhawk around to the west and start down for the

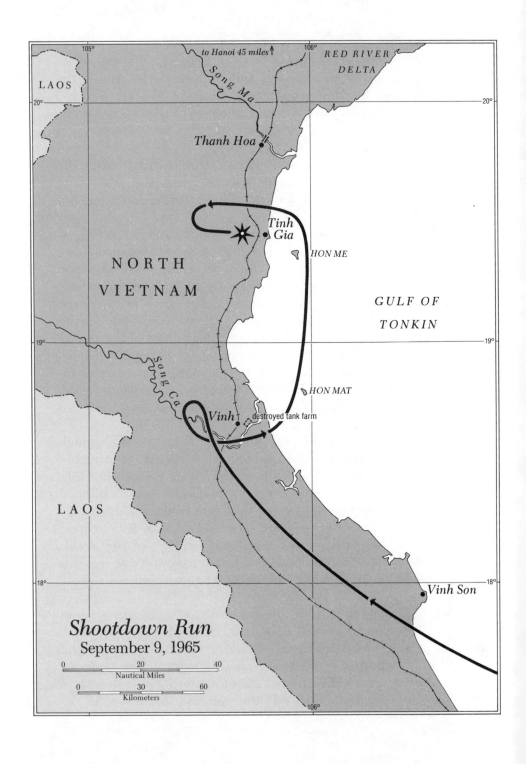

LAOS

to Hanoi 45 miles ↑

RED RIVER
DELTA

Song Ma

20°   20°

Thanh Hoa

*Tinh
Gia*

HON ME

NORTH
VIETNAM

GULF OF

TONKIN

19°   19°

Song Ca

HON MAT

Vinh   destroyed tank farm

LAOS

18°   18°
                                                                    Vinh Son

Shootdown Run
September 9, 1965

0   20   40
Nautical Miles

0   30   60
Kilometers

deck to get set up for the low-altitude drop of all bombs on one run into those trains I can barely see sitting there a few miles inland on my left. Wynne is tucked in close on my right wing, and I casually look down into his face and give him the signal to check bomb switches for "snake-eye" setting. In another minute and a half, I start a wide left turn, adding throttle to accelerate through 400 knots. I am bringing us around to an easterly heading that will prudently have us inbound to the target, heading toward the Gulf. I give Wynne a sort of thumbs-back "hitchhiking" signal for him to slip back into a deep trail formation. Gunsight on, I see the trains coming up in the mist on the horizon, going from ten o'clock to directly ahead. All looks very normal around this familiar dumping ground.

I casually check my cockpit clock at 12:10 P.M. as I line up for the routine drop; we ought to be back aboard the *Oriskany* before 1:00 P.M. I pass down the middle of those boxcars and smile when I see the results of my instinctive timing in the rearview mirror. A neat bomb pattern, perfection! The cloud deck above is at about 3,000 feet and I plan to climb to and remain at 2,000, at least until Wynne can join up tightly for the climb on up to the top for a quick trip home to the *Oriskany*.

Just as I start my gentle pull-up, I hear a sound I don't expect. It has to be the boom boom boom of a 57mm antiaircraft gun! In spite of the roar of the wind and engine noise in that tiny cockpit, which is beating through the air at 450 knots, this sound is loud and distinct enough for me to know exactly where it's coming from. I turn my head to the right and see what I expect to see—that big mobile gun with fireballs coming out of its barrels at point-blank range from just behind my wingtip. I feel impacts, and then I sense that this time my plane is *really* badly hit. I glance at my instrument panel. Fire-warning light on! Hydraulic-system light on! Now all red lights on! My control system is going out and I am thrown against the seat belt by an uncontrollable "zero-g" nose-down pitch. Suddenly my main concern is to get that damned dangling and whipping oxygen mask up to my mouth so I can give Wynne a "Mayday" over the radio. I finally get it up and do get that out, but the g forces by now have reversed to a high positive: I am being pushed into my seat—I can't reach the overhead ejection curtain! I periodically see the Gulf about three miles ahead, but I can tell I'm not going to reach that safe haven where rescue awaits.

As my uncontrollable Skyhawk pitches over and heads for the ground, I instinctively reach with my right hand and pull the alternate seat-firing handle located between my legs. *Wham!* The cockpit canopy is off and I am conscious of accelerating up the ejection track. I look straight up at my parachute canopy as it blossoms; I am shocked to see not just sky behind it but some ground flicking by. That means I am tumbling as the chute is deploying. Just before things get deathly quiet, I find myself saying, "Things didn't go quite right on that ejection," but I can't put my finger on why I'm so sure of that in my excited and confused mind.

Suddenly I am just skimming over the towering jungle trees below me as I drift over the north-south highway (the familiar "Highway 1" on all pilots' maps). Then I start hearing sporadic rifle fire from below, then the whine of bullets as they cut slits in the parachute canopy above me.

Time speeds up as I sink right down toward the little town of three or four hundred people below. I think I'm going to hit that scrub tree on this side of the north-south main street, but I brush by it, my chute above me enveloping it. Snagged, I bob down onto main street like a puppet on a string. No time to think. With my right hand I pop the two quick-release latches on either side of my chest and the parachute straps snap up and away into the tree as I become conscious of a thundering herd bearing down on me from my right.

They are right on top of me, the town roughnecks, running pell-mell from the south, carrying clubs and screaming. I am off-balance and it is the quarterback sack to end them all; every kid has to show off to the crowd, get his licks in, as I am pummeled, bashed, rolled up in a ball. They grab my arms and legs and twist and kick, and then somebody zonks me over the head and I start to get woozy. Through my dim consciousness, I hear a police whistle blowing.

Through all the confusion comes the message that some authority is being imposed; suddenly I am sitting upright in the street, a wide circle of space between me and the crowd, the man with the whistle standing wide-eyed before me in a pith helmet. There are no uniforms; I am surrounded by men, women, and lots of children—the whole village is out. Now two or three boys start cutting my clothes away as the pith-helmet man directs. The action is fast—they are down to those red polka-dot shorts. Dear Syb, help me! Now even the shorts we bought are cut away, lying in shreds in this muddy street.

There go some men with my parachute, wadding it up to hide it; white parachutes draw trouble from the air. What's the man in the pith helmet trying to say? Pointing down—boots? I take 'em off? My God! Look at it! My left leg shattered at the knee, angling out to the side where it isn't supposed to be; no skin broken, but it is bent at least 60 degrees from straight up and down. That changes the whole picture. That is *real* trouble! I am crippled. I will never run again. I'll never be the same again. And just when I need all my strength! I was going to give myself the shot of morphine and run up over the hill. After all those hurdle races I'd run. And I haven't even felt the pain of it yet.

There is the morphine, there is the miniature radio—there it is all out in the street; the kids are rifling my strewn-about gear and cut-up clothes. Another kid rushes up; he has *three* American wristwatches on his arm. He motions for mine. Another shock: My left wrist is clean; my left arm won't raise. Arm flail during that high-speed ejection; I forgot to grab my right wrist with my left hand when I used the emergency handle. Now a broken back or shoulder or both. And the old Abercrombie & Fitch, whipped off and out in the weeds somewhere, "JBS, 1942, Love Dad," lost forever.

I am conscious of aircraft-engine noises overhead as I am lugged naked down the street and laid in a clear area. My guys are up there, in and out of the low clouds, trying to figure out where I am. It's not worth the risk, guys; I've had it. I'll be here quite a while—in this land of night-soil smell.

Men, women, and children circle me at a distance, their eyes always deflected from mine. My nudity is consciously ignored. Two men at my feet, holding hands. What are they, queers?

Then, like a bolt out of the blue, a runner, in civilian clothes, churning up the pathlike main street from the south, working his way through the crowd to eyeball me, breaks in in clear and distinct English: "Are you James Bond Stockdale?"

I yell, "Yes!" He nods knowingly and runs off to the north.

❖

Of everything described so far I am sure. But I fear the account of the immediately following days may seem rather strange in places. The internal bleeding of knee and shoulder, the shock, and maybe even my pent-up fatigue from an exhausting month on the line tended to make me drift in and out of full consciousness. What was I to think after the runner left? There I was, almost to the minute (i.e., at 12:30 local time), 400 days removed from firing the first shot of this air war against North Vietnam, naked, flat on my back in the town square, five minutes' flying time from where it all started in downtown Vinh. Could it be that the United States government had remembered all along that I was carrying lethal propaganda baggage? Was the mysterious, knowledgeable runner merely verifying my presence and starting in motion a prearranged CIA plan for my extrication? Against my better judgment, I dared to believe so. They were going to get me out! That runner was one of several agents who had been given prior notice of my flying today and was now setting up my escape to save our republic from worldwide humiliation.

Relaxed and comforted by such thoughts, I became woozy again. The leg was just starting to lose its numbness. My left shoulder seemed dislocated, but I couldn't get any bystanders to understand that I wanted someone to pull my arm out to try to get the shoulder into its socket. Suddenly I drifted off into a deep sleep in the middle of that crowd in that little town.

The sun was setting when I came to. Now army men were there in uniform, and it was obvious that the drill was to move me out. They tossed me a dirty pair of old blue shorts and a work shirt. There were no motor vehicles in the town; there was not even a stretcher. They were just going to lug me. My leg and shoulder were quite painful now, but like the civilians before, none of the soldiers was the least bit interested in my gestured requests for help in getting them back into their sockets. Cold muscles and swelling were locking them into their misshapen places.

When my porters had struggled maybe a half mile through the woods with me, we came upon Highway 1. It was barely dark, and there they were, at least thirty trucks, all parked under the overhanging trees beside the road, all aimed south, all ready to start down the coast with war matériel for the Viet Cong under their truck beds' canvas covers. There were men and women in and on top of the trucks; a hayride atmosphere prevailed. With soldiers looking after me, nobody paid much attention to where I was being put. In hindsight it seemed strange that I was not blindfolded for this operation.

Once I was thrown up on a canvas cover atop a loaded truck, it was time to move out. With lots of yoo-hooing, yelling, and laughter, we started churning down the road. The trucks had dim, shielded headlights. People on top of the trucks seemed to be watching and listening for airplanes (but there may have been other means of detection I was unaware of). We traveled about ten miles an hour, and every thirty minutes or so the whole convoy pulled over under the trees, turned out all the lights, and all the people went twenty or thirty yards over into the woods. Then the airplanes—*my* airplanes—would come flying down the road just below the clouds and disappear without firing a shot, the pilots obviously convinced there were no trucks down there. This happened four or five times in the two or three hours I was with them.

This was eerie because I had just been flying that same mission over this same road once or twice a week. On a very few occasions, we had caught a convoy out in an open stretch, but I'd had no idea there could be this many trucks along this usually unproductive segment of road. The truckers carried me over into the woods for the first couple of flyovers, but finally I made them understand that it was better for all of us if they just left me on the truck under the trees. It was becoming painful for me to be moved, and it was clear to me that the insignificant chances of a pilot finding these trucks under the roadside trees made the pain and effort of moving me a waste.

By 10:30 P.M. or so, the moon was out, and at what looked like a checkpoint the convoy stopped and the soldiers took me off the truck top, carried me over to the side of the road, and placed me in the custody of four or five civilians who were obviously going to supervise my laying over for another pickup. From my continually prone position, I remember seeing the shape of a tall, hulking man who seemed to be in charge. Although he had a Westerner's bearing, I was never able to see his face or hear his speech well enough to identify the language. Still, for a few minutes I dared hope that he was my pickup man—that it would be he who would arrange to have agent 007, James Bond Stockdale, the prime observer of the Tonkin Gulf affair, removed to a safe haven out of danger of brainwashings, truth serums, and all the rest.

My rescue dream went into eclipse when I realized that the big man had disappeared and it was the short Vietnamese civilians who were carrying me up to a little hut on what I thought of as a cliff overlooking the sea. At least I could smell salt air. It was a little wooden cabin, one room, with a wooden slab bed, and I was laid on its bare boards. With my airborne knowledge of the North Vietnamese countryside around these parts, I fancied I was near Cape Falise.

There was tension in the room among the two or three men who remained with me. A crazed man suddenly burst in with a little milking-type stool and brought it down in the middle of my stomach with two blows before being grabbed and ejected. (I had a vague recollection of some disturbed man being repulsed in a charge against me back in the village about the time I passed out, and now I had the feeling he was still trailing me.) But the real shocker came about twenty minutes later. Again he rushed the door and lunged at me as he came through it. Although the men acting as my guards knocked him off-balance, he managed to fire a big pistol toward me, point-blank, twice. The flashes blinded us and acrid smoke filled the little room as he was thrown out for good. His aim had been deflected; the shots hit below my torso, one creasing my foreleg but not hitting bone, and both rounds splintering the bed slabs, showering wood splinters all over me and that corner of the room.

One man went out and came back with a white rag. He dabbed off what little blood had seeped out of the crease in my leg, then tore the rag into strips and wrapped them around the leg and tied them. I was feeling pretty good about the way these men were protecting me, and I was about to reinstate my rescue theory. But it was dashed again when my new pickup team arrived. It was a trio of sullen soldiers who made it clear that they didn't particularly care for the task. It was now raining as they and some of the older men lugged me down the path to their waiting jeep. I was stuffed behind the seats in the dark rear end with the third soldier, my broken leg forced into a position that made tears come to my eyes.

The soldiers drove off through the midnight rain, windshield wipers going, talking animatedly and yelling what I'm sure was the equivalent of "shut up" when I tried to get them to let me rearrange my leg. Once they stopped and the two in front got out and went into a roadside hut. The third man stayed outside, out of the rain under the building's eaves, casually smoking a cigarette while watching their jeep.

It was barely light when they drove up to a concrete, hostel-type building with a series of doors opening onto a porch. We were on the outskirts of a city. The soldiers lugged me onto the porch and propped me up on a bench while one went to get help.[1] Several men came and opened one of the doors and carried me in and laid me out on one of the two pieces of furniture in the room: a cement slab bed.

Promptly, a short Vietnamese in full surgical array, including white face mask, came in carrying a large black medical bag. He was followed by a crowd of interested townspeople, who filled the room. Without further ado, the country doctor opened his satchel and started laying out his tools on the other piece of furniture, a kind of wooden library table. My heart sank when I saw the first instrument out of the bag: a big surgical saw. All sorts of large scalpels and the like followed. I sat up and started pointing at the saw and at my leg and pleading, "No, no!"

The little man didn't speak a word of English, but he listened attentively and seemingly understood that I didn't want my leg cut off. He gestured like "It's your funeral" and spoke rapidly in Vietnamese, and I got the idea that he would do the best he could but that it was up to him in the final instance.

The leg was terribly swollen and distorted. The skin was stretched tight over some pretty jumbled-up bones near the surface; but even at the inside of what had been the knee joint, the skin was not quite broken. The doctor also examined my shoulder and back, and moved the arm enough to determine the degree of restriction and sensitivity. Then he took what looked like a big veterinary needle and filled it full of a clear fluid. I had to lie back down and expose the inside of my right elbow. Then he shoved the big needle in. I started to count, but before I could get to "three" I was out like a light.

❖

When I opened my eyes and saw the white cement walls and the open door, I had to think where I must be. The shadows were long—it was clearly late afternoon. I had been unconscious all day. A couple of nonmedical men were standing watch, and I became conscious of the fact that my left arm was in a plaster cast that encased all of my upper body except for my right arm. One of the watchmen went for the doctor as I started working my way up into a sitting position to look down at my legs and have that moment of truth: leg stump or full cast? Full cast! I fell back, prayerfully.

The doctor swung in, still dressed all in white, though now it was a little dirty. With him was a man who was able to make me understand "travel casts." I could move my leg a little, and the cast was wide enough to tell me that the leg was not surgically repaired, but just being protected. At least it would not be flopping around in travel, having its blood flow stopped at this angle and that. The doctor gestured in a way that told me he had had everybody in the room pulling on my leg, trying to get it back in its socket, without success. He felt my brow and panted in short bursts, patting his heart as if to say I had been short of breath while under the anesthetic. No wonder. I must have had a shot that would have knocked a horse unconscious.

It was getting dark. The soldiers and their jeep were nowhere to be seen, thank goodness. Two men and a woman came to get me. They had an open-bed, ton-and-a-half truck parked outside. They were clearly civilians through and through, and looked like scavengers, but there was a certain knowing, sympathetic aura about them that immediately got my imaginative mind clicking about *them* being the appointed agents to whisk me out of the country. The little mousy, dirty-faced woman was to ride with me in the truck box, with the men up front. There were a couple of dirty, heavy, quiltlike covers in the back that looked like the padding moving men use in their vans. It was dark as we started moving through the city and I pulled one of those covers around me. In the cast, I had to lie flat on my back.

It was clear that Thanh Hoa was the city we had just come through when I got a look at the bridge we started across just outside of town. It was the Dragon's Jaw for sure, the one I had left the *Oriskany* the day before to knock down. There were signalmen, and all passage was single-file due to cumulative bombing damage. I could look up in the reflected light and see that the girders had been twisted and bent by impacts, probably 500-pounders. I thought of the air group on the ship, now well on their way to Hong Kong. I had listed Harry Jenkins and my operations officer, Paul Engel, as collectors and packers of my papers and gear to be sent home to Sybil. I expected that the Air Group Commander's state-room was cluttered as they worked on that tonight. I hoped Syb's Christmas present, the baroque pearls, didn't get lost in the wrap-ping paper.

Beyond the bridge we stopped, and the mousy little woman went up to the cab and brought back what in the light of a flashlight looked like a dirty little syringe. In a very sincere and confidential manner, she signaled by panting and then by thumping her bony chest that she was to give me an injection for my heart. I yielded the arm, and it was a small and painless shot. She was certainly no nurse; I wondered who had given her the syringes and rudimentary instructions.

I wasn't conscious of any shortness of breath or heart-trouble symptoms, but a pattern was filling in. I'd been in the country not yet thirty-six hours, but I was sensing that the word was out that I was somebody who should be kept alive. There had been the guy in the pith helmet who blew the whistle; there had been the runner who clearly enunciated my name; now there was this ragtag trio who clearly were not part of the establishment. The pattern was still far from clear, but I was periodically hopeful that my move-ments were being monitored by the CIA or some such alert group.

I slept some that night, and at daybreak we pulled into a kind of big country barnyard with limestone karst spires and ridges all around it. We were clearly on a drive-all-night, lie-low-all-day schedule. A San Diego-made Ryan "Firebee" pilotless drone lay crashed in the yard. Quite a coincidence to spend the day right next to one of those. We often used them as targets for our air-to-air sidewinder missiles, and I had shot many of them down in demon-strations at air shows. The one that had coasted into this quiet barn-yard had probably been sent on a photographic mission and either was shot down or malfunctioned before it completed its pro-grammed track back out over the ocean to have its parachute trig-gered and then be picked up by an American helicopter.

I tried to figure out where we were, and it seemed to me that we must be up around the textile city of Nam Dinh where Harry Jenkins and Bill Smith had blown up the petroleum tank-farm a couple of months ago; I remembered flying around karst ridges like these just to the south and west of there. But wherever we were now, it was very rural, very secluded, and very organized. From my supine position, I had seen two or three functionary-type men pass my truck on their way to or from the rather big, French-built frame house a quarter-block away. It was being used as a kind of command post.

I had now been on the ground about forty-eight hours, and although there had been offerings of tidbits to eat, I was in no mood for them. For the first time, however, I felt the urge to urinate, but I couldn't roll over and seemed too weak to generate the hydraulic pressure to squirt against gravity. When the little woman and the scruffy little men who rode in the cab came by to give me another shot (they seemed to be giving me a shot every six hours), I grunted and gestured to try to get the men to roll me over on my side in that big cast so I could at least dribble out into the truck bed. There was, of course, no need for explicitness to give these modest peasants the idea that I had some sort of urinary problem. But they overreacted and went to work in earnest by rushing to the farmhouse for help. Several men came out and carried me up to the big porch. Then I could hear one on the telephone inside repeating a word that I was later to figure out meant "doctor"—it sounded like "*Bock-shee.*"

In a few minutes the doctor walked into the barnyard from behind a grove of trees that screened it from the road. He was brasher than the little man in white; he seemed somewhat irritated at being summoned to see me, though he did speak French and a little English and took the trouble to try to communicate. He thought he had been called because I was passing blood in my urine. When he realized what I wanted, he rolled me over so I could urinate. The interesting thing was that he seemed to have prior knowledge of the nature of my injuries. When he rose to go, he looked at me intently and pointed to my shoulder cast and said, "Minor," and then to my leg cast, and, shaking his head negatively, said, "Major." That was the last I saw of him.

But they left me on the porch for the afternoon, perhaps because it was a drippy, foggy, low-overcast day and the truck bed had been wet. By midafternoon there was quite a lot of activity around the farmhouse. Four or five men, civilian functionaries, crossed the porch repeatedly, chain-smoked cigarettes, and argued loudly among themselves. It all had to do with us and the truck. One of the functionaries then made repeated, agitated phone calls for an hour or so. Again I recognized the word *Bock-shee*, and, to my surprise, frequent use of the word Haiphong.

By dusk, my imagination was racing at full speed. First, there had been the civilian who had been practically expecting me at the shootdown site, verifying my name clearly and running off; second, the nature of my injuries seemed known through a widespread doctors' communication network; and now they were taking me not to Hanoi, where we had been told prisoners were kept, but to Haiphong! Clues kept flooding into my now feverish and slightly delirious brain. After they carried me back to the truck, the old woman busied herself with arranging those heavy, oily quilts so as to protect me from the falling mist. Then she brought the needle and whispered "Saigon" several times and held up seven fingers before plunging it into my arm. Was I to be sedated for seven days while they got me (sold me?) to Saigon?

The shot was another weak one and I remained conscious. I noticed that as we prepared to drive away in the darkness, the second cab-riding man was no longer with us. After a serious talk with the driver, who I imagined to be her husband, the ninety-pound, dirty-faced, scraggly-toothed woman jumped back into the wet truck bed and got over in the corner under her own oily quilt as we pulled out and headed north.

I dozed from time to time while we rattled along up the highway in the light rain. It must have been a couple of hours later when I awoke and took a peek out from under my quilt to discover that we were no longer on a highway but on back roads, curving very slowly through woods. The rain had almost stopped and I could make out the shape of the little woman sitting up in the rear of the truck bed, looking out anxiously. Then the truck came to a quiet stop and she jumped out and ran forward. After a muffled conversation, she jumped back in and her husband continued his hesitant, twisting, and jerky trip. After a while he stopped again. This time he shut off the engine, and there was another whispered husband-wife conference. One of them walked back down the road, out of sight, and came back in about five minutes. It was foggy. My mind flashed back to a similar foggy summer night near Castle Hill at Newport, Rhode Island. Odd, I thought—and then I understood my mental connection: the bell buoy! I could hear a bell buoy in the distance, out in what had to be Tonkin Gulf by Haiphong!

Again we drove, and stopped, and shut off the engine and lights, and again I heard the steps walking away, perhaps to make inquiries, and then coming back. On the fourth stop, they both left and walked back down the road to what I could make out to be a totally dark house surrounded by a high fence. They crept in the gate. I could smell salt air! Several bell buoys were clanging louder now—I could hear at least three. This has to be the rendezvous point for a CIA-sponsored pickup, thought I. Good old Uncle Sam has been tracking me all along and knows I've got to be whisked out of here to protect the Tonkin Gulf story. My little friends are looking for the man who's going to row me out to the junk that has been hired to stealthily move down the coast and eventually deliver me to the Saigon people!

I thought of spending seven days in the hold of a junk—and a spike of fear struck me. In Hong Kong years before, a British detective friend had told me how the smugglers' boats there had double bottoms, and how when police boats approached, they quietly dumped the hot cargo—sometimes including bound and gagged humans—by opening and closing the lower bottom. I can't get to the surface and stay afloat with these casts on, I realized. I at least have to have my arms free!

So convinced was I that I was about to be smuggled out that I set about quietly and vigorously tearing off my upper-body cast. It was thick and tough, but I was finally able to claw it apart with my good right arm. Then I went to work on the heavy leg cast that went from my toes to my crotch. I had it about half torn apart and was panting for breath when the man and woman came back up the road in the darkness. They were quiet and solemn and not the least bit alarmed about my having strewn parts of those casts all over the back of the truck. The woman just got up into the truck and quietly picked up all the pieces and threw them into the ditch. Then she threw the rest of her syringes into the ditch—no more shots. The truck started, she crawled under her blanket, and away we drove.

Soon we were out where there were lights again. My heart

started to sink. And then the truck stopped in a warehouse area and the man walked away as if to get more directions. Crap! He was trying to get out of the suburbs of Haiphong onto the road to Hanoi! Now I was overcome by a new odor; the sea smell was gone, and in its place was an overpoweringly sweet cooking smell, as though from ginger roots being boiled in sugar in some sort of commercial process nearby. It persisted over several blocks as we hesitantly drove on.

My optimism vanished completely when we headed inland. Those sleazy bastards in Washington—half of them probably would not even admit to the other half how we stumbled into this farcical situation.

Soon in the morning light I could see that we were on the outskirts of a city, and I knew it had to be Hanoi. The little driver was evidently not familiar with the city; for an hour we frequently stopped while he went for more directions. It was starting to rain again when, at about noon on Sunday, September 12, the truck suddenly veered to its left and parked at a curb. From my flat-on-my-back position facing aft, I could see a beautiful, French-built public building in a heavily wooded park to my left and a very long prison wall to my right. (I knew it was a prison because of the jagged broken champagne bottles—some clear, some bluish, and some even pink—embedded on top of it.)

I being immobile in my crippledness and what was left of my leg cast, both man and woman left me alone in the truck and walked forward to the prison gate. Little did I know on that morning in 1965, as I looked lazily at the old French Ministry of Justice on one side and the wall of seventy-year-old Hoa Lo Prison on the other, that I would never again be without blindfold or handcuffs on a Hanoi street until I walked out that gate in 1973.

Soon five of them quietly came around the truck and looked in the tailgate—the scruffy little man and woman; two in North Vietnamese Army uniforms carrying a wire-mesh body-contour stretcher; and a third also in uniform, a graying man about my age. The latter spoke in clear English: "I represent the government here, and we are taking you inside."

The two with the stretcher got up in the truck and lifted me into it. One was unusually tall and one was unusually short for Vietnamese. I was to learn that the tall one was probably a sergeant (none of the three who emerged from the prison wore any rank insignia, nor was any Vietnamese ever to wear badges of rank in front of prisoners); he was a jack-of-all-trades—guard, medic, cook—for the few American prisoners who at that time inhabited small segments of this big civilian prison, which was also the administrative headquarters of the whole North Vietnamese prison system.

To us, these Vietnamese military jailers remained not only rankless but nameless, and thus naturally they acquired American nicknames. I was later to find out that my tall stretcher-bearer was "Dipshit." The short stretcher-bearer was a junior officer; I soon learned that he spoke English, claimed to be a mathematics professor, and was called "Owl" by the Americans. The graying man was in charge of this bunch; he had the bearing of a seasoned army officer and was known as "Eagle." As I was being lifted off the truck, Eagle was angrily taking down the truck's serial numbers and writing down responses to the questions he was angrily firing at the hapless truck driver and his wife.

I was carried through the big prison gateway (which could barely accommodate a truck of the sort I had just left). It cut through the fifteen-foot-high outer prison wall, across a dry moat about twenty feet wide (under the surveillance of machine gunners on perches at the wall corners, half a block away in each direction), through a tunnel (which could similarly accommodate a truck) cut in the inner wall, which was in reality a building, and into a courtyard and across it to a door on a porch on its perimeter. I caught the number 24 beside this door as I was lifted up two steps and my stretcher slid onto the floor.

The door of this "24" place was instantly slammed shut and I was alone. I was in a room, not a cell; it was rather large and at the far end I could see another door, which was ajar, and what looked like a little courtyard beyond. My three days of transit had had their ups and downs, but from time to time I had sensed a degree of spontaneity, a look of sympathy, a degree of frankness. An ominous, depressed feeling overcame me inside these walls. They telegraphed the message that from now on everything was to happen according to party line, by the numbers, with bureaucratic humorlessness. Worst of all, I knew I had to discard and forget my pipe dream of being tracked and rescued by an omniscient CIA. I was to be on my own from now on; the Tonkin Gulf secrets were my problem and nobody else's.

Dipshit kicked the door open and set a bowl of rice and a bowl of thin green soup by my side. I wasn't hungry, but I decided I should eat. The problem was I couldn't sit up in the stretcher to manage it; with my left arm and shoulder useless, I needed a back support. I reached out frantically with my right arm trying to grab a little stool, the seat of which I hoped to situate as a backrest, sticking its legs into the wire mesh of the stretcher. Dipshit sneered as he watched me try to snag the stool that was out of my reach. I didn't think Dipshit owed me a thing, but for him to stand there and enjoy my agony seemed unnecessary. After maybe five minutes, he kicked it over to me, and I, trying to make the best of an already bad relationship, said, "Attaboy." Dipshit stormed up in front of me and surprised me with pidgin English: "I am not boy—I am mister." Lesson one in prison: Enragement over colonialism's racial slights was very close to the surface in this country; I was to be paying a lot of French debts.

After I had eaten what I could, Dipshit rolled me out of the stretcher, took out his knife, and cut the rest of my leg cast off. I was shocked at the appearance of my leg; there was no knee anymore, just a wide strip of irregularly swollen meat that connected my calf to my thigh. The lower leg seemed to flop to an unnatural position just about as it had when I first saw it in the street of that little town—swung outboard about 45 to 60 degrees, its axis of bending 90 degrees from the natural one. Eagle came in and helped Dipshit put me up on a high table, and I watched my lower leg sway back and forth like a pendulum as I was moved. It was very painful by then, and I was in and out of consciousness.

I was talking to Eagle about that sweet ginger-root-and-sugar odor I had detected that morning, trying to get him to tell me where I had been and drawing only angry headshakes—as though he knew exactly where I had been and didn't like it—when the door behind me reverberated in response to an authoritative kick. A very confident and mature officer (whom, I learned, preceding American prisoners had named "Dog") swung around and stood at the foot of my table-bed. He laid papers down at my feet where I couldn't see them and said, "I am the commander-in-charge here." Dog addressed me as "Staw-dale" from the *Oriskany* (long *a*, accent on the next-to-last syllable). He asked me to confirm that I was the air-group commander, and then produced the *Pacific Stars and Stripes* with the article about Harry Jenkins's interview in Saigon after the Nam Dinh raid. Dog said, "We know you well and are waiting for Jenkins, too."

So that's where they got their information—they read the damned *Stars and Stripes*. That meant they knew about not only me and Harry, but Jack Shaw and Bill Smith. We'd all been interviewed in Saigon as part of a navy public-relations operation. My God, that meant they must have read about me in the Tonkin Gulf article of August 12 last year! I knew it made that *Stars and Stripes*—I got a copy of it from a friend in Germany. My heart sank.

Dog and Eagle left, and I lay flat on my back on that high library table and thought of my future. Back last May aboard the *Oriskany*, a classified E&E (escape and evasion) publication put out by the U.S. Air Force's Second Air Division in Saigon was circulated among us pilots. It said that after we were captured, not to worry, "there will be no torture or physical mistreatment." Since rough capture in the street, I hadn't had a hand laid on me yet, but the atmosphere in this prison had already made it obvious to me that that document was a lie. Sooner or later they would twist me into a knot and have my testimonial about the Tonkin Gulf on the front page of every newspaper in the world.

I didn't go to sleep until after I had heard the old French church bells of Hanoi ring midnight. It was now September 13; one year ago today, I had sat with mom in that tent beside dad's grave at the Abingdon cemetery and listened to the bugler play taps. Was this taps for me?

The days and nights blended together as I lay on that table, sleeping in snatches and periodically seized with intense burning or freezing sensations in my lower left leg and foot. To stop these flashes, I learned to use my right foot to rearrange my flopping left leg in a new alignment that unblocked the circulation stoppages and got upper-leg blood flowing in the arteries and veins below. I was given a blanket, and that helped ward off the mosquitoes and the chill at night; I rested my head on a matted pile of coarse cloth, which days later I realized was a mosquito net. The activity of my alimentary canal was sluggish. I slurped a little soup once or twice a day; bowel movements stopped, and I could rarely generate enough pressure with my lower body muscles to discharge urine in my old flat-on-the-back position. I would have dreams and hear myself calling out names in the night. I remember waking up while talking with Admiral Cousins's chief-of-staff, Willie House, through some pipeline connection back to the *Oriskany*, telling him, "Willie, we're doing it all wrong over here in this war and we're going to get into a lot of trouble."

Chapter 6

Getting the News

After the trip to Japan, I spent the rest of the summer in Connecticut savoring the precious memories of my vacation with Jim. I was continually thankful I'd made the journey. Each night I'd go off to sleep reliving some of our moments together.

I returned to Coronado with the boys just a few days before school began. Stanford started kindergarten that fall, Sid the sixth grade, and Jimmy his sophomore year in high school. I had only Taylor at home with me, and after school a high-school girl took him and Stan to the park while I did some tutoring at home.

On the afternoon of September 9, I went to San Diego and saw Carol Channing in *Hello, Dolly!* In the darkened theater, waves of nostalgia brought tears to my eyes. It seemed an eternity until Jim would be home in mid-December.

After supper that night, the younger boys asked me to stay upstairs with them until they fell asleep. This old house seemed to have a life of its own; it creaked and groaned at the end of the day and frightened young children trying to go to sleep. I remembered my own childhood imaginings about a wolf in the bedroom closet. Even now, more than thirty years later, I hadn't forgotten my terror, so I was more than happy to stay with Stan and Taylor until they went off to sleep.

About an hour later, I realized I had dozed off myself. I listened carefully, thinking I heard voices downstairs. The clock said almost 10:00 P.M. I sat up and listened more carefully. Jimmy was talking to someone in the living room. I headed for the stairs, and met Doyen Salsig on her way up.

"What are you doing here?" I asked, puzzled. She wrapped her arms around me and hugged me close. "There's been a message," she said, forcing the words out quickly. "Jim is missing." She hugged me even closer.

There was absolute silence as I tried to absorb what she'd said. She'd said Jim was missing. Missing! How could he be missing? It was impossible for a person to be missing. You couldn't be missing if you were alive. You'd have to be *somewhere* in the world. God would know where you were.

"Missing?" I said. "How can he be missing?"

"His plane was shot down and they think he got out, but they're not sure. There's a chaplain downstairs telling Jimmy. He has all the details about what they know so far. His name is Parker. He's a lieutenant."

Lieutenant Parker's voice shook as he told me what he knew. Poor young man, I thought as he told me about Jim's parachute having been sighted but no signs of life after the chute hit the ground. This young lieutenant was just doing his job, and I doubted he'd done this before. Several times I asked him to repeat the meager details. There had been no sound from the radio beeper that was supposed to activate automatically when the parachute opened, nor had there been any sign of gathering up the chute after Jim descended. And that was all they knew. Maybe he was dead and maybe he was alive, so for the time being he'd be listed as missing.

No tears gushed forth. No screams of anguish. Just a puzzling sensation of shock that this was happening to me. Then I began to shake all over. I felt embarrassed to do this in front of Lieutenant Parker, but I couldn't control it. Doyen brought me a glass of sherry, and Lieutenant Parker went over his information once more before he left. He told me to call him if I needed him; otherwise, an officer assigned to help me would call in the morning.

Doyen and I talked about whether I should tell the younger boys now or wait until morning. Jimmy had excused himself and gone to his room while the chaplain was still there. He was trying to be very grown-up and had asked if he could do anything for me. Doyen assured me I should wait until morning to tell the other boys—the words would come once I got started, she said. She asked if I wanted her to stay the night, but I insisted I'd be fine. She made me promise I'd call if I needed her.

After she left, I went to Jimmy's room. He was in bed and music was playing softly on his radio. He asked if I thought Jim was alive or dead. I said I honestly didn't know what to think but that I'd always tell him the truth about his dad. For a long time I sat on the side of his bed and rubbed his back. Then I tiptoed up to my room and got ready for bed. I wondered how to pray, and finally asked God to give Jim and me the strength we would need for whatever lay ahead. Afterward I began to shake again with shock and fear. I remembered all the dire warnings about not talking to the press. I tried to relax but couldn't. I tried to detect whether my intuition told me Jim was dead or alive, but I had absolutely no intuitive feelings about it one way or another. I finally called Doyen and she came back and spent the rest of the night on the sleeping porch.

The next morning I told Sid as best I could and held him in my arms until he'd cried himself out. It was hard to tell how much Stan understood about what was happening. The boys decided it would be best if they went to school as usual; nothing could be accomplished by their staying at home.

Soon after they left, the phone started to ring with official navy messages and friends offering sympathy and support. I still felt only a numb, sleepwalking sensation. The frightening possibility that the news media might descend upon me at any time was an overriding concern in my mind. I felt somewhat reassured by remembering that in the briefing about guidelines if your husband was taken prisoner, the commander had said our government believed the men being held were well treated. If I kept quiet, the navy felt the Communists would continue to treat the men in a humane and civilized way. I felt sure the government had good reason to insist on this "keep quiet" policy.

I did have to establish some sort of premise on which to proceed personally, however. To assume Jim was alive and would return someday made sense to me. It seemed I had three choices really about my personal conduct: I could become an alcoholic and remove myself from reality; I could rant and rave and scream and wring my hands; or I could try to cope as rationally as possible with the uncertainty. The first two choices would only make my life

Jim in a sailor suit, age three and a half, with his father in Abingdon, Illinois, 1927.

Jim at age six with his parents, Vernon and Mabel Stockdale.

Fifteen years old and determined to make the team.

Midshipman Stockdale, age nineteen, in front of Tecumseh at the U.S. Naval Academy.

With his father at the Naval Academy graduation, June 5, 1946.

Sybil Bailey, age one, New Haven, Connecticut, 1925.

Sybil in her dancing school recital costume at age seven.

Eight years old in the garden at home.

Dressed as a farm girl for a festival parade, age ten.

Sophomore year in high school.

June 28, 1947, North Branford Congregational Church.

Sybil and Jim shortly after they were married.

The young "Navy wife."

worse instead of better. I needed to be stronger than ever to take care of the boys now, too. I would try to cope and behave the way I believed Jim would want me to. I'd try to make him proud of my behavior if he was alive and if he did come home someday.

During the next few days, food and condolences poured into the house. Of all those expressions of condolence, the one I knew I would never forget came from my own little Stanford. As I was putting some clothes into the washer, he touched my arm and looked straight into my eyes with his big round blue ones so identical to his dad's, and said softly, "Mom, I'm so sorry about dad."

"Thank you, sweetheart," I whispered, and hugged him to me along with the laundry.

I began to read every item about Vietnam in the newspapers and magazines. I reasoned that a war between a country the size of Vietnam and one the size of the United States couldn't last too long. North Vietnam was such a dinky little country, it certainly wouldn't be any match for the United States. I thought it might be a matter of only a few weeks or months before it would all be over.

But even if it didn't last very long, I did need to know whether or not I'd get Jim's pay while he was missing. As promised, people had been assigned to help me work with the navy to find answers to my questions, but I was completely disappointed by the incompetence of the system. I telephoned every day for two weeks to find out whether or not they'd learned if I'd get Jim's pay. The mortgage payment on the house was due the first of October. If I didn't get Jim's pay, I'd have to borrow on his insurance and withdraw money from our mutual fund. It would take time to process the papers to accomplish those things.

I started calling the commander of fiscal affairs at the naval base. He kept reassuring me that he was doing everything he could to find out. Finally, on the last Friday in September, when he still didn't know, I lost my temper and screeched at him: "I've waited long enough! I'll give you until Monday to find out about that pay for me or I'm going to call the admiral in Washington who's head of all navy personnel!"

My temper tantrum paid off: Less than two hours later, I learned I would receive Jim's pay and the check would be mailed directly to me at home. I'd spend it carefully and save as much as I could. If Jim didn't come home, my pension would be only a pittance against what I'd need for the boys and the house. I'd certainly have to get a job, so I'd better save any extra money I could now.

Living through day after day of wondering and never knowing if Jim was alive became a way of life. I asked the navy for an address where I could write to Jim if he was alive. I was told that any letters I sent should be brief and not "too frequent." I decided once a week was the definition of "not too frequent" for me since I'd always written every day or so.

I wrote my first letter on September 26 and my next on October 3, following the addressing instructions the navy had given me: that each letter should be in an unsealed envelope, enclosed in another envelope addressed to Mr. Abba Schwarz, Administrator, Bureau Security and Consular Affairs, Department of State, Washington, D.C. I was told that the State Department would forward my letters through the Red Cross.

Meanwhile, I tired myself out with long bicycle rides, Taylor in the jump seat on the back. I also continued my schedule of tutoring children with reading problems, and began studying everything I could find about the country where Jim might be alive. I found that there were many who believed this war wouldn't be as brief as I hoped, so I changed my expectations to protect myself, and decided I could cope with a five-year span if necessary. I purposely made this time span far longer than I truly believed would be the case, just to protect myself from disappointment.

Doyen was my confidante and constant refuge in the storm. She and Budd were my social companions, too. They'd go with me to watch Jimmy's football games, and we'd often go to the movies at the Village Theater together. They'd include me in all their dinner parties. I would have been lost without them. I was thankful I had to force myself to function normally for the sake of the boys; their needs gave my days a schedule that helped consume the dragging time. I suppressed my feelings as much as possible so as not to frighten the boys. We had found we couldn't talk about their dad among ourselves—it was just too painful. We all went through the routine of each day in as normal a way as possible. I wrote to Jim every week, but never really expected to hear from him.

My birthday and Jim's birthday were long, sad days. I sorted through and removed mementoes from the two gray metal boxes in which the navy had sent home all his personal belongings. On Christmas Day I opened up and wore the lovely blue baroque pearls we'd bought together in Japan. Wherever he was, I felt closer to him with that necklace reminding me of his love. I knew Christmas would be difficult and had made up my mind to try to make the best possible memories for the younger boys. Budd and Doyen and their family came for Christmas dinner. I thanked God that night when the holiday was over. And I wondered what the new year, 1966, would hold for me.

In the days ahead, as I went about my routine of cooking, laundry, mending, helping with homework, I worried about articles in the newspaper referring to the possibility of North Vietnam holding war-crimes trials for the Americans they held prisoner. They claimed our men had bombed civilian targets and so would be treated as war criminals. The dreadful thought of war-crimes trials nagged at me. I took Jimmy into my confidence about it and asked him to try to keep Sid and Stan from being aware of this threat. He was doing everything in his power to be as grown-up and supportive as possible. When the spring flowers began to bloom in Coronado and the North Vietnamese still hadn't conducted any war-crimes trials, I began to feel easier.

On Friday morning, April 15, as I left the house with Taylor to do errands, I gathered the mail from the front-porch box. I flipped through eight or ten pieces, frowning with disgust as they all looked like advertising circulars of one kind or another. I began to take them into the house—then I stopped dead. Wait a minute, the handwriting on one of those envelopes seemed familiar. I went back through the pile and, sure enough, there, looking back at me, was Jim's handwriting.

I picked up the envelope gently, half-afraid it might disappear if I touched it too much. The paper was cheap and there were no stamps on the front but when I turned it over I saw four stamps across the back, all bearing the word *Vietnam*. There was also a round postmark that said "Hanoi." My eyes then shifted to the envelope just beneath this one, which also had the stamps and post-mark on the back and was addressed to me on the front, but not in Jim's handwriting; instead, the writing was neatly precise and had a European 7 in 547 "A" Avenue.

I stood staring at those envelopes, struck dumb by the magni-tude of what I was holding in my hands, and suddenly fearful. Why was the second letter addressed by a stranger? Perhaps it contained bad news. Maybe I shouldn't be alone in the house with a young child when I read them. But where should I go? I knew Doyen wasn't home. I decided to take Taylor and drive to Gala Arnold's. Gala was another dear friend in Coronado. Heading for the car with hands shaking and heart pounding, I thought how I must drive care-fully because I was in such a state of turmoil.

When Gala opened her door, I half-whispered that something fantastic had happened. I told her about the letters and asked if I could go into her study and be alone when I read them.

In the study, I put the two envelopes down in front of me on the desk and carefully examined the handwriting. On one Jim's handwriting looked completely natural. The other was completely foreign. Which one should I open first? This may be one of the biggest moments of your life, Sybil, I thought to myself. It's possi-ble that he may have written one letter himself and later died. The second letter may be telling you he has died.

I decided to open the envelope addressed in the foreign hand first. If it was bad news, I would rather know about it when I read Jim's letter. As I unfolded the cheap manila paper, I found myself staring at a completely unfamiliar handwriting, but the letter began, "My dearest Syb." It was dated 3 February 1966. I quickly skimmed through the four pages and found at the end it was signed "All my love, Jim." So this letter was from him also, despite the strange-looking handwriting and envelope. Now I turned to the other letter and Jim's very familiar handwriting beside the date 26 December 1965. It began, "My Dearest Syb and Boys."

I sat and read these two letters over five or six times each. The first said the following:

Addressor: James B. Stockdale
                 Detention Camp for Captured American Pilots in
                 the Democratic Republic of Vietnam
                 Via Hanoi Regular Mail

Addressee: Father Mother <u>Wife</u> Brother Sister Son Daughter
Mrs. James B. Stockdale
No. 547 A. Avenue
Coronado, California

26 December 1965

My Dearest Syb and Boys,

Yesterday, on Christmas Day, the authorities granted me permission to send you greetings. How I wish this war would end and I could come home. Detailed and numerous conversations have been held with Vietnamese officials on the status of the war here in the light of International Law and humanitarianism, and the points they make include many sound grievances on both counts. Let us hope that the bombing of the North will stop soon and that peace will be quickly restored in the South.

I have been given your letter of October 3rd describing your football outing with the Salsigs. It is a great comfort to me to know that Hazel has come to the aid of Mother. I was afraid that your New England conscience, Syb, would get the better of you. You have more than your share of responsibility in caring for four growing boys. A winter visit by Mother accompanied by Hazel seems a good tonic for Mother's loneliness while at the same time providing freedom and companionship for all. Please give Mother my enduring love and explain that for the time being that I shall have to write to you alone.

Syb, I'm concerned about your finances. I have a couple of suggestions. Stop by and see that La Jolla man from Investor's Diversified and make arrangements for a regular depletion of those resources. As I understand it, all my allotments continue in effect, and thus there would be a regular (smaller) input as well. At any rate, please consider that fund "living money." Also, with my power of attorney, I should think you would be able to borrow on my insurance. Under these circumstances, I see no disadvantage in that, whatsoever. Having said this, my mind is more at ease, believing you will use the resources. The rainy day is here.

As for my welfare and surroundings, I wish I could report on acquaintences [sic] in my straits, but I have not seen an American since I was shot down. However, I am adequately housed and fed. I'm about 140 pounds. I have a bum knee and shoulder which were well treated in a stay in the hospital here. I'm told that I will soon be able to return to the hospital, where the doctors will finish the job. In summary, don't concern yourself with my physical well being. I'm being taken care of.

In the mental category, I have my ups and downs. Perhaps solitude builds character; I sometimes think of how such experiences gave depth of insight to Dostoevsky and the other writers. Be assured that above all, I have securely found God. My orientation (as I'm sure yours is) is completely in terms of our life together after reunion, of course. I've gone through the autumn and early winter birthdays (JB, Stan, and yourself), living the day with the honored one. I frequently dream of all—Sid and Taylor have been featured of late. How wonderful it is that our children's ages cover such a time span.

Yesterday Christmas was celebrated here. I was treated to light confections at tea in the afternoon and given a fine evening meal in honor of the event. I thought of how sad it is that this life must be blighted by man's inhumanity to man in war, as I mentioned to you when we were last together. In my recollection of our conversations over the years, things left unsaid by me rather than points made, dominate my thoughts under these circumstances. Even though reason tells me that the scope and depth of my emotions were understood without precise statement, how I now wish I had turned phrase after phrase. As you must know, you are the purpose and love of my life, Syb.

My writing time is nearly up, and I must hurry with the more down to earth ideas I've been savoring. I do hope you were able to have Christmas dinner with the Salsigs again. (What with the time difference I visualize you together now.) Our celebration together was becoming a comforting and happy convention. I do hope they stay in Coronado. Pre-Christmas activities should have included the return of the ship, if the schedule held. I hope that evolution went acceptably well for you. I'm sure Bart saw to it that you got the furniture and air-conditioner. I've hoped that the old shipmates that I liked so well stopped by to see you—Don Houck, Paul Engel and all. Incidentally, I wish you would repay Paul a couple of stamp books. Just drop by—he lives right across from Shugarts.

Boys, don't count your old man out for very long. We'll be together soon. I pray by even this summer. Rosey-cheek Taylor, I know you're king of the sandbox set. Stan, how many times I have visualized you marching off to school with your books and pencil box. I've thought of you a lot this week of this big Christmas of your life. Sid, I love you dearly, and wonder how the typical Mr. Regular Boy spent the fall. Flag football, again perhaps. Jim, you've inherited the big load of temporary "Man of the Family" at an early age. You've met our every dream, and I rest more easily knowing your mature and watchful eye is making sure Mother gets as much assistance as you boys can give her. Jim, I'm particularly proud of your quality of character and I know you will be an example matched by your brothers. The last thing you said to me as you rode away to school on your bike the morning I left was, "We'll be praying for you." How much significance that remark has since held for me! Also glad to hear of your athletic achievement this fall. I'll soon be back there with my team again to give you guys a run for your money. Incidently [*sic*], say hello to our old football mates Bobby Tom, Baldy, and Red Dawg.

Syb, I've just been given the word that I may expect to be given a letter a month—perhaps to write as often. Happy Day. It was also explained that my outgoing mail, within this possible ceiling, can go to only one addressee as I inferred earlier. By the same token, only one (yourself) should write to me on the monthly schedule. I'm told that the weight of your letter must not exceed twenty grams. My spirits are climbing already as I savor this knowledge. If God is with us, —————————

All my love,
Jim

Address letters to me as follows:
James B. Stockdale
Detention Camp for Captured American Pilots
In the Democratic Republic of Vietnam
Via Hanoi Regular Mail

And next the carefully hand-printed letter that did not look anything like Jim's own handwriting but which I knew he had written because of the content:

From: James Bond Stockdale
Address: Camp of Detention of U.S. Pilots Captured in the Democratic Republic of Vietnam
Care of Hanoi Post Office

To: Mrs. James Bond Stockdale
Address: 547 "A" Avenue, Coronado, California
United States of America

3 February 1966

My Dearest Syb,

On this chilly afternoon I am so glad to be permitted to write my monthly letter and to let you know that I am still OK. One thinks of Vietnam as a tropical country, but in January the rains came, and there was cold and darkness, even at noon. Keeping warm takes energy, and I lost some weight. February already brings the promise of spring, and I think I will gain it back as the temperature rises.

I am still not used to being alone, but I have worked out methods to keep my mind occupied. My favorite diversion is working for hours at recollecting in detail all of the events that took place on one of our trips together, or during a period in one of our many homes. The trips most frequently covered are our last two: When you met me in Alameda last winter, and when you visited me this summer. Those were really wonderful experiences. I also frequently recollect our days in Norfolk when you and I and Bob and Glo spent so many evenings together (what I call the "portacrib period"). A musical memory we share usually brings this latter period to mind, and it is usually one of the Dorothy Collins/Snooky Lanson musical memories. In the coming years we'll have to update our store of musical memories. At any rate, you would smile at the detail that can be brought back with concentration. Events with Mary Brown and Stan Smith are also particularly pleasant to review; bless them both. There is some good in being able to review one's life as I am doing: One can select the most rich and rewarding course for the future. It is amazing in retrospect how much time and effort is spent on affairs which hold no permanent meaning. More time in sharing interests in detail with the family, and more travel together are my selected courses. We have such rich memories, all too frequently separated by the gaps brought about by my preoccupation with work in the past.

I constantly think of, love, and appreciate you four boys. I do not have a message for each, as I did in my Christmas letter, but assure you together that I am confident that you are helping Mother and doing your best at your activities. My thoughts here deal in detail not only with your achievements, individual traits, and lovable personalities, but with plans about how we will enjoy each other and work together in the future, and how I will help each of you achieve your goals in life. How I miss my sweet old Dad. I certainly gain much from memories of him. He left us all an admirable heritage when he died. Symbolic of his memory is his last gift; his banner which Grandmother presented us, and Mother keeps in my closet. Honor that, no matter what happens.

In the one letter I have received from you, Syb (dated 3 October, 1965), you mentioned the hope that Aunt Hazel would stay with my Mother, and accompany her to California for a winter visit. I so hope those plans worked out and that they are now nearby in their own quarters in Coronado, enjoying the sunshine and the company of all of you. Please give my love to both, my appreciation to Aunt Hazel, and to Mother the assurance that thoughts of her are in my mind and heart constantly. At the end of this letter I copy, as per instruction, the mailing directives concerning letters from the United States to me. No more than one letter per month will be delivered to me, and this letter must be from one of those listed in paragraph 4. I have in mind that letter being from you each month. Please explain this to Mother; I am sure you will include news of her. (I will forego letters from the boys, too.)

Conversely, the maximum number of letters I can send per month is one. That will go to you. Let us both understand that circumstances here or there, or in mail handling, will frequently interrupt this flow. No news will be good news, and we'll hope for the best communication. Incidentally, note 2 below, does not exclude airmail; that is OK. It does exclude mail delivered by the Diplomatic Service, and that with any but the given address (nothing to be sent through the International Red Cross, etc.).

Syb, I hope you took my financial advice and are getting money from our mutual fund or my insurance policies. Please be generous to yourselves.

I can think of no other news here. My knee and shoulder still need some medical attention, and hopefully I will go back to the hospital soon.

I pray a good deal. Every night I remember each of you individually; and I know you do the same for me. I live for the day of our reunion, which I suppose will be soon after the war is over. I have no idea how that is working itself out. Let us think positively and remember the Scripture which goes something like: "All things together work for the good of those who love and serve the Lord." This experience has taught me to love Him completely, and hopefully to better serve Him (and to better serve you all), when I get home.

All my love,

Jim

Note to receiver:

1/ Address to

Camp of Detention of U.S. Pilots captured in the Democratic Republic of Vietnam, care of Post Office Hanoi

2/ Letters must be sent by regular mail through Post Office

3/ Each envelope may contain letters, cards or photos and not exceed 20 grams maximum weight per month.

4/ Only one envelope of 20 grams maximum weight per month. In the envelope may be letters from wife, children, mother, father, sisters, brothers (just immediate family).

He was alive. He really was alive. And he sounded fine—just like his natural self. Even some humor, saying the rainy day is here. We always used to wonder if we'd know when the rainy day had arrived as we saved our money in case it did. How incredible to get these letters from him out of the blue. How wonderful to know he truly was alive. How I thanked God for having watched over him.

Putting my letters carefully into my bag, I went to the kitchen and told Gala the joyful news. She hugged me and we both wiped tears from our eyes. She gave Taylor a cookie for each hand and I drove carefully home. On the way I began to plan how I'd proceed. I'd call his mother first, show the letters to the boys as soon as they got home, call my parents, and show the letters to Doyen and Budd. Maybe they'd have some explanation for the couple of parts that kind of bothered me. They didn't make sense, but all the rest of what he said did. The part about dropping by at Paul Engel's across the street from the Shugarts'—that was strange. The Shugarts lived on the base in Lemoore, California—400 miles north of here. What would make him say "Just drop by"? And that business to the boys about saying hello to his old football buddies—Bobby Tom, Baldy, and Red Dawg. A cold chill slipped through me as I thought of that. It sounded crazy. Baldy Chapman and Red Dawg Davis were fellow aviators, but they never played any football. Bobby Tom Jenkins played football with Jim at the Naval Academy, but the boys had never even met him, and I hadn't seen him in years. He lived in Alabama somewhere—I didn't even know where.

How could most of Jim's letters be so natural and astute-sounding, and those parts be so crazily mixed-up? Maybe they were just momentary memory lapses. But even as I thought it, I knew it didn't make sense. I wondered what that part was at the end of his first letter that was all inked over. Something his censors didn't want me to know, I guessed. I'd have to be sure to remind everyone I told about the letters not to tell anyone I'd received them. The navy would want to know I'd heard from Jim, too. I'd have to remember to call them.

By evening, I'd been over the letters with Jimmy and Sid while Stan and even Taylor listened; I'd read them a couple of times each to his mother and my parents on the telephone; I'd had a long talk with Doyen and Budd about them, fixed supper, and supervised homework and bath time. I felt worn to a frazzle. Even so, I began to think about my next letter to Jim, using the new rules and new address. I felt so thankful I'd kept copies of all the letters I'd already written so I could look back at mine of October 3 and see exactly what I'd said to him. I wondered if he'd understood the symbolism I'd intended when I wrote, "Yesterday afternoon Stan, Taylor, Sid and I went to the beach. We made a lovely sand castle right at the edge of the water. A big wave knocked it down and washed it away but we . . . worked hard to build it up again." It really sounded mundane compared to his. What I wouldn't have given to be an Elizabeth Barrett Browning.

The next morning, in response to my call the day before, two men from the San Diego office of Naval Intelligence came to the house to talk to me about Jim's letters. One, appropriately named Mr. Steele, was a gentleman of the old school; I liked him and had confidence in him immediately. He explained in a thoughtful voice that the navy didn't want to pry into my personal affairs, but that they were most interested in any bits of information about Jim's circumstances other than the purely personal. He told me how much they appreciated my having called to share my letters with them.

I told him I was glad he realized how sensitive I felt about showing Jim's letters to strangers, but that I also knew Jim would want me to cooperate with the Office of Naval Intelligence. I explained that I wanted to do the right thing but didn't want copies of my letters circulated all over the place, either.

After promising to honor my confidence, Mr. Steele asked if Jim's letters sounded perfectly natural as they were written. I told him I felt sure he'd written all but the address on one envelope, even though the handwriting in the second letter didn't look natural. He wanted to know if anything Jim had said seemed unusual or different to me, and he suggested we go through the letters paragraph by paragraph.

I told him I thought the first paragraph in the first letter was carefully worded so as not to offend his captors, and that "detailed and numerous conversations" probably referred to repeated and lengthy interrogations. I felt he used the terms "International Law" and "humanitarianism" because it was difficult to disagree that the Vietnamese might have some grievances in those areas. I felt paragraph two was perfectly natural, and that the financial advice he gave me in paragraph three was accurate and as I might expect. I pointed out that "acquaintences" in paragraph four was misspelled the way he usually misspelled it; that his reported weight of 140 meant he'd lost about thirty pounds in three months—and in the next letter he said he'd lost even more. It appeared to me that he was trying to put the best possible face on the situation so I wouldn't worry too much. "Adequately housed and fed" sounded like low-level conditions to me. He referred to Dostoevsky, one of his favorite writers, and had made that same comment about "man's inhumanity to man" to me when we were leaving the movie theater in Japan after seeing *In Harm's Way*.

Paragraphs seven and eight really worried me. I confided that I was worried about Jim's talking about "stopping by" Paul Engel's to repay him for some stamp books. Not only did Paul live 400 miles away, but also it was out of character for Jim to be concerned about repaying anybody for a few stamps; he used to borrow cigarettes from everyone because he doesn't like to carry things, and he never worried about paying anyone back. I talked about the strangeness of his references to Bobby Tom, Baldy, and Red Dawg as his football buddies. And I told them the most significant part of the letters, the thing that made me feel the saddest, was his phrase "there was cold and darkness, even at noon." I felt sure Jim was referring to the book *Darkness at Noon*, which describes life in a Communist prison so vividly that I shuddered as I sat there talking about it.

Mr. Steele then asked if anything in the second letter seemed to convey a message of any kind. I said that the banner of his dad's he referred to was the American flag from on top of the casket his dad was buried in. It was kept on the shelf in Jim's closet upstairs. I didn't know why his handwriting was so unnatural in this letter. Maybe because of his bad shoulder or being cold and stiff, or both, but I thought it more likely he'd been told to print all his letters. His handwriting is a combination of half printing and half cursive writing, which looks quite unusual if you scrutinize it carefully. I thought someone had told him he had to either write or print, but must not combine the two, so he decided to print.

"His recollections about the past all seem on track and natural to me. To tell you the truth," I said, "I get the impression from both these letters that January had been Hell Week, and since the reward-and-punishment method is so typical of Communist behavior, it seems logical to me that after the rewards of December, he suffered severe punishment in January and then is being rewarded again by being allowed to write a letter in February. I think the tone of the second letter is much more somber than that of the first. I don't find any light touches at all, I'm sorry to say."

Before Mr. Steele and his companion left, they both urged me not to worry too much about the parts of Jim's letters that seemed unusual. I got the impression they knew more about these strange passages than I did.

During the next couple of weeks, I wrote down my comments about the letters as Mr. Steele had asked me to do. A few days after I sent these comments to him, he telephoned and asked if I would accept a phone call from a naval intelligence officer at the Pentagon, Commander Robert Boroughs. Commander Boroughs telephoned later that afternoon and asked me if Jim and I had a favorite song! I thought that was a crazy question but told him we had several that we considered "our" songs. One was "Near You"; another was "Que Será, Será"; a third was "Putting on the Style"; and a fourth was "Fry Me a Cookie in a Can of Lard." I thought he might laugh at that last title, but he continued his questions in a dead-serious tone. At the close of our conversation, he asked if I could travel to Washington at government expense for a conference with him. Excited at the prospect, I called him later in the week and told him I'd be able to go in May.

Jimmy wanted to take care of his brothers, with the help of a daytime sitter, so I'd make the trip as brief as possible. My spirits were at an all-time high since Jim's capture, but I couldn't help wondering what Commander Boroughs wanted to talk about that couldn't be done on the telephone. We'd already talked at length on something called a "secure" phone, so why was it necessary for the navy to pay my way across the country and back? Curious.

Shortly after supper on May 1, a commander from Naval Air Pacific Headquarters telephoned. He said he had been advised to tell me that Hanoi had announced my husband's capture. He said they expected this announcement to appear in the next day's newspaper, possibly with a photograph taken in Hanoi, and he thought I would want to know about it ahead of time.

This news made me apprehensive. The picture, if there was one, might be gruesome. I'd have to get that paper somehow when it first came out so I could absorb whatever they printed and then decide how to handle it with the boys. After a few minutes standing there with my hand still on the telephone receiver, I picked it up again and called the *San Diego Union*. I asked when the morning papers were first delivered to Coronado. A gravelly voice told me they usually came over on the 2:00 A.M. ferry.

I asked Jimmy to sleep upstairs, taking him into my confidence once more about this latest development. Then, a little before 2:00 A.M., I drove down a deserted Orange Avenue to the ferry landing. I sat shivering in my car in front of the Mexican Village Restaurant, waiting for the ferry to dock. But when it arrived there was no sign of any newspapers. The line handler at the dock told me if they missed this boat, they'd be in around 4:00 A.M. I drove back home and paced around until it was time to meet the 4:00 A.M. boat.

I could hear the horn in the fog before I saw the boat, and then watched it bumping against the huge piles. Seeing the banded stacks of papers being loaded into a truck, I followed the truck to the local newspaper office and timidly told the man handling the papers why I wanted one. He gave me the longest, most searching sort of stare out of his tired, work-worn eyes, perhaps wondering if I was crazy, but he silently handed me a paper. I couldn't blame him for wondering at my behavior; hardly anyone in the world knew there were such creatures as prisoners of war. Please, God, I said in my mind as I turned the pages looking for the article, don't let it be too bad. And then I was staring at a picture of my dearest love. His head was somewhat bowed and the picture itself was dark. His face looked unshaven and he seemed to have on a pajama sort of shirt. His mouth was grim, but altogether it wasn't as bad as I'd thought it might be. Thank God, I thought as I went on to read the article below. Directly below his picture, it said "*CDR JAMES STOCKDALE* . . . held by Reds?" And the article in the *San Diego Union*, May 2, 1966, read:

HANOI CLAIMS S.D. NAVY MAN CAPTIVE

Tokyo (AP)—Hanoi's Vietnamese News Agency has identified a San Diegan who, it says, was captured after his Navy plane was shot down over North Vietnam last September. He was identified as Cdr. James Bond Stockdale, 42, of 427 A Ave., Coronado. Stockdale reportedly was assigned to the aircraft carrier *Oriskany* in August 1964, as leader of an F-8 squadron. The agency said Stockdale was captured in Thanh Hoa on Sept. 9, 1965. It distributed a picture of the pilot and released it for publication. Mrs. Stockdale, at her home yesterday, would not comment, a family friend said. Navy officials said they had no further information. The agency identified four other American pilots Saturday and said they also were captured after their planes were shot down last September.

It was straightforward enough, I thought, beginning to read it a second time. That was the first I'd heard about a family friend saying I had no comment, but that was the way the government wanted it, of course, so it was all for the best. I wondered if the wrong address was purposeful or just carelessness. No matter. That was better anyway because of my tremendous apprehension about press inquiries.

Ten days later, early on the morning of May 10, I settled into my seat on the airliner to Washington and luxuriated in the service and in the freedom from household chores. I was to meet Commander Boroughs the next morning at the mall entrance of the Pentagon. Arriving at the appointed place, I saw a man I was sure was Commander Boroughs. He wore a dark blue striped business suit instead of a uniform, and he was about five foot nine", with sandy, receding, thinning hair above a high forehead. We introduced ourselves, and he led me down the long Pentagon halls to his office. I was all eyes, somewhat apprehensive, and anxious to please Commander Boroughs.

Shortly after we passed through heavy security doors, we entered his small and cluttered office. Coffee was served, and once more we went through Jim's letters. Another fellow, named Pat Twinem, was present. When we got to the part about Paul Engel, Commander Boroughs told me that Commander Harry Jenkins lived across the street from Paul Engel. Harry Jenkins was listed as missing, and Boroughs felt sure Jim was trying to tell the navy that

Jenkins was alive in Hanoi. He also said the three men Jim referred to as "football mates" had the same last names as three people missing from Jim's air group—Harry Jenkins, Harley Chapman, and Ed Davis. He impressed upon me that this was classified information and I must not talk to anyone about it. I was excited that Jim had been so clever and that I was allowed to share this secret.

Commander Boroughs then asked if I'd go over to the State Department and ask them what they were doing about our men being held in Hanoi. He explained that the State Department was responsible for protecting the men's best interests since there had never been a declaration of war. Averell Harriman was our ambassador-at-large in charge of these things. Boroughs wanted to know what Harriman's people had to say about what they were doing to promote Jim's best interest. I felt a little puzzled about all this but agreed to do it.

The next day, Pat Twinem escorted me over to the State Department, where I had an appointment with Mr. Philip Heymann, one of Ambassador Harriman's assistants. We were a few minutes early and were asked to wait in a large outer office with a desk at the far end. The thick carpets muffled our footsteps as we approached. Behind the large desk sat a man intent on his paperwork while a young woman stood behind him looking over his shoulder. They were so engrossed in their reading that they didn't even realize we had arrived until Pat Twinem cleared his throat, startling them both. Pat Twinem began to inquire about Mr. Heymann—but while he was doing that, I was transfixed by the papers these two had been reading: They were clearly copies of Jim's letters. I was stunned. These people were fairly slobbering over copies of my precious letters from Jim.

My heart pounded all the way through my conversation with Mr. Heymann. The essence of his message was that everything possible was being done to ensure that our men were well-treated, but unfortunately these things couldn't be talked about. He told me Ambassador Harriman was tremendously experienced and I was really most fortunate to have him on the problem at the time.

All the way back to Boroughs's office in the taxi, I railed and ranted at Pat Twinem about passing out copies of my letters. He had recognized them, too, so there was no denying it. Back at the office, I shouted at the sober-faced Boroughs that if they passed out my letters to anyone ever again, I'd never let them know if I received another one. I was a little shocked at my own behavior, but I'd so hoped to hear something encouraging at the State Department that finding strangers reading my love letters seemed like an extra blow. Commander Boroughs promised to personally handle all my mail in the future. That made me feel somewhat better.

He then asked if I ever sent Jim any pictures. I explained that I hadn't even taken any pictures. He said he wanted me to think about cooperating with Naval Intelligence in a scheme to get a secret message to Jim. It would involve my sending a picture with each letter from now on.

"That sounds dangerous," I said. "What if he gets caught?"

"That's why I want you to think it over carefully before you give me your answer," Commander Boroughs replied, still looking at me steadily.

"Well, I don't know. What guarantees are there that Jim would be protected if he got caught?"

"None. He'd be on his own."

"And I'd be responsible for having involved him."

"That's right. But I think you have to consider whether or not he'd want you to involve him."

"I guess he's already answered that in part by sending those messages out in his letters."

"Yes, I think you could say that. But I don't want you to give me an answer now. Think about it, because you're right, it is a dangerous business, and you are taking his life into your own hands, so to speak."

He went on to say he'd need to know my answer sometime in the next month. If I agreed to cooperate, he'd want me to send my special letter and picture at a time when the North Vietnamese would be most likely to give it to Jim for Christmas, probably in early October. Naval Intelligence would need several weeks to get a special picture ready if I agreed to send it. He reminded me how important it was not to tell anyone about this, especially for Jim's sake. I nodded and said I'd let him hear from me after I'd thought it over. Meanwhile, I agreed to begin immediately to include a photograph with each of my monthly letters.

Thinking about it on the plane home, I was almost sure that I would cooperate with the Intelligence people. I thought Jim would want me to. But I'd sleep on it to make sure. It was nothing to decide lightly. My spirits absolutely soared.

In late May I wrote Jim about our plans to leave for Connecticut on June 21 and that we'd have the same Sunset Beach cottage we'd had the previous summer. On June 20, 1966, I cleared out my desk as I prepared the Coronado house for summer tenants. I would take my most recent, precious letter from Jim with me. It had been written in March and arrived on June 12. I reread his last paragraphs before I put it into my bag for the journey to Connecticut.

> Please don't worry too much about me. I'm holding up and doing OK. God has become my roommate and he's taking care of me. Your views on determinism certainly apply to my situation when one considers the religious conviction I've realized "for God works in mysterious ways his wonders to perform": I remember on our last day together last summer when you said "I just can't believe God won't send you back to me." I see no reason to doubt that He will. Let us just pray that it's soon. I hope that the many problems of running a big home and guiding a big family have not been overwhelming, Syb . . . I worry about you worrying too much with all of the responsibilities that have fallen on you, Syb. Please relax, have faith and just do your usual wonderful job. No more could be asked.

I decided to take a letter I'd just received from Ambassador Harriman also. I was worried about Jim still being listed as missing when I'd had mail from him; I felt this let Hanoi off the hook to take good care of him. I wrote to President Johnson expressing my concerns and asked for an explanation. Instead of receiving a reply from the Executive Department, I received one from the State Department. Why a question I'd addressed to one department received a reply from another somewhat baffled me, but I had a great deal to learn about the ways of Washington. Ambassador Harriman's reply in part said:

> . . . I quite understand your concern about the fact that your husband continues to be listed as "missing in action" when you have received letters from him in North Viet-Nam. This terminology stems from traditional Navy practice of carrying a man as "missing" despite the fact that there are indications he is a prisoner of the enemy. It has nothing to do with your husband's status as a prisoner of war. As you

correctly point out the Geneva Convention applies in the Viet-Nam conflict. North Viet-Nam adhered to the Convention in 1957, and a state of armed conflict between two or more of the "High Contracting Parties" does exist. Unfortunately, the North Vietnamese authorities have argued that the Convention does not apply in the present conflict. . . .

In part because of your question raised in your letter to the President, the Navy and other services are presently reviewing the terms used to designate men being held by the Communists in Viet-Nam. I am informed the Navy will be in touch with you directly. . . .

On the evening of July 5, I was sitting on the seawall in front of our cottage watching the sunset change colors from red to rose to pink and then lavender. I never ceased being amazed at this lavish celestial display just before twilight, and I was somewhat surprised to see that my mother and father weren't in their usual beach chairs watching the sunset, too.

"Sybil." I was startled to find my father touching my sleeve. His ruddy face was unusually sober, making me immediately attentive to his quiet words. "I don't like to tell you this, Sybil, but I think you ought to know. We've just been watching the news and they showed some pictures of prisoners marching through the streets of Hanoi. The news isn't good, Sybil, but I'm sure they won't go through with it."

"Could you make out anyone you thought was Jim?" I asked in a hushed and frightened tone.

"No, I couldn't make out faces very clearly. It all went so fast. They said more, but I'm sure they won't go through with it, Sybil, but I think you should know for the boys' sake as well as your own."

"What, father? What is it they said?"

"They said they're going to try the prisoners with war-crimes trials, but I'm sure they won't go through with it, Sybil."

And then again, in a stronger voice, he concluded, "I'm sure they won't."

I could see in his eyes the agony of having to tell me about this dreadful threat. He gave my arm a squeeze as he settled on the seawall beside me, and we watched the last piece of sun sink below the horizon. From far down the beach, I heard the boys' voices as they shouted and cavorted with their friends. I was already beginning to wonder how I'd handle this new threat with them.

Later, lying down in the old-fashioned iron bed in my Spartan bedroom, I prayed as I had never prayed before that these trials would not become a reality. "Dear Heavenly Father," I whispered into the darkness, "please don't let it happen. And if it does, I'm going to need extra help only you can give me."

The horror I imagined was of Jim blindfolded and handcuffed, standing against a stone wall and being executed by a firing squad, all while the boys and I watched on TV. Jimmy was at camp and not here to help me protect Sid, Stan, and Taylor. I wondered what he might hear about this at his camp off in the wilds of Michigan. I couldn't sleep and turned on the radio to hear if anything more was being reported. The voice of a slaphappy disc jockey burst into the room, telling me about the million-dollar record he was going to play. It was better just to have the quiet, with the lapping of the waves in the distance. I would think about our days and nights in Japan together and see how much of the detail I could recall.

At breakfast, I gently told the boys not to be concerned if they heard rumors about war-crimes trials; the Communists were probably just trying to frighten us, and whatever the future held, Jim would want us to face it bravely. I wished I felt as confident in my heart as I sounded.

During the next few days, my heart literally ached with agony and I hated the feeling that neighbors were looking at me pityingly and thinking, poor thing, poor thing. Finally, after almost a week of this suspense, my emotional dam broke completely. My mother held me like a small child as I sobbed and sobbed. "I can't stand it. I can't stand it," I cried out over and over again. "What am I going to do?"

"It's no good to try to hold it in all the time. I think letting it out some will help you hold up for the boys."

I looked into her eyes and saw all the pain a mother feels for a child when she can't help. She went on gently: "You've got to hold up for the boys, you know. You don't really have any choice. That's what Jim would want you to do."

✧

In the following days, I resolved to heed two of Jim's favorite axioms. One is "Always try to turn a disadvantage into an advantage," and the other, which was really more his dad's than his own, "When in doubt, see the manager." At the end of the week, I called Commander Boroughs and asked him to make appointments for me to see Admiral McDonald, the chief of naval operations; and Ambassador Harriman. I had added one of my own axioms: "Nothing can take the place of a personal visit."

When I arrived in Washington a couple of weeks later, Commander Boroughs met me at the airplane. On the way to the Pentagon, I told him I'd decided to cooperate with Naval Intelligence in their attempt to communicate covertly with Jim. I'd already begun sending Jim a photograph with my letter each month so that it would seem like my routine procedure to the Vietnamese. Commander Boroughs's face lit up with a broad smile; he wanted me to meet with his photographic specialist while I was in town. "He may want you to think of a way you can signal Jim in the text of your letter to soak a picture in water without the North Vietnamese catching on. We will have prepared the picture ahead of time so it will pull apart when soaked and he'll be able to read an enclosed message."

That night before I went to sleep, I figured out a way I could do it. It involved a picture of a stand-in for Jim's mother, taken bathing in the ocean. The next morning, I met Bart Connolly at the Pentagon. He was there on shore duty now. He explained I had to be interviewed by the navy chief of information before I could see the chief of naval operations: they wanted to be sure I wasn't going to cry and carry on in front of the big important people. I passed inspection, and when I saw the CNO (chief of naval operations) I told him I wanted Jim listed as a prisoner of war and I wanted the navy to launch its own anti-North Vietnamese propaganda campaign. I left feeling unsure whether either would become a reality.

The next day I was once again escorted to the State Department for my meeting with Ambassador Harriman. This time, however, Pat Twinem waited in the reception room, with a secretary who postured like a *Vogue* model, while I went into a large room that was heavily carpeted and handsomely furnished.

Ambassador Harriman was in his late seventies and looked more heavyset than I had envisioned. I noted that he wore a hearing aid. This made me feel more at ease because my father wore a hearing aid also. I told myself that I must remember to look straight at him when I talked to him, as that would make it easier for him to understand me. Maybe if he thought I was a thoughtful person, he'd try even harder to do whatever he could to help Jim.

After assuring me that he was encouraged by Hanoi's muting its threats about war-crimes trials, and telling me that the things the State Department was doing on behalf of our men being held captive covered a wide range of activities—none of which could be publicly disclosed—he began to ask me some questions that puzzled me a little.

"Mrs. Stockdale, how are they treating you over at the Pentagon?" he asked.

I wondered what kind of a question that was. Weren't these people all members of the same government? Well, I figured, there was no way this department was going to get me to say anything uncomplimentary about my Jim's navy, even if there *were* some things that had been frustrating me.

"The navy's doing a fine job and trying to be helpful in every way they can, Ambassador Harriman. I just hope the army and the air force are doing as well by their wives."

"How do you think your husband is getting along, Mrs. Stockdale? I understand you've had mail from him. Can you tell very much about his circumstances from what he says?"

"Ambassador Harriman, have you ever seen a letter from a prisoner in Hanoi?" I asked, amazed that so many others had read my mail but this man in charge of the welfare of our imprisoned men might not have.

"No, I haven't," was his simple reply.

I handed him Jim's first letter, and his eyes glistened like those of a small boy opening a Christmas toy as he unfolded it and began to read. When he came to the part with Jim's advice about my finances, he frowned and looked genuinely concerned. "Mrs. Stockdale, you aren't having any financial troubles, are you?"

Despite my flippant urge to compare Jim's earnings to his, I told him everything was just fine, that the navy was sending me Jim's pay. Also, as I departed, I told him I planned to send a newsletter to the other wives in my circumstances, telling them about the reassurances he had given me. He agreed that was a fine idea.

The next day I was escorted to a separate complex of low buildings on a hill adjacent to Arlington National Cemetery. Here I was
to see Admiral Semmes, the head of the Bureau of Naval Personnel,
who had signed the original messages telling me Jim was "missing."
He seemed extremely impressed that I'd had a two-hour visit with
Ambassador Harriman. I wondered how he knew about this and
how long I had stayed. Admiral Semmes had a smooth and charming
manner, but I didn't feel I was making a social call.

"Admiral Semmes, I think you should write to the wives from
time to time after your initial letters about their husbands' circumstances. It's lonely enough without feeling completely cut off from
the navy and thinking everyone's forgotten you."

He replied with something like "If there is no news, what
would I say?"

"I think you should just say you're thinking about them and
haven't forgotten them. You know you're dealing with the female
psyche in this situation and I remind you that it's somewhat different from your own. For example, if on your wedding day you told
your wife you loved her and then considered that job done, you'd
be in for trouble. You have to tell her you love her over and over
again. It's the same with the wives of the men who are prisoners
and missing—you need to tell them they're being remembered and
their husbands are also."

"Well, I'll have to see about that," said he, looking over at his
assistant, who was also in the office with us and who wrote some
notes on his pad.

"Also, I want to send a newsletter to other wives in my circumstances, telling them about my visit with Ambassador Harriman. I
understand the navy won't give out a list of the names and addresses of these people, so I'd like to send my letter to you and ask your
office to address the envelopes for me. I'll put the stamps on and
everything. Do you think that will be all right?"

Although his reply was noncommittal, I didn't have a glimmer
of an idea that his office would take my letter and rework it, do
nothing further about it, and, five months later, send out their own
say-nothing bureaucratic letter, which satisfied no one and was not
what I had in mind at all.

I concluded, however, that I was making some progress about
doing something to help Jim—for when I returned home from my

Washington trip, I found this telegram waiting:

July 29, 1966
To Mrs. Sybil Stockdale Report Dlvy Care
· · SM Bailey Sunset Beach Branford, Conn.

      The Secretary of Defense has determined that the best inter-
est of the personnel missing in action in Vietnam will be served if
those personnel who we have reason to believe to be prisoners of
North Vietnam be so listed. Accordingly your husband, Cdr. James
Bond Stockdale, 485624/1310, USN is now listed as captured instead
of missing in action. This determination does not indicate that the
Navy Department has received any additional information over that
given you previously. Be assured that if any additional information is
received I will communicate it to you immediately. We regret the
continual refusal of North Vietnam to comply with the provisions of
the Geneva Convention and to furnish the names of the prisoners
being held.

          Vice Admiral B. J. Semmes, Jr.
          Chief of Naval Personnel, FM BuPers

At the end of the summer, before we left Connecticut to return
to Coronado for the school year, we said goodbye to Jimmy as he
left for Mercersburg Academy in Pennsylvania. We were careful to
keep our emotions under control; we wouldn't see him again until
Christmas because he'd spend Thanksgiving with my parents. Sid,
Stan, Taylor, and I made the flight back to California by ourselves.

Back in Coronado, after catching up on the summer news with
Doyen, she told me she and Budd were shocked that Jim had not
been promoted a year early to the rank of captain. That was the
usual procedure for outstanding naval officers and would have been
appropriate with Jim's record. I was pretty crushed about it, too,
but tried not to think about it; it seemed trivial compared to other
things. In the September 14 issue of *Navy Times*, I read an article
saying servicemen overseas in a combat zone could invest any
amount they could save from their pay in a 10-percent savings program with the U.S. government. I was excited at this prospect, but
when I called Washington, I was told Jim didn't qualify for the
program. I couldn't believe it. They double-checked. He didn't
qualify. When Congress passed Public Law 89-538, they neglected
to include the men in North Vietnam. It was an oversight. My spir-

its hit rock bottom. The whole United States Congress just completely forgot there were any Americans in North Vietnam. It made me feel sick.

My spirits lifted a little the following week when Commander Boroughs and two of his specialist cohorts came to Coronado to work out details of my October letter and picture for Jim. They had Budd Salsig stand in for Jim, and when he figured out my signal to soak the picture, they felt it was safe to send it. I was to mail the coded letter on October 9. I hoped there'd be a chance they'd give it to Jim; I hadn't heard from him since his last letter to me, written on May 2. One of the parts I liked best about the project was working out the way Jim would let me know if he got the covert message encased in the picture he was to soak. Commander Boroughs asked me to think of a way Jim could begin and end a letter that wouldn't alert his captors but would assure me he'd gotten the message. I said if he started a letter with "Darling" and ended it with "Your adoring husband," we could feel sure he had the code.

The days began to pass more quickly as October 9 came closer. When the day to mail the special letter arrived, I carefully folded the letter dated October 9, 1966, and placed the picture inside the one sheet of folded paper. It was a photo of a woman who closely resembled Jim's mother. The North Vietnamese wouldn't know it wasn't his mother, but Jim would know it right away. That was to be part of the signal to alert him that something was up. I could only do what I thought was truly in Jim's best interest, my inner voice whispered as I wrote his name on the envelope. And as I bicycled with Taylor toward the post office, I purposely turned my mind to other things.

A couple of days ago, I'd had my first meeting with other local wives whose husbands were missing or captured. There were thirteen of us altogether. Through the grapevine I'd heard of several other wives in San Diego who were in the same boat. I'd telephoned a couple of them, but they were so terrified they'd hardly talk on the phone. I could understand their fear; for all they knew, I was a reporter. But recently another POW wife, Patsy Crayton, had called me and said her husband had been shot down and that some of the other wives would like to get together. So I'd invited all those we knew about for lunch.

The lunch stretched into an all-afternoon affair. An avalanche

of words poured forth from all thirteen of us. Often, we were all
talking at once, pouring out what so-and-so had said about what
we'd been told by Captain or Commander somebody, or what the
commanding officer's wife had heard might be the case, and on and
on and on. Lorraine Shumaker was our "old-timer" in the group.
Her husband, Bob, had been shot down in February 1965 and she'd
had mail from him. At one point she mentioned someone whose
name I didn't recognize. He'd told her something she felt was as
reliable as anything she'd heard.

I said, "Who is he?"

And Lorraine replied, winking, "Oh, you know. He's my contact with those people in Washington we never talk about. You
know who I mean."

Now, pedaling along on my bike on the way to the post office, I
felt a sense of relief: Maybe I wasn't the only one taking risks. I
hadn't questioned Lorraine about it, but I'd listen carefully for anything of special interest she might say at our next gathering. We'd
decided to meet each month just as squadron wives always do.

At the post office, I inspected the letter in my hand one more
time and was horrified to see that in my turmoil I'd neglected to put
stamps on it. God Almighty, what a dumb thing to do! I hoped it
wasn't prophetic. I stamped it now, blew a kiss on it, dropped it
into the slot, and heard it thump onto the bottom of the box.

"It's on its way, Taylor. For better or for worse. There's no
taking it back now."

A little more than a month later, writing my monthly letter to
Jim, I included a paragraph mainly for his captors' information.
Commander Boroughs had asked me to include it so the North Vietnamese would be prepared for the arrival of some Christmas packages for our men. From my reading and Boroughs's instructions, I'd
become more knowledgeable about prisoner-of-war conventions
and procedures. It was all laid out in the Geneva Convention Relative to the Treatment of Prisoners of War, which North Vietnam as
well as the United States had signed. Among other things, it required that prisoners of war be allowed to receive a limited number
of packages of a specified weight during each year.

So far, however, the North Vietnamese were not abiding by the

Geneva Convention. They still hadn't even published a list of the men captured, nor allowed the required mail flow, nor allowed the International Committee of the Red Cross to inspect the camps where the men were being held. They claimed they had reserved the right not to abide by this Convention and, furthermore, that they were not in a declared war. The last part was true, but Article II of the Convention says that it applies in case of declared war or *armed conflict* if both parties have signed the Convention.

Why hadn't the U.S. government taken the North Vietnamese government to task in the press about their violations of the Convention? The cause must have had something to do with the secret negotiations Ambassador Harriman alluded to at the State Department. It seemed to me it would be better to have it all out in the open.

At any rate, if we were going to try to get packages in to our men, I felt they should contain the world's most nutritious dehydrated food. I contacted our old friend from test-pilot days, John Glenn, about arrangements to have astronaut food sent in our packages. John came through with flying colors, and the Pillsbury Company donated all the astronaut food we needed. As I packed Jim's box, I tried to imagine what the North Vietnamese would think of the tiny dehydrated roast-beef sandwiches sealed in see-through airtight packets. Then, carefully, I wrote the paragraph Commander Boroughs had suggested:

> Our government is very much in hopes that your captors will allow you to have a small package for Christmas. With this hope in mind, they will receive packages addressed to those of you who have been allowed to write in the past and from whom mail has been received. This includes only eight Navy people, and the packages delivered are intended for everyone whether or not mail has been received from them. The packages contain highly concentrated and nutritious foodstuffs similar to that used by our astronauts and were prepared and packaged by Pillsbury Mills of Minneapolis, who developed them under Navy contract. They have donated the contents as a public relations gesture and the packages contain the equivalent of eighty meals altogether.

No more mail came from Jim, week after week, as the calendar slowly gave up on 1966. Among the numbing days and nights of worry and fear, however, were some tender moments as well. On the morning of my birthday, November 25, Stanford and Taylor awakened me singing "Happy Birthday" and, beaming from ear to ear, presented me with breakfast in bed. I laughed and hugged them as I smacked my lips over my dry cereal, dry toast, and glass of Hi-C! Sid came in with their gifts, lovingly wrapped in wads of Scotch Tape and mismatched, wrinkled paper and ribbon. I ooohhed and aahhhed over my package of peanuts from Taylor, an Almond Joy candy bar from Stanford, and a gallon of root beer from Sid! Not a mouthful was left by the time we left the bedroom.

A month later, on the night before Christmas, all four boys were in and around my bed, where I was propped up against pillows. I hoped my seeming ready for sleep might convince Stanford and Taylor to go to sleep earlier. That year, for the first time, Sid would help with the presents. But no one helped with the stockings. I always did those by myself.

Jimmy said earnestly, "Okay, now this is the way we'll do it in the morning. I'll go down first and see if Santa's been here. Then I'll bring the stockings upstairs and we'll see what's in them up here before we go down to the tree. That way, mom will have a few minutes extra to sleep."

How proud Jim would have been of his sons. How I prayed 1967 would bring him home.

Chapter 7

Learning the Ropes

Navy survival school was a "better than nothing" preparation for the North Vietnam prison experience. But it generated one big false impression that led to unrealistic expectations there. That was that it all happened in the first month or two, and that "if you hang tough through them, the jailers will put you aside as a waste of their time and leave you alone." Well, that might be the way an efficient American would run a propaganda farm, but that wasn't the way things worked in North Vietnam. They were neither that efficient nor that impatient. The profile of the typical prison experience in North Vietnam did not have shock and anxiety peaking out at first, and then petering off. Quite the opposite in the case of us early captives (and I was just #26); the problem was slow in generating. I started out as a stretcher case, and isolation and total neglect typified my predicament for the first months; during that time the prison administration ("The Camp Authority") was still gearing up for the long pull. The whole cast of characters—prison officials, interrogators, guards—was being changed from ordinary army men (Dog, Eagle, Dipshit) to experienced extortionists (Cat, Rabbit, Pigeye). The opening kickoff hardly set the pattern for my football game; it was a continuing struggle of parrying tactical changes throughout all four quarters—and each quarter was more than one year long.

The aeronautical map lay on the table untouched until just after the noon hour on October 25, 1965, when the guard came in and took it away. I had just refused the Vietnamese's first demand.

After a month of delirium on that library table in room 24 of Hoa Lo Prison, I had been barricaded in this back room of Don

Thuy Military Hospital in Hanoi. They had brought me here to make me what they called a "functional criminal," to "get my leg under me" so I could conform to some sort of prison routine. It had been ten days since I had been covered over with sheets and rolled in the night to the operating room for the first of what was to be a series of three operations. To test my "gratitude" before proceeding, Eagle had been sent over by someone he called the "general staff officer" to try to get me to provide some "military" information. He had brought an aeronautical map on which I was to draw the navy in-flight refueling areas. The map had come from an airforce airplane on which such areas were printed.

The navy didn't have any special fueling areas; they just did it wherever it was convenient, usually over water. That stood to reason; I think Eagle knew that, and I told him so. But he said he had to have a "secret" mark on the map to show my "Good attitude." The only thing I could figure was that they had copies of our Code of Conduct and would have tried to use it as a blackmail wedge if I had drawn some fake ones in to get more medical treatment. It was sure enough easy to tell that these political officers wouldn't know a 500-pound general-purpose bomb from a kid's water bomb if they saw them side by side, but they were experts on blackmail bombs. They didn't know beans about using technology, but they knew how to use shame.

Late that afternoon, Eagle's sidekick, Owl, entered, shut the door, and solemnly announced, "I bring word from the general staff officer. You have made a very grave error; things will not go well for you." And then he left. About ten o'clock that night, I was awakened by the arrival of a young functionary officer I called "Mickey Mouse" and a jeep driver. I was blindfolded, carried out on a stretcher, and then placed in the jeep's front seat, my first time upright in over six weeks. After six or seven blocks and some hard turns late in the ride, there was a stop, a clanging, bright lights of what I assumed to be Hoa Lo Prison's dry moat penetrating my blindfold, then muffled reverberations of a quick trip through the inner tunnel and a stop at the far end of the prison courtyard.

The blindfold came off and Dipshit loomed out of the darkness bearing a huge pair of old, worn crutches. He signaled silence with finger across lips, and I was pointed toward a green door on the right wall of yet another tunnel, through a building I had never seen before. The crutches were for a man half a foot taller than I, and I vaulted along, my left leg held clear of the pavement, fearful of falling and without any hints as to the amount of weight I should put on a stiff but somewhat straightened leg from which the stitches had been removed only the day before.

The few vaults in the cool night air had been as exhilarating as the scene inside the green door was depressing. The floor of the short hallway I faced was littered with debris, including a goodly batch of blood-and-pus-soaked bandages. The ceiling of this building was very high, the walls a dirty white, and four bolted cell doors were on either side. All were padlocked except the first door on the left. A barred window above each cell door had been boarded up. The jeep driver ran ahead and opened the next-to-the-last door on the right. Inside were two crumbling cement-slab bunks, one on either side of a very narrow aisle, leg stocks at the foot of each slab, by the door. These stocks were attached to lock-actuating handles controlled from the hallway. A "rathole" open to an outside gutter was between the bed heads, opposite the cell door; a mosquito net was rigged over the bunk to my left.

Mickey Mouse threw two pairs of thin khaki prison pajamas, a bar of soap, a washrag, a pair of automobile-tire sandals, and a drinking cup on the cement slab to his right and said in a tough, low voice, "Keep silent." The cell door was slammed and bolted, and two pairs of footsteps retreated out the green door.

Pasted on my door was a fresh sign: "The Camp Regulations— October 20th, 1965." In pidgin English, they went like this:

> —The criminals are under an obligation to give full and clear written or oral answers to all questions raised by the camp authorities. All attempts and tricks intended to evade answering further questions and acts directed to opposition by refusing to answer any questions will be considered manifestations of obstinacy and antagonism which deserve strict punishment.

> —The criminals must demonstrate a cautious and polite attitude toward the officers and guards in the camp and must render greeting when met by them by bowing all the way down at the waist. When the Vietnamese officers and guards come to the rooms for inspection or when they are required by the camp officer to come to the room, the criminals must carefully and neatly put on their clothes, stand at attention, bow a greeting and await further orders.

—The criminal must maintain silence in the detention rooms and not make any loud noises which can be heard outside. All schemes and attempts to gain information and achieve communication with the criminals living next door by intentionally talking loudly, tapping on walls or by other means et cetera will be strictly punished.

—Any obstinacy or opposition, violation of the preceding provisions, or any scheme or attempt to get out of the detention camp without permission are all punishable. On the other hand any criminal who strictly obeys the camp regulations and shows his true submission and repentance by his practical acts will be allowed to enjoy the humane treatment he deserves.

—Anyone so imbued with a sense of preventing violations and who reveals the identity of those who attempt to act in violation of the foregoing provisions will be properly rewarded. However, if any criminal is aware of any violation and deliberately tries to cover it up, both he and the perpetrator will be strictly punished when this is discovered.

I pulled up the net, sat down on the slab under it, laid the crutches across the several pieces of my prison gear Mickey Mouse had brought, contemplated the dismalness of it all, and thanked God to be with Americans. For the first time since leaving the *Oriskany*'s flight-briefing room forty-seven days before, I was within whispering distance of Americans. Just think, if I should have a heart attack now, I could call out my name and chances were good that sooner or later Syb would know more or less when and where I died. In the hospital, I had spent lots of time thinking about dying a secret death and rotting in an unmarked grave in a foreign land. As experiences went in this prison system, being able to get a death-bed exclamation to an American's ear was security!

I looked down at those leg stocks at the foot of the cement-slab beds, then up above them at the feeding chutes within reach of a man in stocks in a sitting position, then back over my shoulder at the "rathole" with the small, open excrement bucket beside it. This cellblock was built for efficiency; a man could be locked in stocks for months and the only jail labor required was for an attendant to open the food chute once or twice a day and hand in a bowl of rice to a hungry prisoner who would sit up and take it. It was up to him to get his crap out the rathole.

The illuminated bare light bulb hung from the ceiling high

above this dirty little bunk space at the bottom of what was actually a tall, rectangular shaft with ventilating holes twelve feet above me. Those nineteenth-century Frenchmen knew how to build a self-ventilating, no-nonsense prison. A minute after first lying back on the straw matting (tightly woven, the thickness of cloth), I sprang up and took off the old blue shorts and work shirt that had been given me in the town where I'd been shot down, put on one pair of prison pajamas Mickey Mouse had brought, and draped the other over the top of the mosquito net to keep the bare-bulb light out of my eyes.

I lay awake that night of October 25, 1965, for a couple of hours, heart pounding in excitement. I had not received one word of advice about when I could put weight on this leg. There was a big scar down the center of the knee where they had just taken the stitches out. The leg was toed-in, ugly, and crooked, but under me; there was no joint action at all. The tendons behind what had been the knee were all changing shape. I was amused to discover that if I lay back and extended the stiff leg directly over my head, I could count my own heartbeats by watching a misplaced pulsating vein on the top of my left foot.

The first indication I had of American activity was the sound of someone urinating into a bucket somewhere along this little hallway. I felt so good to be a part of a group for a change. How long would I be here? How long would it be before I got to a real prison camp, with the barbed-wire enclosure, cellmates, and maybe a little campfire at night where we could sit and talk about home? Probably I'd have to wait till I could get around well on crutches. There was a chance I would never walk without them; my part of the work in camp would probably be just keeping records on a clipboard.

I was awakened by the rhythmic clang of a prison gong, the ever-increasing frequency of a beat of a hand-held metal pipe against a railroad iron dangling from a tree, topped off by the ruffle-pattern "signature" of the beater. Next came the martial music on the street loudspeakers on the other side of the prison walls. And finally I heard the rhythmic clapping of the prison staff's group calisthenic exercises in the courtyard. It was still dark, but the prison day was now in session.

Bang! The key was in the lock holding my door bolt home. Dipshit flung the door open and yelled in Vietnamese, pointing to my mosquito net (I gathered I should have had it down and folded). He then impatiently pointed to the little toilet bucket and to my bar of soap and washrag, waving me out into the hall. He was in a hurry as I worked to get all of this in hand, including the bucket full of some predecessor's week-old excrement, and myself onto those giant-sized crutches. Dipshit strode toward the green door and threw open the last cell door on the right, number 8, indicating that that was my destination. As I struggled along, Dipshit's head turned and I glanced to the left and upward and saw a grinning American face looking down at me through a crack from a vantage point he had acquired at least three feet above his door.

Elated by that quick shot in the arm of seeing an American face, it took me a second to realize that Dipshit had led me into a replica of the cell I had just left, except that there was a water spigot over the rathole on the wall opposite the door. The obvious idea was for me to dump my bucket and wash my face and hands. When Dipshit slammed the door behind me, my crutches skidded and I panicked as I nearly fell. (My lower left leg still swung sideways at what had been the knee, and a fall on it at that time might well have brought about its amputation.) I then realized that I had slipped on and was standing on stale piss all over the deck. God, it stunk. Who would do that?

In this stinking mess I stripped down and, for the first time since I had been shot down, looked down at my now very thin, dirty, and deformed body. "Syb, you would hardly know me now; I didn't look at all like this in the Fujiya hotel's Dream Pool where we took our daily nude baths together just three months ago. Who would have thought all this could happen?"

I should have doused myself all over, but I wasn't up to it. I was shivering. The faucet just dribbled and the water was cold. It was clammy in this cellblock. It was like living in the bottom of a dark cement silo, perhaps cool enough in summer, but cold even in these tropics after the fall air arrived.

As soon as the other five solitary occupants had each in turn been taken into cell 8 for their dumping and washing, Dipshit slammed the green door at the end of the hall and left. The "Camp Authority" was not Dipshit's cup of tea. He had joined the system as cook/medic/police chief of a floating population of a very few Americans. The population of prisoners was increasing steadily now, things were getting organized, and he was losing his freedom as a roving monitor who could ignore or pester Americans as he chose. He was now supposed to sneak around and make sure we didn't talk, but that was too dull a chore for him. We didn't know how lucky we were.

So for the next few days, this place, which I was soon to be told by my blockmates was known as "Heartbreak Hotel," was the scene of comparatively casual visiting. I immediately heard whispering from the guy I had seen high above the end of the hall, and fell to the floor and spoke under my door. His name was Dave Wheat; he was off the carrier *Independence* and had been shot down the week before. Not to worry about the piss on the floor of cell 8—that was part of prison life in North Vietnam. This prison was full of Vietnamese men and women civilian inmates, and their men and women civilian guards would come into our hall and piss on that floor while on their rounds every night rather than go to more distant latrines. Dave could watch them.

Nimble Dave Wheat, from his high observation perch, not only had a way of secretly seeing inside hall activities but could also see Dipshit for a couple of strides before the latter hit the green door. Wheat's "all clear" and "danger" signals were neither complicated nor subtle. For the former, he would softly whistle a line of "Mary Had a Little Lamb," and for the latter "Pop! Goes the Weasel." If a person was caught talking, Dipshit would just open his door and rant in Vietnamese. The communication "trip-wire" system, with its swift sequence of apprehension, arrest, torture, confession, apology, and atonement, had yet to blossom.

But it was not far away. In fact, it was during these very days that the driving power behind that trip-wire system, systematic torture, was being tested and perfected by a specialist in the field. His practice victim was a young shipmate of Dave Wheat's, shot down on the same day he had been. We heard all about it the next day, October 27, when he was brought in and put in the only vacant Heartbreak cell, number 6, across from me in number 3. He was Lieutenant (jg) Rodney Knutson.

Knutson had arrived at Hoa Lo Prison on the morning of October 18. He was put first in room 18, a large interrogation room on the front side of the prison, just off the main, "Heartbreak," court-yard. There this brave and confident young officer was tested under the new regulations that had recently been glued to my door: ". . . refusing to answer any questions will be considered manifestations of obstinacy and antagonism which deserve strict punishment." He refused to answer questions beyond name, rank, serial number, and date of birth, the only questions that international law held he was obliged to answer. He was then threatened with death.

Once left alone, Knutson yelled down to another cellblock and told some other Americans what was happening to him. A guard heard this exchange, and Knutson was moved to still another cell-block, around the corner, in a place Americans came to know as New Guy Village. There he was put in cell 2, well out of earshot of Heartbreak Hotel, and it was here that over a nine-day period he was beaten (his face cut and bruised, eyes swollen shut, three teeth broken), tightly bound, whipped, and kept in leg stocks, all to no avail—he would not answer the improper questions. Finally, on Sunday, October 24, his interrogator informed Knutson he had received permission from "high authority" to do what was necessary to get him to talk. When Knutson again refused, this interrogator, a rather tall Vietnamese officer with pronounced protruding ears, brought in a small, muscular man whose distinctive features were a receding hairline and expressionless eyes.

Methodically this man slapped Knutson about the head and shoulders, knocked him down, and laced manila hemp rope around his upper arms, shutting off his blood circulation and bending him double, producing excruciating pain and claustrophobia until Knutson was forced to submit. There was no option of death for Knutson; this new torture expert knew how to apply pressure while positioning his victim in a way that took that alternative out of the equation.

The questioning of Knutson that followed was not provocative and Knutson's answers were innocuous, but that wasn't the point. By carrying out a new policy action, North Vietnam had crossed a boundary. Henceforth, Americans were to be allowed to stay within the bounds of name, rank, serial number, and date of birth only at North Vietnam's sufferance. The "rope trick" had been incorporated into their system and would be selectively used as they chose.

Knutson's interrogator became known as Rabbit; the torture expert as Pigeye; the "high authority" who authorized this first "torture" in the classical sense, the "general staff officer," the Cat.

Pigeye was the first of the three I got to know. He replaced Dipshit as our turnkey. Ours was not a confrontational association, it was just that Knutson had identified him, and I studied him as he opened my cell door and awaited my bow and the picking up of the bowl of pumpkin soup I ate twice a day, and as he took me back and forth to the cell 8 bucket dump and faucet each morning. He was older than the other guards—perhaps thirty-five or forty. His manner was that of a master gymnast—perhaps an athletic trainer, at the very least a professional masseur. He was trim and moved with a catlike glide, never betraying what was going on behind his cool countenance. In a word, he was a study in aloofness, a very impersonal technician.

The jug-eared officer called Rabbit was hard to mistake. I met him at the first interrogation to which I was called during my Heartbreak Hotel stay. It was a cold night in early December when Pigeye came to my door and gave me the "sleeves" signal (cutting action of hand across other wrist). I took that to mean roll sleeves down and prepare to go meet an officer, and was apparently correct. I exited the green door for the first time, and followed him out of the tunnel and across to room 24 in the rain. It was slick; I nearly fell on my crutches getting up the steps. I went into that room in which I had spent a month flat on my back. My library table was gone. The jug-eared officer was sitting behind a small table draped with a blue cloth; a lamp on the table was the only light. A silent man about my age sat back in the shadows. I bowed as instructed, and Rabbit told me in good English to have a seat on the low stool before him.

This quiz, or interrogation, started out as what I would call an "attitude check." How was I? Was my clothing adequate? Was the food adequate? And so on. I had a lot pent up inside me and welcomed a confrontation; I was getting damned tired of sitting there in Heartbreak watching all these other new shootdowns spend about ten days there and then have the heavenly experience of being taken out and put in a jeep and taken to a real prison camp of the sort I dreamed about. I brought up the question of the Geneva

Convention of 1949 concerning treatment of prisoners of war. I complained about solitude, filth, and the unfinished medical work on my leg.

My truculent attitude got the silent older man out of his chair; he took Rabbit's place at the table and let Rabbit interpret the short speech he gave in Vietnamese: "You have no right to protest; you are a criminal and not entitled to Geneva Convention privileges. It is true that my country acceded to the Geneva Convention of 1949, but we later filed an exception against those captured in wars of aggression. You are nothing but a common criminal, guilty of bombing schools, churches, and pagodas, crimes against humanity. You have medical problems and you have political problems, and in this country we take care of medical problems only after political problems are resolved."

He stomped out into the rain, after getting from Rabbit what I presumed were keys to the jeep. Rabbit then dismissed me after telling me that I had just made a grave error, that I had offended an officer of great influence, an officer who sits on the general staff, an officer who had handled the French prisoners after the glorious victory of the people of the Democratic Republic of Vietnam at Dien Bien Phu in 1954.

I had just met the Cat.

Back in cell 3 of Heartbreak, I continued to watch the one-way flow of new shootdowns come and go on to that wonderful place out there somewhere—a place like the prison compound I lived in during both my trips through survival school. The fact that I was being treated differently was really starting to worry me. When was the Tonkin Gulf shoe to fall? How in God's name was I going to handle it?

In mid-December I started getting some valuable lessons on the reality of the Hanoi situation. They were delivered by the first exception to the one-way flow of prisoners—a man who had been to that outlying camp and was sent back. Only there was no camp-fire; he hadn't had a cellmate. Robinson Risner, an air-force lieutenant colonel shot down nine days after I was (and my successor as the senior American in Hanoi), was suddenly put in the cell next door to me, Heartbreak number 2, that cold December night. Risner, uninjured at shootdown, had gone through the standard ten days at Heartbreak while I had been over in room 24 on the table. A very popular and natural leader, "Robbie," as he whispered his own introduction, had then been taken out to a place he called "the Zoo," two or three miles south of Hoa Lo, on the outer fringe of Hanoi. There, in fulfilling his role of leader, he organized a program of drilling whispering holes through the walls between cells and started issuing standardized resistance instructions.

During the last week in October, about ten days after Knutson was hauled in by the new "Camp Authority," Robbie had been caught in these activities and arrested. On the night of October 31, he had been brought back to Hoa Lo Prison and stuck in one of the four cells in New Guy Village, where Knutson had been tortured. There they socked him into leg irons and put him on short rations for about a month and then closed in for the "kill." He was blindfolded and walked into trees and ditches until he got banged up and disoriented, and then they gave him Pigeye's latest version of the rope trick. Robbie was a strong man, yet he told me they overcame him. His story gave me some very serious things to think about.

Robbie was a gold mine of information about how Americans were doing in prison. He had memorized the names of all the prisoners at the Zoo, several of them old friends of mine: my Naval Academy classmate Jerry Denton; my fellow instructor at Test Pilot School Bill Franke; and my Spad pilot aboard the *Oriskany*, Ed Davis—the same Ed Davis I had declared "killed in action" in August! He had miraculously climbed out of the Spad in the vertical dive that night, pulled his rip cord, and almost immediately found himself standing upright on the ground. His being in here and listed KIA with only weeks of married life behind him seemed tragic to me. Wouldn't the poor girl think of remarriage in a year or so?

On those cold December nights, Robbie gave me lessons in how to tap messages through the wall. What had started in August as the "Smitty Harris tap code" (named after the prisoner who had come across it by accident during a coffee-break conversation at survival school years before) had taken on a standardized form of American Hanoi prisoner usage. Robbie instructed me to call him up with the "shave and a haircut" beat: tick tick ta tick tick. He would let me know he was ready to receive my first word by answering tick tick. Then I would spell it out using the five-by-five matrix I had memorized: tick tick tick tick tick (pause) tick tick (w) tick tick (pause) tick tick tick (H) tick (pause) tick tick tick tick tick

(E) tick tick tick (pause) tick tick tick (N)—WHEN—and Robbie, understanding it, would acknowledge with a tick tick. Then my second word: tick (pause) tick tick tick tick (D) tick tick tick (pause) tick tick tick tick (O)—DO——YOU———THINK———WE——WILL—— GO——HOME? After he tick-ticked acknowledgment of the HOME, I ended my message with another "shave and a haircut," and he would tick-tick and then give me a "shave and a haircut" and start his answer—which in those days most felt compelled to answer in phrases like THIS SPRING.

Many refinements to this code had been worked out already at the Zoo. Robbie gave me a number of abbreviations that had become standard. For instance, on the very first day of his instruction, I learned not to laboriously spell out WHEN DO YOU THINK WE WILL GO HOME?, but to use WN DO U TK WE GO HOME? Robbie taught me to "buy" a word with an early tick tick as soon as I had heard enough of it to guess what it was. If I guessed wrong—i.e., if my word didn't make sense in the context of what followed—I would just have to give a series of ticks (the error signal) until I backed the sender up to where I could get it retransmitted. With constant practice and refinement, my tap communication became more accurate and almost as fast as talking.

The Smitty Harris Tap Code

	1	2	3	4	5
1	A	B	C	D	E
2	F	G	H	I	J
3	L	M	N	O	P
4	Q	R	S	T	U
5	V	W	X	Y	Z

Eliminate K, (use C instead)

First digit: row
Second digit: line

Examples

S: 4 – 3
T: 4 – 4
O: 3 – 4
C: 1 – 3
K: 1 – 3

✧

On Christmas Day of 1965, in the afternoon, I heard Pigeye come and take Robbie out through the green door. In maybe half an hour, Robbie was put back in his cell and I was taken out. Pigeye took me across to a little-used carpeted "céremonial" room next to 24. I nearly dropped my crutches as I bowed, shocked to see the Cat sitting there in what looked like a brand-new Sears Roebuck suit. Rabbit was at his side as interpreter, and I was again bade to sit down on the stool in front of the table. Pigeye took his place at the table with the other two. Cat made a big thing of Vietnamese democracy, where Pigeye—"an enlisted man," as he called him— sat at the table with officers. Christmas tea was served.

Although our first meeting had been stormy, Cat was clearly not trying to make trouble on Christmas Day. In fact, he was acting his holiday part with disgusting greasiness. He had even arranged to have a male turkey "gobbling" outside as a guard pestered it in the prison's free-fire-zone dry moat right under the window. With an ingratiating simper, he invited my attention to its gobbles, which he thought surely would make me feel right at home.

But just about then his holiday role called for him to get serious. "Staw-dale," he enunciated, in a rare use of a personal name, "you and I are the same age, we are both lifelong military officers, we both have sons the same age. But we are from different social systems. There is a wall between us which will always be there." In saying that, he gestured as to how the wall was situated up and down right in front of our faces. "The wall is there and will remain there, but you and I must try to see through it. We must join together and bring this imperialist war to an end. Together we can do much to bring that about. You must help me make the other criminals realize that it is in their interest as well as ours to stop the war. You will help me. You do not realize it now, but you will. . . ."

I was breaking into a cold sweat. This was his master game plan. I was being solicited to entice my junior officers to betray their oath of office, their Code of Conduct, their country. It was my guess he had probably told Robbie the same thing. He had us pegged—we were the leaders of the only prisoners he had, air force and naval service (navy and marine) flight crews. He knew the

Code of Conduct and that we were responsible, and our juniors responsible to obey us.

I was so flustered that I wasn't sure I was picking up all he had to say. There was a semijovial remark about "your government" saying it would cease bombings. "But we know all about the invidious nature of your government's so-called bombing interruptions. As you know better than I, we've been subject to their 'on again, off again' bombing ever since that black day of August fifth, over a year ago."

Was he saying he knew all about the August 5, 1964, bombing? Was he hinting that he was going to take me over there where he had Knutson and Robbie taken and get the Tonkin Gulf story out of me? I was so goosey about that, yet dimly realized that I had to keep a placid face in spite of my anxiety or the world would come tumbling down on top of me. What's this? He's handing me an envelope! It's Syb's writing, forwarded from the International Red Cross in Geneva, Switzerland!

"Now go back to your room and think about what I've told you, Staw-dale. You are very old and you are not well. You must think of yourself. You must think of your family who wrote you that letter. You must help me end this war."

Back in the cold cell on that dark Christmas Day, I let my crutches crash to the floor as I sat down to read what Syb had written in longhand months before.

October 3rd, 1965

Dearest Jim,

It is early early morning here and the world is waiting for the sun to rise. The world seems very special in these moments before dawn. It seems to be pausing and waiting to hear the birds begin to sing.

We have been having a Santa Ana here this week much like the one we had at about this same time two years ago. ["That was that great day I took command of Fighter Squadron Fifty-one at the ceremony at Naval Air Station Miramar; she's trying to raise my spirits."] It made it difficult for our team to play their best football Friday night. Doyen, Budd, Sid, Ben and I went out to Poway to see the game. J.B. ["That's what Jimmy likes to be called now"] played particularly well but in spite of this our team lost by a few points. He and Mike looked very grown up when they came into the stands after the game.

Yesterday afternoon Stan, Taylor, Sid and I went to the beach. We made a lovely sand castle right at the edge of the water. A big wave knocked it down and washed it away but we didn't let ourselves be discouraged and worked hard to build it up again. ["That's symbolism of hope, plain enough."]

I don't know whether or not I told you in my last letter ["I'll bet she's writing me via the Red Cross every week just like when I'm on cruise"] that Peg and Bob Selmer visited here recently ["Special trip from the East Coast; our best friends during test-pilot days at Patuxent"].

I talked with Mabel again this week and Hazel is still with her. They both may come here for a visit this winter and I am looking for a suitable room where they can stay.

The sun has come up now and I can hear the birds beginning to sing. We are all fine here Jim and send you

All our love,
Syb

That letter, one picked at random from dozens Syb had probably written, told me all I needed to know: that everybody was well, that they were hopeful for the future, and that they loved me. It was a real shot in the arm. The velvet-glove treatment continued the next day, December 26, when Rabbit came to the door with paper and pen and a sheet of instructions about how Syb was to properly address mail to me (no more International Red Cross stuff). I was told I could write a short letter to her, to copy the instructions from the "Democratic Republic of Vietnam" about addressing mail and enclose it. Then he gave me a sheet of paper delineating how my return address was to read.

My mind was thousands of miles from that prison as I wrote to my darling family, paper on the cement bunk across from where I sat, crutches beside me. I had thought about how to get Ed Davis's name out as a live prisoner, and buried that and others in double-talk in the text. Rabbit came and got my envelope and letter an hour later.

Five days later, December 31, the iron fist struck. I had anticipated it; there was a menacing aspect to the way Pigeye had been

shadowing me the last couple of days. In a prison, one gets to know when one is being stalked. Besides, I just had too much information on what was going on to believe that I could walk the middle road without a showdown, crippled or not. In midafternoon on that last day of 1965, the Vietnamese made a big production of a pinch they could have pulled off most any day of recent weeks. More than once I had been detected lying on my cell floor retrieving with a crutch slid under my door a cigarette some nonsmoker had tossed down. (Pigeye would peek in the green door, see the crutch, and rush in and bang on my door.) But they saved this "trip-wire" theatrical production till they got word from Cat that now was the time to close in. Nonsmoking Robbie tossed down the cigarette, my crutch went out, and—bang!—Pigeye was in the green door yelling, others right behind him, and I was had.

I was taken before Rabbit and Mickey Mouse. I was proclaimed guilty not only of violating the camp regulation prohibiting communication (prima facie evidence of making a prior arrangement for the cigarette with Risner), but of moral turpitude—to wit, "ingratitude for the undeserved humane and lenient treatment Ho Chi Minh was providing you." The "general staff officer [Cat] will be very disappointed to hear that you have let him down and stooped to such a crime." I would see; I would be made to repent and to atone for my crimes against the Vietnamese People.

About the time the prison gong signaled evening tattoo, the green door banged open and I knew it was time to say goodbye to Robbie and take my lumps. I was moved out, lock, stock, and barrel—net, bucket, blankets, and all. I rolled all my earthly possessions up in a blanket as Mickey Mouse directed and they were taken by a little scruffy guard we had not bothered to name. I was not blindfolded, but moved cautiously around Heartbreak courtyard on the normal-size crutches they had traded for my high ones on Christmas Day. I was led into a doorway that was new to me and motioned to climb a circular staircase. On the second floor I transited a hallway, and then came down another circular staircase and into a dark hall that had four cell doors on the left and a blank wall on the right. This had to be the New Guy Village cellblock Knutson and Risner had described. The third door was opened and I looked into a somewhat narrow but much longer cell than I had left. The concrete bunks were broader and much higher than those in Heartbreak Hotel, but offset, head to toe rather than side by side.

"Get up on the bunk!" shouted Mickey Mouse, pointing to the one in the back of the cell, below the high window, a broad window not boarded up but one that I noted was much too high for me to reach with my current climbing ability. The cell was particularly eerie because of the etchings on the dirty walls—large, crude pictures of hunchback, African-type antelope with long skinny horns, mixed in with big ostriches. Remembering that there had been Dien Bien Phu–vintage newspapers on the hospital windows, I somehow jumped to the conclusion that these drawings must have been the handiwork of prisoners taken at Dien Bien Phu in 1954. African Foreign Legionnaires? Was Cat working with them right here in these cells?

After talking to Risner I pretty well knew what to expect in this cell. I hobbled on my crutches over to the bunk and the guard took them away as I managed to swing myself up on it; the big locking bar of the leg irons was raised, and I was relieved to find that even though my left foreleg was permanently toed in about 20 degrees, the left leghole was big enough to accommodate my half-broadside anklebone without a permanent pinch. The bar was lowered and padlocked and my arms bound behind me while Mickey Mouse ranted on and on about my bad attitude and failure to repent for the crimes I had visited on the "people of the Democratic Republic of Vietnam." I was amazed at how seriously he seemed to take this dressing down. He didn't appear to feel the least bit sheepish about what I'm sure he could see was a patently fraudulent frame-up. So help me, I marveled in amazement at the effectiveness of the little device of always basing the infliction of punishment on the technical legalism of having violated one of their written documents. Professor Bob North at Stanford had told me how legalistic most Communists are, but I was not prepared to see how such a simple contrivance just seemed to lock up the case for the eager Mickey Mouse.

There was no blanket that night. Scruffy and Mickey Mouse took the crutches, marched out, and locked the cell door. I spent the night slumped over in irons, arms bound behind. I mainly remember how cold and shivery I got. I could change position by resting for short periods on my right elbow, but never on my left; there was just no way I could stretch my body to the left against the pressure and pain of that asymmetric built-in twist of my leg. I picked up the two sets of Hanoi church bells at 11:00 P.M. I was waiting for them at midnight on this New Year's Eve, and as they rang I said, "Happy New Year, 1966," and thought of Syb and our boys on a winter's morning in Coronado. I decided that little Stan (age six) and Taylor (three) were playing with Christmas toys at home, and that Jimmy (now fifteen) and Sid (eleven) were down at the park playing touch football.

Having talked to Risner, I programmed myself for thirty days of softening up in those irons. At the end of the day on January 1 the ropes were removed from my wrists in back and tied in front so I could lie back the second night. A blanket was thrown over me and I gratefully worked it up around me. For three days my arms were bound in back by day and in front by night, but then the ropes were left off. My rations were cut short, but food was such a low-priority item with all the anxiety I had within me that I made a deal with myself not to bitch about it. Every morning I was let out for about ten minutes to use my bucket. I took care not to drink much water and was really glad not to eat much because this way I nearly stopped needing the bucket; I couldn't reach it from my high perch in irons, even with arms free, and any unscheduled toilet actions had to go right under the blanket with me. But one aspect that did give me a little trouble was the fact that there were no Americans within earshot. I pounded on the walls and talked loudly at safe times after about the fourth day, but all I got were some Vietnamese giggles immediately next door to my left. I had been spoiled in Heartbreak.

I was totally surprised when, on about the twelfth afternoon, Pigeye brought in the crutches and unlocked and lifted the big three-foot-long shackle bar. I was going to quiz. I followed him through new territory—out the door to the left about three steps past cell 4. (Cell 4 was where the Vietnamese prisoners were; I could hear at least two of them chatting happily as I went past.) Then we turned right and came into a small courtyard (New Guy Village Courtyard, I was sure, remembering how Robbie had described it), with what looked like a horsetank directly ahead, a separate building on the bias down by the wall to the left (which had to be the toilet), and a passageway now coming up on my right as I passed what looked like a locked cell. Pigeye motioned me to the right and down the passageway toward the big courtyard, but just before we entered it, it was a hard right turn into a big room.

I had caught a glimpse of the number by the twin green doors—it was room 18. A little woozy from being upright, I was left alone. Pigeye stepped outside, closing the doors and padlocking their knobs together from the outside with some strange iron contraption. (In later months I was to become intimately familiar with these "contraptions"—they were what we grew to call "traveling irons," leg irons that permitted their wearers to waddle about to perform such chores as toilet-bucket use.) Room 18 was rather large, maybe twenty-five feet deep and thirty feet across. In it were a big table and a little table, a blue cloth over each. The floor and walls were rough and dirty. The distinctive feature was up over my head, hanging from the high ceiling—a giant hook, like a big meat hook. In the corner was a slop bucket, no lid, half full of excrement. I was trying to find a peephole in the white-painted glass panels in the top half of the twin green doors when I heard Pigeye manhandling the improvised traveling-iron locking device and sprang back.

Rabbit, scowling, marched in purposefully and sat at the little table. I bowed nervously in accordance with camp regulations, and, following Pigeye's nod toward the little stool in front of the table, hobbled over to it on my crutches.

This was it; I was ready for the worst, and Rabbit got right to the point: "It has been decided that you must write to your government and explain to them the true story of the Vietnamese people's willingness to fight for four, eight, twelve years to defeat you imperialist aggressors. You must explain the determination of the Vietnamese people and that the U.S. people will in time understand the plight of the Vietnamese people and that the war is illegal and immoral. You must recommend to your government that this illegal and immoral war must be stopped."

I went into my song and dance about the Geneva Convention of 1949 and the improper nature of Rabbit's demands. He wasn't even irritated, just waved it off as so much hogwash and pushed a paper out in front of me. It was handwritten, I felt sure by him, a communication to, so help me, the "U.S. Foreign Secretary of State." "This is what you must write," said Rabbit. "You are an old

man; you must think of yourself. Go back to your cell and work on
it."

As I swung on my crutches along the walks and passageways,
retracing my steps, Pigeye at my heels with paper, pen, ink, and
Rabbit's "document," my mind was racing. I clomped along thinking to myself, It's a no-win situation, but think of where you would
be if Rabbit's paper had said what you were really scared to death it
would say: "I have come to know the Vietnamese people and now
find it in my heart necessary to expose the fraud of the United
States government's trumped-up charges in the Tonkin Gulf a year
ago last August. L. B. Johnson hoodwinked the United States people and Congress into passing a joint resolution giving him war-
making powers in Southeast Asia on the basis of an event that never
took place. I know this to be true; I was an eyewitness." Now *that*
would be something else!

When we came down the passageway toward my New Guy
Village cell, its door was open. A guard had left a full bowl of pumpkin soup and half a loaf of French bread on the unused bunk. There
was to be no getting up into the irons! Pigeye put the writing material beside the food on the bed slab and left, slamming and locking
the cell door. I skimmed the words Rabbit had written for me and
my heart sank. It was sheer degradation; how could I think of
playing that game? The bottom had just dropped out of my life.

I scarfed down the soup and munched the bread, taking no
time to enjoy either. I was busy thrusting back a tempting urge to
delay commitment to the ropes, to "play it smart," to "use my
cleverness." I knew that a straight copy of the whole of Rabbit's
text—a demeaning, childlike recitation—would be read by any intelligent American for what it was—childlike pidgin-English propaganda. So I thought, Why not waffle, see if you can put them off,
stall, appeal to their expectations, "be reasonable," as they say?
Oh, where are those great booming voices from on high that shout
down maxims of patriotism, messages from God, when one is at the
razor's edge of moral decision? Isn't all of that supposed to be coming down to me about now?

No, it's just me down here; I'm stuck with myself. I've just got
to come to terms with this dilemma by logic, intuition, and gut
feeling. That's it! Gut feeling! There was never any doubt when
Eagle brought that air-force map to the hospital. It came to me so

clearly then that what was being asked was just a litmus test, the top of the iceberg, just the opening ploy. The total phoniness of Eagle's mission and his obvious embarrassment in performing it made that case more transparent, but isn't this the same? Isn't credibility of defiance what it's all about in the long run around here? Where is your ego? Who are you to be shoved around? Isn't this what you set out to prove to your dad when Bill Stanforth was coming down that sideline?

I left the paper, pen, and ink where they lay, picked up my crutches, and walked back and forth. This cell was three times as deep as the one in Heartbreak, and at the far end I could look up through the high window and see the top of the outer wall with its embedded pink, blue, and clear champagne-bottle shards sparkling in the winter sun that was rapidly sinking behind the prison. After those days in irons, it felt good to move around, and to have made up my mind in a way that would have made my dear old dad proud. Next summer it would be twenty-three years since dad took me on the train from Chicago all the way back to Annapolis just to see and hear me take the oath in Memorial Hall. "Do your best to be the best midshipman here," he'd said fondly as he turned on his heel and walked erectly down the steps. Funny I should think of that just now.

It was dark when the key went into the cell door lock. Pigeye let Rabbit in first. I held my crutches in one hand and bowed as he marched to the front bunk and contemptuously flipped through the blank sheets of paper. "You will learn," he said as he marched out with Pigeye. They locked the door and I'm certain headed for the Cat's office to get permission to escalate.

It was not Pigeye but the little scruffy guard who unlocked and swung open the cell door about half an hour later. One look at the expression on his face as I bowed and I knew Rabbit and Pigeye had got the permission they wanted. He picked up the papers, ink, and pen and nodded me out and to the left. The door of cell 4 was slightly ajar and a civilian guard stood chatting with two male Vietnamese prisoners inside. Civilian guards were older, like retired master sergeants; they wore light tan uniforms. The Vietnamese prisoners peeked searchingly at me when they heard my crutches

clicking by. It looked like they had some of their personal belongings from home in there with them. What incongruity, thought I;
little prison households set up within a few yards of where bones
are broken.

I followed the now-familiar route to room 18 along the dimly
lighted passageways, walked between its open green doors, and
shifted the crutches to my left hand and balanced on my right leg as
I gave the usual bow in the general direction of Rabbit and Mickey
Mouse in the brightly lighted room. Sullen silence met me as
Scruffy laid out the papers, ink, and pen on the small table, then
went back and slammed the doors shut. About then I caught sight of
Pigeye in the dark corner slightly behind me and to my right; with
his right hand, he was holding on to a heavy iron upright bar, its
end resting on the cement floor. The bar was longer than Pigeye
was tall, and was threaded through two big ankle lugs that rested at
its bottom; in his left hand he had a coil of manila hemp rope, about
three-eighths of an inch in diameter. Rabbit gave me time to absorb
the dramatic effect of Pigeye and his equipment, then spoke. "You
are insolent and obdurate. This is your last chance. Write the paper."

I shook my head "no" and the scruffy guard "eeowed" as Pigeye let the iron bar go with a crash. Rabbit and Mickey Mouse
joined the chorus as Pigeye leaped toward me, popping my jaw
with the heel of his hand, showing me stars, and knocking me off-
balance while deftly flipping the crutches aside as he wrestled me
to a sitting position on the floor. He then sprang up astride my legs
and, making the same "soft fists" of the heels of his hands,
whopped my jaws alternately, making loud slapping noises on contact, but (unknowingly?) telegraphing a certain reluctance to break
facial bones. Meanwhile the other three raised a din that was a little
too obviously designed to telegraph a commitment to kill.

Little Scruffy held my arms back while Pigeye went for the bar,
his eyes searching over my shoulder for a signal as to whether to
connect my legs to it or not. Sure enough, off came the lugs, and my
wobbly crippled leg got stuffed into a lug and onto that bar. My legs
spread-eagled and extended, I facing the closed doors, Pigeye went
to work on reeving the manila hemp rope about my upper arms in
some complicated pattern he obviously had well in mind. With a
crescendo of shouting by all, I could feel his foot in my back as he

pulled my arms and shoulders together in jerks. I cried out about my left arm and shoulder—the former unable to be raised and the latter broken in ejection and painful—but the ropes continued to tighten by jerks. As my shoulders compressed, I heard shouts of "Down! down!" and Pigeye's arm pressure on my back bent me forward at the waist.

In a flash I saw Pigeye's sandals fly by my right side as a result of his kicking them toward the door. He put a bare foot on my right (thank God) shoulder and mounted my back as my head slumped toward my knees. Then the rhythmic jerking continued as he pulled up on his rope end, cinching my shoulders and arms ever tighter. I was yelling by this time; the idea was crossing my mind that Robbie might hear me, as we had heard others being trussed up in this room from Heartbreak, when a rag went into my mouth. It was probably little Scruffy's handiwork. There was no feeling but tingling in my lower arms; the blood had been stopped for some minutes. Then Pigeye's bare heel was on the back of my bowed head. So help me, my head was pressed to the bricks between the calves of my legs. I wouldn't have believed it. And in that position all action stopped; the rag came out of my mouth. "Keep silent! Keep silent!" I heard Rabbit shouting in my ear. Then I was suddenly worried about getting my breath. I started to panic! I knew from survival school that I must quit thinking about suffocation and get my head "out of the box," but everything was closing in: the tremendous pain of lower arms and shoulders—the claustrophobia—the hopelessness of it all.

I suddenly realized that I was listening to Rabbit's fading voice at what seemed like a distant location. "Do you submit? Are you ready to comply?"

"Yes, I submit, I submit," I murmured.

Pigeye kept the pressure on for a minute or two as if to put an exclamation mark on his performance. Then he dismounted and I raised my head as he methodically started loosening the arm bindings. I'd never felt such relief in my life, even as the blood surging back into my arms induced its own form of throbbing pain. Pigeye slid the bar out of the ankle bolts and took them off with positive tenderness. His work was done for the day. I don't think either I or Pigeye would have believed it if a fortune-teller had correctly forecast the future for us at that time: that in the years ahead, we were to go through this routine fourteen more times together.

I could hear Pigeye pacing outside as I worked to hold the old-fashioned dip pen straight. My right hand's grip was very flaccid after the ropes, and the pen kept sliding out of the notch. As soon as I copied the disgusting piece, I turned and gave a signal through the gap between the doors. Pigeye took the irons off the gapped doors, and came in, tossed my sandals over to me, and walked to the table. He read no English, of course, but he did make sure there was about the right amount of writing on my paper. Satisfied, he went over and picked up my crutches, put them beside me, and waved to me to follow. He clutched both Rabbit's and my papers as I followed him back to New Guy Village cell 3. It was late now, and cell 4 was quiet. I was not put back into irons, but the agony I felt in my heart that night was worse than any that could have been generated by physical restraining equipment. I did not sleep. I heard the chimes of every hour from the church bells. How to live this down? What to do now?

✧

The scruffy little guard came early the next morning and gave me the "sleeve" signal. Rabbit was waiting for me at the quiz table in room 24. He was acting cool—he let me bow and sit down and then he slid across the paper I had taken the ropes for, his letter to the "U.S. Foreign Secretary of State." "This letter must be put in its proper form," he said. Then he laboriously explained a format for letter submission that must have come right out of a French or Vietnamese fifth-grade composition book. He wanted a double-size left margin, and the fresh paper on which it was to be recopied must be creased in a certain way so the writer could follow the new margin, etc., etc. Then he dropped the other bomb: "Also, improve the expression—make it sound like you."

I was learning, step by step. Why did I waste a second considering what he had requested without taking torture? Now he's asking for a new letter. I'm right back behind the eight ball.

That did it; I grasped at an idea that had occurred to me the night before as I tossed, iron-free, on that hard slab: The thing I've got to do, figuratively at least, is "get up and fight on my feet." The psychology of being flat on my back and crippled and just volleying back Rabbit's thrusts, cringing in wait for his slams, was driving me bats. My mind went into high gear as I sat there staring at him.

You've got to go on the *offensive* and figure out a way to change the wording of that missile and deflect it. If it goes into the public domain, you've got to get it into the hands of friends in Washington who know you well enough to recognize what's going on over here. Either Bill Crowe or Bob Monroe is sure to be stationed in OP-06, Plans and Policy, in the Navy Department. That office sent all three of us through postgraduate school and it's there that we were all to serve at least one "payback" tour. Your friends are in that office in Washington, and if you are being forced to disgrace yourself, the least you can do is let them know what's happening to you and make your boss the addressee.

I spoke to Rabbit: "There is no way I could make this sound like me. Senior military men follow certain procedures. If I violated those procedures, my superiors would immediately know there was foul play afoot."

Rabbit broke in. "Watch your tongue. Don't forget your status as a criminal." Then, his eyes squinting as he perked up, he said, "Go ahead. What is your idea?"

"American naval commanders do not dare write directly to the foreign secretary of state. They must go through the military chain of command. This is a political document you've had me copy. Everybody in my government knows that I would have sense enough to send it to the Political Military Policy Division of the U.S. Navy Department. They would take my remarks and forward them up the chain. The crossover to the foreign secretary of state occurs at the highest level. Also, your words are those of your national radio propaganda. I should have to use the U.S. Navy style of speech."

Rabbit dismissed me immediately, saying, "We shall study your proposal."

I was led back to my cell, worried sick. This is risky business, thought I. At least with the address I gave them I feel sure the thing will wind up in OP-06. But now you're sounding like you *want* to write the damned thing. What about that credibility of defiance? Are you blowing all the credibility you suffered for last night?

There were just too many angles to this one. Half the time I wished to hell I had just kept my mouth shut. But what would I be doing right now? I'd either be writing it again or taking the ropes and getting ready to write it again. I was just out of gas and I was not ready for that rope trick again this morning. Anyway, I'd committed myself to another course now. Live and learn, live and learn. The rules of this ball game would change as we went along. But for now, *I* was spinning the web, and I liked it better on this side of the fence. Time would tell.

Rabbit came to my cell that afternoon. He had paper, pen, the old letter as I had copied it, and ink. "The general staff officer said for you to write a letter to the Political Military Policy Division of your navy, making the same points but using your military style of expression."

"I can't say the same things, exactly, because American naval officers wouldn't say some of the things you did."

"Shut up and write it your way; I'll pick it up in a few minutes," said Rabbit, turning on his heel and slamming the door. Funny guy, Rabbit. Smart as hell, and independent. He was dangerous because he seemed to have an intuitive grasp of our Western way of thought; he knew when he had me over a barrel. But it was clear he thought Cat made a mistake by letting me go with this, and that gave me hope. Now, what line of reasoning would Rabbit expect me to take in explaining the "plight of the Vietnamese" people to the Navy Department?

I took the pen and started to write furiously for the record (there was no such thing as a "rough"; they counted the papers they left with me). Graduate school was the best of all preparations for this life of "fire and fall back," "cross and double-cross." I went after that paper as if it were a bluebook in an international-law exam and started cranking out the bullshit.

I was dotting the final i's when Rabbit himself unlocked the bolt and burst in with a sneer. He took the pen, ink, all the paper, and left. My line in the letter to the Political Military Policy Division *vis-à-vis* the "poor Vietnamese people" had been one of disingenuous pity with a touch of ridicule, liberally sprinkled with obscurantism. It was a flowery piece of "constructs" with a lot of big words with double meanings alluding to the woeful primitiveness of the Vietnamese people. This was all a setup to allow me to wind up the last paragraph explaining how the American people should know that I am locked up in the custody of the most determined "primates" I have ever known.

But although no American could have read it without knowing it was a spoof, that didn't mean I was laughing up my sleeve all the way; it caused me tremendous worry. It made me somewhat more attractive to the Cat, and I was thus forced to work "closer to his horns." Working close to the horns has certain advantages—you learn better what exactly the bull is capable of and what he is not capable of—but you pay for this vantage point with continual anxiety, the gross expenditure of emotional energy. Knowing that a visiting left-wing American could blow the whistle on me should Cat show the letter to him accounted for much of my expenditure of emotional energy. Had he done that (and I luckily sneaked under their wire, because cross-checking prisoner writings with the American radicals later became commonplace), the North Vietnamese retribution would have been swift and severe.

❖

That was a bad winter for me, 1966. I was alone in New Guy Village. I was to taste "the ropes" again as Rabbit methodically forced me to "fill in the squares" required by the Camp Authority—my filling out of personal biographic forms, a confession of my misdeeds toward the Vietnamese people, a begging of their pardon, a promise to make amends, then more biographic forms. These were all part of the fear-and-guilt package that any extortionist knows is the key to the breakdown of human will—and guilt and fear I acquired in bulk. I felt guilty at my failure to do better in the ropes, and fear of swift and severe retribution.

What brought the most fear, however, was my imaginative extrapolation of where I seemed doomed to go after the war: into a life of continuous shame without friends or self-respect. What I had given up in the ropes seemed trivial in comparison with what I was sure I was eventually going to have to give up—military secrets, Tonkin Gulf facts. When I took stock of the power the Vietnamese had over me, my weakness and crippledness, my sinking mental state, it seemed clear that they had me on a downhill run that would force me to the bottom.

On those endless cloudy days of that clammy winter, I would crutch myself back and forth across the length of New Guy Village cell 3 and imagine a return to America that would disgrace my family, my hometown, and my service. The nightmare always came to an end with my turning my back on society and eking out a living on Rolling View Farm—the one thing the Vietnamese could not rob me of. That farm of mom's saved my life that winter.

And then spring came, and I began to make more sense out of this loneliness. I started keeping exact track of the time of day back in Coronado where Sybil and the boys were, and indulging myself regularly in "strolls down memory lane." I found my dried-out mind manifesting an entirely new dimension of memory. If I searched delicately, didn't clamp down on the past scene too abruptly, I could bring out unbelievably clear and distinct details of first viewings of baby boys, birthday parties, and family outings. But I also learned that such periods of reverie had to be rationed because I missed Syb and the boys so that if I stuck with them too long, it all became too real and I would start feeling guilty for the lonely life I had condemned them to as a sailorman. I would then slip into a self-defeating funk. This was particularly bad on birthdays, as when, on that April 3, I felt the need to cover every facet of little Taylor's life as he was becoming four years old.

One afternoon Rabbit came by my cell and solemnly announced, "I am to take you to see an important person tonight. Be ready."

I was really dirty; I had not had a bath since being shot down over six months before; I had several weeks of beard, and my clothes were filthy. That didn't seem to matter, but what did matter was ridding me of my crutches before he took me to see this guy. He said, "You're walking well enough without these now," took them, and left.

After dark I was blindfolded, led to a jeep in the courtyard, handcuffed, and driven several blocks while Rabbit repeatedly warned me to "be polite" in the presence of this important personage I was to see. When the jeep stopped, I was led inside a door, the handcuffs and blindfold were removed, and I looked ahead up a long flight of stairs. I negotiated them one at a time, and was somewhat dizzy at the top, where they turned me to the right and down a long hall that led into a room at the end. The room turned out to be a regular French bathroom, with flush toilet, lavatory, and all. This was only my holding point for about two minutes, but I was overcome by the fact that, for the first time in all those months since shootdown, I was in an actual room, a room with a wooden floor, plaster walls, central heat, and no direct vents to the open air.

The next turn of events was even more of a shock. I was taken out and led around the corner into the first door to the right, where I saw the backs of about fifteen men already assembled. All were sitting quietly, and all save two were in military uniforms. The room was smoke-filled and carpeted; everybody was seated either in chairs along the wall or in chairs here and there facing the man in civilian clothes seated on a sofa against the wall opposite the door. Every person there was my age or older except my personal day-in, day-out, one-on-one antagonist, the jug-eared Rabbit. After he indicated to me the low stool in the center of the room on which I was to sit, he took a seat in the very back corner, note pad in

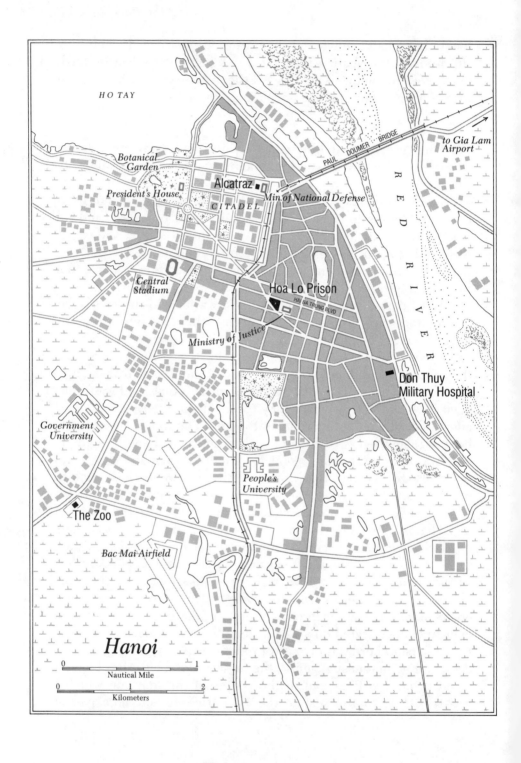

HO TAY

Botanical
Garden

President's House

Alcatraz

CITADEL

Min. of National Defense

PAUL DOUMER BRIDGE

to Gia Lam
Airport

RED RIVER

Central
Stadium

Hoa Lo Prison

HAI BA TRUNG BLVD

Ministry of Justice

Don Thuy
Military Hospital

Government
University

People's
University

The Zoo

Bac Mai Airfield

Hanoi

0   1
Nautical Mile

0   1   2
Kilometers

hand. Limping forward awkwardly, I concluded that I must be surrounded by general officers. (They had removed their rank insignia, of course, in accordance with Vietnamese standard practice in the presence of prisoners.)

As I eased down onto my assigned seat, a vaguely familiar interpreter's voice started to speak in clipped English. It belonged to the other man present in civilian clothes. He was seated between me and the man on the couch, the latter being the obvious object of deference of all the other Vietnamese in the room. I knew the silent man on the couch had to be important when it came to me that the interpreter's voice was that of one of the two announcers on the "Voice of Vietnam," their English-language propaganda program that was broadcast daily over all of Southeast Asia.

The unwary radio announcer started addressing the important one as "Vien" until Rabbit came forward and whispered to him what I suppose was a reminder that criminals like me were never to hear a proper Vietnamese name. But I had all I needed. "Vien" had to be Nguyen Khac Vien, a name with which I had become familiar through my research in graduate school. Vien is a medical doctor and a longtime resident of Paris. He is a master Communist propagandist, a better-than-average writer in English, and an intellectual of sorts, a former acquaintance of Albert Camus. He led the Viet Minh propaganda and agitation campaigns and demonstrations in Paris and in the French countryside during 1953 and 1954, efforts that had a part in discouraging the French people and French government from pursuing their war in Asia. Moreover, Vien is known to be a longtime close personal friend of Premier Pham Van Dong.

During our ensuing talk through the radio-announcer interpreter, it became clear that as far as Vien was concerned, the master game plan for this war had been well in the works for a long time: It was to be a replay of the Dien Bien Phu era, including the propaganda-induced political disillusionment of the Western adversary.

What actually happened during that night of conversation gave me lots of food for thought. The first thing that was vividly displayed to me was the difficulty an educated person has in keeping his intellectual roots obscure. Vien was committed to remaining anonymous; he slouched in the middle of the broad couch in a rumpled European suit, slender hands dangling before him and crossed at the wrists, the very embodiment of the fabled enigmatic Oriental. But his questions tracked right out of a textbook of old-fashioned Western Philosophy I.

"Are you a Catholic or a Protestant?" (Being a Protestant, so the conventional wisdom goes, I must rely on conscience as the ultimate guide to action; as a Catholic, it would be authority.) "As a professional military man, where in the field of warfare does your conscience find its limit?" He zeroed right in on the obvious limiting case, the failure of the German army to overthrow Adolf Hitler. He then went on to a discussion of justice.

We had an hour-long verbal Ping-Pong game. For me it was sheer entertainment after so long a drought to again talk to somebody who actually knew who Plato was, someone who could openly smile when I deflected his discussion of the definition of *justice* to the arguments of the all-night debate about that same subject on Cephalus's porch in Piraeus 2,400 years before. Vien and I held opposite views on almost every point raised, but what a change it was to talk to a man urbane enough to take a hit when I ridiculed the idea of any sane person comparing LBJ to Hitler, and then tacitly grant me the point without going into a theatrical rage.

Only the interpreter and the two of us spoke aloud during the meeting. By Vien's facial expressions, I could tell he understood my English well. The Vietnamese officers sat quietly, sipping little cups of hot tea served by old servant women who crawled through the disorganized array of chairs, never getting up off their knees, never being so bold as to raise their eyes, and backing out the door rump-first rather than offend the exalted intellectual on the far side of the room. That performance in itself was quite a commentary on those "new" socialist mores of old Indochina.

The evening's interview seemed short. He dismissed me with a smile at one of the points when we were at a standoff. Obviously, I was there to have my brain picked. He was probably going to write propaganda booklets and had asked to talk to an "American intellectual" from the dungeons. I doubt he knew or bothered to inquire about the details of conditions under which we were living; one look at my filthy clothes with their leg-iron rust stains and my unshaved face probably gave him a good clue, but he was too sophisticated in the ways of Vietnamese prisons to be alarmed. Good Party form would have had him consider it none of his business, and it was my impression that this was the way he looked at such things. But I couldn't help believing that he left convinced that his work was really cut out for him if he was going to write persuasive propaganda for the likes of me.

Still, by the time I had hobbled back down the long flight of stairs, a step at a time, I was conscious of being consumed with a new feeling of horror, horror at the great patience of the DRV ruling hierarchy, and their great confidence in the ultimate success of their programmed saturation propaganda-bombing of the West. Vien had calmly told me, "Our country has no capability to defeat you on the battlefield. But war is not decided by weapons so much as by national will. Once the American people understand this war, they will have no interest in pursuing it. They will be made to understand this. We will win this war on the streets of New York."

As Rabbit and his guard took me back through the rain in the jeep and the blindfold and the handcuffs, I thought over the total performance. I gave myself pretty good marks overall, but hoped I was able to conceal the sense of horror that crept over me as my worst fears had been confirmed. America had set herself up to lack self-confidence and moral leverage at the very turning point when she most needed it.

The last and most important lesson of that 1966 winter-spring season of isolation in New Guy Village I learned in late May. I was called to quiz in a newly soundproofed room in New Guy Village Courtyard. (I had watched the progress of this work in late winter on morning trips to and from the latrine. Blobs of plaster had been affixed to the walls to diffuse the sounds of cries; I called it "the knobby room.") It was a hot night. Cat was there with Rabbit, Mickey Mouse, and Pigeye, and from the moment I bowed at the doorway it was clear that tension was high and that Cat had a deadline to meet. It was time to clean me up for the first time and take me downtown to a press conference.

I should have anticipated this. Some days previous, Cat had summoned me to tell me that I would be "severely punished" for communication. (Their trip wire had caught me in a whispered conversation with my oldest friend in Hanoi, Jerry Denton, back from the Zoo for punishment.) Thus, as was his standard procedure, Cat made his demands only after I had been placed under a cloud of prior guilt. Moral leverage is never forgotten in Communist squeeze plays.

". . . Tomorrow you will go to the press conference. There will be foreign newsmen there who will ask you about your views on the American imperialist aggressors' bombing of the Democratic Republic of Vietnam. . . . The whole world is watching America try to squirm out of her illegal position. . . . Even Senator Fulbright says America has guilt on her conscience . . . even Fulbright, who supported the trumped-up charges of so-called Vietnamese PT-boat attacks nearly two years ago now. . . ."

Cold sweat broke out on my brow. Was this it? Were they closing in for the kill on the Tonkin Gulf fiasco? All I could do was hang on as they ranted and raved.

"You will tell the world that the bombing of the DRV has been illegal. . . ."

I shook my head and tried to be calm as I told them that I would not go downtown. Cat pointed to Pigeye. "You know that this man can make you submit. You are old; you are crippled; you are foolish. You must think of yourself."

This went on till after midnight, and still no rough stuff. There was a sense of urgency. It was clear they had to have me intimidated by midmorning, yet they couldn't afford to rough me up— we were too close to curtain time. More and more frequently, the three Vietnamese officers would digress into animated conversations among themselves in their native tongue. Finally Rabbit announced, "You will go to the press conference tomorrow." He reached into his case and slid a handwritten paper across the table toward me. "You will sign this now and read it at the press conference tomorrow. If you misbehave, you will be severely punished."

This was the showdown, and I blew my stack. Had it not been for my deep anxiety about the Tonkin Gulf, and their mention of its being in the news—in a recent *Look* magazine, no less—prudence would have kept me in my chair. But I bolted up and wiped Rabbit's paper off the table and shouted at the top of my lungs, "I am not going to any press conference!" I ranted and raved and waved my arms and shook my fists in ways that I never would have dared had not all that emotional tension of those August 1964 days been pent up within me. I didn't care. What had I to lose? Better to go down in flames *here* than drag my country through muck in front of the whole world.

Then I realized that my three antagonists were sitting wide-eyed, openmouthed. Why hadn't they sicced Pigeye on me? He could have had me in the ropes crying like a baby and signing any paper they wanted me to sign long before now. Cat's face showed real panic; my mental snapshot of his distorted face became the most valuable icon I was to acquire that first year. That guy was actually in trouble! He was really worried. The hierarchy had stuck him with a pop-up requirement, he had gotten a late start, and I had turned into a wild-eyed, erratic lunatic. He wasn't even thinking about siccing Pigeye on me; he and Rabbit and Mickey Mouse were becoming immersed in an excited conference in Vietnamese. They were shaking their heads and were very sober as they walked out, yakking away, all but ignoring me. In an hour or so, a regular guard came in, walked me back to my cell, and slammed and locked the door.

I got up on that high New Guy Village bed slab and rested my head on the ankle stocks, thanking God for sparing me from being in them, and stared through the high cell windows, across the dry moat, past the broken French wine bottles embedded atop the fifteen-foot outer prison wall, to the rosy-fingered dawn of the Hanoi sky beyond. My mind was running at full speed. These political cadres—Cat, Rabbit, Mickey Mouse—are not ideologues so much as they are just ambitious bureaucrats! After all those months of hearing their impassioned ideological rhetoric, it had somehow escaped me that, like all too many of us, Communists also can get twisted around the axle of chain-of-command bureaucracy, the axle of careerism. Cat had a deadline to meet. Some foreign left-wing press group had decided they wanted to interview an American prisoner about some big article in *Look* magazine. The setup was tailor-made for what he had been saving me for—and then I turned out to go bananas and he could not risk his career on taking an unknown factor like me out in public.

Wow, are there lessons in all this! What's that old crap I used to hear about how military officers should maintain their bearing, remain calm and courteous, and project personal dignity, no matter what? By holding to that ethic, you automatically volunteer to have a ring put in your nose and be led downtown to be slaughtered at a

Communist press conference. These Communist bureaucrats have careers at stake and, like our bureaucrats, have a zero-defect mentality. They dare not chance a public incident. Ergo, for self-protection, I should construct a subtly unstable personality and climb into it—climb into it like a wetsuit and internalize it.

I was beginning to learn that indispensable attributes in this deadly game of extortion and pain are not only tough-mindedness and physical courage, but skill in the dramatic arts as well. School plays as well as football were valuable preparation. Mom and dad's lessons were *both* prophetic.

But dramatic skill will by no means get you by, day in and day out; it is a capability useful only in down-to-the-wire circumstances. And the penalties for being unmasked in a put-down are high—the ropes, for starters. But there are lessons to be learned about the pain and claustrophobia of that rope experience, too. The good news is that though it is imperative for credibility of defiance that you hang in there for a good hard-won "submit," if you keep your wits about you it is difficult for the extortionists to get information that they don't know you have. The bad news is that if they know the truth, and they know you know the truth, and they want you to document it, you are in trouble. Which leaves me with the question: Why, of all times, didn't they close in on me for Tonkin Gulf documentation tonight? Do they have that *Stars and Stripes* of August 12, 1964, or don't they?

A lot more than I had counted on had been accomplished that night in the knobby room. I had failed Cat in the clutch and he temporarily dropped me out of his personal surveillance stable and put me on ice. A couple of nights later, I was told to "fold up," and with all my personal belongings I struggled down to room 18, where I was told to wait. I heard a prisoner being marched by that room toward New Guy Village, and then I was taken to Heartbreak cell 1. Robbie Risner and I had changed places. The next day I was given my first shower since being shot down nine months before.

Heartbreak was full of new shootdowns. It was like a holiday for me to be out of isolation and back in regular solitary confinement where I could hear all the noises of people coming and going and do a little whispering and tapping. My cell was first on the right, just inside the green door; across the hall was cell 8, the shower, the bucket-dump area, and the night bathroom for all the civilian guards, and I heard them all night.

Cell 1 was traditionally in charge of hall clearance, but although I had shed my crutches, I was hampered, being unable to get up and look out the top peephole where Dave Wheat and a dozen others since that October '65 morning had watched. I came to rely on help from Sam Johnson, cell 6, a guy with two broken shoulders, a loping gait, and a Texas drawl, who had been shot down in an F-4 on the night of April 16; and Jim Lamar, cell 3, with a fused elbow and an Arkansas twang, shot down in an F-105 on May 6. We were able to chat frequently. Talking to people, particularly these guys fresh from home, was like a breath of air. In those days, there were three ways to live in a Hanoi prison: with a cellmate; in solitary like I was now in Heartbreak Hotel; and in isolation like I lived from December to June in New Guy Village. In neither isolation nor solitary did you commonly see another American; but in going from isolation to solitary, you covered 90 percent of the distance to having a cellmate.

In that first week of June, I was called to quiz with Rabbit. He said the general staff officer was considering sending me to an outlying camp. Hallelujah! thought I; maybe I can get away from this one-on-one situation with you, Rabbit. But my elation was short-lived; Rabbit then said that the staff officer insisted that he visit me there. "Your time will come when you will work for us. Mark my words. Your time will come. You will pay for your keep. In the meantime," he added, "I will make sure you do not communicate."

Two nights later, my Heartbreak cell 1 door was swung open by Pigeye. He made a "roll up" motion with his hands, meaning I was to pack up all my possessions in blankets and get ready to move. My heart danced! I had set the record for tenure here in Hoa Lo Prison and I was glad to be rid of it, glad to be getting away from Cat's and Rabbit's and Pigeye's headquarters.

Sam Johnson, Jim Lamar, and I were individually blindfolded, handcuffed, and stuffed into a single jeep. After about fifteen minutes, we pulled up at a curb. We were at the Zoo. Sam and I were put in solitary and isolated by being sealed off from the rest of the camp by a cell of Asians. The Vietnamese knew we had talked at Heartbreak and we were put side by side, as a mutually contaminated pair. His cell had two bunks; mine was a big one with three. Lamar was stashed in another building.

It was in that summer of 1966 that Sam and I perfected the art of rapid, expressive, terse, arrest-free wall tapping. We kept from being apprehended by watching shadows, planting tiny mirrorlike reflecting pools of drinking water or urine just inside our doorsteps, and perfecting the danger-signaling art of "light bump and go" (lightly brushing our common wall with a shoulder and moving deliberately and innocently toward the center of our respective cells as predators rushed toward our cell-door peepholes). Sam had heard about the wall-sound-amplification capabilities of our farm-pump-style "porcelain" drinking cups. We learned to get nearly opposite one another, put our respective cup lips against the wall, and lean our heads against the cup bottoms. A light tick with a fingernail came through an eight-inch wall like the beat of a snare drum.

As we worked the wall together, we learned to be sensitive to a whole new range of acoustic perception. Our tapping ceased to be just an exchange of letters and words; it became conversation. Elation, sadness, humor, sarcasm, excitement, depression—all came through. Sam and I would sign off before dark with abbreviations like GN (goodnight) and GBU (God bless you). Passing on abbreviations like conundrums got to be a kind of game. What would ST mean right after GN? Sleep tight, of course. And DLTBBB? I laughed to think what our friends back home would think of us two old fighter pilots standing at a wall, checking for shadows under the door, pecking out a final message for the day with our fingernails: "Don't let the bedbugs bite."

As autumn set in, the continual arrival of new prisoners brought about the need to utilize all available bunks. The other bunk in Sam's room was taken by Jim Lamar. The Asians were moved out of the cell to my right and three brand-new Americans took their place, but they would not tap on the wall. This told me that the initial torture sessions were getting very bad and that the intimidation they produced ("You will now go to a regular cell, and as long as you strictly obey the camp regulations and do not communicate, you will be humanely treated") had a lasting effect on more and more new shootdowns.

Meanwhile, I continued to limp around my massive three-bed abode in splendid isolation. And in this continuous solitude, I was getting very depressed. Jim Lamar's arrival understandably meant less tap with Sam. New guards were mean (especially two—one we named Big Ugh, a moon-faced big country boy of about seventeen who had just joined the army and was strong as a horse and had eyes like a cat; and an older, tough snake in the grass we knew as "Jake"). The cell loudspeakers were full of pidgin-English diatribes about how we were going to be held accountable for our acts before war-crimes tribunals. It was wearing to be stalked, baited, and watched week after week.

Also, in that fall of 1966, I was getting the feeling that America was not conscious of the momentum that was generating among these peasants over here. They were starting to snicker at our "measured escalation." And Dr. Vien's words were starting to ring in my ears: "We will defeat you on the streets of New York."

Christmas Eve, 1966. I'm still in solitary, still not in the Zoo communications network, still being awakened by leg cramps at night, and still unable to stand up for more than a few minutes at a time.

But I'm having a good chat with myself tonight, thanking God for his blessings, and even feeling the spirit of the holidays. Try living with yourself locked up and totally alone for a year or two. You, too, will become more introspective, and probably find yourself whispering an almost continuous soliloquy during your waking hours. You'll also get to know yourself, and the longer you're alone, the more frank and truthful you'll be with yourself.

And being frank and truthful with myself on this second Christmas Eve alone up there, I have to say that, for me, in this isolation, holiday thoughts can often be an abomination, a self-flagellation. It just tears me up to think of dear, sweet Syb and those four lovable, rough-and-tumble boys of ours missing me on this, their early day-before-Christmas morning. (I now visualize the time of day the people I'm thinking of back home are experiencing; Coronado, California, is fifteen hours behind Hanoi in the winter.)

I ask myself, Are you nuts? Would you rather have them *not* missing you? Of course not, I admit; it's just that I'm so soft-hearted about people I love when I'm so alone. I seem compelled, driven, on each holiday, on each family birthday, to talk myself through the whole family holiday experience, working back, anniversary by anniversary, to the earliest account my memory can dredge up. Sometimes I get so transfixed, so carried away in this process, I could be watching a movie screen and hours and hours go by like seconds.

But my Christmas movies and birthday movies somehow get to be sad movies, and I want to put this one off till tomorrow during daylight. I'm so despondent tonight, so tired of this existence, this private hell. I'm tired of being stalked and baited and hammered and watched. I can feel the Cat out there, and his puppet, the Rabbit, and his personal arm twister/animal trainer, Pigeye. "There will come a time, Stockdale, when you must do things for us. You will see. You will perform your duties. You will pay for your keep." I'm tired of being deformed and weak, and in pain whenever I'm on my feet. Most of all, I'm tired of the isolation and the fact that I'm having to fight these battles all by myself, half the time without even the comfort of knowing that if I disappeared, some American prisoner could make a good guess as to the date of my death. I've never been so far out on a limb, so short on help or hope.

It's getting past my bedtime. I wish I could lie down on these boards under this damnable ever-lit naked bulb and drift off to sleep. But, no, there is too much action out there in the courtyard. I can hear cell doors slamming. I'm sure these clowns are putting on their Christmas act tonight. Last year it was Christmas afternoon for Robbie and me and that turkey gobbler outside; but step by step these Vietnamese are learning our customs and refining their program to squeeze every ounce of propaganda blood out of us. "Take advantage of the American national and religious festival days to confront criminals individually, to show Democratic Republic of Vietnam generosity with a holiday fruit or sweets, and to criticize them and make them criticize themselves in order to emphasize guilt for the American imperialist war of aggression."

Guilt and fear, guilt and fear are the age-old primary tools of these manipulators; it is they that beat you down, particularly when you are lonesome and despondent. All of this torture seems to me a mere accelerator of the basic process of unhinging a victim with fear and polarizing him with guilt. Only the prisoners' comradeship and loyalty to each other can effectively deter this repeated tearing down of a man.

Here it comes—the big key is in the door lock. Enter Big Ugh, the guard. I bow at the waist. "Follow me," he signals with the universal hand motion of peasants. (This new recruit doesn't yet even know the monosyllabic pidgin-English commands most guards use.) We're off.

I hobble across the empty, dark courtyard, listening to the straps slap against the stock of the drawn rifle behind my head. Big Ugh is ever vigilant as he marches a man who couldn't walk three blocks without collapsing, through a walled enclosure he couldn't possibly scale. I go to the lighted open doorway; stop and bow on the guard's order; and then, as has become second nature to me by this time, take my seat in the inferior position on the low stool before the Vietnamese officer seated erectly behind the blue-draped table. ("Ho Chi Minh blue," of course, as they always remembered to tell us.)

This official is new to me; I've never seen him before. He is not part of this camp's administration, but that is not unusual on holidays, when they send English-speaking cadres out to all outlying camps from headquarters. He is of course without rank bars but I judge him to be a senior captain or junior major. Their officers are usually a little older than our American counterparts, so he may be thirty-five or thirty-seven. He is intense, frail, and, you can tell at a glance, political rather than combat. This comes through partly from his unexercised thinness and soft, delicate, long-fingered hands, and partly from his supersensitive, almost effeminate countenance. Already I don't like him. There is something about his protruding eyeballs, higher-than-normal cheekbones, and oversize long neck with its pulsating blue veins going at about eighty cycles per minute that signals cunning intelligence, perhaps treachery. Sam has described such a person and given me the name that has to be his: Chihuahua.

Chihuahua is all smiles tonight as he follows his holiday operating instructions. He seems somewhat relieved because he does not have to assume any theatrical posture, because he does not have any particular ax to grind with me. I am not his to play with; he knows I am worked only by his boss, the Cat, through the latter's picked agent, the Rabbit. Chihuahua doesn't know the state of play with me and doesn't dare upset it; I can tell old pulsing veins just wants to breeze through the planned routine with me and send me back to my cell.

Chihuahua's patter starts out in typical North Vietnamese holiday change-of-pace fashion: "On the occasion of your religious holiday, in accordance with the humane and lenient treatment of the Democratic Republic of Vietnam, you are provided sweets. . . . Did you notice the ashtray on the table? Our artisans fashioned it from the wreckage of a war criminal's F-105 Thunderchief. Your imperialist air pirate was brought down by our brilliant gunners in Nghe An Province. It was the fifteen-hundredth American aggressor aircraft to be destroyed by our people."

Both his invective and his statistics are a bunch of crap, the numbers by at least a factor of three. I spend hours and hours of my time playing with shootdown numbers. Hanoi Hannah (the Vietnamese version of Tokyo Rose) always gives "the count" of American airplanes shot down on her daily propaganda radio program, which is usually piped into our cell loudspeakers except when her schedule calls for the discussion of something we prisoners are not to know about. Hanoi Hannah's numbers don't jibe with the prisoner count, which can be rather closely deduced by everyday camp observations.

From myriad little bits of visual and audible evidence, and from occasional slips of the tongue of interrogators, I'm pretty sure that right now they have about 150 American aircrewmen here in the North Vietnamese prison system. Further, it's my conviction that of every two pilots parachuting into North Vietnam, one either dies from infection in the jungle or is killed by exuberant mobs of civilians in the capture process. Throwing in the factor of increasing numbers of multiseat fighters being used each year, the numbers now come down to the fact that 150 aviators in prison means about 400 airplanes shot down. And I'm supposed to believe that that ashtray is made out of the fifteen-hundredth? Why reply? Why appear tractable?

"In honor of your religious holiday, we also offer you a banana. These were brought here by Cuban visitors from that fraternal socialist country in your native Western Hemisphere."

I take it and stuff it into my mouth. Then he reaches for the drawer. This is a switch—a pair of envelopes! Before I can extend my hand, I am startled by bright lights flooding the room behind me. I am suddenly conscious that there are people moving in back there—and now a movie camera starts to whine. This is all new; it's all too quick as my bug-eyed friend starts his speech into an old-fashioned hand-held microphone he suddenly produces. I've been mousetrapped!

"In accordance with the humane and lenient policy of the Democratic Republic of Vietnam, on this occasion of Christmas, my government presents you these letters from your wife—one from last September, and one from last October." I take them and clutch the already opened envelopes. "Also, here are two photographs—one of your wife and children, and one of your mother."

Pictures! Another switch! Those I grab and frantically scan. Yes, there they are, out in front of the shore house at Branford, Connecticut. Syb looks tanned, determined, and tired; each of the four boys seems to have grown about the right amount. At least they were all alive last summer.

But this other picture? That can't be mom. She looks so drawn, so unnatural, and she's aged so. . . .

As if from another world, I make out a faint voice in the distance talking to me. The interrogator with the neck veins is saying something. "What?" I ask.

He very articulately enunciates, "What do you have to say about your Christmas letters and photographs?" as he holds the old stick mike in front of me.

I blurt out, "That's not *my* mother." Nobody seems to understand me, and then cut! The klieg lights go out, the camera stops, there is a lot of self-conscious tittering and chatter in the back of the room. My mind is reeling at the thought of this mail and the suddenness of it all. It flashes through my mind that my last impulsive remark might have spoiled the production, but the Vietnamese seem happy about the whole thing. The idea of pulling off a surprise movie is leaving them giddy, never mind what the sound track has on it. They'll check that later. Or will they?

As a matter of fact, I'm not sure my spontaneous remark was audible throughout the room. I'm getting better at spoiling propaganda fodder, but this was inadvertent. The time will come when

I'll hope those last words were too indistinct to be read by Vietnamese off the tape, but right now my mind is spinning because I'm so worried about that picture, about my mother. Is she that old woman? For an instant I wish I had never seen that picture; I have the impulse to wad it up and throw it down. Then I'm conscious that everybody is suddenly up and milling around, and it becomes clear that it's time for the next prisoner, time for me to leave. Another guard comes and grunts me toward the door, and the next thing I know I'm locked back in my solitary cell with Syb's unread letters, two envelopes, and two pictures. Merry Christmas, 1966.

In the dim light of the naked bulb, I read Syb's wonderful letters of September and October with absolute reverence. They are full of love and information. She and the three younger boys are living right there at home in California, in our old house on "A" Avenue in Coronado. Jimmy is in his junior year at Mercersburg prep school; he's now six feet tall, weighs 185, and made the varsity football team. Syb is thus carrying out the schooling plan we worked out together (except we were to have been on duty in Washington this fall). Syb is again taking tutorial reading students every afternoon in her upstairs study on the glassed-in porch. I marvel at the variety of people who need remedial reading help. She has students from second grade to junior year in college. Thank God she picked up on that cross-dominance therapy from our neighbor Mrs. Arnold when little Sid started getting C's and having nightmares. I think that must all be behind him now. For all practical purposes, he's cured, and Syb has a new teaching specialty to follow on from her master's degree. Sid is the family dishwasher now, burning up the junior-high intramural football league, and even liking cotillion. Stan takes his lunch to first grade. And Taylor—the little ice-cream eater who was having his third birthday as I left on this cruise—is now in nursery school.

In all, wonderful news from my little family. Syb included a sermon Jimmy had written at boys' camp in Michigan last summer in the first letter, and closed each letter with a loving sonnet.

But my mom! That picture really works on me. From the way Sybil describes her actions, it sounds like she's lost her marbles. The heck of it is, the last time I saw her it seemed possible that she might be going 'round the bend, and this picture tends to confirm it. When I returned to California for Christmas in 1964 and she arrived from Illinois to visit us, I was privately shocked at how different she was beginning to look. Dad had been buried four months before. She had lost weight, had aged more than normal for the period, and had overdone her hair tint.

But it's the more radical changes in her habits that Syb describes that makes me think I had observed a trend that has accelerated in the last two years. Syb's September letter said mom was preparing the country house for sale and had bought a smaller, more practical one in town; then, zingo, according to Syb's October letter mom bought an airline ticket to California, and arrived unannounced in a taxicab—to pay a short visit and do some swimming! She said that all she needed was a good soak! Mom has to have set a record for personality change. All her life she found it difficult to leave work unfinished, was afraid to fly, hated for visitors to arrive unannounced, and was afraid of swimming. Is the poor dear thing headed for a mental institution? What kind of a life is that going to leave Syb with?

My solitary soliloquy continues as the days pass—one, two, three after that Christmas 1966. I daily converse with Sam Johnson and Jim Lamar through the wall, tapping lightly as usual with just my fingernail, my cup lip pushed against the wall by my head, ear against its base, eyeballs glued to the light strip under the door, poised to give the one-beat danger bump with my shoulder and walk smartly toward the center of the cell at the flick of a telltale shadow change. Thus braced, we talked over the Christmas events and my frustration at my mother's visage and behavior.

Except during those precious minutes of communication, the prison routine continues to deaden my sensibilities. The guard now always comes in right after the early-afternoon gong and ransacks the cell. What is he looking for? He seems to leave the letters and pictures alone. What if I wanted to get rid of the damned demoralizing picture? It's really getting to me, and my emotional stability and defenses are starting to sag. It would be dumb to give it back to them. What would I say? "I don't think it's my mother"? "I don't love my mother anymore"? Perhaps it's silly that I should be in a quandary over this, but it would be typical of the Camp Authority mentality to use the destruction of a picture as justification for starting me down the torture road on the grounds of ingratitude for the "humane and lenient" distribution of gifts.

It's noon. I've had it. I've got to destroy the picture. It's poisoning my whole outlook. I'll just tear the thing up in tiny pieces and mix 'em with the crap in my bucket.

But wait a minute—it's dumb to throw away something from the States without doing more with it. James Bond would soak it in piss and see if a message came out of it. I'll try something like that just for the hell of it. The guards never come before the afternoon gong, and that must be forty-five minutes away. My drinking-water jug is half empty; I'll piss it full to the brim, mix it up, and stick the picture in it. I hope the damn thing disappears in a cloud of smoke.

Nope. She just floats there and stares back at me—a sallow-skinned, hauntingly peculiar mom, standing in the surf on our Coronado beach in a black bathing suit. I pace the cell and let my mind drift back to pleasant thoughts of sand castles being built on that same beach by my little boys, as described in the letter from Syb that I received at Christmas 1965.

She's now been in that jug nearly half an hour. No smoke, no fire, no coming apart—just that cheesy Polaroid paper starting to fray at the edge. What ho! I can pull the back right off! Nothing on either side, of course—just white as a sheet, both faces. I'll take it out and lay it here on the bed slab while I go get the crap bucket. There's not much in it to hide the scraps in. I hope I can tear the picture into small enough pieces to do the trick. Okay, let's go to work.

Wait a minute! Am I seeing things? This cell is so dingy and dark; I'll take this peeled-off picture back over to that little light crack between the boards nailed across the window. So help me, I see specks on this paper! My God, as I watch it happen, a whole paragraph of small print is coming out on the inside of the picture back as it dries! In this dim light, I can squint and start to make out words! Thank God for these 20/20 eyes—I wouldn't have a prayer if they were any less.

I can hear doors slamming. The gong is about to go. Why didn't I start this James Bond spook stuff earlier? The guard will be here in a minute—I've got just so many seconds to burn the meaning of this thing into my brain. Now read and memorize!

> The letter in the envelope with this picture is written on invisible carbon. . . . All future letters bearing an odd date will be on invisible carbon. [I make a quick check—yes, the October letter is dated the

ninth.] . . . Use after you write a letter. . . . Put your letter on hard surface, carbon on top and copy paper on top of that. Write message on copy paper with firm pressure but not enough to indent the papers below. . . . Best to write invisible message on lines perpendicular to lines of plain language of letter home. . . . Use stylus directly on invisible carbon if copy paper not available. . . . A piece of invisible carbon can be used many times. . . . Begin each carboned letter with "Darling" and end with "Your adoring husband." . . . Be careful; being caught using carbon could lead to espionage charges. . . . Soak any picture with a rose in it. . . . Hang on.

This is the real thing! This message is cut to fit just Syb and me. Only she would know that I would never normally use "darling," and that complimentary close, "Your adoring husband," is about as far from anything I would say as I can imagine. Syb really gave them a couple of absolutely positive check signals.

So that wasn't mom in the picture at all. It had to be a professional model about her age and shape, probably from a San Diego agency. No question about it; the background clearly made it the Coronado surf—I could make out Point Loma. What was I thinking about? Mom flying out unexpectedly to relax and swim! Why was I so blind to the hints Syb left me? Syb's letter even said, ". . . all your mom needs is a good soak." That shows how mixed up my mind can get in this oppressive gloom of solitary confinement.

The gong! Tear up the scraps of that picture. What to do with this little decal-like thing with the message on it? I've only read it once; I'd like to go over it one more time to check the accuracy of my memorization of it. These modest peasants never check your private parts. Fold it up and stick it up your ass! Okay, all picture pieces mixed in crap in the bucket—lid back on, bucket in its place. Footsteps outside. What if this is a setup and they do come in with guys who know how to inspect, even in private parts? This might be a frame-up for those espionage charges! War crimes, War crimes, War crimes—that's all we hear on that squawk box. Maybe they're going for some *real* espionage charges—maybe they think if they get the goods on me, I'll make a deal with a Tonkin confession! That message up my ass is so soggy and wadded up, I probably couldn't make it readable again anyway. Pop open the prison pajamas and dig it out. The key is in the door! Eat it!

The guard misses the fact that I'm chewing and gulping as he comes in. "Wall!" he shouts. He does not speak English, but he knows that word will get me to assume the cell-inspection position, nose to the cement wall, hands flat against the wall as high as you can reach (for me, with a broken back and a broken left shoulder, that's not very high with my left hand). I hear things being shoved around, bucket moved, opened ("Be with me, God"), lid slammed back ("Thanks, God"). The guard grunts for me to turn around. He shouts, "Bow!" and I bow. Out he goes, and the door clicks shut.

It takes me a while to realize that a whole new world has just opened up. This was targeted right to me, which means they have confidence that I can get out the information. That close, "Hang on," sounded like we're in for a long siege. It's no consolation, but at least my predictions are tracking. And what a shot in the arm to be assured you're still on the first team! There *are* people back there, Naval Intelligence people, people like Syb, who think, and care. God Bless America. As long as I can keep that letter of Syb's, that beautiful letter on the white stationery with the odd date, I can really land some body blows on this North Vietnamese war effort, I can really fight back. All I need is a chance to write a letter home in private, and a "little bit o' luck."

I just hope those people back home realize where the real war effort is focused over here in Hanoi. You can't spend time in this city, even in this prison system, and not have your eyes opened to the power of propaganda. "We will win this war on the streets of New York." Dr. Nguyen Khac Vien, Pham Van Dong's pal and the man who made that boast to me nearly a year ago, is cranking out what may be the propaganda seeds of our destruction. But the one thing they can't stand is bad press in our big, liberal, high-circulation newspapers that they read so avidly. I've got 'em by the balls now. Once I go out with the gross violations of the Geneva Convention here in these prisons, there'll be some changes made. My government will see to it that my stuff is leaked to the *New York Times,* the *Washington Post,* and all the rest.

I can't wait to get this news through the wall to Sam and Jim. God, what a piece of information! Sam's excitement is clear from his touch. Jim comes on the wall after Sam. He's really agitated about the new Americans on my right not communicating; we're as boxed in as we were with the Asians there. Jim thinks "Soak any picture with a rose in it" is a general signal that needs to get out to all hands. These new and very cautious Americans boxing us in are also dishwashers for this building; Jim plans to recycle a note message he has left for them before: "You are ordered to get on the wall"— plus enough tap code to get them started.

Throughout the rest of Christmas week, I refine my list of verified prison names. Jim Lamar had picked up many while he was in the main Zoo communications loop. Except for those of us the Vietnamese have chosen to name publicly on propaganda broadcasts, no other prisoners have been permitted to write or receive mail; there is no reason to believe that the North Vietnamese have notified anybody of the capture of the rest, the vast majority. Those prisoners' names will be the first-priority subject for the invisible carbon, if and when I get to use it.

I go over my list time and again with Sam and Jim. No names will be included unless the person has been sighted or heard (by whisper, tap—you name it) by another American prisoner. Sam, Jim, and I conclude that together we have had contact or bona fide reports of a contact with only about forty American prisoners. That means less than a third of what I consider to be our total population—all camps—can be positively identified as here until we get more communication from the rest of this camp. I go over this "positive ID name list" every day, a habit that will stay with me throughout my imprisonment.

New Year's Day comes and goes. I think of my last New Year's experience, lying in my own crap in irons. I thank the Lord for this year's blessings. On the next day, a sunny January 2, after the gong, and after the guard has been in to make his daily cell inspection, I am conscious of a commotion outside my door. I hear the voice of a young political officer known as "J.C." (named for the Christ he appears to think he has replaced on earth). He does not work me for propaganda—Cat does not trust anybody but himself or Rabbit with that chore—but he does have authority to involve me in some regular camp routines. An attending guard opens the door and a harassed J.C. comes in with a stack of paper and envelopes! I bow; he ignores it—he is on a rush errand. Can this be the moment I've dreamed of? So soon?

J.C. speaks: "The American women's delegation, Women's

Strike for Peace, is leaving for the United States tonight. They want to carry criminals' mail back to their families. You will be permitted to write one page. Do you want to write? Take the pen and paper. Address the envelope in accordance with the instructions. Act quickly—I must pick up soon." He and the guard leave and the door is locked behind them.

Fast! Fast! Fast! Get that paper down on that bed slab and start writing. "Darling," colon. Blah blah blah blah blah. For God's sake, just keep saying noncontroversial things, platitudes, whatever. Don't say anything about God—Lamar says he heard they now make you rewrite the letter if you mention Him. In a hurry today, they'd probably just throw the whole letter out. I rush through a full page of innocent chitchat with Syb and then ". . . I am in good health, I hope the boys are fine. . . . Your adoring husband, Jim."

Now flip it over! Turn it 90 degrees to cross-thread it so they can read it better! Get that stashed sheet of blank copy paper out from under the bed board. Syb's carbon letter on top of the new letter. Then the copy paper—now press hard, but not too hard.

It's all been memorized. "Following men here in prison," then the forty-plus names . . . I'm almost out of room. Quick, get all you can in to make it clear that there is torture, irons, solo—I hear a door down the way. Got to quit. Chew up that copy paper. Swallow it. Are there any telltale indentations on my "Darling/Adoring husband" letter? On the carbon? No. Put Syb's old carbon letter back where it always stays.

I am just finishing the address on the envelope when J.C.'s guard opens the cell door. J.C. takes the letter and envelope, quickly scans the letter, sneers, and slams the door. He is really a jerk—a "fonctionnaire," as they say. Poor sweet Syb, what a sketchy, messy letter I had to rush off to you. But you'll understand. How lucky I am to have married a smart woman—a smart woman with guts. We're in this together all the way, just the two of us: "Darling" and "Your adoring husband."

Before I can even tap the good news to Sam and Jim, their door is opened. There are guards in their cell—lots of shuffling, toilet cans scraping across the floor. They're being moved! They cough as they come out. There they go—I can see the shadows of their feet walking by my door, toward the building to the right we call the Barn. What a mixed-up day. I am by turn elated and depressed.

First I strike a solid blow into North Vietnam's solar plexus, and now there go my only everyday contacts with America.

But no time to sink into depression. My door is unlocked again and in comes the guard, giving me the "roll up" signal. I'm to move. Pack everything up, especially those precious letters and the picture. The guard indicates to never mind my toilet bucket. Okay, out I go—goodbye, home. Now what? Turn left? I'm only going next door into the end cell that Sam and Jim just left. Now back next door for the bucket, back into the end cell, and the door slams and locks. Now there's rustling around in my old cell, more than one moving in. More doors slamming. A general room shuffle is in progress. More shootdowns are coming in every week and they have to reorganize the cell assignments every so often.

This old cell of Sam and Jim's looks about like they described it. In the three-bunk cell I just left, on Rabbit's orders I had to sleep by the far wall (he pretty well knew who was communicating and who wasn't), but now I swear I hear someone rustling around the bunk right by this room's wall. When things quiet down, I walk to Sam's old communication station (I can see a faint oily place where he must have tapped to me all those months). Cautiously, prayerfully, I lightly tap a "shave and a haircut." The "go ahead" signal, "tick tick," comes back. Hurray! At least I'm not out of communication. Then, cup on wall, I get serious, give my name, and ask, "Who you?" I am elated to find out there are *three* guys in there. Two have rather serious ejection injuries—Will Gideon, air-force major, shot down last August; and Will Abbott, air-force captain, shot down a month later; the third is fit, and able to communicate—Tom Browning, air-force first lieutenant, shot down last July.

Well, think I, in these two cells they now have four prisoners living where three used to live. More coming in all the time. While wishing no individual the poor luck to get shot down, I see my only hope of ever getting a cellmate is their being crowded into it. Sooner or later it's got to happen (I naïvely thought).

During the next few days, I feel great; I'm really emerging into the swim of things. There are new people to communicate with, new names to memorize. The big news is that this whole building underwent a change of tenants, and now all are communicating. The tap code seems to be a universal language now. Bill Franke, my old test-pilot flying pal of years ago, is the only other solo in this building, and he is in the other end room. He is working on trying to get communication by whisper or note with the Barn, a building quite similar in appearance to this one, located right in line with us to the southeast.

I feel great for other reasons, too. I'm getting back at the Vietnamese through the carbon. I'm going to turn off their torture machine. I heard on Hanoi Hannah that Patricia J. Griffith and her group from Women's Strike for Peace got off for home on January 2. "Deliver the goods, Patricia. Deliver the goods."

I am now told it looks like it will be a week or so until Bill Franke is able to furnish regular communication from the Barn; but meanwhile, this intrabuilding communication is quite stimulating for a person like me who has never had an opportunity for main-line communication. It turns out that my next-door neighbor Will Abbott was shot down while on air-force exchange duty with a navy fighter squadron flying off my old ship, the *Oriskany*. Boy, will the Vietnamese have trouble understanding his case! Only within the last month or two have all the interrogators seemed finally to understand that navy pilots fly off ships, and air-force pilots off fields. Now right away they're hit with a rare crossbreed.

Late last fall, Hanoi Hannah had been gloating over the tragic shipboard fire of the *Oriskany*. Although Will Abbott had been shot down a little over a month before it happened, he had been able to obtain some of the sad injury and death details from prisoners shot down after the event. One tragedy that gave me particular pause for thought was the suffocation death of the *Oriskany*'s new air-group commander in my old CAG's stateroom. He suffocated in the very bed in which I had slept during my last six months of freedom, the bed from which I arose and departed into this hell. Fickle chance. ". . . the race is not to the swift nor the battle to the strong, neither yet bread to the wise, nor yet riches to men of understanding, nor yet favour to men of skill; but time and chance happeneth to them all."[1]

January 17 was a cold and rainy day, during the morning of which I was again jolted by a surprise visit by J.C., again with pen, paper, and envelope in hand. This was too good to be true—nearly a year without mention of outgoing mail, and now twice in two weeks! This time the Reverend Muste, the good Presbyterian minister and Hanoi visitor whom Hanoi Hannah just commended for labeling his native land a "criminal" violator of international law, has offered to take war criminals' mail back to their families. Sweet guy. Since not many of us write, and they don't dare tell the reverend the truth, and he needs a load of mail to make him feel pious, I'm up again! Poetic justice! Okay, Reverend Muste, how about taking a little target list back so we can start hitting important targets that need hitting and get this Mickey Mouse war over with?

Quick, quick. It really pains me not to have more time to give Syb and the boys a more thoughtful letter, one that would more vividly describe my hollow-stomach feeling of missing and loving them. But I have to press on, fill the page with noncontroversial platitudes, and just try to get as much feeling in as I can, on the run. Now, "Adoring husband," sign it "Jim," flip it over, put the carbon on again, now another copy sheet out of stash (this is my last one till the opportunity comes to swipe another); and now, in big clear print, write at 90 degrees to the lines of my "open" letter to Sybil.

On goes the list of prisoners, starting with the names I've acquired since January 2. Then I write on, explaining that the solar plexus of this war machine is the Hanoi propaganda radio station, the pump-up motivator of the whole country. That *must* be destroyed. I give them my best estimate of where the prison camps are, and I tell them that the main railroad tracks running north and south along the coast are about a mile and a half due east of this place, the Zoo, and that we can hear the trains roll out of Hanoi heading south every night just after dark. I tell them what questions are being asked and what new weapons the Vietnamese are curious about in recent military interrogations of new shootdowns, and so on.

I'm still doing the bold print frantically and almost out of room when—bang!—the door flies open. My heart sinks. I'm caught red-handed. I'm dead.

I see the mean guard, Jake, bearing down on me and for a second I consider grabbing the copy sheet and stuffing it into my mouth, but a voice inside me says, "No—that would rip it all. Stay cool, and watch your *eyes*—get that guilt out of them!"

Jake yells, "Wall!" He has a newly enlisted guard with him and he's going to demonstrate a room inspection for the neophyte. My stack of papers is right there on the bed board, all piled up in order, new letter on the bottom, Syb's last letter next, and on top the copy

paper with boldly printed lists of prisoners' names, important Hanoi targets, and statistics about torture—all in very, very plain
sight. Even if one didn't read English, the stack would look odd,
particularly that sheet on top with the outsize letters, lines running
the long dimension of the stationery instead of the short.

I press my nose into that wall and pray like I've never prayed
before. I hear them ransacking the room. They're talking excitedly
in Vietnamese. I'm saying the Lord's Prayer silently, my head swimming. This can't be happening. This is curtains! What is that thing I
see? My God, I haven't thought of that for years! It's the face of
Christ in the big stained-glass window behind the altar of the Naval
Academy chapel. He's looking right into me just like he used to
when I was a plebe sitting before Him at mandatory chapel every
Sunday morning, praying that I could make it at Annapolis. What is
this, a religious experience? I just don't have those. What does it
mean? That I'm going down the tubes? That he is "welcoming me
aboard" in heaven?

I feel Jake slap down hard on my shoulder; he spins me around
roughly. He sticks his hand under the waist band of my pajama
pants, jerks and breaks the string, and laughs for the benefit of his
new partner as the pants fall down. While he shows his apprentice
how to frisk me, I sneak a peek over his shoulder at the paper stack.
Just as I left it! J.C. probably warned them not to foul up his rush
project of supplying the friendly reverend with lots of paper.

I bow on command, the door slams, and they lock it from the
outside. I can't believe what's happening to me. It's like a reprieve
while standing before a firing squad. I'm weak as I chew and swallow the copy paper, put the carbon back, and sit down to address
the envelope. "From: Camp of Detention for U.S. Pilots Captured
in the Democratic Republic . . ." J.C. is at the door. He haughtily
waits while I finish the envelope, casually glancing around the cell.
I can see that he suspects nothing. He takes the envelope and paper
and leaves as I bow.

I'm left exhausted, but with a secret glow in my heart. This life
does in fact have meaning. These past three weeks, since Christmas
Eve, have been a very eerie and very lucky interlude. I'll have to
mentally put all this on the back burner now and patiently wait for
another breakthrough. It's liable to be a long time. "Go, Muste! Go,
man, go! Praise the Lord and pass the target list!"

Chapter 8

Making Connections

After the holidays were over for another year, all the trimmings packed away in the attic, and Jimmy back at Mercersburg, I applied and was accepted as a full-time remedial reading teacher at Southwest Junior High School in nearby Chula Vista, to begin January 30, 1967. I was both excited and scared, as I hadn't been in a full-time classroom since 1949. I didn't think I would be neglecting my duties at home. Taylor had started nursery school, and even with my tutoring, the long days alone were getting the best of me. My spirits were dragging until I got the message about my new job; then my morale shot up to the top of the scale. I hired a peppy little white-haired grandmother to be with the boys while I was in school, and became very industrious, vacuuming, catching up with the ironing, and even cleaning out some drawers and cupboards I'd planned to do long ago. I marveled at how much I accomplished in so little time.

Brushing my hair before bed one Sunday evening early in January, I started with surprise as the phone rang. Who would call me at ten o'clock on Sunday evening? I answered quickly so the ringing wouldn't awaken the boys. A hurried, harsh voice said, "This is the *Sunday Herald Examiner* calling from Los Angeles for Mrs. James B. Stockdale. Is she there, please?"

I surprised myself by saying quietly, "No, Mrs. Stockdale is out. May I take a message?"

My caller left a number.

Feeling sure something newsworthy must have happened, I immediately called the duty officer at BuPers (Bureau of Personnel) in

Washington to see if he knew anything. He sounded sleepy, knew nothing, and asked me to call him if *I* learned anything! I then called the newsroom at the *San Diego Union* and said I'd heard that some news had come in about American servicemen captured in Vietnam and asked what it was. I was told four U.S. women had brought back twenty-one letters for the families. Two were for San Diego women, one of them me.

The next day was full of calls from the news media, but no one knew whether or not the letters had been mailed. The American women were probably some of the Women's Strike for Peace crowd who were welcomed in Hanoi by the North Vietnamese and then came home and babbled the North Vietnamese propaganda line about treatment of prisoners like so many windup robots. They seemed not to care whether we ever got the mail as long as they got credit for the North Vietnamese in the newspapers. You'd think the U.S. government might say something about these people. I thought they were giving aid and comfort to the enemy, but there was just the usual silence from our side. A fellow at the State Department said he'd call me in a day or so if he found out anything about when the letter would be mailed. I wondered whether he'd try harder if his son was a prisoner over there.

On January 11, at 7:25 in the morning, I was in the kitchen packing lunch boxes while the boys' favorite breakfast hash was browning. The doorbell shrilled and I pulled my bathrobe closer around me as I went to the door. Through the French windows, I saw a red, white, and blue mail truck standing at the curb. I felt the sharp January air through my light cotton robe as I opened the door.

"Mrs. Stockdale?"

"Yes."

"Special delivery for you."

The envelope was from one of the four women I'd read about in the news. I quickly ripped it open and found one inside addressed to me from Jim. Taking a deep breath, I slid my finger under the flap and carefully pulled the letter out. It was dated January 2, 1967—only nine days ago—but my heart was already beginning to hammer inside me when I saw that, in Jim's own handwriting, this letter began, "Darling."

I couldn't believe it. It just seemed too good to be true. Quickly

I flipped the single page over and searched for his final endearment. There it was—"Your adoring husband, Jim."

I was sitting in the wing chair reading when Sid came into the living room. "Mom, is breakfast ready? I don't want to be late."

"Sid," I said, and I know he sensed the excitement and importance of the occasion in my voice, "I have a letter from dad."

His eyes widened and fear flashed across his face.

"He's okay, Sid. It's all right. But I want to read his letter once here by myself. Will you help with breakfast? It's all ready to serve and the lunches are packed. I'll be there in a minute and read dad's letter to you. Okay?"

"Sure, mom." And he wiped the tears that being even this close to his beloved dad brought to his eyes.

I turned back to Jim's letter.

January 2, 1967

Darling,

I just received the pleasant surprise of being informed that a visiting delegation of American women has offered to carry mail back to the United States. Accordingly, I write this quickly composed note.

Less than an hour ago I read my "Christmas mail" for at least the twentieth time. On Christmas night I was given your September and October letters, including the pictures of you and the boys, and the one of Mother. What a welcome addition! This was a holiday!

I feel so up-to-date on everybody, now, having heard about your summer, and being aware of your winter activities. J.B., I'm so proud of you for being a leader at camp—for being in such tremendous physical shape—for making the varsity team at school—for developing such a good attitude toward life and faith. Your composition [I had sent excerpts in my September letter] stressing the service of yourself through God was well written, and original. I've incorporated a request to remember such a wise admonition into my daily prayers. Sid, my heart runs over for you as always. Your generosity and helpfulness to Mom will never be forgotten. . . .

Then came a somewhat strange paragraph that would have frightened me a few months ago but now only made me smile. In that paragraph, Jim was signaling me not to lose track of where Felix Greene lived in the United States. Felix Greene, occasionally in North Vietnam and in my opinion an enthusiastic apologist for their behavior, was one of the trendy ultra-liberals we had once met socially while at Stanford. Such "visitors" were used, possibly sometimes unknown to them, as stalking horses by the North Vietnamese to serve as backdrops for propagandistic photographic coverage of American prisoners. This was against the prisoners' code and many took torture in an attempt to "decline" such "invitations." Jim probably had in mind turning the tables on him in some way should he ever be forced to confront Greene.

Jim then went on to say:

> Stan, I know how much you enjoyed your Grandfather this summer, and I hope he is with you now. Taylor, I think it is wonderful that you are going to nursery school. . . .
>
> Let all know that all is the same with me. . . . Syb, know my thoughts and prayers are with you especially, in all your activities as you care for our wonderful family. Your letters were so complete, and the thoughts therein will sustain me for many hours of enjoyable memories. I try to remember a few lines from each of your poems— thank you for the thoughts.
>
> I'll think of your prayers at 5:00 A.M. [I had told him I would wake up early and say special prayers for him then], together with those of our boys, big and small, at night. I'll think of Coronado this winter, and how I hope my mother and your parents are enjoying a sunny Sunday afternoon stroll along the Hotel walk. I'll think of you, most of all, and continuously.
>
> Your adoring husband,
Jim

The minute the boys were off to school, I went to the telephone and dialed the by now familiar number of Commander Boroughs's office. When Boroughs came to the phone, he called me Syb. I was still a shade offended that he used Jim's love name for me. The first time he'd done it, I'd been shocked into silence, yet I thought it would be pretty stuffy of me to ask him to call me Sybil instead. Since Jim called me Syb in his letters, Commander Boroughs probably thought everyone called me Syb. That morning I had such good news, I decided to call him Bob. I blurted out that the women had brought back a letter from Jim that started with "Darling" and ended with "Your adoring husband." I could hear him chuckling on the other end, and we made arrangements for me to send the letter to him as quickly as possible. Before I hung up, I reminded him he'd promised to always tell me the complete truth about Jim's circumstances, no matter what. He said he'd keep his promise. And he did.

A few days later, I stood in the crowd at the San Diego airport waiting for the passengers to get off the plane from Washington. I was there to meet Bob Boroughs, who was coming because he had something he wanted to show me.

When he arrived, he was in a sober mood. He wanted to go directly to the Office of Naval Intelligence in San Diego. On the way, there was no light banter about the others in his office or much to say at all. I prattled on about my teaching and my children until we pulled into the parking lot beside the long, low, functional building. A high chain link fence completely surrounded the parking lot and the gray structure. Inside the front door were the typical navy-office pale green walls, pale gray asphalt-tile floor, and occasional tired brown leatherette settee. We went through a second door and down a long hall to a larger room where several people were working at typewriters and doing desk work. Commander Boroughs introduced me to a fellow at one of the desks, and this gentleman led us out yet another door and into a small room off a narrow hallway. In this barren room there was just one folding metal chair placed in front of a wide built-in shelf. I saw a manila folder on the shelf. The office worker who had led us here had already disappeared. Bob said he was going to leave me alone to study the folder. He said it contained the message Jim had sent back on the special paper as Bob had instructed him to do. I was to take my time and come back down the hall when I had finished.

After he left, as I sat there alone on the cold metal chair, I thought about what a cheerless place this was. Then I opened the folder. I found myself staring at the chemically developed message Jim had managed to send through in his "Darling" letter of January 2.

"Experts in Torture   Hand and Leg Irons   16 hours a day. Alive here are: . . ."

There followed a long list of names of men who were listed as missing and were now for the first time known to be alive. I recognized a few on the list. One was Bill Franke, whose wife, Jackie, was here in San Diego and had years ago shared a hospital room with me when our second babies were being born. His being alive would be a surprise to many because he'd been declared killed in action and Jackie had collected his insurance. She'd said all along she felt the navy was wrong, but they insisted he was dead, and now here was his name on Jim's list. Will Abbott was listed, too. His wife, Sharon, was here in San Diego also. He'd been on exchange duty with the navy from the air force when he was shot down.

But, oh, my God, the horror of that first line! "Experts in Torture   Hand and Leg Irons   16 hours a day." There was no turning away from it. It was what I'd suspected but hoped was not true. I felt a sour, bilelike stuff creeping up into my throat. I swallowed and wondered if I was going to throw up. I eyed the wastebasket in the corner and pulled it closer to me. I swallowed again and took a deep breath. I thought I was going to be all right. But, oh, my God. My own dearest, beloved Jim. "Hand and Leg Irons— 16 hours a day." Oh, God.

Later I commented to Bob Boroughs, "At least now our government knows for sure how our American prisoners are being treated." I couldn't help but think that before too long some action would be taken to change the horror of this truth we'd learned.

In mid-February, as if to make absolutely certain there was no mistake about his having received the code, yet another letter arrived from Jim with that precious "Darling" at the beginning and "Your adoring husband" at the end. This one had been brought back by a group of world travelers from the religious community, who may have meant well, but who, like the women's group, I saw as serving the propaganda aims of the enemy. This letter was dated January 17, 1967, and began:

> Darling,
> By another stroke of good fortune I am able to communicate with you quickly through the kindness of an American Delegation visiting Vietnam. As the American Women's Group took my note of January 2nd, so a delegation of clergymen will mail this in the States upon their return home.
> I am still in good health and receiving the same good treatment.

I paused in my reading here and took a long, deep breath. I knew only too well from the covert message in his last letter what this "same good treatment" consisted of. Yet his spirits seemed

high. Thank God I'd taken the risk of giving him a chance to communicate covertly. That had given his morale a tremendous lift.

Most of the remainder of this letter was to or about the boys
and included such thoughts as the following addressed to Stan:

> . . . How I wish I could spend time with you now—You are at an
> exciting age when you are learning so much of the world of nature.
> The other night I imagined myself explaining the stars to you.

And to Taylor:

> . . . I think of you daily at your Nursery school work, and your eve-
> ning walk home . . . Know I love you very much and dream of our
> reunion.

About Jimmy:

> I've been wondering if J.B. will go to camp again this summer. . . .
> I hope he got his license at Christmas.

And to Sid:

> I had just been thinking how much you are like your grandfather
> Sidney. . . . You're OK at any rate. I think of you at cotillion.

To his mother he said:

> I thought of you particularly on your 78th birthday. I pray for
> you daily and often include those I'm sure are in constant touch with
> you in Abingdon.

And to me at the close, he said:

> . . . I have great plans for us. I miss you and the boys terribly
> now, but as you pointed out we have many blessings for which to be
> thankful. I love you . . . and am proud of you. You're doing a *swell*
> job.
>
> Your adoring husband,
> Jim

My heart overflowed with gratitude at that final sentence.
"You're doing a *swell* job." That was his way of telling me he approved of my cooperation with the Intelligence people and of my
taking the risk of involving him. Even in the throes of torment and
torture, he was thinking of ways to make me feel better. No one
could ask for more.

❖

Two months later I once again met a plane from Washington at the airport in San Diego. Bob Boroughs had brought another expert with him this time—a Mr. Bruce Rounds, who said he worked for the State Department. The way he laughed when he said it made me think he really worked for the CIA. Bob had said on the phone they'd treat me to dinner at the Mission Valley Inn before we had our conference. I was still in the dark about what this conference concerned, but at least we were not in the ominous ONI building on the other side of town. Both Bruce and Bob seemed in very good spirits during dinner and it was a fine treat for me to be dining out with two men who seemed to enjoy my company.

Soon afterward we settled down in the conference room to the serious part of the evening. Bob Boroughs explained that he hoped the North Vietnamese might give Jim a special letter from me for our twentieth wedding anniversary, which would be coming up on June 28. The Intelligence people wanted to get another code in to him that would be easier for him to use. Even if the Viets were watching him write every word, he'd be able to use this new code. Bob said he would show me how to encode all my future letters, but suggested that my first letter be one that Bruce Rounds had written for me, which I could copy. Bob handed me the letter, and it read something like this:

> Dearest Jim,
>
> The boys and I not long ago took a trip to Disneyland for ourselves. We came upon this bright idea as a way to treat ourselves for our boy Taylor's birthday. We all spent a most enjoyable time together and I especially enjoyed eating some ice cream and chocolate eclairs. . . .

When I finished reading, I told Bob and Bruce I didn't think it sounded like me, and that it would really depress Jim if he thought I was eating sweets, since he knew I had to watch my weight. Bob lit another cigarette while one still burned in the ashtray. He said the only other way to do it would be for me to use the cryptographic code he would teach me. Writing my letters would be slow at first, but if I could have one done in time for them to take back to Washington with them on Friday, they could get it ready to be taken to Hanoi by someone they trusted.

Bob and Bruce spent the next hour or more teaching me the intricate encoding process. By the time I went home, I knew I'd have to take a couple of days off from school to have the letter ready by Friday. I went to school the next day, Monday, and set everything up for my absence Tuesday and Wednesday. I told my aides and the principal I didn't feel well. Sympathy was not hard to come by in this situation.

On Wednesday afternoon I was propped up in bed against my pillows, playing the not-feeling-well charade to the hilt. I had at last finished a long encoded letter to Jim dated May 25, 1967. It was actually April 19, so of course the Mother's Day I'd just written about had not yet taken place. My vivid imagination was serving some practical purpose at last! I had meticulously checked my letter against the code Bob and Bruce had given me Sunday night. I'd been through the whole thing twice already, and now, after a shower and in a fresh nightgown, I decided to check it one last time. It read in part:

> My Dearly Beloved Jim,
>
> At the outset of this letter I want to ask the Vietnamese authorities a very special favor which will mean so very much to us both. I hope that June Twenty Eighth, which is so very memorable in our minds and is our twentieth anniversary, the Vietnamese authorities will give you this anniversary letter. History tells me gentleness and kindness and compassion are traits which the Vietnamese treasure and consequently I am now appealing to them to give this letter to you as my gift. . . .

I went on to tell him about our day in Disneyland to celebrate Taylor's fifth birthday and about Mother's Day. I told him how thrilled I'd been to find the beautiful roses shown in the enclosed photograph waiting for me in the living room on Mother's Day morning. I told him how proud I was that Jimmy had called his grandmothers from prep school as well as me at home. I then wrote at length about memories of our life together. I felt pleased about how natural my encoded letter sounded as I came to the close. At the end I was allowed a few words that were not encoded. I used them to include a poem I'd found by an anonymous author.

> God keep you, dearest, all this lonely night;
> The winds are still,

The moon drops down behind the western hill;
God keep you, dearest, 'til the light.

We all love you with all our hearts and always will.

Your own SYB

The following evening, Bob Boroughs and Bruce Rounds stopped at the house to pick up my masterpiece.

"Let's all have a drink to celebrate," I suggested.

"Bob doesn't drink, but I'll have bourbon on the rocks," joked Bruce.

They seemed to be in a better-than-average mood, I thought as I broke the ice cubes out of the tray. How good it was to hear male voices in this house and have the fun of making drinks and exchanging nonsense remarks.

Drinks in hand, we settled into our easy chairs, and Bob's face sobered as he said, "Syb, I have something that I'm truly happy to be able to tell you at last. But this information is for you alone. I don't want you to share it with anyone else at all until it's announced later this summer."

"Later this summer?"

"Yes, that long, and you'll see why in a minute."

"You look sober as a judge, for God's sake. What now?"

"I know you were disappointed for Jim's sake last summer when he wasn't selected early for captain along with some of his classmates. The truth of the matter is that he was early selected then but the navy kept it quiet."

"He was early selected?" I interrupted. "Are you sure?"

"Yes, I'm sure, and I think you rate knowing it now. Everybody in the puzzle palace where I work doesn't agree with me, but I convinced the right people so I can tell you now. You can't tell anyone else though."

"Nobody else knows?"

"Practically nobody, no. The powers that be are afraid the North Vietnamese might think he was promoted early for his activities in prison. In my opinion, he *should* be for that alone, of course, but we don't want to give the slant-eyes any reason to watch him any more closely than they already do."

"How will the navy ever announce he's been promoted then?"

"They'll publish his name on the promotion list that comes out this summer with all the rest of his classmates on it. That will give him the protection he needs."

"Is there any way we can tell him about it? It makes me feel so much better about everything to know that when it's important, the navy really is careful. I can put up with a lot if I know they're really being careful when his life is at stake. We've got to figure out a way to let him know."

"I knew you'd be after me about that," Bob said, draining his glass. "I've already decided how we'll do it, but you'll have to trust me to do it my way."

"Why not put it into your secret message in my next letter? Just make it part of the encoded information."

Bruce raised his eyebrows at Bob quizzically. Bob smiled and studied the melting ice in his glass. "Trust me, Syb. Just trust me on this one."

After they'd gone with my May letter in hand, I took a glass of sherry up to my bedside table. This was my celebration for my dearest love's so well deserved early promotion. Ordinarily, I was puritanically careful about drinking alone, but these few moments tonight were special. Here's to you, Jim. It's almost noon tomorrow where you are. God keep you, dearest.

A few weeks later, on a Monday evening in May, I was curled up on the sofa working on lesson plans for the next few weeks. The front door was open and the boys' midstreet baseball-game sounds made me smile. Only in Coronado can a full-blown game of baseball go on in the middle of the road without churlishness on the part of auto drivers. If I had to be in this hellish situation, thank God I was here, 1 thought as I studied my plan book. And thank God I had my teaching to keep me exhausted enough to sleep at night.

I scrambled to my feet as the phone shrilled. It was Jimmy calling from Mercersburg, and his tone told me he was greatly upset. He said the school was an artificial atmosphere and he was fed up with it; he planned to leave a note and run away the following evening. He didn't want to add to my troubles, so he was telling me, but I must promise him I would not call the headmaster. His life there was just too superficial, so he was going to get on a bus and find out what real life was like. He had about $50 and would get odd jobs as he went along.

I was horrified, but I tried to sound calm. I warned him about getting robbed and getting rolled. I wanted to keep him on the wire until I could think a little more clearly. Finally I suggested that if he really felt leaving was the right thing to do, he should shake hands with the headmaster, tell him the school wasn't right for him, and walk out the front door; there was no need to sneak away. To my immense relief, he agreed this was a good idea and promised me he'd call again the next day before he departed.

As soon as I hung up, I called Doyen. I implored her to ask Budd for any advice he thought would be helpful. She reassured me, and even made me smile by reminding me of our all-night search for her oldest son during the summer of 1963 while Jim and Budd were at sea. She had been frantic then as I was now, but it had all ended okay.

The next day when I arrived home from school, Doyen was waiting for me. She said Jimmy had called their house when he couldn't reach me at home. Budd had talked to him and told him in no uncertain terms he was to stay there at school and finish the year, that that was what real life was all about, and that that was what his father would want him to do. Jimmy had said he'd think about it and would call me that night.

That evening when Jimmy called, he said he'd decided to finish the year at Mercersburg. He said it didn't have anything to do with what Captain Salsig had said to him—he had his own reasons for changing his mind. I told him I thought he'd made a wise decision and changed the subject to plans for the summer. What a blessed relief to know he'd stay there safe and sound at school. And what a blessed piece of good fortune to have friends like Budd and Doyen.

In June, as I traveled east once again with the boys for the summer, I thought back over some of the events since my trip last summer. It had been a busy year. The biggest event was getting the first code in to Jim successfully. That was really a stroke of luck. I wondered how long it had taken Jim to figure out the signal I'd given him in the text of my October 9 letter. Knowing that his mother couldn't stand surprise visits of any kind, was terrified of flying, never rode in taxicabs, and never went swimming because of her fear of the water, I'd reasoned that if I included a paragraph about her doing all of those things, Jim would suspect something was up. And when he saw the picture of a strange woman standing in the surf, someone who resembled his mother but wasn't, he would *know* something was up. I could still remember my signal paragraph verbatim.

> I surely do hope you have received the pictures I have sent in my last two letters. And speaking of pictures, I am enclosing one of your mother in this letter as we had a most unexpected surprise last week. Your mother arrived in a taxi. She said she had decided on an impulse to fly out and stay with us a few days and treat herself to a good long soak in the water. I took the enclosed picture while she was here.

However long it may have taken him to figure it out, he had gotten all the information perfectly. He knew how to use the special paper my letter was written on as a carbon, and he knew that any future letter with an odd date would be on the same special paper. He knew to soak any future pictures with roses in them. I smiled as I thought about those Mother's Day roses I'd sent a picture of in my May letter. I'd had Sid take a picture of me arranging them after buying "seconds" at the florist to serve the purpose. Bob Boroughs didn't think the carrier was going to get into Hanoi at all with my anniversary letter; it would be sheer luck if we got two codes to Jim in one year. We could always use the picture-with-roses method now, though. Thank heaven I'd taken that risk when I'd had the chance. The upset with Jimmy had come out well, too. He was going to summer school to make up for failing French and chemistry. In my letter, I'd told Jim that Jimmy was "below the minimum standard in a couple of courses." I was pleased with my gentle way of phrasing it. My poor dear Jim certainly didn't need any additional bad news in his life.

A couple of weeks after settling into the Connecticut cottage, I went to Washington again to keep an appointment with Ambassador Harriman. I wanted him to know that the wives in the San Diego area would like to have someone from the State Department come and tell us what steps our government was taking to ensure humane treatment for our men. I'd learned a lot about the provisions of the Geneva Convention Relative to the Treatment of Prisoners of War. In view of Jim's covert message about his treatment, along with other signs of Geneva Convention violations, it seemed to me our government should be doing something besides keeping quiet. Also, I'd heard from some Virginia Beach wives that two representatives they'd talked with from the U.S. State Department believed our American prisoners were being held in private homes, living an easy life as teachers (of English, I presumed) in Vietnam! That infuriated me, and I decided to let Ambassador Harriman know how I felt about it if I possibly could. One State Department representative also predicted the war would last at least four more years. I intended to ask Ambassador Harriman what information that prediction was based on. When I told my mother what I planned to say to Ambassador Harriman, she said, "You're getting feisty as you get older, aren't you?"

When I saw Ambassador Harriman in Washington, he was as gracious as before and always the proper gentleman, but again not very informative. He did say it was "stupid" of the fellow to predict the length of the war, and he reassured me that much was being done to ensure humane treatment for our men, but it was of a secret nature and he was not at liberty to give any details. Our conversation was almost identical to that of a year ago. A whole year and nothing new to say. How could the most powerful military might in the world be unable to overwhelm that small, backward strip of territory? When I sharpened the tone of my questions with Ambassador Harriman, he didn't appear to pay any attention. It was almost as if he were giving a monologue. I left feeling frustrated and depressed.

Following my appointment with Ambassador Harriman, I had one with Senator Dirksen. Jim's mother had implored me to see him as her Illinois senator and the one man she trusted in Washington. I'd had the appointment for weeks, but still I waited almost an hour. I was tired and upset after hearing Ambassador Harriman mouth meaningless phrases. While I waited, a tall, slick, well-tanned man in his late thirties half-tiptoed into the reception room. With a look that canceled me out completely, he sidled his tight-trousered behind onto the sleek-looking secretary's huge desk. He

Sybil and the four boys at Sunset Beach, August 1964, just after the Tonkin Gulf raids.

Jim's squadron pilots aboard the *Ticonderoga* after the Tonkin Gulf raids. Left to right, top row: Gerry Mitchell, Jere Francis, Dick Hastings, Bud Collicott, Lee Bausch, Tom Klein, Bill Moore. Bottom row: Buff Oistad, Bill Poppert, Russ Baker, Jim Stockdale, Tim Hubbard, Gene Corbett, Roy Miller.

Jim's Crusader about to hook an arresting wire.

Jim's last visit with his dad, in Illinois, March 22, 1964, just before he left on "Tonkin Gulf" cruise.

Jim at home at 547 A Avenue, Coronado, California, the day before his deployment, April 1965.

A routine pre-flight briefing aboard USS *Oriskany*, September 1965.

Jim emerging from his Skyhawk on the flight deck of the USS *Oriskany*, one week before he was shot down.

Checking notes just prior to the final flight, September 9, 1965.

turned his head sideways as he whispered in her ear. I saw the long sideburns and neck hairs curling near his collar. She simpered and glanced over at me as they played their flirtatious games in front of me. They seemed typical to me of many I saw in the State Department and congressional offices. Why did I have to sit here and struggle to control my emotions while these two wriggled and smirked in front of me?

When I was finally ushered into Senator Dirksen's presence, I asked him to please tell me the truth about whether or not the military commanders were being given a free hand to prosecute the war in a way that would enable us to win as quickly as possible. I expressed my fears that Secretary McNamara was calling the shots at the Pentagon and, with his lack of military expertise, was preventing the military from fighting the war in the way that would bring the swiftest victory. He absolutely assured me in his most solemn and resonant voice that nothing could be more incorrect and that Admiral Sharp and all the other military leaders were completely free to conduct the war as they chose. Three times I went over this ground with him, and three times his answer was the same. Why would he lie to me? I wondered. We were here alone, in a back corner of his office. Would an honorable person lie to someone in my situation about something this important? And yet it made no sense whatsoever for our country to be struggling to overcome that tiny country.

Shortly after I returned to the beach from that Washington visit, Bob Boroughs telephoned with more depressing and frightening news: The Bureau of Personnel had so screwed things up that the news about Jim's early promotion to captain had been printed in the July 8 issue of the *Journal of the Armed Forces*, where, he felt sure, the North Vietnamese would see it. That news made me feel absolutely sick.

On August 1, a new chief of naval operations, Admiral Thomas Moorer, took over. I wanted to see him in person to make sure he knew about Jim's covert communications. I didn't feel I could trust anybody but Bob Boroughs in Washington. I asked Bob to try to get an appointment with the new CNO for me, but he reported I couldn't see him while he was so new in his job. I was angry about not getting a fifteen-minute appointment before September; I had to see him before I went back to California. While I was fuming with frustration, I saw this newspaper article in Drew Pearson's syndicated column in the *New Haven Register* on the 8th of August:

DISTURBING REPORTS ON U.S. PRISONERS
by Jack Anderson

Washington—Disturbing whispers have leaked out that the Johnson administration has not done all it could to arrange better treatment for American prisoners in enemy hands.

One high official complained to this column that prisoner problems have been given a low priority at the State Department. He quoted Secretary of State Rusk as telling aides that the captured Americans are not prisoners but hostages, that the communists would demand a quid pro quo for treating them decently and that he has no intention of granting any concessions.

In the Pentagon, the brass-bound generals are so embarrassed over the unmilitary-like behavior of a few captives that they have slammed the lid shut on all prisoner information. The prisoners' families have been warned not to talk to reporters lest the slightest publicity be used against the captives to increase their torment.

Actually the North Vietnamese are sensitive to world opinion and probably take better care of the publicized prisoners. The great Pentagon hush-up seems to be aimed less to protect the prisoners than to protect the authorities from criticism. . . .

Before I went to bed that very night, I had my telegrams to Secretary Rusk and Admiral Moorer on the wires. Both telegrams said essentially the same thing:

My husband, Cdr. James B. Stockdale, has been a prisoner of war in North Vietnam for two years. I am certain all the families of war prisoners were shocked by the Drew Pearson article referring to the great Pentagon hush-up today. Do you feel that this report is basically true or false? We earnestly beseech you to support these men who make such a staggering sacrifice for their government and to relay our concern to all members of the Defense Department.

Respectfully yours,
Mrs. James B. Stockdale

Two days later, during our late breakfast, a Branford taxi driver arrived at the beach and handed me a Western Union envelope.

"Do telegrams arrive by taxi in Branford?" I asked, finding this somewhat mystifying.

"Sometimes they do," the rotund driver replied. "Mostly when they want them to get there right away, I think."

"Who's it from, mom?" Sid asked soberly.

"It's two pages," I said, my voice showing my surprise at its length. "It's signed, 'Sincerely T. H. Moorer, Admiral, US Navy, Chief of Naval Operations.' I'll tell you guys about it after I've had a chance to digest it. It's business stuff—there's nothing new about dad."

Sitting alone on the front porch in the old cane rocker, I read:

August 10, 1967

1.   In reply to your telegram of yesterday please let me assure you that every effort is being put forth by responsible officials of your government to secure the release of prisoners as well as bring the Vietnam conflict to an early successful conclusion.

Let me further assure you that your government has made strenuous attempts to assure humane treatment for American prisoners of war and to obtain more information for their families. I know of no basis whatsoever for Mr. Anderson's accusation of neglect of responsibilities in these matters.

2.   We in the Navy clearly understand the shocked concern which must have been generated in the families of our Navy prisoners in North Vietnam upon reading Mr. Anderson's article. However, I am sure you and the others understand that so long as we enjoy the valuable privilege of freedom of the press, the publication of such material is bound to occur.

3.   It is my understanding that you plan to visit in Washington next week, and that you have expressed an interest in talking with me. I cordially invite you to lunch in my office at 12:30 on Wednesday, 16 August 1967.

Sincerely, T. H. Moorer,
Admiral, US Navy,
Chief of Naval Operations

Lunch in his office! I'd never heard of anyone having lunch in the CNO's office. That sounded exciting. I'd have a chance to meet him before I went west after all. I quickly sent off my acceptance and began making plans for the trip. I was also going to write down exactly what I wanted to say to Admiral Semmes, with whom Bob Boroughs had gotten an appointment for me. I was going to tell Admiral Semmes what a rotten job I thought he was doing on Jim's behalf.

On the day of my big visit and lunch, I was shocked when Bob Boroughs told me that Admiral Semmes and Mrs. Moorer would have lunch with Admiral Moorer and me—that time together would be my official appointment with Admiral Semmes. I hadn't planned to have his new boss hear the harsh criticism of him I'd written, but now it was that or nothing and I decided Admiral Moorer would just have to know right now how I felt about Admiral Semmes.

After meeting Admiral Moorer for the first time and saying hello to Admiral Semmes, I took a deep breath and said, "Admiral Moorer, in these few minutes we have together before Mrs. Moorer joins us, I'd like your permission to read what I have to say today. What I have is four pages long and takes seven minutes to read. Will that be all right with you?"

Looking sober, he nodded his permission and I read my treatise. I told him of my dismay at the U.S. government letting the North Vietnamese fill our media with propaganda and never responding. The enemy's flagrant violations of the Geneva Convention were totally ignored; packages sent to our men at Christmas were refused; our participation in the savings-deposit program was prohibited; and one wife was told she was lucky to be getting her husband's pay, because he wasn't doing what he'd been sent to do. I asked if there was any one officer who was in charge of prisoner affairs to the extent that his career would be damaged if he made life-threatening mistakes. I explained in detail that Jim's loyalty and risking his life in covert communication had been rewarded by sloppy bungling at BuPers after I had been assured his welfare was being carefully protected. I said Jim might sacrifice his life as a result of the gross incompetence at BuPers and that I wanted an explanation in writing to give to Jim if he did come home someday. I explained that up to now I'd had faith that my government would do the right thing in the end, but that now my faith wavered, and one had only to examine the record of events to know why.

The total silence that followed my reading was interrupted by Mrs. Moorer joining us for lunch. We all breathed a sigh of relief.

We walked over to the lunch table set up in the middle of Admiral Moorer's office. There were place cards on the table even though there were only four of us present. I was on Admiral Moorer's right, Admiral Semmes on my right, and Mrs. Moorer across from me. The napkins were so stiff with starch, I had trouble unfolding mine. I looked the table over carefully, wanting to remember every detail. A steward passed a tray of celery, radishes, and carrot sticks, serving me first. I wished Mrs. Moorer had gone first so I could do everything she did and not make mistakes, but so far so good—the celery and carrots went on the bread plate.

Admiral Moorer began to talk about the children, and I relaxed some as we discussed their summer activities in Connecticut. The steward then placed in front of me a lovely-looking cold plate with roast beef, turkey, ham, and potato salad. We waited for the others' plates to arrive, but instead the steward returned and removed my plate. I thought this was a little strange, but we continued talking about the boys. I saw Mrs. Moorer frown slightly when she looked over my shoulder and saw the steward arrive with my cold plate again. Admiral Moorer commented, "Well, I don't know what that was all about."

I replied, "It looks delicious, Admiral Moorer, and I know I'm going to enjoy it."

Then, to my complete amazement, Admiral Semmes, Mrs. Moorer, and Admiral Moorer were served plates with hot sirloin tips and gravy, mashed potatoes, and creamed peas. Mrs. Moorer's eyes darted disapproving glances at Admiral Moorer, but no one mentioned this unusual arrangement. Well, I thought, maybe when you're in the big time, you don't all get the same thing.

As we began to eat, Admiral Semmes asked me if I'd consider coming to work for him as a civilian in BuPers. He'd match my teaching salary and move me to Washington. He said when other wives in my circumstances came to see him, I could tell them what the navy was doing to help them. I felt he was trying to buy me off, and I was genuinely enraged that he still didn't understand the depth of my disillusionment and dismay about the way his department had mishandled Jim's welfare. What did it take to make this smooth-talking senior officer understand? Bluntly, I told him that if I told others like myself about his performance, they'd be more inclined to jump out the window than leave feeling better. For the first time, I just said exactly what I believed, without any reservation.

As this heated conversation took place, Mrs. Moorer tried to calm the situation by asking how the other wives in San Diego were getting along. I was grateful to her for changing the subject.

For dessert, I was served a dish of lime sherbet. All eyes focused on it, wondering whether or not it would stay put. Then Admiral Semmes was promptly served Boston cream pie, Admiral and Mrs. Moorer were given vanilla ice cream, and we all proceeded as if this were perfectly normal. The whole arrangement seemed strange to me—but for all I knew, maybe it was supposed to be all mixed up. Mrs. Moorer's eyes made me doubt that, however. I guessed Admiral Moorer would hear more about this luncheon that evening.

At the end of the summer, while flying west, I once again spent some of my time reviewing events. At that luncheon with Admiral Moorer and Admiral Semmes, I realized I was losing some of my inhibitions and felt freer to state what was on my mind. I knew I had to be careful not to become shrill or too emotional or I'd be written off as an unbalanced female. But I also knew that for the first time I had focused the attention of Jim's leaders more clearly on his dire situation. I knew, too, that there was just so much I could do. I could only criticize my own government privately; there was nothing the enemy would like better than to have me criticize the U.S. government publicly. There was no doubt I was caught in the middle, and it was frustrating and disheartening.

Back in Coronado once more, I sat at the antique desk at the end of our living room and made the final copy of my September letter to Jim. It was all encoded but sounded natural as I reread parts of it:

> . . . . when I wrote my last letter I said our last word arrived from you in January. This regrettably is still true but maybe soon you will be allowed to write again. . . . Sid, Stan, Taylor and I left Connecticut the first day of September and flew to Los Angeles together. Sid left us there and went up to Collins for a week and the two little boys and I came on home. This dearly beloved house looked very good to me and I feel this is my true home now. My school meetings started the

following Tuesday, so it didn't leave much time for unpacking and settling in but we did it as quickly as possible. Jimmy stayed on in Connecticut with the Grandparents two days and then visited friends in Wayne, Pennsylvania, before going back to Mercersburg for early football practice. He really looked forward to getting back to school and had a good summer. He did a wonderful job at summer school and became a close friend of his roommate from Wayne. They have invited him for Thanksgiving, which pleases him. He calls every Sunday and seems so well adjusted and relaxed this year. I am so grateful he has seemed to find himself so well. He is very interested in applying at Ohio Wesleyan and we have some small West Coast colleges in mind also.

That was the good part, I thought. There was so much I wished I could tell him, both good and bad. I also wondered what he would think if he could read just parts of my mail for the last month or so—for example, the letter Jim's mother had sent to me, which she received from Senator Dirksen.

July 27, 1967

My dear Mrs. Stockdale,

     Your daughter-in-law came to see me concerning Commander Stockdale's imprisonment by the North Vietnamese and whether anything can be done to bring about his release. . . .

We hadn't talked about my wanting to bring about his release. That was a flat-out lie about our conversation. It made me sound as though I wanted to violate all the rules of honorable conduct for military prisoners. The only honorable way Jim's release could come about before an end to the war would be if all the prisoners of war were released to a neutral country like Sweden and held there instead of in Hanoi. Senator Dirksen's letter made me sound cheap and shallow. Why hadn't he written Jim's mom about what we really discussed? She scolded me on the telephone about not having talked with him about the conduct of the war. I wasn't sure she really believed this letter from him was just a bunch of junk, a figment of someone's imagination.

She also told me on the telephone that she was going to the hospital for tests and observation the first of October. That wasn't like her unless something serious was wrong. Guilt pangs shot through me. She wanted to come and live in California with me this coming winter. I knew it wouldn't work—our personalities were both too strong for us to live together in the same house. I wished she'd liked the retirement community I'd found in nearby Lemon Grove. That would have been just the right amount of closeness for us both; she could have visited us a couple of days a week. How would I feel if something happened to her now? But I knew Jim would understand we couldn't live together. I thought so, anyway.

I wondered what he'd think if I could tell him about the information sheet the State Department called a "white paper," where they described what was happening to him like this: "We reluctantly come to the conclusion that some of the US airmen were being subjected to emotional and physical duress, which is a flagrant violation of the Geneva Convention." I supposed it would be too ungentlemanly to use the words *torture*, or *leg irons*, or *handcuffs*. Besides, we wouldn't want to upset the American people. I was really getting kind of cynical and sarcastic. I'd have to be careful. Those were traits best not displayed if you wanted people to take you seriously.

I had sent the State Department's "white paper" to a number of news people with the following cover letter:

> Gentlemen,
>
> My husband has been a prisoner of war in North Vietnam for two years. I *beg, beseech,* and *implore* you to print the enclosed information in your publication so that the world may know the *truth* about the treatment of our prisoners.
>
> Yours sincerely,
> Mrs. James B. Stockdale

It seemed so mild and controlled compared to the way I felt. But, my God, there was that article from the *San Diego Union* dated September 5, 1967, which was enough to scare anybody.

> Washington (UPI)—North Vietnam is keeping alive the possibility it may put US prisoners on trial for war crimes and has sought to involve black power militant Stokely Carmichael in the proceedings, diplomatic sources reported yesterday. . . .

Ambassador Harriman kept insisting that the war-crimes trials were not going to happen, but how could I tell what to believe or who was telling the truth?

When I arrived back in Coronado, I found a letter waiting for me from the carrier of my anniversary letter. He hadn't gotten into

Hanoi and had returned the letter to me; I sent it later in the regular mail, explaining the delay to the North Vietnamese. I'd written to the attorney general asking how the world travelers who were admitted to Hanoi could keep their passports and go in and out of North Vietnam like commuters even though that country was on our State Department forbidden list. The simple answer I received was that their passports weren't stamped in North Vietnam and so there was no legal evidence that they'd been there, even when they broadcast the details of their trips on the front pages of the newspapers. It was just one more disheartening bit of evidence that the United States didn't want to make things too difficult for North Vietnam.

By October there was still no mail from Jim. Nothing since January. I couldn't help but wonder if he had been killed or died. Bob Boroughs telephoned every few days, and one of the things he said was that we wives in San Diego who had been meeting informally each month must formalize our organization, elect officers, and adopt bylaws. I felt overwhelmed at the idea of taking on another project, but he was so insistent that I knew I'd have to convince the other wives we had to organize more formally.

Jim's mother was very sick in the hospital and I took a week off from school to visit her in Illinois and talk to her doctor. Just before I left, I got three other San Diego POW/MIA wives—Karen Butler, Jenny Connell, and Sandy Dennison—to promise me that they and our group would elect officers while I was away. When I returned, Sandy Dennison called me and said they had elected officers and given our group a name—the League of Wives of American Vietnam Prisoners of War. At the last meeting, I had suggested we use the term *league* as the dictionary definition seemed appropriate. Sandy was the secretary and she'd ordered stationery printed for us and had rented a post-office box.

I felt particularly close to Karen, Jenny, and Sandy. They were much younger than I, but we all seemed to share a newfound spirit of assertiveness. I felt that my willingness to take the lead in whatever we did gave them the courage to follow. Debbie Burns was another like the rest of us. She had recently moved to San Diego from Lemoore, as had Karen and Jenny at an earlier date. We didn't differentiate between POW wives and MIA wives—we felt it was more positive to assume all our men were alive. Our meetings weren't sad, sober-faced affairs, but were frank and openhearted exchanges about our feelings and information. We always drank wine and laughed. We knew some of our behavior might seem ghoulish to others, but among ourselves we felt free to do and say whatever we felt. Being together gave us all strength.

One of the first official decisions of our League was to direct our secretary to write to the Departments of State and Defense and request that some official come to San Diego and give us whatever information was available. We had been writing these same requests as individuals for months. Bob Boroughs felt we'd be more effective as an organized group, and we could only hope he was right. We were encouraged shortly thereafter to learn that Congress had amended the savings-deposit program and we were now allowed to invest whatever we could save from our husbands' salaries at the 10-percent rate. Our organization had written about that injustice as well. More important than the money involved was the satisfaction of feeling we had achieved some small measure of acknowledgment for our loved ones.

I had still had no mail from Jim since the previous January, but in my October letter I brought him up to date on family activities. It took me only three to four hours to encode my letters now. I told him about Sid's love for flag football and drum lessons. I raved about his helpfulness with his younger brothers. He was thoroughly enjoying junior high school. Stanford was in the second grade and loved to read a story to us all every evening. He also thrived on games of living-room football organized by Sid and played with a pillow. Taylor joined in the games but was most proud of being able to ride a two-wheel bike. He was in kindergarten and told me each night how much he loved his daddy. I kept pictures of Jim all over the walls in the boys' bedrooms. At the end of my letter, I told Jim his mother was desperately ill and not expected to live. I told him I'd hired special nurses for her and that she was sleeping comfortably most of the time.

Jim's mother died of leukemia on October 29, two days after I mailed that letter. I was executrix of her estate and was now the manager of the 222-acre farm in Illinois. I told Jim about his mother's death in every letter I sent. I felt he would want to know the truth and that it would be cruel for him to return someday and learn she'd been dead for some time. I wondered if the sad news would make Jim's captors more inclined to give him a letter. I was becoming more and more frightened at not having heard from him in so long. Maybe he had been caught sending covert messages. Maybe my encoded messages had somehow been apprehended. I faced another holiday season in a worried frame of mind. At best, the holidays were a harrowing time. My prayers became more frequent and more fervent.

Along with my Christmas cards that December, I opened a letter from the Bureau of Personnel of the U.S. Navy addressed to Capt. James B. Stockdale, 547 "A" Avenue, Coronado, California.

> Dear Captain,
>
> You have just been selected for deep draft command. Please accept my most sincere congratulations on this achievement. We will be attempting to place you in your command at an early date. However, priority will be assigned to those officers in YG-44 and YG-45 who have not as yet had their deep draft command. In the event you are just commencing a tour or have been there a relatively short time, we will not order you to command at sea, short of an emergency, until you have completed a minimum tour. . . .

How could they possibly be so incredibly screwed up? Wasn't there any system of coordination? What could I do to impress upon them that Jim was in prison in Vietnam, being tortured? My Christmas spirits didn't improve when, a few days later, the little brown packet containing medicines and a few candies that the navy had advised me to try to send to Jim for Christmas was returned. Only one tiny glimmer of optimism came my way during this sentimental season. Admiral Moorer invited the San Diego missing and prisoner wives to have lunch with him at the Officers' Club while he was visiting the naval air station at Miramar, nearby. After lunch, during his talk, he emphasized that fourteen- and fifteen-year-old boys were now among the North Vietnamese casualties found on the battlefield. Historically, when an army committed those so young to battle, it was an indication that their resources were almost depleted and victory for the opponent should not be far away. As 1967 gave way to 1968, I grasped at any small shred of hope I could find.

In January 1968, I watched the capture of the USS *Pueblo* and its crew on my television screen. Publicity about the welfare of these men ran rampant through all the media. The tremendous amount of attention the incident received in the press doubled my frustration and agony over our guidelines for silence about our men in North Vietnam. The wife of the *Pueblo*'s captain was extremely critical of the U.S. government in the press. There was a bitter feeling of resentment about her among the POW wives in San Diego. We felt her public criticism of her own government demeaned her service and her country in the eyes of the world. It was also terribly frustrating to have all the hullabaloo about the *Pueblo* prisoners going on in the press while nothing was being said by our government about our men in North Vietnam.

Our feelings about the wife of the *Pueblo*'s CO were so strong that when Congressman Mendel Rivers came to San Diego to talk to us POW wives in February, we refused to sit at the same table with the wife of the *Pueblo*'s CO. Mendel Rivers was known for his frankness, and in his talk to us he lived up to his reputation. He made no bones about the fact that the North Vietnamese were barbarians; that our men were living in hell itself; and that if he had his way about it, he'd bomb North Vietnam into the Stone Age. I was shocked as well as refreshed to hear him shout all these things at the top of his lungs. Almost everyone else patted us on the head, told us to pray and try not to worry, but here was one Washington official who was not afraid to tell the truth about his perceptions. No reporters were allowed to attend this meeting, however, so his message was not publicized, and we were still advised it was in our husbands' best interest to keep quiet about their circumstances.

By March, it had been fourteen months since I'd had any mail from Jim. Neither Bob Boroughs nor anyone else had any explanation for this long and agonizing silence. I poured out all my worst fears to God as I drove back and forth to school, and I communicated with formal prayers both morning and evening. I just had to trust that Jim was okay. I didn't have any other choice.

Then, on a Thursday morning, March 14, at about eleven o'clock, I heard a familiar voice at the back of my classroom at school say "Mom." I looked up and saw Jimmy, who was home for spring vacation, waving a letter in his hand and silently mouthing the words "From dad." My students didn't know anything about my personal life, so as calmly and quickly as I could, I turned my class over to one of my aides and rushed out into the hall where Jimmy was waiting. Carrying the unopened letter, we raced down the hall and found an empty classroom where we could sit and read it. It was postmarked "2–1" from Hanoi. That meant it had been sent on January 2, as the North Vietnamese use the reverse of our month and day on their postmarks. When I opened the letter, I immediately noticed that Jim's handwriting was completely different from any he'd used before. This letter was all in script and was dated December 19, 1967—three months ago.

> My dearest Syb, J.B., Sid, Stan, and Taylor, Syb, the letter I've had from you was written some months ago today. In it was the wonderful picture taken in our living room on the Sunday before Christmas. That picture has been in my hand every day during my prayers, since I got it, and I trust you are all in the same robust health this Christmas. I pray that the grandparents are well, your mother particularly, in her 80th year, and I hope my mother is in her own home in town. I wrote you some months ago and I want to assure you that my health is still good, thanks to good food here.
>
> J.B., I figure you to be a senior at Mercersburg and the thought makes me very happy. I hope that you are able to study with ease and relax, and I pray your college plans are going well. Mother and God are your best guides in all. Sid, I know you are Mother's right hand man; play tennis with her and use my good racket. Stan, I know you're still the leader in your class and a wonderful boy, thanks much to Grandfather Bailey's guidance during the summers. Taylor, Mom tells me you're her littlest angel and that's the way I often think of you, even though I know you're a big kindergarten boy riding a two wheel bike. Thanks to all of you for your prayers. I love each of you four guys with all my heart.
>
> Syb, I hope you get to Palo Alto to be with our friends Bill and Kathy. Tell Kathy I can hear those nuns praying for me. Please stop in and see the Greenes.
>
> Syb, I visualize you to be teaching, hopefully at Coronado High. I know how busy and stimulated you must be with job and home. God will guide you in Jim's college placement. Do not let tuition limit you—just pick the right college. If events have made the Academy available, it's completely up to Jim.
>
> Syb, in my thoughts each day, I go by your time (my days are mentally spent with you the previous evening). I imagine your events

hour by hour, particularly on birthdays and such. Needless to say, I miss you constantly, and especially on such days as our 20th anniversary last June. I love you completely.

I often think of Red and wanted to include a message, but it is impossible; tell him perhaps next time.

My thoughts are with you all this Christmas, and my prayers and love constant during 1968, and always.   Jim

His reference to Red was his way of telling the Intelligence community he couldn't send a covert message in this letter; Jim knew Red Rayborn was head of the CIA at one time. The letter he referred to with the picture had been written a year to the very day before he wrote this one, long before his mother died. He hadn't been given my anniversary letter, he had never received the new code, and he didn't know his mother was dead. His completely unfamiliar handwriting appeared to me to have been forced out through pain and anguish.

I was a mass of mixed emotions, shedding tears of relief that he was still alive, and tears of pain for the dreadful torture he was surely enduring. I couldn't help but be impressed by the discrepancy between what I knew was happening to him and the calm, clear tone of his letters. I knew he was undergoing gross, barbaric torture, and yet his letters had a serene, poetic feeling about them. Maybe the good Lord had answered my most frequent prayer—to give Jim the strength he needed to withstand his ordeal. I felt that Jim's faith was sustaining him. He'd never been as demonstrative about his faith as I was. I had been tremendously relieved when in an earlier letter he had said God was his roommate. His faith must be far stronger than mine for him to be able to write as he did while he existed in a living hell.

A few days later, I saw another direct result of our League organization: Ambassador Harriman's assistant telephoned me, saying he would be out to talk to our group in early April. Bob Boroughs had us request that a reporter be present during this meeting, but the State Department denied permission; no one but primary next of kin (wives, or mothers and fathers if the man was unmarried) with valid identification cards would be admitted. Anxious to hear what this State Department representative was going to say to us, Bob asked me to wear a hidden tape recorder to the meeting and return the tape to him. I had no idea whether this was legal or proper, but agreed to wear the machine, which arrived air express.

I was both excited and frightened as I got dressed and ready for this meeting. I pinned a tiny microphone to each side of my bra and snapped two diminutive reels of tape into the machine, a black metal box about the size of a paperback book. Running the cord down my side from my bra to my girdle, I tucked the cold metal box into the top of my girdle and ran another cord out the bottom to just above my knee, where there was a small on/off switch. To conceal my lumpy midriff, I wore a loose dress with a Mexican quechquemitl.

Afterward, however, I couldn't imagine why Bob Boroughs had been so anxious to hear what this man said to us. He simply reiterated the few scraps of information we already knew about our prisoners and assured us our government was doing everything possible to see they were humanely treated. Our government still had no reason to believe that keeping quiet was not the best way to proceed and still hoped our men were being treated humanely. I marveled at the detached, casual attitude of this man. Didn't he know Jim was being tortured and kept in hand and leg irons?

That night I fell asleep after sobbing into my pillow. I felt so incredibly helpless. Somehow, some way, I had to find something I could do to help Jim.

Chapter 9

Strength in Unity

January 26th, 1967. I was still alone, but I really felt like I was up on my feet fighting. I had sent two coded letters off to Washington that month, and gotten into the Zoo's main communication link for the first time. Rabbit had called me to an "attitude check" quiz a couple of days earlier and betrayed his doubt about the U.S. Navy actually having a political-policy division! That had to mean that the bogus letter was on hold. Things were certainly looking up on the propaganda front; I'd skewer those bastards yet. This state of affairs had seemed out of the question one year ago as I faced the sting of their overwhelming leverage and looked up the road from New Guy Village.

And I had a hunch I might get a cellmate. With all the air-raid action we'd been hearing last month, the place had to be loading up. I'd just heard that Jerry Denton and Jim Mulligan got put in together this week. My guess was that they might put me in with Bill Franke, down at the other end of this building. We were the same age, and what with those interminable biography demands they threw in whenever they had you down and out, they might have figured out that we'd been together before at Patuxent River. They tended to try to compartmentalize mutual familiarity to minimize the spread of new information; that's why I still think they chose Sam to go alongside me behind the no-communication fire wall.

The night of January 26 was cold. I put on both of my pajama shirts and added a flourish I learned from Sam and Jim on how to keep your feet warm in these clammy cellblocks in the winter.

They called it "putting your pants on upside down." You took off your pajama pants and closed the waist by pulling the drawstring all the way up and tying it. Then you stuck your legs into the cuff ends of the pant legs and pulled the cuffs up to your crotch. That left your feet together in what became a kind of warm little bag.

I'd had a look at my broken leg at the same time. It seemed to be straightening itself out a little bit. Nature is a great healer: Give the old body a break with a positive mental attitude, and it will do wonders. I still had nighttime cramps and the circulation wasn't right, but I could tell that new blood routes were being formed down there in that mashed-up bone and gristle. I just hoped I wouldn't fall and tear apart the calcification.

All in all, things were coming up roses. I drifted off to sleep on the bed board, under my blanket, covered by my net, with the always-present lit and dangling bare bulb above. There was peace in my heart. . . .

✧

The keys. I heard the rattling of the keys out front. That sound was always the first sign of trouble at night. Now suddenly they were in my door lock. It was opening.

"Don! Don!" ("Don" was my Vietnamese name—they give every prisoner one that is pronounceable by the guards.) "Llole up" [roll up]. The guard watched me unwinding the blanket from my legs. "Llole up," he repeated, and then held up five fingers and left. I assumed he meant that I was to be packed when he came back to get me in five minutes. Damn, I thought, they wouldn't be getting me up to go down and move in with Bill Franke at this time of night. I heard doors slamming down the way. A big move must be on.

Don't forget Syb's letter—the papers, the magic carbon papers. Do we take our toilet buckets? I think the guard would have me dumping it now if we were to take them. We must be moving out of this camp. Take off the outer pajama shirt; it will be warmer outside this concrete-walled refrigerator, even in this late-night air. Don't forget that porcelain drinking cup, whatever you do. Who would have thought that such an ordinary thing would be my communication link with my civilization?

The keys again. The door opened. It was "Spot" with Jake.

Spot was something like a noncommissioned warrant officer, senior to a guard but not quite a commissioned officer. He spoke English. "You will move far away to another camp. Keep silent—any communication and you will be severely punished. Leave bucket."

Jake put a tight blindfold on me. I felt for my blanket roll, picked it up, and followed the pressures of the hand that gripped my arm, down the three steps and then left toward the bright lights and murmuring commotion around what had to be a truck parked in the roadway just inside the gate to my left. I recognized the voice of Fox, the regular military camp commander of the Zoo, as he quietly gave terse orders in Vietnamese. No wonder they wouldn't allow us to learn any Vietnamese words. How could they run complicated evolutions like this and still keep us in the dark on what they were up to if we could make out what the leader was saying?

Prisoners were climbing into the back of the truck, one at a time, controlled. Locks clicked as they were handcuffed, once up on the truck bed. I could tell by the touch on my arm and the murmurs that the big problem now was what to do with me. Somebody took my roll, and a man on each side quietly lifted me up to a third in the truck, who got his hands under my armpits, hoisted me aboard, and stood me up on the rear sill. I was down from a normal 170 to about 125 pounds, true, but that last guard was strong; it was probably either Jake or that mean, ham-handed boot apprentice of his, Big Ugh. I tried very hard to be cooperative and "can-do" when they were having transportation problems with me, else I might have been declared nontransportable and put back in that devilish one-on-one status with Rabbit in New Guy Village. God, I thought, it's great to be out in this stimulating action, this absolutely intoxicating action that makes you feel like you're living again. All this mixing arouses your competitive spirit.

Here I was, right in the midst of things; I couldn't believe it. There must have been five or six of us prisoners in that truck, and almost as many guards, plus Spot, whom I could hear. I'm being cuffed behind (i.e., hands behind my back) with the regular Dick Tracy-type ratchet-and-hinge cuffs, not those damned rigid two-piece, screw-bolt manacles, thank God. Some guard notices that I'm off-balance trying to sit down with one good leg and my hands constrained to the small of my back. To keep me from falling, he supports me as he pulls me into a sitting position up against the truck's starboard side. My tire sandals come off on that maneuver. I can't reach to find them, but they're not critical. The papers and the cup are all I have to worry about; they're buried in the middle of my blanket roll, and I feel sure they'll get that roll to me wherever I go.

This has to be something like a ton-and-a-half "stake" truck of the sort I was brought to Hanoi in, a year and a half ago; but with the muffled sounds and bright lights in here, it has to be canvas-covered. Spot gives us all another lecture on the dire consequences of communicating. The guards are climbing in and out among us, making sure all blindfolds are tight.

I concentrate on a vaguely familiar intermittent noise that's been haunting me ever since I was lifted into this truck. It is a quiet, guttural, half snort, half throat-clear. It is not a signal, it just goes on and on. That pleasant lowing sound has been part of my life some-where. Who have I known with such a persistent postnasal drip? Think. Think. Think. USS *Oriskany*. Ready room 5. It has to be my old shipmate, my pal, my favorite squadron commander, Harry Jenkins! Check the azimuth of that postnasal drip! He's butted up across from me. We're almost foot-to-foot.

Pressure, pressure, foot pressure without motion. The foot of my good leg is up against something warm and soft. A foot? A thigh? A guard? The ball of my right foot presses slowly, deliberately, rhythmically: dum dum da dum dum ("shave and a haircut"). I feel a slow and careful realignment of that soft and warm thing. It is a foot, a foot belonging to a guy with a wonderful postnasal drip. It eases itself into a position toe-to-toe with mine. Slowly, deliberately, without detectable motion, it answers: dum dum ("two bits").

As the cab door slams and the engine starts amid loud Vietnam-ese talk outside, I come on with "push push—push push push push push [pause] push push push push—push push push" ("J.S."). The friendly foot comes back with "H.J."

What a moment to savor! Here I am with a guy I love as much as any man. I know his wife and kids, his father and mother. They've been to our house to have dinner with Syb and me. As his air-group commander, I was shot down flying one of his airplanes. And during those first weeks I was a prisoner, how I did pray that

Harry would never be shot down and captured. What a shock it had been, lying helplessly in that stretcher, hearing that first menacing lecture in Hoa Lo Prison: "We know about you on the aircraft carrier *Oriskany*. We know about you and Jenkins and Shaw and Smith." Dog had shown me Harry's picture in the *Stars and Stripes* article about the Nam Dinh raid. It was authentic. ". . . we are waiting for Jenkins, too," he had said.

Of course I knew that Harry did get bagged in November of that year of 1965. I had about ten days with him in Heartbreak a year ago last month. I even knew that Harry was later moved to the Zoo, because in a bathhouse a few weeks ago I saw his little greeting etched near the baseboard with a nail: "Hi CAG, Saint." I've got to be the only air-group commander in prison, and I was Harry's CAG when he was the skipper of "The Saints." But what a coincidence to be right here touching feet with the man who had been my closest friend during those wonderful days when we were at the peak of our flying careers.

As the truck driver grinds gears and chugs along through crowded city streets for twenty minutes or so, and as guards move among us in the bright light, clicking their pistols, checking blindfolds, and shouting "No!" to suspiciously shifting prisoners, Harry and I go into high (but motionless) gear, "tapping" with mere pressure through our foot soles. In this heady, fresh, January air, balmy air free of all that cellblock clamminess, I am transported into another world—the world of the aircraft carrier and its pilot ready rooms full of good and highly respected friends. I try to give Harry as much information as I can, as briefly as I can. "Next door to me has been Will Abbott, captain USAF, shot down while exchange pilot with VF 111 on *Oriskany*. Will Abbott was shot down a month before the *Oriskany* fire . . . Gordon Smith was shot down and badly burned, but rescued by helo . . . Wynne Foster had his arm shot off in his cockpit but got back to destroyer and ejected. He is now in hospital in USA. He is trying to stay on active duty . . ."

Harry replies with information obtained from his new shootdown contacts. He gives me the names of some of our friends lost in the *Oriskany* fire in October, only three months ago. He also tells me of some of the heroes of the fire, like Paul Engel, who was trapped behind sheets of flame and smoke for more than an hour, but shoved all the bombs stored on the quarterdeck sponson over the side before fire consumed the area. Harry is in the midst of an exciting account of Dick Bellinger shooting down a MIG a few days before the fire when we are jerked back to reality as the truck grinds to a halt.

"Keep silent! Keep silent!" shouts Spot as Harry and I "tap" off with fond farewells. In the North Vietnam prison system, you never know whether you're saying goodbye for six years or a couple of minutes. We disembark into what I make out through the blindfold to be a lighted street, the cuffs are removed, and I am given my precious blanket roll, which I clutch to my stomach. We are lined up in silence and then led in a column through a narrow pedestrian gate. The guard with each one of us then draws us to a stop, and we are taken along one at a time, each shortly after the cell door of some prisoner ahead is heard to slam shut and be locked. As I am moved along in my turn, it seems as though I am going through a labyrinth of very narrow passageways. We stop, a door is opened, and I am thrust into this brightly lighted place, my blindfold removed, my tire sandals tossed on the floor by the guard escorting me, and the door locked behind me after he exits.

I am in a small cell that has very little floor space, but four bunks (upper and lower slab bunks on each side, each with leg stocks and locks). The surprise is that the place is relatively clean, the walls freshly whitewashed and the wood bunk planks still smelling new. These walls are brand-new brick and mortar!

Throughout the cellblock, door slams, footsteps, muted Vietnamese whispers, and other sounds make it clear that our whole truckload of Americans is moving in here. Each cell is being occupied by a solitary prisoner. Harry and I are neighbors! And who else is here?

It takes us just about thirty minutes to get the layout and the lineup figured out. It takes a good deal less time than that to figure out what all this fresh brick and mortar is about. From the familiar smell of the piss-encrusted deck, the appearance of the dry-moat lights, which I can see through a high window, and the unique taste and smell of recently boiled drinking water in the jar on one of my top bunks, I conclude that we are back in Hoa Lo Prison. But this is another part of the big, block-square prison, a part in which I've never been. Still, we came in the pedestrian gate, and that's on the front, on the street where I was lifted out of the stake truck a year and a half ago. This has to be on that northern side, to where Robbie Risner said he saw them wheelbarrowing all those bricks and sand the autumn before last.

It's hard to believe, but these dumb bastards have taken these big communal cellblocks—cellblocks that have housed scores of Vietnamese prisoners ever since the French built this downtown prison in the last century—and honeycombed them with small cells for us Americans, taking great pains, and lots of construction resources, to make sure none of us shares a common wall. "Aha," I can hear them saying. "We have stopped the wall-tap communication of the American criminals!" My God, I thought, they'd extended the partitions clear up to the twelve-foot ceilings.

Those new Vietnamese walls may have hampered the summer ventilation the French had in mind, but they were a farce as far as being wall-tap stoppers. The investment of a year's construction work was about to be canceled out by a few old farm-pump drinking cups.

We all had outside walls, and in minutes, we were tapping "round the bend" with the help of those cups. It was soon clear to us all that the labyrinth design of that little cellblock resembled a "ticktacktoe" layout, with only one hallway instead of two cutting down the middle, paralleling the sidewalk outside. The big news was that there was (luckily for us) only one door for all in-and-out traffic. My cell was at center front, number 3, my door facing the entrance passageway, thus I could watch shadows and count every guard in and out. Our standard, multipurpose operating signals would do it: first guard in, one thump ("Danger," "stop," "no"— any negative connotation); last guard out, two thumps ("all clear," "yes," "okay"—any positive or safe connotation). Interesting thing about the new walls: A moderately light thump with the heel of your hand came across like a bass-drum reverberation. Moreover, it was almost omni-directional—the guards couldn't tell where it was coming from.

In our midnight exuberance, we went to thumps for simplicity. Each guy sounded off with his location:

"First cell on the right, Jerry Denton."

"Right-hand back corner, George Coker."

"Center, back side, Harry Jenkins."

"Sam Johnson, all the way around on the front."

That made five; that must have been our truckload.

We finally quit for the night when a nasty little English-speaking officer, infuriated by the thumps that were so difficult to localize, gave us short, individual, threatening speeches as his twitching left eye filled our peepholes each in turn. On the basis of his "bug eye" and short, fat build, somewhat like a ladybug, he was forthwith permanently named "Bug." It crossed my mind that we would see a lot of him—but even in this brief encounter, it came through that he was no Rabbit. He was mean, but he didn't have that dangerous cunning streak; I predicted Bug would stick right by their book, a slave to prescribed doctrine. That meant this gang in here could play him like a violin.

After Bug left and I gave the "all clear," I recognized Sam Johnson's touch as he thumped for us all to hear: bump bump— bump bump (pause) bump bump bump—bump bump bump (GN— "good night"); bump bump—bump bump (pause) bump—bump bump (pause) bump bump bump bump—bump bump bump bump bump (GBU—"God bless you").

I'd arrived. I was finally in the mainstream. That was one of the happiest moments of my life.

The guys said that Robbie was still in isolation back in New Guy Village. That meant I'd be the senior man in the system, the boss. This was where I was supposed to be. This was my life. We had to shut off that torture machine, and I now had the tools to do it, if Uncle Sam would just get the specifics on North Vietnam's violations of international law into America's public domain, into the *Washington Post*, into the *New York Times*. Vietnam would have to come off it; without propaganda, without American public opinion, they'd be sunk. Even Dr. Vien said that. "We will win this war on the streets of New York"? Ha! Come on, Muste, come on, Patricia Griffith, at least one of those letters had to be in the chemical lab by now.*

I was getting sleepy again. I *liked* this gang. Who was this kid Coker? I'd heard he looked like Jimmy Cagney, and had been acting like Jimmy Cagney in Sing Sing ever since he got here . . . Jimmy Cagney . . . Jimmy Cagney . . . Jimmy Cagney . . .

*See Appendix 3.

Clang! Clang! Clang! . . . I'd been asleep. It was the morning gong. I was back in Hoa Lo Prison again.

Bang! My door swung open. I'm number one to dump my bucket, and guess who is here to escort me: Jake. They'd moved that mean son of a bitch in last night on the same truck we came on. I grabbed my bucket, went out the little door, and came face-to-face with more new construction. Bricklayers were at work already that morning, building a wall between our building and the single-story houselike shed straight away. Jake turned me right, and down a sidewalk. Suddenly we entered a big prison courtyard with cellblocks all around. On the outside these cellblocks formed the inner wall of the dry moat of Hoa Lo. The fifteen-foot-high, five-foot-thick outer prison wall framed the outside of the moat and loomed above all, with its sparkling jagged champagne-bottle shards pointing skyward and gleaming in the sun. In the middle of the courtyard, a shed of ten bath stalls was in the final stages of construction. These were arranged five on a side, back to back, each with a big slate laundry-type sink and faucet. The doors on each stall were equipped with peepholes for guards' anticommunication checks.

A depressing feeling came over me. It was clear that last night's truck or trucks had brought just the first contingent. There might not be any other Americans here yet besides those in our cellblock, though I thought I heard whispers just then coming from the high windows of the building on my right. But the place was being renovated for many Americans—in a long-range project that had started in late fall 1965. There were surely thirty-five or forty cells here. That meant a crowd, even if all were kept in solitary as all were now. But if each cell had four bunks like mine—and mine was a tiny cell—what was in store for us? I was daily becoming more convinced that my initial five-years commitment was but an optimistic pipe dream.

Jake turned me to the right at the corner of the courtyard and motioned for me to dump my bucket in the hole on the moat side of an anteroom that had wooden cellblock doors closed on either side. The noise of my scrubbing my bucket with the stiff-bristled bamboo broom echoed through long, empty hallways on all sides with ominous resonance. I was what the navy calls a "plank owner" here, part of the commissioning crew. This was my new home, my new command. As I was steered back to where I came from, I noticed that my home had artwork. This prison had upstairs apartments for what I presumed were senior wardens and their families, and staring down at me from a beautiful gilded frame in a prominent window overlooking the door of my cellblock was a heroically sized V. I. Lenin, eyes ablaze.

We five in our little cellblock were soon spread out and moved to random locations as the place filled up to about forty prisoners. Still in solitary, I was put in the very end cell in the northwest corner of the complex. Knowledge of the tap code was practically universal in that compound, and we soon found out exactly where we lived. A very innovative and aggressive prisoner by the name of Dave Hatcher was moved into our first cellblock and almost immediately sized up the compound and spread the word that he had just named this northeast corner of Hoa Lo Prison a "camp" called "Las Vegas." Our old place, where Dave lived, was Stardust. Right around the central bath area were Desert Inn, the Mint, Thunderbird, Golden Nugget, and Riviera. There were numbers on cell doors, which we matched up with these names, and my address became Thunderbird 6 West.

We were all learning the importance of having a "map" of the complete camp in the mind's eye of each prisoner. This required that descriptions and names of landmarks be put into the communication network as soon as an authoritative prisoner identified them. It also required that cellblock leaders promulgate descriptions of the cell layouts of their blocks so that everybody in camp had a good idea of exactly where Mint 1, Desert Inn 5, Riviera 3, and Thunderbird 6 West were.

Within a week a guard appeared at the door giving me the "sleeve" signal. I was led down by Stardust, then to the right, away from the Stardust door, out of Las Vegas, through a gate in the now-completed eight-foot wall, and over to that single-story, houselike shed, now made invisible from inside the camp. There they were, in a big room, sitting side by side behind a long quiz table covered with the inevitable "Ho Chi Minh blue" cloth: Rabbit and Cat. I instantly made a mental note of what would be our official name for this place: Cat's quiz room (CQR).

As always, Cat started the quiz, even this "welcome aboard"

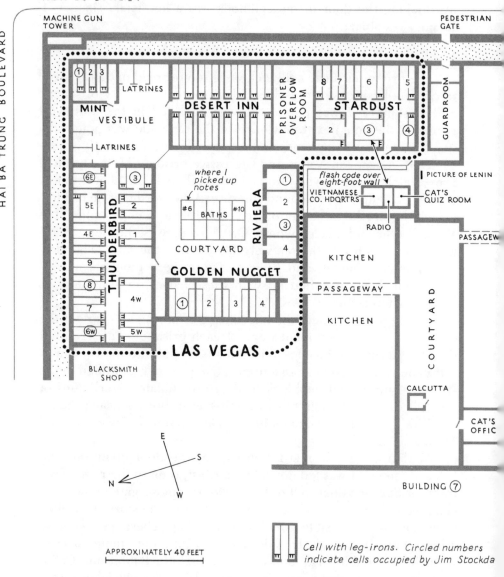

HOA LO STREET

MACHINE GUN TOWER

PEDESTRIAN GATE

HAI BA TRUNG BOULEVARD

① 2 3

LATRINES

MINT

VESTIBULE

LATRINES

DESERT INN

PRISONER OVERFLOW ROOM

8 7 6 5

STARDUST

2 ③ ④

GUARDROOM

⑥E ③

5E 2

4E 1

9

⑧

7

⑥w

THUNDERBIRD

4w

5w

where I picked up notes

#6 BATHS #10

COURTYARD

GOLDEN NUGGET

① 2 3 4

RIVIERA

① 2 ③ 4

flash code over eight-foot wall

VIETNAMESE CO. HDQRTRS

RADIO

KITCHEN

PASSAGEWAY

KITCHEN

PICTURE OF LENIN

CAT'S QUIZ ROOM

PASSAGEW

COURTYARD

CALCUTTA

CAT'S OFFIC

LAS VEGAS

BLACKSMITH SHOP

E

S

N

W

BUILDING ⑦

APPROXIMATELY 40 FEET

Cell with leg-irons. Circled numbers indicate cells occupied by Jim Stockda

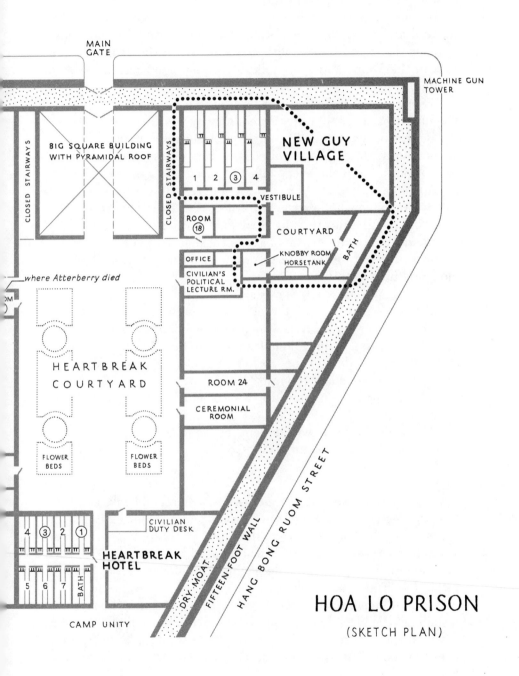

MAIN
GATE

MACHINE GUN
TOWER

CLOSED STAIRWAYS

BIG SQUARE BUILDING
WITH PYRAMIDAL ROOF

CLOSED STAIRWAYS

NEW GUY
VILLAGE

1 2 (3) 4

VESTIBULE

ROOM
(18)

COURTYARD

OFFICE

BATH

KNOBBY ROOM
HORSETANK

where Atterberry died

CIVILIAN'S
POLITICAL
LECTURE RM.

OM

HEARTBREAK
COURTYARD

FLOWER
BEDS

FLOWER
BEDS

ROOM 24

CEREMONIAL
ROOM

HANG BONG RUOM STREET

CIVILIAN
DUTY DESK

4 (3) 2 (1)

HEARTBREAK
HOTEL

5 6 7 BATH

DRY MOAT

FIFTEEN-FOOT WALL

CAMP UNITY

HOA LO PRISON
(SKETCH PLAN)

version, by trying to put me on the defensive. "My officer has told me of the impolite manner in which you and your four cronies behaved the night you were brought to this place. You and those with you that night are establishing yourselves as the blackest criminals in the Democratic Republic of Vietnam and you have been separated.

"Staw-dale, I meant what I said on one of our first meetings. The illegal war brought upon my country by your American imperialist aggressors continues. Hundreds of American criminals are now in my custody. My job, and yours, is to direct these criminals in the path of peace, to make every effort to bring this aggressive war of Johnson and McNamara to an end. As I have said, you will help me, you will help me whether you know it or not. The time is nigh. You have your own battles to fight, Staw-dale, battles of age and battles of wounds. I know the battle of age because you and I are the same. I have instructed my people to provide you clothing, shelter and food, and time to think.

"Think and get well, Staw-dale, but let me warn you: Do not tamper with our work with the other criminals. Things can go very bad for you very quickly. I can have you made into a domestic animal, if necessary. But I do not want to do that. I think you have a certain understanding of the world that could make you a force for peace. Do you have any requests?"

"Yes. I have been alone for a year and a half. I want a cellmate."

"We will study. It will depend on your attitude. Obey camp regulations. Do not communicate. Go."

My thoughts were very sober as I was marched back to TB6W. Cat had decided to take a chance on me and put me right into the system while he lay out there in the bushes, waiting for me to come around or screw up. Either way, he figured he could win. He gave me the usual crap about helping him, but I wondered what he meant by "The time is nigh."

Almost immediately, a work crew circulated through Las Vegas, installing little black loudspeaker boxes, out of reach high up on the walls, in each of the camp's thirty-eight cells and a large prisoner overflow room. They were all wired up within a matter of days, and, like at the zoo, each morning and night we were being "entertained" by Hanoi Hannah's and Dr. Vien's interpreter's "Voice of Vietnam" disinformation propaganda broadcast to the American servicemen in South Vietnam. Interspersed would be daily propaganda readings by either Vietnamese voices I could recognize (Rabbit, Bug, and, rarely, Chihuahua) or Vietnamese voices much less practiced in English, unrecognizable and almost unintelligible.

It was still early February when my first leadership crisis occurred. It had to do with these loudspeakers—or squawk boxes. A very bright young officer, an idealistic MIT-educated aeronautical engineer with whom I had whispered extensively at Heartbreak in the fall of '65 and now located a couple of doors down the hall from me in Thunderbird, was called to quiz. The interrogator said, "We want all American criminals to hear the latest news from their homeland, but some of our interpreters do not have enough language practice to be understood well on the camp radio. You are going to read the *New York Times* to your fellow criminals over the camp radio."

The interrogator had his guard brandish leg irons, and this smart young American, weak from a bout with dysentery, decided to go ahead on the spot and outwit the Vietnamese with cleverness. The *New York Times* articles to be read on these local loudspeakers were those written by Harrison Salisbury on his visit to Hanoi during the 1966 Christmas season. Although the articles were very uncomplimentary to the United States, and loaded with what we had all been getting for months as the official Central Committee propaganda line, my friend made them sound very funny with his phrasing and pronunciation. Ho Chi Minh became "President Horse-Shit-Minh," and so on.

This reading act was going over as a real morale booster in the cells; you could hear muffled chuckles up and down the hall every time he talked. But it worried me—for a very good reason.

One of the graduate courses I remembered best from my recent study at Stanford was called "Comparative Marxist Thought." It was taught by an old Kremlinologist who knew all its strands; we read only primary material, no criticisms of Communist dogma, just the translations of what their ideologues themselves wrote. (It had already become clear to me that I knew more about what Lenin actually said than anybody I had confronted, including Cat and Rabbit, both Party members.) But in midcourse, our professor had taken time off for a week while we listened to tapes of psychologists who had studied the much-publicized "brainwashing" issue of the North Korean prisoner-of-war camps. There, Communist inroads were frequently made in what are called "criticism/self-criticism" sessions, in which Americans were assembled for face-to-face discussions led by an experienced Party cadre. These discussions did not work "black magic," but a description of their results pointed out to me that certain people are quite susceptible to peer pressure in an atmosphere of imposed fear and guilt.

The Vietnamese had so far robbed themselves of this method of exploitation by insisting on treating "American criminals" as non-persons, and thus not worthy of holding open discussions, of having opinions. In fact, as I reviewed what those psychologists had said about the Korean scene, the thought crossed my mind that with good tap communication, which could keep our morale up, we prisoners might be better off if we didn't come face-to-face with each other except when assigned together permanently as cellmates. (That association was too close for psychological trickery.) But in this case I sensed that in having America bad-mouthed by a fellow American, even in a comic way, there was an element of man-to-man contact that might later be expanded and manipulated to our detriment.

On the fourth day, a second American voice, that of the cellmate of the first, took over the reading of Salisbury's articles. This voice was self-conscious and ponderous in a way that gave an ominous, serious aura to the recitation. That did it. I put out the order: "To talk on the camp radio requires a license. The license costs one week in leg irons. The license is good for one week and then must be renewed."

I got the order out just in time; about five more Americans were asked to read the next day, and all refused. As a result of totally unanimous refusal, only the two who had already read for the squawk boxes went into leg irons, and they for less than one week. The reading requirement was dropped from the Vietnamese agenda for the time being.

Many indicators came from that little drill. It showed that the Vietnamese read unified pressure very well; they clearly judged it counterproductive to their long-term propaganda goals to go to war over that issue with all the American prisoners in Las Vegas. No American voice was ever heard on the Las Vegas squawk box again that year. Lesson learned: Unified prisoner commitment, clearly perceived by the Vietnamese before they had been able to get a significant number on the hook, could win. Effective resistance was not built so much on desperate goal-line stands, heroic displays of high thresholds of pain to salvage losses, as on unified, timely, persistent, committed signals to the Vietnamese that they must punish one and all, day after day, to get what they wanted.

In short, unity was our best hope. And in our prison, unity came automatically. Men of goodwill of the sort that inhabited those dungeons, faced with a torture system that made them write, recite, and do things they would never think of doing in a life of freedom, wanted above all else to enter a society of peers that had rules putting some criteria of right and wrong into their lives. Authority was not something that had to be imposed from the top; to be led, to obey fair and universal orders within the capability of all, was a right that this community of Americans demanded. A life of perfection was for them out of the question, but they all elected to take pain in a unified resistance program, to fight back against degradation. To tell them "Do the best you can and decide for yourself how to resist" was an insult. They demanded to be told exactly what to take torture for. They saw that it was only on that basis that life for them could be made to make sense, that their self-esteem could be maintained, and that they could sleep with a clear conscience at night.

Our campwide communication system seemed indestructible that spring of 1967. Our style in Thunderbird took its form from a young air-force pilot who had been shot down nearly two years before, in April 1965. His name was Ron Storz. A bright and aggressive fellow, Storz picked up on the fact that his cell (TB3) was an ideal location from which a person could act as hall captain during those precious noon-hour and early-dusk minutes when the only real threat to our privacy was a slim force of patrolling guards. By intricate, self-determined means, Storz arranged a peephole lookout system by which he could be warned of any guard's approach. This opened up the possibility for low-voice chitchat of the sort I had known in Heartbreak.

It was a pleasure to be under the sway of the commanding self-confidence and presence of Storz when those magic vocal-communication times came 'round and the lookouts reported "All clear." He kept the subject pertinent, the news flowing, and talked just loud enough to be understood, utilizing the services of one relay man in the middle of the cellblock.

Intercellblock communications were also the province of young, alert, imaginative guys like Storz who concocted a seemingly never-ending stream of bath-stall whispering and across-court hand-flash schemes. (Our five-by-five-matrix monotonal tap-code system directly lent itself to hand-flash signals.) Hardly a week went by without a seemingly disastrous breakdown in cross-camp communications—another wall built, another guard post established, a key American communicator moved. A long period for the development of a new route would be solemnly predicted by me or some other senior, and an innovative young Yank would almost immediately announce that he had us back in action way ahead of schedule. In Hanoi I had a lot of tactical decisions to make, and my bias of error was always in the same direction: I invariably overestimated the ingenuity of the Vietnamese and underestimated that of the Americans.

Storz's hallways produced a lot of laughs, as well as some sobering thoughts. One of our last unoccupied cells (TB9) was filled late one morning by a big, tall marine who had been kept out of our communication range and only seen entering and leaving torture/isolation areas since arriving in Hanoi just before the previous Christmas. As soon as the "all clear" signal was given, he announced his arrival into the prison community with the following words: "My name is Orson Swindle. I'm from Georgia Tech. Are there any ATOs in this cellblock?"

Orson always kept a self-confident and robust frame of mind in that foreign land. Those little people gave him no concern.

Another remark I'll never forget also came from a new arrival in Thunderbird, this time a very young pilot. When he learned that Bill Franke was there in TB8, he said when cleared: "Commander Franke, I went to your memorial service on the *Midway* flight deck a few days after you were killed in action. I want you to know the chaplain prayed you right into Heaven."

As laughter filled the hall, my mind flashed back to Bill's wife, Jackie, an old friend of Sybil's and mine. She and their kids had been sitting on a "killed in action" report for a year and a half. I thanked God I had gotten his name out as alive and well.

In late February 1967, I was taken to Cat's quiz room again. I wondered if it was already time for me to be made into a domestic animal as he had threatened. No. He was positively sweet. For the fifteenth time I was told about how quaint it was to have the cloth on the interrogator's table be the identical color of Ho Chi Minh's pajama-uniform when he was sneaking across the border from China, setting up the Viet Minh in the very early 1940s. He handed me a letter from Syb in which she had enclosed a striking living room snapshot of herself and all four boys. No roses. Casually, I allowed my eyes to catch the letter's date: December 19, 1966. More carbons! Then came the big announcement: I was to get the cellmate I had requested. To hear Cat tell it, he had made an exception in my case in view of my age and feebleness.

The fact was, the cellmate program had been the rage of the Thunderbird hallway for the past three days. It was happening all over the camp—new young shootdowns were being put in with old senior solos. Two days ago, First Lieutenant Dave Gray had been moved in with Bill Franke, two doors down from me in Thunderbird. Gray had been shot down in late January and stashed in New Guy Village, where he had seen Risner. Then the day after that, First Lieutenant Ron Mastin from Thunderbird had left for New Guy Village to share a cell with Risner.

With Cat, I of course played the part of the dumb ass, to whom the idea of a cellmate was a revelation. As I departed, Cat's last words were "Take care of him, Staw-dale; he is a very young man." I followed the guard back to my cell in Thunderbird, and there he stood, a bright-looking little fellow, a real, live American, Lieutenant (jg) Danny Glenn.

Danny Glenn and I had a wonderful association. I was nearly twenty years older than he, and I remember him saying in our second week together, "The guards treat me like your son—so if it's okay with you, in their presence I'll act like it."

To get to know Dan Glenn's mind was for me like taking a drink of cold, cold, refreshing water. He was an architect by education and could hold forth on both art and construction engineering. I say "hold forth" in the most complimentary sense because it was common in that mind-drained prison circumstance for cellmates to take turns delivering explications of serious subjects; it was wonderful therapy for the giver, and like an afternoon in a good library for the listener. Dan came into the cellblock already practiced in the tap code. I was amazed and asked him how he'd managed that. "Oh, I've been practicing alone," he said. "You know, the code and how you use it is all written out on the bottom of the quiz table in the knobby room. I spent my first night in Hanoi tied up on that torture-room floor. I looked up at the bottom of that table, and there some Yank had written 'All American Prisoners, Learn This Code.'"

Dan had been shot down on December 21, two months before he moved in with me. He had spent Christmas Day, 1966, in that old French-built farmhouse with the barnyard near Nam Dinh, where I had heard the Vietnamese making arrangements on the phone to take me to Haiphong. The difference was that he was in good physical shape and "the system" was refined to the point that new shootdowns were being met at way stations, not by villagers and country doctors but by Camp Authority hard-line political interrogators. Dan was tough and gave them nothing, and spent much of that Christmas Day suspended from the ceiling on a hook, upside down.

I issued a group of standing orders to all POWs while Dan was with me. It became obvious to all in Las Vegas that our camp was a more or less permanent residence for the senior prisoners, but a holding point between the initial shakedown at Heartbreak and an outlying camp assignment for many others. That population in transit through Las Vegas in the spring of 1967 provided a unique courier service for the dissemination of standardized orders all over the North Vietnamese prison system. Dan served as a sounding board and source of advice as I tried to build a foundation of fair and easily understood law. That law could not be vague; to just give the order "Obey the Code of Conduct" would have been the biggest cover-your-ass maneuver of all. The Code, as good as it is, is like a constitution—arguments can go on endlessly about how it should be applied to specific situations. I had to spell out our Hanoi-specific applications, to select out certain of Cat's key programs that we would likely be able, by corporate effort, to defeat.

Writing law in any circumstance—and particularly in this extortion-prison circumstance—requires sensitivity, an appreciation for how deeply each element of the constituency is on the hook. The Vietnamese worked each prisoner on a "ratchet" system. If, ordered to do *x*, the prisoner refused, that was often a minor offense. At least it was minor compared to refusing to do *x* after having done *x* on demand before. The latter case was one of changing your category, downgrading your pliability. That was always a major offense. That's when they broke bones. To blindly order people to immediately take on all the ratchets they had become trapped behind was to demoralize the encumbered and drive Americans apart.

For instance, to just issue the order "Do not bow" would have been folly and ultimately destructive of prisoner unity. The Vietnamese had gotten the drop on us with this bowing to every one of them at every meeting, and right now an order to refuse would have meant the beating of most of us into submission. That is, if the offense was committed inside the camp. But they couldn't afford to show their viciousness in public, and I had learned that ex-post-facto punishments were more often than not halfhearted. They were overloaded with public appearance commitments and had to concentrate on short-term payoffs and often let long-term "lessons" slide. It was in public that the real prisoner humiliation came in, so "Don't bow in public" was a good, practical, useful law.

Here in Las Vegas we had just proved that as long as we all stuck together, as long as we provided no exceptions, no deviationist cases off which they could play the weak, we could all "stay off the air"—no broadcasts, no recordings.

It would be the height of ignorance to order sententiously, "Make no confessions"; the toughest of the tough were forced to make them from time to time. But I thought that if everybody applied his post-torture skill and cunning to the problem of avoiding the use of the word *crime* in confessions, we could do it, and thereby take a lot of the emotional steam out of what they published. "Admit no crimes" thus became a law.

One of the greatest booby traps I saw on the horizon, one on which they could surely capitalize, given the euphoria all would feel at release time, was the "let bygones be bygones" scene when we left for home. By the time we got to that threshold, I reasoned, all the chips would be in; they wouldn't dare turn people back in public. I felt sure all could hold to the figurative expression "Don't kiss them goodbye."

My whole concept of proper prisoner-of-war behavior was based on sticking together. We were in a situation in which loners could make out. If, after the initial shakedown, you refused to communicate with Americans, there was tacit agreement that the Vietnamese would leave you alone; there would likely be no more torture, no confessions, no radio broadcasts, maybe not even another tough military-information interrogation. One interested only in keeping his own nose clean could score lots of points by remaining a loner. I asked everybody to give up this edge of individual flexibility and get in the swim, communicate, level with your American neighbors on just what-all you compromised, what information you had to give up in the torture room, to freely enter into collusions with Americans, to take your lumps together and, if necessary, all go down the tubes together. In this circumstance our highest value had to be placed on the support of the man next door. To ignore him was to betray him. The bottom line was placing prisoner unity over selfish interests. It was "Unity over Self."

This first set of Hanoi-wide laws was put out in easy-to-remember acronym form—Bow, Air, Crime, Kiss, Unity over Self: BACK US. These orders were absolutely prohibitory—that is, you were required to take torture, forcing the Vietnamese to impose significant pain on you before acceding to these specific demands. In the spring of 1967 the orders were carried to every camp in the Hanoi prison system under my name as the senior American communicating in that system.

I then became obsessed with getting more and more "lowest common denominator" positive prohibitory orders out before Cat's sensitive antennae detected our collusion and brought down my leadership team in an inevitable purge. Dan's newness showed in his optimism on that score. He didn't know Cat, and wanted to assume the system had no leakage and that my regime was safe. I said, "No, it has a life-span, and it will probably be very short." I didn't ascribe my feelings to great wisdom, but to the experience I had gained in my year and a half of working very close to the horns. To understand Cat was to know that a purge was inevitable and soon to come.

It was early May 1967 when Rabbit got on the Las Vegas squawk box for a policy announcement that sent chills up and down my spine. No sooner had Rabbit started reading into the mike than Dan and I could hear cell-door peephole covers flicking open and closed all the way up and down the Thunderbird passageway. Ours opened in turn, not once but many times, and in each case we stared back at the exposed portion of the peeper's face and ultimately concluded that a crowd of senior Vietnamese (Cat included) were on hand to catch our reactions to Rabbit's groundbreaking speech. He was laying out the early prisoner-release policy of the DRV.

The script was repeated about three times that afternoon. It started out by scolding the prisoners for their poor attitude, their uncooperative attitude. "You are criminals. You must work for us. You must pay for your keep. You have obligations to the DRV. You must atone for your crimes and thereby enjoy the historic leniency and generosity of the Vietnamese people." Then he got down to facts. Some few Americans are cooperative and willing, but some are diehards, blackest criminals. However, most of the American criminals are noncommittal, in between. The latter must devote themselves to proper behavior—i.e., atonement for their crimes by service to the DRV. First, they must throw off the evil influence of those blackest criminals who break the regulations of the Camp Authority by communicating and inciting others to oppose the Camp Authority.

Rabbit concluded by telling us what was going to happen: A place is being prepared for those black criminals who persist in inciting the other criminals to oppose the Camp Authority. It is a dark place to which they will be banished. All the rest of the criminals must strive to be worthy of Vietnamese lenience and generosity, "and those who repent, show true repentance in actions as well as words, will be permitted to go home even before the war is over."

There it was—the ultimate challenge to our "Unity over Self." Get the Americans to compete for early release; only those who come out winners in hate-America speech contests on the radio get to the finals. As the fever sweeps the camps, they may even have a little movie-taking, perhaps a banner-waving demonstration of "American prisoners against the war."

As always, my immediate reaction, my flight of fancy, underestimated the Americans and overestimated the Vietnamese. A rehash of Rabbit's message during the evening Thunderbird hallway communication session revealed a universal repugnance and dread regarding what he had to say. There was little concern in any American's mind about the possibility of the Vietnamese throwing anybody out to defame him; we now knew the Vietnamese well enough to be sure that any early releasee would have to buy his way out by groveling on his knees before the Communists, bad-mouthing America. I gave their new release program a name: FRP—the "Fink Release Program," and that was the way it was to be known. I also issued an order that started on its way to the other cellblocks of Las Vegas and with subsequent movers to the camps elsewhere in the city and outside it: "No early release; we all go home together."

I shook my head as I got up and left my whispering spot under the door and said, "Once that gets all over the system and Cat gets hold of it, he's really going to be mad. That Fink Release Program had to come out of his general staff group as a national policy. He'll close in for sure." Good old Dan looked at me skeptically.

The next day I got a very interesting report, relayed from the DI (Desert Inn) cellblock. Right after Cat's speech, the Vietnamese had made a series of "attitude checks" at about three locations, bringing in sample prisoners to get their reactions to the great prospect of early release. The friend who reported this to me had a young interrogator who let slip the Vietnamese names of their three categories of prisoners: the willings, the partial-willings, and the diehards.

Those names fit the Vietnamese psychology: They had to think that every American was either politically enlightened (willing) or on the way to enlightenment (partial-willing); and that except for a few diehards, a dynamic transformation of partial-willings into willings was imminent. That was dogma; that was the way it had to work; that was the way they ran their country. Their Party members were the "willings," who swayed the "partial-willings." Already I'd had enough looks at the goings-on in the civilian side of Hoa Lo Prison to realize how their "diehards" were treated. Their event chain went from apprehension at "wrongdoing," to interrogation, to forced confession, to "instruction," and finally to atonement through public pledge of reform. They liked to think a standard remedy for "diehards" was applicable across the board—from Vietnamese thieves to irresponsible street hoodlums to tough-minded American professional military aviators. The basic problem of all was a social maladjustment.

It was a hot night late in May when lots of moving started around the camp. Dan and I were taken out with all of our things rolled up, and were stashed together in a bath stall. Then the guard came and motioned for Dan to follow. We shook hands; that was the last time I ever saw him in prison. In due course I was picked up and escorted down two doors from where I had just moved out. There I was, in Thunderbird 8, moving in with Jim Lamar. The "mixing" of youth and age had been inexplicably ended, and age with age and youth with youth was the general pattern now in overflowing Las Vegas.

It was overflowing because, starting right after the first of April 1967, the skies cleared and our air-force wings and navy air groups started plastering Hanoi at least twice a day. This was a great boon to our morale; for the first time we could see things happening that could, if kept up without interruption for several months, conceivably bring the North Vietnamese around. For instance, city water mains were cut and we had no running water in Hoa Lo Prison in central downtown. (The water table was so near the surface that shallow wells could be dug in the Las Vegas courtyard from which buckets of brackish water could be extracted for once-a-week sponge baths.) City electric power was off half the time, and transportation facilities were nearly at a standstill because of torn-up roads and fuel shortages. (This was given as the excuse for our being short of food; the little we had was mostly rice from the prison storerooms.)

Just a few days after moving in with Jim Lamar, I was called out to quiz. It was down to Cat's quiz room again, and there he sat, with dark rings under his eyes and a haggard face. He said it was time for me to help him. He was worried about us criminals, he said. The summer was unusually hot, there was a shortage of bathing water, many had bad skin problems, many were sick and there was no chance to get fresh air. He asked me what I thought of his idea of giving us Americans an opportunity for lots of fresh air outside the prison, with a chance of plenty of bathing water. He would make all this possible if we would just clear up the debris from the cluttered, bomb-damaged streets. And of course, he added, we would get the benefit of "redemption from sin" (he used that very term) by making up for the damage we had "wreaked on the countryside." Did I agree that my fellows would benefit from this benevolent concession? Might I agree, in this one case, to announce this good program on the camp radio?

No, I said, I would not. Furthermore, I was not personally interested in any excursions outside the prison gates. My skin was bad and I had boils, but I would just put up with them.

"Well, I am sorry," he said in a strangely reconciled way. "I just want you to remember that I gave you a chance to do something good for your fellows, under my own auspices."

As soon as I got back in with Lamar, I told him about this bomb-debris cleanup program. Both of us thought it was a trap—that for every prisoner, every shovel, there would be two cameramen snapping propaganda shots continually, and there we would be in the world press: "American prisoners of war go to the aid of North Vietnamese patriots as Yank bombs rain on the city of Hanoi." As for the repentance and repayment, we made up yet another general order for promulgation during noon hall talk: "No repent; no repay; do not work in town."

That order made the rounds of all cells before the pidgin-English formal request for volunteers was put on the camp radio after the "Voice of Vietnam" that night. Every day afterward for a week, we got reports of interrogations in which a hard sell for volunteers was pushed and our unified block resistance obviously noted with frustration. Our signal was out, and our unanimity read by the Cat.

As soon as the afternoon gong rang on the eighth day, a guard was at our door and I was given the "dress for quiz" signal. On a hunch, I shook hands with Jim Lamar. I was not to see him face-to-face again for four years.

My armed escort directed me past the bath shed and down to Riviera 3. I entered, bowed, and was confronted by a hostile young English-speaking political officer who went by the name of Greasy, along with another junior officer and newcomer to the scene whose real name I took to be Vy (at least that was the name written in one of his books left on the table after a quiz I'd had with him some weeks before). Several excited guards, including Jake, were there, too. This was all very strange; it was a setup in which, apparently, neither Rabbit nor Cat wanted involvement.

Greasy spoke: "I have been going through your records. Your biographical file is incomplete and misleading. Take these sheets of paper and write a description of your duties at each military post at which you have been assigned, ever since you entered the service. Be specific about secret briefings you have attended and bombing missions you have flown."

Cat was clearly giving me a "last chance" signal. I had been through all that crap, with ropes, in New Guy Village that first winter. "No!"

"You are making a very serious mistake. Do you refuse to obey the order of the Camp Authority?"

"I refuse."

"Stand facing the corner."

Out they all trooped, running in a pack as if they all wanted to share in the excitement. Back they came three minutes later. I could tell what Cat's decision was by the looks on their faces. He had said, in so many words, "Throw the book at him."

Jake came out of the pack with cuffs and spun me around. He locked my wrists behind in bolted manacles ("squeeze cuffs," not ratchet cuffs) and marched me out to bath stall 10 on the south end of the shed, where leg lugs and a long iron bar were already laid out. Jake signaled for me to sit down on the concrete (which takes a bit of doing for a person with no knee on one leg and both arms trussed up behind), and then on went the lugs (the bad way, open end up), then the heavy bar threaded through and laid on top of my ankles. This was the way I would be for three days—open air, mosquitoes at night, tropical June sun beating down on me by day.

There were a few highlights during these three days. First of all, I had noticed that this bath stall had been out of use by prisoners for several weeks, and now I knew why: It had become a storeroom for splints and crutches. Then the first night the Stardust dishwashers boosted up one of their number, Fred Flom, to give me a smile and thumbs-up. That told me that by noon the next day everybody in Las Vegas would know where I was and how I was trussed up. Such assurances were golden.

That second night, as I dozed, I was abruptly awakened by a guard who stood astride me and cuffed me back and forth with his fists—on the grounds, as best I understood him, that I had been "communicating." (I had been muttering in my sleep.) I raised some ruckus, and after he left, in the still night, I heard a towel being snapped in Desert Inn: snap snap—snap snap (pause) snap—snap snap (pause) snap snap snap snap—snap snap snap snap snap (pause) snap snap—snap snap snap snap snap (pause) snap snap snap snap—snap snap snap (GBU JS—"God Bless You, Jim Stockdale").

Late the third morning, I called "*Bao cao,*" the only emergency signal we were authorized to use, because I thought I was about to pass out from sunstroke. The same guard came in, slugged me five times in the face, and right on his heels was Greasy to assure me "My guard can do anything he wants."

But the real climax of this "softening-up" process came at high noon of that third day. Jake came in with a pair of regular Dick Tracy "ratchet" cuffs, removed the manacles, and then put my arms behind me again and clamped the ratchets on them way up by my elbows. He really bore down and closed them well beyond the point where mere blood stoppage took place.

It was obvious that they were getting me ready for a showdown. In thirty minutes I was in agony and crying out; Jake swept in and stuffed a rag down my throat and cinched up the ratchets another notch tighter. The heat and the choking and the pain were bad enough, but I was really getting worried because Jake was so erratic and emotional.

How I wished Pigeye had been on that job! Your hands were numb for some time after he put you through the rope trick, but he seemed to have a sense of getting the job done short of maiming damage and I had grown to have confidence in his reliability in that respect. Oh sure, there was lots of shouting and excitement when he was going for a submit, but Pigeye was an aloof and cool cat and not a political fanatic like this crazy Jake.

As best I could with my crooked leg, stiff and jammed sideways into the irons, I rolled over on my side and started banging my head against the bath door to get *anybody* to come. Piercing pain racked my body when my deadened lower arms bumped the concrete abutments of the bath stall. Pretty soon the door opened, and who was it but the warrant officer, Spot. Jake was right behind. Spot looked concerned without seeming to let on; I could see he was telling Jake to take the rag out of my mouth and to blindfold me. He did both, and then I could feel the leg lugs coming off. Then they had to lift me up to get me on my feet and I was led off toward what I thought was Stardust.

I sensed I was going over toward Heartbreak, and my anxiety was high enough, with the cuffs still at full ratchet, that I called out my name: "Stockdale, heading for Heartbreak!" In the midst of the noon-hour quiet, I knew some prisoner would pick it up. Position reports become an obsession when you realize how close you are to permanent isolation or even death. But nobody slugged me for crying out; whoever had me by the arm seemed to be in a hurry.

I stumbled along, oblivious to where we were, blindly following the arm pressures of my escort. We walked and walked, and suddenly we turned left and I was nudged to step up, and then it got cool! We were out of the tropical sun.

The blindfold came off. It had been Jake with me after all; he had apparently been calmed down by Spot. We were in room 18 and there was Bug! Bug looked sleepy, as though he had been awakened from his noon siesta to handle my case. He said he'd been told that I had disobeyed an order of the Camp Authority, and he told me I was to sit quietly and contemplate my crimes. I blurted out that I was going to lose my arms if they didn't get some blood into them. Bug reluctantly walked around behind me and had a look at them. He yelled to Jake, presumably asking for a cuff key, and then left on the run.

In a minute or two, he ran back in, and he and Jake went to work on the cuffs and arms I couldn't see. There seemed to be some hang-up, and Bug was excitedly shouting to Jake. Finally one and then the other ratchet popped loose, and then came pulsations of almost exquisite pain as blood surged into the arteries. I looked at my blue and swollen forearms and felt the cool air of that high-ceilinged room and breathed relief as I had seldom done in my life before. Bug was sober-faced, but couldn't resist making a self-congratulatory remark: "I might have saved your arms." He added, "That will teach you to obey the orders of the Camp Authority. Now, complete these sheets as the officer asked." He and Jake locked the door of room 18 and left.

I sat down at the familiar long quiz table and, as best I could with a pen I could hardly hold, wrote again what I had written before—brief descriptions of stops in a twenty-four-year naval career. Some of my accounts matched reality and some did not, but they had been consistent throughout, and that was the important thing—including that "Mediterranean cruise in VF 32" I took "in the summer of 1964." When I finished, I left the papers on the table and lay down on the dirty red tile floor and breathed deeply.

It was late afternoon when I was awakened by "Mo," a more or less agreeable guard from Las Vegas who wore his pistol in the middle of his back. Mo took me back and put me in Riviera 3, where I'd had that stand-up quiz and gotten sent to the bath a few days before. The room was set up to be my new home; my clothing and blankets were there. As soon as Mo left, I dived into the pile to find the precious carbons. Yes, the old letters were buried in there in their dirty envelopes, all sheets intact! Then and only then, and as a matter of relatively minor interest, I took note of how the little quiz room had been equipped with a bed board on sawhorses for sleeping, and a small chamber pot instead of a bucket for toilet use. I found all my gear from Thunderbird 8 except my automobile-tire sandals, which I never saw again.

Riviera was a low-ceilinged, rickety wooden building with lots of unintended peepholes that allowed occupants better-than-average views of what was going on in the prison yard around them. It was not used as living quarters except for people on "stashes" in the midst of punishment tours. Bombing was consistent and getting even heavier by that time, and it was not uncommon for the concussion of nearby impacts, even the shock waves of low-flying supersonic planes, to blow the rickety Riviera doors nearly off their hinges. They would pop open and remain ajar until some frightened guard rushed by, latching them. Meanwhile, I could see the dozens of pounds of light metal shrapnel that had fallen from the sky into the Las Vegas courtyard. All of that would be cleared away before any Americans were walked through the yard.

I lived there in Riviera 3 for just over two weeks. Riviera 2, on my right, was an interrogation room; and to my left, what amounted to Riviera 4 was by then a headquarters for a new camp official: a bespectacled little older Vietnamese man who was apparently a medical doctor—at least he often carried a hypodermic needle with him, and he frequented the end bath stall checking on crutches. The rate of influx of new shootdowns was obviously going up and the Camp Authority was becoming more all-embracing.

It was during the quiet, sultry noon hours that I was able to observe those Americans in punishment status being brought individually to the baths for their once-a-week shave. Two men I was shocked to see for the first time in prison were old flying buddies of mine. Their cases had been aired in the Thunderbird hall. Bob Shumaker was being kept in irons in the Desert Inn on the charge of making "halfhearted" bows to the enlisted guards on his way to and from bucket dumps. A young Crusader pilot, Bob was the second-longest-held prisoner in Hanoi, having gone down in February 1965. He was a very smart young fellow with three years of postgraduate education in aeronautics and electronics. He looked to be holding up pretty well, though the cuffs of his prison pajamas bore the unmistakable rust rings of continuous stays in irons.

The other old friend did not appear to be holding up well at all; he was staggering along, and unbelievably thin. His name was Nels Tanner, and I knew him as the best, most stable landing-signal officer in the Pacific Fleet. In the Crusader training squadron he had trained my old squadron LSO, Tim Hubbard. Nels had been shot down in the fall of '66 and they had tortured him to obtain the names of his "fellow pilots who gave up flying because of the illegal and unjust nature of the war." There were no such men, but Nels gave them a couple of ringers—navy lieutenants "Clark Kent" and "Ben Casey." The North Vietnamese gullibly blew up this "revelation" as a great news story, and many American newspapers exposed the farce as the biggest joke of the war. American leftists wrote the North Vietnamese government exposing Nels, and he had been in leg irons ever since. He was kept in one of the tiny dark cells in the Mint except for these once-a-week hobbling visits to the deserted yard for a face wash.

✧

Soon Pigeye started attending my door, and I could tell it was nearing time for me to perform. A day later I was taken before Cat himself. After I'd bowed and taken my place on the stool (still barefooted), he said, "Ah, Staw-dale. I have been out of town. I have been told that you have had some difficulty in my absence. I am sorry I was not here to intervene. But you disobeyed orders of the Camp Authority and you must make amends. The opportunity is afforded tonight. You will be taken downtown to meet some foreign guests. All I ask is that you be civil. You must be civil, Staw-dale. Do you understand?"

"I do not want to go downtown. I do not want to meet anybody. I will not answer any questions. I will say nothing."

"We will see! You will be there, and I warn you to use good judgment. I trust you have learned your lesson. Now return to your cell and remember that what has just happened to you can happen again and again."

As Pigeye took me back to Riviera 3, I thought of the difference between this session about going downtown and the one a year ago May. Before, there was the specific requirement that I say such and such; this time it was just "be civil," a considerably less stringent demand. Maybe Cat had decided on going around the other way, just trying to "break me to halter" on a trial run or two.

That night Pigeye came to the door with the "dress" signal. I signaled that I had no sandals. Pigeye was not a detail man, and, like many a good fighter pilot, affected a studied indifference to mundane affairs. He shook his head and ran off toward Thunderbird to get sandals from some other prisoner. When I was ready, he took me around to the pedestrian gate through which I had come blindfolded with Harry Jenkins five months before. (In Thunderbird hall talk, it was positively confirmed that this and the big gate through which I was carried after shootdown were the only breaks in the outer prison wall.) Pigeye and I waited inside the dry moat, near an open guard's bunk room that faced the pedestrian gate. Then we heard the approaching jeep and he put the blindfold on me—in a remarkably sloppy way that allowed me to see out.

It was an eerie ride through the streets of Hanoi; our destination seemed to be only six or eight blocks from the prison. I could see that many of the downtown windows were boarded up. Smudge pots lined the streets, and on that sultry night groups of people were huddled in alcoves, seemingly cooking over open fires. There were no streetlights illuminated; it looked like a city under siege.

The jeep pulled into a courtyard and parked next to what may have been a large restaurant or hotel. Pigeye took off my blindfold and motioned for me to wait quietly until he got the signal for us to move to the nearby porch. We could hear a crowd chatting inside (it was made up mostly of an East German movie crew that was in Hanoi to make a documentary, and other Communist-bloc correspondents).

My mind was racing as we waited; I vowed that there would be no bowing in public, and damned little talking. Pigeye nudged me and I walked up onto the porch, turned left, and headed for a lighted room. I saw no other Americans, though others were to follow me. A voice yelled "Bow" as I crossed the threshold, and I brushed by whoever yelled it, shaking my head no. A spotlight seemed to be trained on me as I walked across what might have been a dance floor; somebody motioned me toward an individual table on which there were bottles and food. I stopped dead, faced the light, and stared down whoever was murmuring out there behind the klieg lights. Suddenly I recognized Cat's voice ringing out in clear English: "Leave! Take him away—get him out!" Pigeye took my hand and led me out into that wonderful darkness of the porch and back down to the jeep.*

Eighty-six new shootdowns entered Hoa Lo Prison during the summer 1967 bombing campaign. Throughout July, all cellblocks of Las Vegas were full to overflowing. Almost every night one or more new shootdowns would be hauled into Heartbreak for initial torture and shakedown for our bombing targets of the next day. Every few days a draft of usually junior officer prisoners would be taken in jeeps to one of the four or five satellite camps around the city.

About a week after my downtown trip, there was an urgent need for space in Riviera 3 for someone else. I was moved first to

*See Appendix 4.

my old Thunderbird 6 West, alone, and eventually down to the other end of the hall into Thunderbird 6 East with Sam Johnson. Sam and I devoted all of our energies to communicating my "standard operating instructions" to the floating population of Las Vegas. To the best of our ability, we kept the prisoner communications lines full of BACK US—WE ALL GO HOME TOGETHER—NO REPENT, NO REPAY, and general "hang together" philosophy. We were capitalizing on the chance of a lifetime to unify all American prisoners in North Vietnam.

Every evening during the prison staff's dinner hour, the Thunderbird hall was cleared in accordance with procedures inherited from Ron Storz (who was by then in the Desert Inn), and I lay on that cool cement under the door of cell 6 East and followed the conversation. It was as I lay there one evening in the early part of August 1967 that I had my first word of Syb since receiving her "carbon" letter of the previous December. And in the same message I got word of my year-early promotion to captain in the navy. All this didn't come out loud and clear the first time. The news came from the lips of Bill Lawrence at the very far end of the hall. Bill had been shot down on Syb's and my twentieth wedding anniversary, June 28, 1967. He had been one of my best students at Test Pilot School a dozen years before, and this was his first opportunity to communicate with me in prison. I first heard my name mentioned, then something about "Sybil," and finally something about "captain." I grew anxious as the full message was passed from mouth to mouth up the hall, and then I got it! "Bill Lawrence says he saw Sybil aboard the carrier *Constellation* in San Diego this spring. Sybil looks great and all four boys are doing fine. Your name was on the last captain selectee list; you made it a year ahead of your Academy class."

As usual that night we made sure all the new arrivals in the hallway understood my standing orders and my name. A week later the Camp Authority became tense and ruthless and the Thunderbird hallway started to be vacated, cell after cell each day. One of those who got the orders, a young and dedicated navy pilot, had come into prison on the crest of such a wave of new shootdowns that he had just that afternoon been stashed in Thunderbird, even before he'd had his initial shakedown torture for current bombing-operations information. We didn't ask him how long he had been down, but had no idea he was that fresh-caught and inexperienced. That night they took him out and put him in the ropes and demanded that he give certain information. He innocently replied, "No, sir; that is against my commanding officer's orders." Cat was called immediately, the ropes tightened, and the young man, like the best of men, was forced to give what they now knew he knew: what the orders were, and what my name was. The purge for more particulars about the complete chain of command was on. I knew it had been inevitable.

This purge affected many people, bringing torture to many and death to some. Norm Schmidt was taken to interrogation and never came back. Dan Glenn was tortured and in irons two months, interrogated mercilessly, and never let anything crucial escape his lips. Nels Tanner, on his one hundred and twenty-third day in leg irons in the Mint, was caught at communications, tortured, and made to reveal before movie cameras the content and meaning of my orders. Ron Storz was buttonholed and told to come across with information on me, and his response was to take the pen they asked him to write it with and jam it nearly through his left arm. He carried a big scar from that the rest of his short life. Marine Warrant Officer John Frederick was kept blindfolded in leg irons for a month while Rabbit tried to make him reveal "Stockdale's connection with the CIA." He knew no details and kept silent. (Five years later he died in prison of disease.)

But they would not arrest Sam and me until they caught us "red-handed" in some overt violation of their legalistic regulations. They called Sam to quiz and told him to tell me that now was the time they were going to make a "domestic animal" out of me. But as they caught and arrested people step by step on our hall and moved them out over the next couple of weeks, they left two occupied cells within communication range as a trap, cells 3 and 5E, and set up a surreptitious round-the-clock guard post in the alcove between cells 3 and 2 across the hall from us. Even then, with stealth, patience, and porcelain cups, we were able to exchange daily well-wishes with our good friends Tom Curtis and Will Forby in cell 3, and Al Brady and Fred Crow in 5E.

Then one day in late August, Sam noticed a guard up on the high prison wall behind the moat unscrewing the bulbs of the emergency lights that shone in on our cell even when prison power was cut. Good old smart Sam was intuitive about all things, and calmly muttered, "Something's going to happen tonight."

Sure enough, we were cast in total darkness about 8:00 P.M. when the prison power was purposefully cut. Sam and I talked quietly, sitting on bunks opposite each other. We both could sense a stealthily gathering crowd of people forming up outside our cell. I guess the idea was that they expected us to whisper to the occupied "bait" cells in the totally unprecedented absolute darkness.

With some muffled coaching from behind, the regular roving guard opened the peephole, beamed his flashlight on us, uttered a common pidgin-English phrase, "Be silent," and tried to provoke an argument. Sam and I grumbled a little and then recognized Rabbit's voice coarsely whispering to the guard. The door was thrown open.

It was hot; we had boils from accumulated filth; we were angry and ready for a showdown. The space between the bunks was just wide enough for one, and I took the lead and walked out into the flashlight glare, identifying Rabbit with about four others. He made an enraged charge at me, yelling "You and your communication!" and pushed me back into the cell. I and Sam behind me were crowded back, and then I countercharged and threw Rabbit right back out into the hall.

That was all he needed. The door was slammed and locked, the inside prison lights came back on, and in about three minutes Rabbit's voice came on the camp radio: "A criminal has just made a provocation against an officer of the Democratic Republic of Vietnam. Totally strict camp discipline is going into effect. All American criminals can expect severe punishment if further attempts to communicate with others continue."

Doors started slamming all over Las Vegas. The halls were full of Vietnamese guards and officers; it seemed that everybody was being moved. Sam was moved out; a few minutes later, I was taken out with all my gear. They took me right around the corner into the Mint, cell 1 in the corner. Once in the Mint, I was treated to a whole series of door slammings and movings in and out of the other two tiny cells throughout the next hour. What was happening was this: Rabbit still needed a "red-handed" communication charge against Sam and me, apparently to please Cat. He decided the quickest way to get it was to put me in Mint 1, Sam in Mint 3, and torture the guy in the middle to admit that Sam and I communicated in the Mint. The problem was, prisoners started acting up when they were put into cell 2 with instructions to inform on us, and they had to be moved out again. What we wound up with was Sam next to me in cell 2, and in number 3 at the other end, Howie Rutledge, an old friend, fellow Crusader pilot, and hard-line prisoner.

Rutledge, Sam, and I were all three locked into leg irons in the Mint. But irons didn't mean much in the Mint; the cells were so small, there was no way to walk beside the bunk—you just had to inch along sideways. The Mint was the bottom of the Las Vegas barrel.

We in the Mint were individually taken out to wash in the brackish water from the improvised wells every week. Rutledge was covered with boils, worse than either Sam or I. I had crotch rot from continuous filth; my pajamas were caked with pus, and I would alternate putting the pants on frontward and backward every time I was let out of the irons to go out to wash.

A new twist to my washing was what I called "the Ted Williams shift," named after the special defensive formation that great baseball player faced every time he came to bat. The Vietnamese defensive posture against my poisonous influence on the "other criminals" was to clear *all* the baths, the courtyard, and surrounding areas of Americans whenever I emerged from the Mint.

But Cat didn't give up on the possibility that in my torment he might squeeze out a little concession, maybe a little propaganda. I was amazed when the guard brought a razor out to where I was washing my face in deathly silent solitude. He gave me the "shave" motion. I complied—I hadn't yet the sense or guts to use self-defacement as a defense—and sure enough, it was out of the bath and into the quiz room in Riviera. There sat Vy, the young interrogator who had teamed up with Greasy to send me into punishment in June. Yes, the general staff officer had decreed that I was to meet with some of his friends. I would not be taken downtown but to another prison. "You must keep calm; do not make a disturbance or you will be severely punished."

Strange fellow, this Vy. He seemed to be an outsider. In May I had hinted broadly to him that if he could rig an escape for me to come along, I would set him up with a job as a translator at the Hoover Library at Stanford. Now, in closing out this conversation, he leaned over to me almost as if in confidence and said, "You have made a lot of trouble for the general staff officer. He is very very angry. Criminals at camps miles away all know your rules. The general staff officer says that you have set back the Camp Authority two years. You are in danger and must be very careful how you conduct yourself."

Whatever Vy's motive, he couldn't have done more to raise my morale. God, two years' setback! My life *has* served a purpose. This is *not* a pointless existence!

As they put the blindfold on me, I couldn't believe what was going on. I had no shoes; my trousers were covered with encrusted pus fore and aft; the trouser legs bore broad rust rings from the leg irons. Could this be a serious, politically sensitive meeting? Why in the world was Cat doing this? What did he think he could accomplish? Of course, thought I, this may be one more attempt to break me to halter. Maybe he is trying to save face with his bosses on the general staff. Whatever, my morale was soaring. I had told myself I wouldn't go, but now I *wanted* to go to this crazy meeting and rub Cat's nose in it!

Pigeye took me in hand and we mounted the jeep for a drive to what I later learned to call "the Plantation." It was an improvised prison set up around the manor house and outbuildings of an old French residence, in the very northern part of the city's Citadel section, about eight blocks north of Hoa Lo Prison. After my blindfold was off, I was marched into a rather large meeting room. There, around a very large, four-sided table, sat about a dozen Vietnamese officers, including Vy, and two burly Western men in civilian clothes. Pigeye nodded toward a regular place at the table beside Vy. I was to sit right beside him! No inferior position! No stool! I sat down without bowing. Cat, whom I had not actually seen since the night I went downtown in June, came in on the opposite side of the table, and arranged it so that he sat between the two men in civilian clothes. Cat looked at me and said in English that the guests were Russians and that one (the bigger one) was a novelist who wanted to talk to me.

The Russian asked me very ordinary questions, and appeared to have been bamboozled into being a straight man for this "last-chance attitude check" Cat was giving me. "How do you feel about the war?" "What possible gain can the U.S. have by continuing the war?"

My answers were relatively hostile, though I didn't realize that I seemed to be directing my answers to Cat, and not to the so-called Russian author. Cat motioned to Vy and the little fellow went over and listened as Cat whispered in his ear while the Russian continued his laborious questioning. Vy came back and whispered to me: "The general staff officer says you are to quit looking at him. You are not to look in his direction."

Finally the Russian got to his "question of the day." (These public political quizzes always had a central, planted question, designed to produce an American response that would be quoted in North Vietnam's propaganda broadcasts—with credits.) "Don't you as an American see a certain similarity between the American Revolution and the revolution in Vietnam?"

I had learned that you had to jump all over those propaganda feed-ins and kill the whole subject by overstating the case. "No, there is absolutely no comparison. In 1776 we were Englishmen who were merely trying to relax the ties between us and the motherland." The Russian sneered.

At that point, the old Vietnamese linguist who was translating between English and Russian, and keeping a Vietnamese commentary going for the benefit of the table, seemed overtaxed. Vy was called on to take his place and did a magnificent job. So Vy spoke Russian! I remembered that when I had mentioned escape, he had told me he could get to the West easier over the Russian border than via China, even though I had contacts with Hong Kong detectives. No wonder!

The Russian novelist was fed up. Through Vy, he told me it was time for me to ask any final questions I might have.

"Yes, I have a question. How are the Russian-U.S. track meets coming?"

After a lot of puzzled facial expressions and question-asking in Russian and Vietnamese around the table, the Russian scoffed and spoke in broken English himself: "Do you mean sport?"

"Yes. I remember seeing a great track-and-field contest between the Soviet Union and the United States at the stadium of Stanford University in 1962. Are they still being held?"

"No, they have been stopped because of the American imperialist war of aggression in Vietnam."

"What was the name of that great Russian high jumper of those years?"

"Valery Brumel."

Cat broke in. He had had it. "That's all; the conference is finished."

❖

When I got back to the Mint and into the irons, I tapped the whole story to Sam and Howie with glee. That two years' setback Vy mentioned had really set me up. My morale was high. Howie sensed that, and delicately gave me some bad news he had been holding. The Vietnamese had been documenting the evidence against me with great care. Not only Nels Tanner but others had been tortured to make a movie explaining all my orders and their meaning.

All I could think of was the war-crimes trials the camp radio was always threatening.

❖

Cat had made his last try to get me to cop out before he let the ax fall. His guards now became vicious. The next morning, as always, I got the "shave and a haircut" from Sam about daybreak. I put my cup to the wall as he was giving me his "Good morning": tick tick—tick tick—tick tick tick—tick tick (GM), when a war whoop echoed through the alley behind us. A guard we called "Jap" had been in the machine gun tower atop the fifteen-foot wall behind us looking down into my bed, waiting for me to put that cup to the wall. That was it! Caught red-handed! Time for me to go into the meat grinder!

I was taken out of irons immediately and walked by Jap down to Cat's quiz room, where Greasy was in charge. The place was a shambles; it had been used as a torture chamber. I recognized one of Jim Lamar's sandals with a strap broken, lying in a corner. Jake laid out the big iron bar and the coiled rope as a gesture of psychological warfare while I sat on the floor and denied communicating with Sam. "Why fool around with nonsense like that?" I shouted. "Let's get on with it. Let's talk about 'BACK US,' 'WE ALL GO HOME TOGETHER,' 'NO REPENT, NO REPAY' . . ."

Greasy brushed all that aside; he was not empowered to take up the meat of the case yet. Everything had to be controlled, have Cat's okay.

But they had a plan on this day of arrest. Jap got the reward of catching me: He got to beat up on me. I was blindfolded and he took me out into the courtyard where the shallow wells had been dug that summer and walked me into the dirt piles and a scrub tree as I fell down, cut my head, and prayed that regrown gristle in my knee would hold together. That went on for maybe half an hour, and I tried to cry out signals that would be picked up in the cell-blocks. Finally Jap stood me up against a wall (I feel sure, of the Desert Inn) and sent four bruising blows into my kidneys and knocked the wind out of me and I sank. Then it was back into Cat's quiz room, out of the blindfold, and into irons for the day while they arranged for my "trial."

About ten the next morning, I was marched to the sound-proofed knobby room in the New Guy Village courtyard. An unprecedented array of people and paraphernalia were there to meet me. A long table was against the wall opposite the door; and behind it, arms resting on its "Ho Chi Minh blue" cloth, were at least half a dozen Vietnamese officers I had never seen before. The man in the center was portly and spoke English. I mentally nicknamed him "Mao." Behind me was a semicircle of about ten riflemen, bayonets fixed and pointing toward the floor. Pigeye was up front where I expected to see him, and he had there as his assistant torturer the big kid who had been at the Zoo as a recruit, Big Ugh.

Mao opened the proceedings by stating, "I have not been here long, but I have heard a lot about you and it's all bad. You have incited the other criminals to oppose the Camp Authority."

Then it was Pigeye with a clout to the jaw (soft fist, as usual), and into the ropes amid extraordinary shouting from both the table and the ring of soldiers behind. Somewhere in this excitement, as my head was being forced down into the claustrophobia position for my "submit," Pigeye, I think by mistake, looped the rope under my *left* (broken) leg and around my neck and took a purchase on forcing my head down to my left knee, rather than to my right knee as he had done before. My leg was bending backward, giving at the knee, when suddenly—*pop!*—there went that hard-won cartilage.

Pigeye heard it, everybody heard it, but nobody could acknowledge it. I was out of business. I submitted, and told them all they wanted to hear. Yes, I had opposed the Camp Authority and I had incited the other criminals to oppose the Camp Authority. The whole thing ended there sort of self-consciously, with everybody filing out and me sitting there on the floor. I was not to be able to get up for over a month.

Three weeks were spent on the floor of that knobby room while I was worked over alternately by Greasy and Vy, with able assistance from Pigeye or Big Ugh as needed, as "war crimes" dossiers on myself and all my leading senior compatriots were compiled. I wrote the papers, and I signed them. But I made them beat it out of me. I felt like two cents when it was done.

Of course, it was never said that it was war-crimes dossiers that were being compiled. Actually, the heart of what they wanted, through the medium of literally dozens of "statements" from me, was a description of how my chain of command worked, who the principals were, how communication was handled, and then a statement of duties performed by each of the principals. I was filling in squares, squares that never really captured the secret of what drove our prison resistance system. But as Greasy and Vy came and went, and conducted their little torture sessions to get this and that out of me, it was clear to me from the items that they had been sent back with for rewrite and focus change that a legal mind was at work at headquarters.

All of this happened to take place at a time when the "Voice of Vietnam" blaring from the outside loudspeaker had much to say about war-crimes trials. It also happened to take place at the very time the Communist world was warming up to celebrate the fiftieth anniversary of the October (Bolshevik) Revolution, and Russian music from the Vietnamese public radio would saturate the prison yard on into the night. As I hiked my butt across that concrete floor at night to urinate under the door because my bucket was left full (hoping I would not get caught and slapped by the guard for doing it), I would be transported into quite a gloomy frame of mind. I felt closely integrated into world history.

My first overall problem in that siege was to protect the Young Turks who had so much to do with the success of the prison organization—the Ron Storzes, the Bob Shumakers, the Sam Johnsons, the Nels Tanners, the George Cokers, the George McKnights. They were buried down in the pack on the seniority list, and to make reference to them was really to finger them. The first list Greasy and Vy were sent to get was that of my "central committee." No, I said, we did not work that way. "Americans are always organized according to strict authoritarian lines," I said. My junior tormentors went away, and then came back with their instructions: "A central-committee list must be produced." I didn't have one.

Big Ugh gave me the ropes, shut off the blood circulation in my arms, and scared me to death because he was so ham-handed and erratic. Vy supervised that torture session and showed his true colors by giving me a kick in the bad knee with some clodhopper shoes he had acquired. "Tell me more about your escape ideas," he taunted.

Finally, after several days, and at a point where I was afraid I was about to spill my guts, I told them to give me a pencil and paper and let me be alone and I would give them my "central committee." I came up with a long-shot solution: I wrote down the name of every prisoner on my list (except Risner, of course, who was stashed back in the cellblock around the corner from me there in New Guy Village—and whom I watched wash at the horsetank just outside my door nearly every day). I gave them a list of 212 American names, in (as best I could figure) rank order. When Vy and Greasy returned, I held it up and said, "This is our organization. It is a lineal responsibility list. It is like a snake you can't kill— the head will always grow back: Take me out and Denton will take over; take Denton out and Jenkins will fill in."

Out to headquarters they went with it.

A day later they came back. No, it would not do—"You *must* have a central-committee list!"

But that list of 212 names impressed them. Forever after I submitted it, I felt we were all a little bit safer in having them know that everybody knew the name of everybody else in the prison system; that way, they were accountable for each one of us. Others were killed in torture later, perhaps just due to unprogrammed overshoots, but knowing of our general communication capacity and ingeniousness couldn't help but make them more conscious of their need to be prudent. After all, there was the chance that they would be held accountable someday.

"My central committee? Why, yes, right here, the top of this name list." I drew a line under the junior air-force lieutenant colonel and said that every name above it was central committee. And that stuck.

Then it was time to write my statement of the duties these commanders and lieutenant colonels performed. They all went like this: "Jeremiah Denton carried out my orders as criminal in charge of the Stardust. His duties consisted of inciting the other criminals to oppose the Camp Authority. He carried out his mission well."

But an interesting wrinkle developed on these reports of individual duties ("crimes"). They were bounced by Cat's office as incomplete in one unusual respect. Greasy was sent back to say, "You have forgotten an important element of proof. You neglected to say that this man has the *innate* ability to incite these criminals to oppose the Camp Authority."

That flashed me back to a loud discussion I'd had with Rabbit some months before. He was the only Vietnamese political cadre besides Cat who had ever volunteered to tell me that he was a member of the Communist party. In the heat of discussion, I had said, "Okay, you're so proud of being a member of the Party, maybe you would tell me what the criteria of membership are."

Rabbit had replied quickly, assuredly, and emotionally: "There are only four. First, you have to be smart enough to understand the theory. Second, you have to be seventeen years old. Third, you have to be selfless and willing to work without the aim of personal gain. And fourth and most important, you must have the *innate* ability to influence others."

Okay, so I methodically started correcting all the sheets, inserting the phrase "and he has the innate ability to do so" in the right place. It was late in the afternoon; I was dragging my feet, and Greasy was getting impatient.

One by one I worked through the stack, but one sheet Greasy grabbed from my hand, wadded up, and threw away. "Forget it, he's harmless," he said. I went right on to the next one, trying not to let my amazement show. The man bypassed was a perfectly honorable fellow with high standards of personal conduct. But Greasy was right; I knew him well and he *was* harmless. That was what the political cadres were figuring out during those hours and hours of individual prisoner "attitude checks"! You could put this officer in a cellblock as senior man and he would do nothing discreditable himself—but on the other hand, it would be a rare day when he organized trouble for the Vietnamese. What were leaders to one side were troublemakers to the other, and these political cadres had a truly amazing eye for that key man—the leader/troublemaker. They were used to looking for them. It is the leader/troublemakers who make communism work.

By the time all of this had been extracted, I was really run-down. I remember one afternoon seeing one of my fellow floor-dwellers, a beetle, on its back being eaten alive by ants. The poor thing was helpless because it couldn't get its feet under it, and it was being slowly lugged toward the doorsill, still moving while the ants were all over it, eating holes in it. I felt just like that beetle, being eaten alive by ants—and yet didn't know my greatest challenge of the Las Vegas purge of 1967 was still ahead.

One night about the first of October, I was lugged back to Riviera cell 1, in the central Las Vegas courtyard. There was no bed and no mosquito net. Then in walked a nasty guard we called "Drut" with a pair of ratchet handcuffs and a blindfold. As I was blindfolded and cuffed behind, I heard a slightly tipsy Greasy talking loudly in the Vietnamese officers' mess area in the little courtyard by Cat's quiz room behind Riviera. "Even Don bowed down, even Don bowed down," he was drunkenly repeating to his messmates.

As the weeks in blindfold wore on, I got more and more depressed. The instability of my rehealing knee cartilage, plus the problem of being cuffed behind and without the strength or balance to get up on one leg, meant that my locomotion was limited to just hunching along on my behind on the filthy floor. I could not ward off the mosquitoes; I could not use the filthy slop bucket I could smell in the corner. I was just a blind, crippled animal, shitting on the floor. And the worst part was, I could think of no reason why I should not expect to spend the rest of my prison career in those straits.

The blindfold and one handcuff came off once each midday when I was given a bowl of what we called "sewer greens." At about the beginning of the third week in those circumstances, a peculiar thing occurred early one afternoon when the guard came · to take the soup plate and put me back in cuffs and blindfold for another twenty-four hours. The old bespectacled "doctor" from the other end of Riviera literally sneaked in behind the guard, looking over his shoulder apprehensively. He lifted me up onto my feet, felt my knee, and walked me around a little to show me that I was gaining strength in the stiff leg. But what he was clearly worried about was my eyes, to see if they were being damaged by the continual pressure of the blindfold. He eased me over to the light and stared into them, and then moved his finger back and forth to see if I could still track it. Then he put me down, exchanged some angry words with Drut, checked the courtyard, and crept out. He was clearly upset about the way I was being kept. And clearly afraid of letting certain officials of the camp know it.

I had never been so depressed and anxiety-ridden in my life. Whether I got any sleep each night depended on a very fickle factor: which guard came to take my soup bowl after the noon meal and put my cuffs back on behind me. If it was Drut, he always closed them up that extra ratchet that pressed the wristbones; that meant twelve hours later, after midnight, the wrists would be puffed up and I would be in bone-tingling agony. In such circumstances, when one has no voice in what happens to him and randomness and chanciness determine his fate, one lives in a worse hell than if continually pestered by a mean but *predictable* antagonist. Chance and continual uncertainty are the ultimate destabilizers.

My uncertainty extended to America's national resolve. As October wore on, it was clear, even to one whose only contact with the world was aural, that the bombing raids that were finally doing the job late that summer had dropped off. No longer did the siren scream all day. No longer were the Riviera doors being blown open by concussion. Just when America had finally gotten the idea of how to get this war over with, it was clear that we were being betrayed by the very men who couldn't wait for the right justification to start it.[1]

For the last three years or so, ever since those three days in August 1964, I had had premonitions about getting left stranded high and dry on this LBJ Vietnam venture. And now the bottom was dropping out. Those conscience-stricken pissants who ran our government had suddenly "got religion." And my life was about to turn inward, away from all matters international.

My life made that turn on the night of October 25, 1967. I was dozing in the corner of Riviera 1, smelling my own stench, now numb to the mosquitoes on my back, against which I had no defense, when a key was inserted in my door. What's this? A quiz? Hands started fussing with the blindfold knot, then it came off, then the guard gave me the "roll up" signal. Hallelujah! *Anything* was better than this setup! The guard helped me to my feet; the old doc had shown me that I could hobble, and I picked up my blanket roll and staggered out behind my guide/guard. At the pedestrian gate, we came to a waiting jeep; my stuff went in the back, I got into the seat, and back on went the blindfold. We were under way!

About eight blocks later, we parked in what smelled like a wooded area. All I could hear were a distant dog barking and nearby crickets. This unfamiliar guard had me envelop my messy blanket roll in my arms and limp along as he guided me through the grass, onto a sidewalk, into some light; then there was a left turn and a wait while a squeaky gate was opened. He nudged me forward as I heard impatient voices muttering below. I felt for a down step with my stiff leg, committed to it, and established myself on it. Then I tried to repeat the action, one step farther down, but I had apparently lost my directional sense and got off to the side, because once I had committed, I suddenly could find no step, and lost my balance, and fell headfirst down several steps and splattered onto what was apparently a sidewalk below. My cup banged down the cement, there was a lot of self-conscious whispering, people picking me and my things up, then a limp of a few steps ahead, a right turn, a few more steps, a cell door opened, I went into the light, and off came the blindfold!

I was in a cell just a little bit bigger than those in the Mint—maybe nine feet long and less than four feet wide. The difference was that this one had no bunk—just a raised portion of concrete floor where one spread out to sleep. In fact all but the first couple of feet inside the door was raised. The guard motioned me to hang my mosquito net and lie under it on a very thin rice-straw mat he furnished. Then he went away and came back with the portable "traveling irons." They were locked on, and I lay back as if in heaven. This little white box was the biggest blindfold I had ever been in. I had been on the verge of a nervous breakdown an hour before. Now I had the feeling I was back among friends. Tomorrow was going to be a great day!

We christened this tiny dungeon "Alcatraz." It was on the grounds of the North Vietnamese Ministry of Defense. It had been a high-security political prison for the highest-ranking Communists under the French; had been allowed to run down after 1954; and according to a nameplate date etched in new concrete, had been reclaimed in June 1967. It was thus the "dark place" Rabbit mentioned was being prepared for the "darkest criminals, who persist in inciting the other criminals to oppose the Camp Authority" in his early-release announcement in May of 1967. After the Las Vegas purge, their list of darkest criminals had been made up, and here we were in leg irons, in windowless cement boxes that were dark by day, bright at night.

First thing the next morning, one by one we started dumping and scrubbing our buckets at the privy on the raised concrete platform. Within an hour, we all had the "lineup": cell 1, Howie Rutledge; cell 2, Harry Jenkins; cell 3, Sam Johnson; cell 4, Bob Shumaker; cell 5, Ron Storz; cell 6, Nels Tanner; cell 7, George Coker; cell 8, George McKnight; cell 9, kept empty; cell 10, Jerry Denton; cell 11, Jim Mulligan; cell 12, kept empty; and I was in cell 13. The lineup was in fact my leadership team at Las Vegas, in spite of my attempts to protect such standout juniors as Shumaker, Tanner, Storz, and Johnson. And included in what we would call the "Alcatraz Gang" were those other "Young Turks" Coker and McKnight, who on a dark night two weeks before had escaped from a nearby lockup called "Dirty Bird Annex," swum down the Red River into the countryside in darkness, and been discovered buried in a mudbank the next day and brought back.

Thus eleven of us had truly reached the bottom of the Hanoi barrel. We all had pedigrees of which we were proud, and we started our new adventure with mutual admiration and high spirits. We would be Brer Rabbits in the briar patch.

To watch, harass, and interrogate eleven of us, approximately twenty-five Vietnamese were fully employed. We ultimately learned that we were within a block of the Plantation, where I had talked to the Russian author about track-and-field competition. Our camp commander was also in overall command of "the Plant" and thus was not one of the twenty-five full-timers but part-time help. He was not a political officer but a short, very pedestrian older man who spoke no English and bore all the marks of a long army career. He looked like the nickname we assigned to him, "Slopehead." Second-in-command was an English-speaking political officer, full-time. He was a rather simple, decent fellow whom we knew as the

Rat. He was no Rabbit, not even a Bug, but he did have a modicum of competence as an interrogator and judge of character.

Our guards at Alcatraz were varied and plentiful. Even though we were all kept in locked cells and in locked leg irons within those cells except at midday, the Vietnamese seemed convinced we would figure out a way to escape. Sometimes two guards were on armed patrol out front all night, sometimes one. There was never an instant when our little courtyard did not have at least one armed guard on patrol.

The Alcatraz routine was fixed. Every morning at the gong, a duty guard would make the rounds, taking each prisoner out of his traveling irons and then one at a time out through the little yard and up to dump his bucket. We were all expert communicators, and from the first day forward, each person would "scrub out" a little message as he swished the stiff bamboo broom through the crap and water in his bucket. It might be only one's call letter. (In this tight little company, we reverted to single-letter calls: I was s, of course; Shumaker took b for Bob; and Sam Johnson, to avoid duplicating the j of the senior Jenkins, took l for some reason I never understood.) So a typical bucket wash by Shumaker might sound like this: swish swish—swish swish swish (pour in more water) swish swish—swish swish swish swish (hi) (dump out the water and put more in) swish swish—swish swish (pause) swish—swish (pause) swish swish swish—swish swish swish (pause) swish swish—swish swish (gang) (dump water) swish—swish swish (signed Bob).

Jerry Denton, whose cell was right at the foot of the steps up to the bucket dump, was always the last to dump and was then made to wash down the whole toilet platform. That gave him a license to give the Alcatraz Gang a five-minute speech with his broom every morning. Jerry would appear to be very serious about cleaning up the area as he deliberately and methodically swept out a joke, a prayer, or some hot dope he had picked up at quiz.

Then all the leg irons would be stowed in cell 9. The day's routine would be over by about 3:00 p.m. when, after the second meal's dishes were picked up, all prisoners would be locked back into irons. Our communication times were pretty well limited to the irons-off period, but there would be thousands of words passed each day. Communication between the long block of ten cells and my and Mulligan's little block of three was connected through an

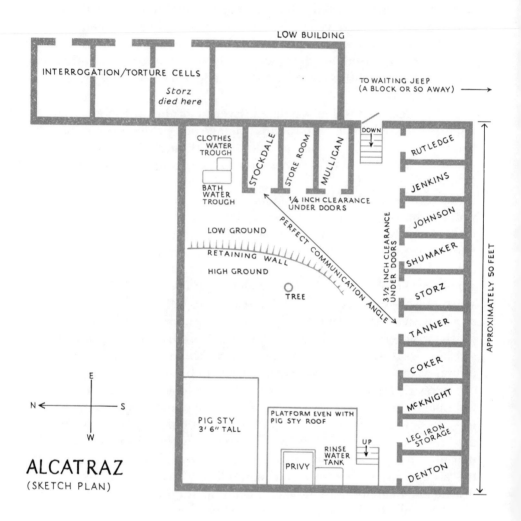

LOW BUILDING

INTERROGATION/TORTURE CELLS

Storz died here

TO WAITING JEEP
(A BLOCK OR SO AWAY) ⟶

DOWN

CLOTHES
WATER
TROUGH

BATH
WATER
TROUGH

STOCKDALE

STORE ROOM

MULLIGAN

RUTLEDGE

JENKINS

JOHNSON

SHUMAKER

STORZ

TANNER

COKER

McKNIGHT

LEG IRON
STORAGE

DENTON

¼ INCH CLEARANCE
UNDER DOORS

3½ INCH CLEARANCE
UNDER DOORS

PERFECT COMMUNICATION ANGLE

LOW GROUND

RETAINING WALL

HIGH GROUND

TREE

APPROXIMATELY 50 FEET

E
N ⟵ ┼ ⟶ S
W

PIG STY
3' 6" TALL

PLATFORM EVEN WITH
PIG STY ROOF

UP

PRIVY

RINSE
WATER
TANK

ALCATRAZ
(SKETCH PLAN)

under-door flash link between me in cell 13 and Nels Tanner in 6.

Never have I seen such universal sensitivity to sound, sight, and communication. With a quiet throat clear, I could summon Nels and immediately see his finger under his door, ready to receive my message.

On a cold winter's night in February 1968, four months after we got there, I was taken out of the irons to go to quiz. It was Rabbit! My heart sank. He was acting cool and said he "was in the area and just stopped by to see how things are." Then he moved to his favorite subject with the question "Does your navy really have a political-policy division?" I felt like I was being pushed back into the quagmire. I assured him that it did, but could tell from the way he was acting that my paper written two years before had still not been sent, was still being checked for foul play. Then he inadvertently dropped in an item that I could use: "Our review board is not sure there is such an office. You know, now the Camp Authority has

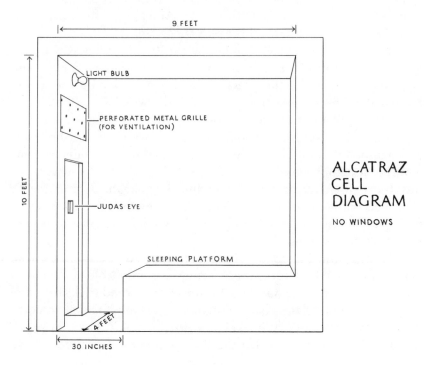

9 FEET

LIGHT BULB

PERFORATED METAL GRILLE
(FOR VENTILATION)

10 FEET

JUDAS EYE

SLEEPING PLATFORM

ALCATRAZ
CELL
DIAGRAM
NO WINDOWS

4 FEET

30 INCHES

set up a review board to screen all of the material we send to your country. In the past we have been badly damaged by criminal trickery."

"Is that so?" I asked with a straight face.

"Yes, but the criminals have paid for their trickery, just as you will pay if we find falsehoods in your material. In any event, the general staff officer wants you to reword parts of that paper. You will hear from us."

That was it; I was taken, shivering from the cold, back to my cell and into leg irons.

That night I came to realize that I had to kill that damned paper before it killed me. My mind went into high gear. The next morning, as soon as it was safe, I gave my little throat clear and immediately saw Nels's finger under his door where the guard couldn't see it, ready to receive my message. I flashed with my finger, "Do you feel like the Clark Kent and Ben Casey matter inoculated you against having to produce more propaganda?"

"I think I know what you're getting at," Nels flashed back. "The answer is yes. I have never been asked to write anything to be sent out of this country since the gooks' American left-wing friends sent them that front page of the *San Diego Union*."

Okay, I said to myself. I'm on the right track. Luck is with me! Spook (our Alcatraz turnkey, an English-speaker) had left my peephole open by mistake the previous week while Denton was giving his morning broom speech on the privy platform. When Spook happened to look up and saw me blamelessly watching Denton, he realized he had left the peephole open by mistake and rushed over and snapped it closed. In the world of extortion, such minor events have great significance. That meant I could admit I knew Denton was there in Alcatraz without giving Slopehead an opening to charge us with communicating. That simple eyeball transaction that took place between Spook and me was golden. Truth was a very useful weapon around there.

At that point I needed writing materials. For a crayon, I had to make an artificial rat turd, there being no serviceable real ones in my cell just then. This was done by sneaking burned sticks from the crapper and mixing the charcoal with soap crumbs. The next morning as I swished out my bucket, I swiped a crude piece of paper toweling from there, too. During the noon hour, I printed a large note to Denton in big capital letters. I gave it a childlike ring and it went something like this:

Dear Jerry,

I saw you through my peephole when the guard forgot to close it last week. I feel very sad that back at the other camp I had to write some very bad things about you. I hope this has not brought harm to you. I am very worried about an old letter I wrote to the U.S. government. It was addressed to a fake office in the Navy. It was full of dirty tricks against the DRV, much worse than the Tanner letter about Clark Kent and Ben Casey. When the word gets back here about how I made fools of the Vietnamese people that bastard Rabbit will have my ass. I am very worried about this slander of the Vietnamese people. God Bless You.   Jim Stockdale

(I put in that sentence about "that bastard Rabbit" having my ass for authenticity; the Vietnamese always expected idioms in our secret correspondence and took great pleasure in "breaking our code." Also, they would expect me to have some nasty things to say about Rabbit.)

I then contacted Denton, as I did every day, through Tanner. I told him that one of these mornings as I walked down toward his cell door on my way to the bucket-dump stairs, a note in brown paper would come sailing through the rather large crack under his door, and that he was *not* to touch it. I said that I was not going to throw it under his door unless the guard was watching me, and that it was being planted as a false intercept. Jerry got the picture and sent a message right back saying he would steer clear of any notes I threw and was already laughing at whatever I was pulling off.

I stood on my toilet bucket and found a place to hide the note under the grille over my door where the Vietnamese didn't think I could reach. Each morning at bucket-dump time, I got it down and folded it up, hid it in my belt, and, by glancing back at the guard escorting me, looked for a condition wherein the guard was not right on my heels (which would make a note drop incredible) but not so far back that he probably wouldn't notice my throwing it. In other words, I wanted to get caught doing something that looked genuinely sneaky, not like an act put on or so stupid that the Vietnamese would smell a rat.

Five mornings went by fruitlessly; the guy was either on my heels or lagging way behind and not paying enough attention. After each unsuccessful sortie, the note would go back up under the grille.

On the afternoon after my fifth unsuccessful try, I happened to be taken to the horsetank for my weekly sponge bath. As always for an Alcatraz bath, I was stripped nude out in the open, the attending guard watching me from nearby. While I was washing, Spook, our turnkey, just happened to come into the yard with a class of neophyte guards who were undergoing initial training over at the Ministry of Defense. He was taking them on their first tour of a real, live prison camp. Seeing my door open, he chose my cell for his demonstration of how to properly inspect a criminal's room.

He was giving it hell. I could hear them banging around in there like they were taking my whole cell apart. Then came his war whoop! "Don! Don! Come here!" My regular guard tagged along and in I went, stark naked. Spook had my note to Denton. The kid guards were all wide-eyed. And did Spook ever read me off—in both languages, so the kids would learn how to really be tough!

A theatrical performance was called for yet again in prison. I became shocked! Guilty! Frightened! I pleaded for mercy! I begged his pardon! I left no doubt among the guards that I had suffered a tremendous setback.

My clothes were brought in and I was left in the torn-up room, all soapy, my door slammed and locked. The whole troop of guards were off to see Slopehead or Rat to present the incriminating evidence! I had to get down and peek under the door before I clapped my hands for joy. This was better than the original Denton-cell maneuver I had planned! It was a perfect way to deliver the bait.

One week, two weeks, everything normal. Undoubtedly the Camp Authority's "review board" was in full deliberation! I put all my faith in the Vietnamese seeing this as too much of a loss of face to recycle the project. I kept the Alcatraz Gang up to speed on where I was on this thing. At about the three-week mark, I was called to quiz. Slopehead was presiding, Rat interpreting, and Spook playing "disciplinary guard." (On seeing the lineup, I tingled with joy; this thing was already dead, or Rabbit would have been sitting there. They were finally sick of the damned letter.)

Slopehead said the charges against me were very serious: calling a Vietnamese officer a bad name, and communicating. I dodged the bad-name part, but denied that I had communicated. I was playing "sea lawyer," and it is a game Vietnamese Communists take very seriously in all their legalistic simplicity. Rat translated a long diatribe from Slopehead as "the camp commander says you violated camp regulations." Playing along in mock seriousness, I stated that there was nothing in camp regulations about *writing* a note, only *passing* a note. Slopehead fell glum. He cleared the court, and I was sent outside with Spook.

When I was called in, Slopehead had turned smug. He had Rat translate the following decision: You are guilty as charged. You are wrong about the camp regulations. They say you may not talk, tap, leave notes, et cetera. "This is et cetera!"

So into the irons I went, round the clock for a month. I couldn't have enjoyed irons more—and I never heard another word about the Navy Department or its "political-policy division." My letter had flunked the screening of the Camp Authority Review Board and was shelved, shelved with an Alcatraz laugh.

But there was agony as well as humor at Alcatraz. During the year, Rat was ordered to obtain yet another confession of "crimes against the Vietnamese people" from all of us. Since they were going to have to give each one of us serious torture to get anything, the physical layout dictated that they do us one at a time. Each man stayed in the torture room longer than the one before him. The process started out at about two days per man, and wound up at more than twice that. I think Rat started to get a message about then. George McKnight spent hours and hours on his knees, hands up against the wall. I'll never forget the raw-hamburger appearance of his legs as he washed at the horsetank near my cell—nor will I ever forget the big wink, the big grin, and the "thumbs up" he flashed to me as I peeked at him from under my door.

There was also love for fellow prisoners at Alcatraz. The most meaningful citation I've ever received came from a "chain message" that each of the other ten guys planned and swished out in sequence at the bucket scrub on the morning of September 9, 1968, the third anniversary of my shootdown: "Here's to CAG for three great years. We love you. We are with you to the end."

Each member of the Gang had his moments of bitter sadness at Alcatraz. Mine came on Christmas night, 1968. The loudspeaker outside my cell was carrying a special Christmas program, playing an old recording of a haunting tune called "Till" by an American piano player named Roger Williams. This was vintage 1956 and I liked it. I was missing Syb and the boys. I hadn't had a letter for nearly two years. Suddenly, as I lay under my net, a key went into my door lock. I waddled over to the door in my traveling irons. The door opened, and it was just the guard on duty; he thrust a letter into my hand and slammed and bolted the door.

It was from Syb! The bare bulb was quite dim, but I could make out the words as I read fast the first time through. It was a lovely letter written only about two months before, with photos. All the boys were okay. Jimmy was a college freshman at Ohio Wesleyan. Sid was a high-school freshman in Coronado, with leg casts on. (He was having a bout with Osgood-Schlatter disease—a temporary condition that accompanied too-fast leg growth.) Stan was doing fine in second grade, and Taylor was in kindergarten. Everything sounded good in our Coronado household. And then I came to it: "I have sold your mother's house in town and put all her things in storage." There were some more remarks that allowed me to piece together the fact that mom had been dead for a year and two months. Syb had undoubtedly been giving me details of that month after month in her undelivered letters and was now winding it down. Mom had died while I was at my low point—hunching around on that excrement-covered deck, blindfolded, in Riviera 1.

Oh God, what a shock. How I dearly loved her and sweet old dad. My mind leapt to where they now surely lay, side by side in that little Abingdon cemetery. And I thought of that emotion-packed September morning when I arrived back there to visit the two of them for the last time.

If the Naval Academy bathrobe in dad's hospital room was a symbol of his influence on me, that Beecher Chapel into which I peered right after leaving his bedside symbolized all the inner power and confidence mom had imparted to me. Of course, that power came not from the organized religion of the chapel, but from the artistic action that took place there: the contests, the recitals, the plays, the oratory.

Neither my mother nor my father were anything like traditional churchgoers. They almost never attended services. As a matter of fact, the social amenities and politics of the churches as institutions formed the basis of a good deal of the humor in my home. Not that my parents were cynical about religious faith; they both honored the Protestant beliefs of their pioneer mothers. They just did not indulge in "churchiness." I was never told to attend, but voluntarily took it up as a high-school kid in order to be with the girls at Epworth League on Sunday night. In a very casual way in the spring of my senior year in high school, I decided to join the church. I had not even been baptized, so this had to be done at the same time. That fact was of absolutely no concern at home.

But almost everything else in my life was of great concern there. My childhood was never carefree or even particularly happy, because from my earliest memories I was always behind, always had debts to pay. It wasn't that I was nagged so much; rather, it was that I grew up understanding that I must excel—excel across the board in studies, music, oration, drama, athletics. From the time I entered the first grade, an inner voice periodically said to me: "To dope off, to just smell the flowers, is a waste, is lazy, is inconsiderate of your parents, and must be paid for with conscience-stricken remorse." And I believed it.

I always imagined myself being seen by outsiders as the spoiled little rich boy. My mother was insensitive to this in the elementary grades: If it sprinkled, I was driven to school; when the blizzards came and everybody took a lunch box, I had to take one fully equipped with napkins and silverware. I hated it when my classmates gaped in silence. I vowed under my breath that someday they would learn that I was as tough inside as the next kid.

In my solitude at home, I developed imaginary friends with whom I talked, usually in my swing in the backyard, where I had privacy. I would spend hours out there swinging gently, enacting in my imagination scenes of athletic triumphs, sea fights, and shipwrecks. I had a theory that if I fantasized hard enough and long enough about an achievement or challenge, it would come about in real life, if perhaps in a slightly diluted, less dramatic way. Somewhere along the way, that awful drive, that tough-minded determination never to be put down, developed within me. You just couldn't grow up in that house in that little town, with all of that personal attention from proud parents, all that embarrassment, and all those big dreams, and not get the feeling you had a continual obligation to push yourself to the limit.

Mom was a tough critic. She was a skeptic, an intellectual, and a very determined, proud, and private person. Despite her dignified image, she was quick with earthy stories, and when I was a boy and we were alone together, we would often enjoy eye-watering belly laughs about anything from the pompous self-righteousness of the town's leading figures to the latest barnyard joke. A casual acquaintance would never have believed what it was like to go out to Rolling View Farm to work with her—spraying her beloved fruit trees in the orchard she'd personally set out tree by tree, or just walking the fields pulling bull nettles or velvetweed, carrying them back in gunnysacks to be dried and burned.

There were times as a young teen-ager when I really felt that I was being touched by greatness on those special days in the wide-open spaces alone with her. She had taken a lot of foreign language in college (she was still our substitute Latin teacher at the high school and I would keep my head lowered at question time in class; she had agreed never to call on me there) and out in the fields she liked to recite German poetry. I didn't understand a word of German, but it was beautiful, and she would interpret special passages for me—she really loved it. But her specialty was Shakespeare. She had coached many of his plays, read and studied his works time and again, and could go on and on reciting lines. She wasn't showing off, she was just having her kind of fun—and she was teaching me. "Do you know what he meant by that? . . . Listen to that line again— isn't that true to life? That's what's so good about William Shakespeare—he really put his finger on the foibles of human nature."

In the spring there would be oratory contests in the high-school auditorium in the evening. All the bright contenders would come to mom for coaching. She worked on their diction, stage presence, even hand gestures. For me, she even fashioned the oration I was to give. The year was 1940. England was at war, and my speech was about Churchill. I still remember parts of it:

> . . . His ancestors had served England and fought her wars and led her peace for as far back as one could remember. But he was the younger

son of a younger son and therefore, and fortunately, poor. What does a young man of spirit do, with quick blood in his veins, no money, and a great tradition behind him? He goes to his country's wars. . . . Around you, Winston Churchill, is a gallant company of ghosts. Elizabeth is there, and sweetest Shakespeare, the man who made the English Renaissance the world's renaissance. Drake is there, and Raleigh, and Wellington. Burke is there, and Walpole, and Pitt. Byron is there, and Wordsworth and Shelley. Yes, and I think Washington is there, and Hamilton, two men of English blood, whom gallant Englishmen defended in your Parliament. And Jefferson is there, who died again, the other day, in France. All the makers of a world of freedom and of law are there, and among them is the Shropshire lad, to whom his ghostly author calls again: Get ye the men your fathers got, and God will save the Queen. . . .

We had some powerful times with real play performances. I hate to think of the number of nights I spent as a grade-school boy in the high-school auditorium as the second or third act of a school or home-talent play was rehearsed "one more time." She would stand in the back and shout, "No, no, no—you are emphasizing the wrong word. . . . Enunciate, enunciate, your diction is sloppy. You must speak more slowly and clearly for people to understand you back here. Now, go back and start where the maid comes in. . . ." Watching all this from the back row night after night, I got to know every line in the play.

And then it came time for me to be in plays, some of which she coached, and all the rest she attended. Occasionally I would score an extra point with her, even when she was not the coach. I had the lead in every high-school play, and she knew most of those plays very well. We would talk about my interpretation of the parts at home. In my last play, my senior year, we began arguing about the male lead's part. From the way I described my feelings about it, she was convinced that I was off the track, that I was creating a character quite different from the one she would have her actor portray. I was confident that I knew what I was doing, but I was nervous when I peeked out before the curtain went up and saw her and dad making their way down to their orchestra seats.

From my first entrance, however, I forgot about everything but doing what I wanted to do, my way. I could tell in the second act that we had a real barnburner going—my timing was good, and the audience was quick with a sigh or a laugh in the right places. As the curtain fell after the last act, the applause was good, but I became concerned again about mom's reaction as I went back to change. One of my close friends out front sensed what was going on; I looked up apprehensively as he came into the dressing room with a smile on his face. He said mom really liked it—that as people were congratulating her, he saw her wipe away a tear. Now that was something! That was not like her.

The only other time I knew I'd really scored with her was in that Beecher Chapel on the first Saturday morning in May of 1939. Public schools in our part of the country in those days had competitive spring festivals almost like those of the ancient Greeks. The big one in that part of Illinois was known as the Military Tract Competition (so named because the competing high schools were all located in a "military tract" that President James Monroe had set aside for land grants to veterans of the War of 1812). It was a large grant and about twenty high schools competed for a full day in every sort of literary, musical, and track-and-field event. In music the events were piano, violin (both instruments that I had been given lessons on, of course), and men's and women's voice. As a freshman, I had taken first place in the Abingdon High School piano contest earlier that spring, and thus had earned the right to represent my school in this very important competition.

On that Saturday, I thought I had surely gotten in over my head. I was only fifteen, representing one of the smaller schools. Each of us contestants filed in one at a time at about ten- to twelve-minute intervals, mounted the stage, sat down at the concert grand, and played his or her memorized selection. Out front was a small audience of music teachers and parents, and in the first row were the judges—two old lady musicians plus the chairman of the music department of Knox College. These three kept making notes solemnly on their grading forms. When all of us had finished, we filed back in together and sat behind the audience as the head judge read out the winners, starting with fifth place. I watched the back of mom's head, and she visibly flinched when my name was called last, for first place. I think I was the only freshman in history ever to win it, but I didn't feign modesty. I knew I had talent, and I had paid my debts. I had been taking lessons and practicing for an hour a day since I was five years old.

The head of the music department presented me with a gold medal. As we all started leaving, he came over and began telling me that I had to major in music; that on the piano keyboard could be found the complete range of satisfactions, achievements, and emotional lifts that any profession offered. This was an interesting way to look at it, and one I thought a lot about later. But at the time he was telling me these things, my mind was wandering. I was thinking that I had just scored five points for my school in the overall competition and that I was already late to Knox's Willard Field locker room to get dressed for the afternoon's track-and-field events. I had other debts to pay. There was this business of dad's ambition for me to go to Annapolis. And I was to shed the image of being a chubby little mama's boy who was always at the top of the honor roll but unable to fight his way out of a paper bag. . . .

"Till" was still coming out of the outdoor speaker and suddenly seemed so appropriate as I said farewell to dear old mom. On that Christmas Night, 1968, I stood there in my leg irons and wept.

Sometimes there was resentment in Alcatraz. The Gang was there for the public demise of both McNamara and Johnson. It was hard to tell which departure the Vietnamese more enjoyed rubbing in. The loudspeaker in the Alcatraz yard would yowl, "Even McNamara and Johnson have quit. How can you persist in your diehard support of an immoral American government?"

But there was also originality and vitality at Alcatraz. We broke the record on communication improvisations. One of the favorites was Jerry Denton's famous "Vocal Tap Code." This was used for short oral messages, usually of an urgent nature. He first asked everybody to "desensitize" the guard force by hawking, spitting, nose snorting, and sneezing as we moved to and from our bucket-dumping duties. Then it came: noise substitution for tap-code numbers. A 1 or a 2 was respectively one cough or one snort, or two of either. A 3 was a throat clear; a 4 was a hawk; and a 5 was either a loud spit or sneeze, depending on the range. A member of the Gang would come back from a quiz at night, snorting and wheezing, giving us in the cells a full report, and the guard would be oblivious to it all.

We also covered every future communication contingency we

could think of. Each member of the Gang picked a song that had to do with his home state as an emergency self-identifier. The thought was we could at least whistle our tunes as a last-ditch maneuver just before we bit the dust. Shumaker chose "The Pennsylvania Polka," Tanner "The Tennessee Waltz," and so on. I picked "Chicago," but George McKnight complained about the tune being hard to remember and switched me to "I Used to Work in Chicago in a Big Department Store." Mulligan requested a waiver on the state-song idea. He wanted "When Irish Eyes Are Smiling." We let him have it.

There was a special personal commitment in Alcatraz. It was unity over self, no matter what the cost. Joseph Conrad could have been describing the Gang: "A certain readiness to perish is not so very rare, but it is seldom that you meet men whose souls, steeled in the impenetrable armour of resolution, are ready to fight a losing battle to the last." [2]

There was illness at Alcatraz. We all ate identical rations from the same pots, but had different diseases. Half had intestinal worms that could "make their toilet buckets fairly boil," in Harry Jenkins's words. Some became very emaciated, particularly our spark plug, our hero Ron Storz. He ultimately became depressed, lost interest in eating, and failed rapidly.

And there were sometimes short tempers in Alcatraz. It was a cold winter's night on January 24, 1969. By that time, the Gang had been in leg irons there for fifteen months. Harry Jenkins, laden with big intestinal worms, was seized with stomach pains and called "*Bao cao!*"—the authorized emergency call. The guard on duty started out grouchy—and wound up mean. He had picked up enough English to mutter things that sounded like "Sleep," "No *bao cao*," and so on. Harry got mad. His voice pitch went up. He added a few expletives. That got us all up. We waddled to our doors in our traveling irons and commenced to shout "*Bao cao*" in unison. Then we started banging on the doors. Soon the yard was full of furious Vietnamese officers. We shouted them down from behind locked doors. Finally someone said Harry would see the "*Bock-shee*" and our anger dwindled off.

But I thought this was the time to vent our wrath about this continued solitary-confinement-and-leg-irons thing. It had gone on long enough—too long for sick people. Before the first gong early the next morning, I got down on the floor by my door with my irons still on, called Nels Tanner, and put out an order: "Everybody goes to the food pot when we are taken out to get our rations, but nobody takes any food for three days."

So that's what happened, and by evening meal there was a regular lineup of enraged political cadres watching and scowling. We were demonstrating organized resistance to authority, and that is the highest crime any group can commit in a Communist country. Sure enough, that night many of us were dressed down in quiz by Rat and others. They were obviously getting material to make a report to Cat.

Before daylight the next morning, my door flew open. There were about five people outside in the darkness. A voice said, "Roll up." They had no cuffs, but I was spun around and a piece of thick, stiff wire was bent tightly around my wrists. Then I was blindfolded and marched off into the faintest of winter dawns. I was stuffed into a jeep and driven through city streets. (In their haste with the blindfold, the Vietnamese had left me a tiny peephole and in the dim light I could make out scores of bicycles moving along the road as we wove through them.) Then we stopped and I could smell it: Hoa Lo Prison. I knew every step of the way in my blindfold—I could tell when we left the outer moat and got into the tunnel through the inner building; it rang like an echo chamber to the heel clicks of my escort. Then a left turn, a few steps, and left again. Ha! So it's room 18, is it? They are not screwing around this morning!

Blindfold off, twin green doors clamped shut, I found my mind floundering for a cover story that would minimize blame of those wonderful guys I'd left behind, minimize their implication in my hunger-strike decision. I knew room 18 so well. I found myself edging right toward its only peephole, an ill-defined area of blurred paint on one of the small windowpanes. I knew right where to stand to see out it. And who was coming up from Cat's office area on the far side of the main courtyard? Rabbit, and, two paces behind him, Pigeye.

It was just daylight when they rounded the corner and threw open the double doors. I bowed. Rabbit brushed such a gesture aside and bluntly said, "It is you who has caused me to be brought back here from my new office. I don't like it. We'll get you this time, you son of a bitch. I don't want to talk about what happened at the camp you just left. I want to know only one thing: Will you be my slave or not?"

"No!" I shouted. And twenty minutes later Pigeye had me roped and screaming for mercy. It was 7:00 A.M., January 25, 1969.

Chapter 10

Going Public with the Truth

Each morning as I read the newspaper during the spring and summer of 1968, I wondered if it was possible that someday I would look back on these days and feel anything except despair. The spring was one continual starting and stopping of the bombing in North Vietnam. It seemed to me almost deliberately planned to allow the North Vietnamese to recover from the damage of one siege and prepare to withstand another. I was becoming more and more desperate in my need to do something I felt might help Jim in some way. The North Vietnamese were insidiously clever and our leaders such patsies for the enemy's propaganda ploys. Bob Boroughs suspected even worse was the case: He thought that some State Department officials were too friendly with those Americans who happily spread North Vietnamese propaganda in the United States.

In May, I received word that a navy man who had been released early from imprisonment in Hanoi would visit San Diego and reassure us about his treatment. He reported that it was rough but not unbearable. No one pointed out that this man's release, good condition, and reasonable treatment were part of the enemy's propaganda campaign. When this fellow made these statements, I felt certain he was telling the truth. What was not said was that probably he had been separated out soon after his capture and accorded special treatment with the idea that one day he might do just what he was doing now—spreading enemy propaganda about the treatment of prisoners.

Furthermore, I was dismayed that my own government encour-

aged and applauded these early releases. For a military man to accept parole and come home early was forbidden by the Code of
Conduct. Yet our government encouraged and condoned this sort
of release. What kind of honorable situation existed when our own
government disobeyed the code it had sworn our servicemen to
uphold? Not only was there no outcry by anyone that the enemy
abide by the Geneva Convention, but now the U.S. government was
flagrantly encouraging the military to disobey its own code. I was
not encouraged by a newsletter from the new head of the Navy
Bureau of Personnel, dated May 20, 1968, which said, "The news
concerning negotiations with North Vietnam gives hope and cautious optimism. . . . I believe we are reaching a turning point and I
pray that the matter of prisoner release will be one of the earliest
resolved."

I was the one reaching a turning point. More and more I was
beginning to think about going to the press myself and telling the
truth about Jim's treatment. I would keep the intelligence parts
completely quiet. Just making the information he had written in his
letters public, along with the facts about the Geneva Convention,
should stir the public to take some sort of action. On my way to
Jimmy's graduation from Mercersburg, I made the rounds in Washington and asked Bob Boroughs to begin thinking about my going to
the press.

The graduation ceremony was an informal, outdoor affair, but
very pleasant. The beginnings of the social revolution of the youth
in our country were apparent in the boys' exaggerated casual dress,
combining wildly clashing plaid coats with checked pants and pais-
ley neckties, tied as sloppily as possible but still passing the coat-
and-tie requirement. During the graduation exercises, I felt close to
Jim and spent most of my time wondering if he had any sense of
where I was or what I was doing.

As that summer progressed, I felt overwhelmed by an avalanche of trouble. I received a letter from the writer Felix Greene,
who had recently returned from Hanoi.

> . . . I am very surprised that your husband has indicated that he is in
> solitary confinement. I wonder if in fact you are correct in assuming
> this. From what I have seen and from what most other reporters from

Europe have observed, the usual practice is to allow a number of U.S. prisoners to be housed together. For what comfort it might be to you, I might say that those of us who have been able to see prisoners in North Vietnam have concluded that their treatment has been good. . . .

As he and others broadcast this sort of misinformation, I felt more and more inclined to tell the truth publicly. All my reading about Communist treatment of prisoners throughout the world led me to believe that telling the world the truth about Hanoi's treatment of American prisoners might be our only hope.

That June, Sid graduated from the eighth grade as a leader in his class. All spring he'd been complaining about a painful knee and I kept hoping that eventually his complaints would disappear. When we returned to the cottage in Connecticut for one more summer, I realized Sid was sitting out the neighborhood football skirmishes and his tearful eyes clearly reflected he was really hurting. I took him to a doctor, who said, "If it's bone cancer, we take the leg off right about here." With the side of his hand, he chopped at a place in his right thigh between the hip and the knee.

I could hardly breathe during the next three days. I couldn't believe these terrible things were happening to me. I kept looking at Sid across the yard as he sat with his friends, resting his leg. My gift from God for my twenty-first wedding anniversary was word that Sid had Osgood-Schlatter disease (arrested development of growing ends of bones with involvement of shinbones, causing local pain and swelling just below the kneecap) instead of bone cancer. Jimmy had had O.S., too. It was no picnic, and if Sid's became worse, he might have to wear leg casts, but I knew eventually he'd be okay.

I think of the remainder of that 1968 summer as my Branford Library summer. I was still seriously considering going to the press with my story about Jim's plight as it was revealed in his letters, and contrasting it with the requirements of the Geneva Convention and their flagrant violations by Jim's captors. It seemed clear to me that we needed to spotlight the truth about North Vietnamese treatment of American prisoners, but I needed to be absolutely sure that public exposure of the North Vietnamese was the right course of action for me to follow. It was also extremely difficult for me to accept the idea that the U.S. government could be wrong about their "keep quiet" policy, even though my reading strongly indicated otherwise.

Long into the endless hot, humid, sleepless nights, I pored over *The Prisoners of Korea, The Road to Calumny, In Every War But One, In the Presence of Mine Enemies*, and many more books and articles of a similar nature. They were depressing, and when I would finally fall asleep, I'd have nightmarish dreams. Often Jim would be about to come across a narrow bridge leading out of prison, but just before he crossed he would have to return for something he'd forgotten and would disappear. I would wake up feeling sweaty, exhausted, and nauseated.

On July 20, I wrote a form letter to my friends, asking them to write their elected representatives requesting that everything possible be done to effect humane treatment for all prisoners in Hanoi. I also told them I planned to vote for Nixon if he was nominated, wouldn't have a copy of Dr. Spock's book in my house (Spock was a baby doctor turned vocal war protester), and felt that Eugene McCarthy had prolonged the war. McCarthy seemed to think that just a little more love of our enemies would solve our problems. Further, he planned a slow withdrawal from Vietnam, along with a halt to our bombing. I feared that this would mean sure death for many, many Americans and prisoners.

I followed that part of my letter by saying that my oldest son felt my ideas were saturated with emotionalism and lacked intellectual reinforcement. I used Jimmy as a sounding board for my ideas about the progress of the war. He wasn't sure that Nixon's secret plan to end the war actually existed. I insisted it made sense that he had one, but I secretly suspected I was my own victim of wishful thinking. Jimmy would argue with me about my hopeful conclusions, but he was gentle and sympathetic in expressing less optimism than I felt about Nixon. I felt President Johnson was hopelessly trapped in a morass of generalizations. That spring Johnson had announced he would not run again, but I felt any Democrat would follow the same policy and that we had to have a change of party leadership.

If I was absolutely honest with myself, I probably felt Nixon would bomb the enemy into submission and end the hostilities in a few weeks. The kind of bombing Johnson kept starting and stopping did little damage and only encouraged the enemy to hold out.

✧

By the end of that long, hot, tedious summer, I had convinced both myself and Bob Boroughs that I should go to the press with my story. After seeing Jimmy off for college at Ohio Wesleyan, I flew back to Coronado and started the school year for myself and Sid, Stan, and Taylor. I felt encouraged about my plan to write something for the press by an article in the *San Diego Union* on September 1, 1968. Entitled "Red Brain Wash Teams Work on US Pilots," it had been written by Edward Neilan of the Copley News Service and in conclusion said, "Many experts believe the prisoners will be paraded and exploited—in flagrant violation of all established codes—at various stages in future negotiations on the Vietnam question."

In response, I sent the following telegram to the new secretary of defense, Clark Clifford, and the same to Averell Harriman:

> A recent article in the press by Mr. Edward Neilan of the Copley News Service describes the ruthless treatment of prisoners of war in North Vietnam. In conclusion the article reads, "Many experts believe the prisoners will be paraded and exploited, in flagrant violation of all established codes, at various stages in future negotiations on the Vietnam question." My husband has been a prisoner of war in North Vietnam for 3 years. What steps are being taken to prevent these present and future violations of the established codes?

Clark Clifford had replaced Robert McNamara as secretary of defense. I was glad to be rid of McNamara. In my opinion he was a smart theoretician who knew nothing about waging war. I remembered hearing him say on the radio when he left the Pentagon for the last time something to the effect that no one would have dreamed the war could last so long. I thought, anybody who fights a war the half-baked way you have should know it can go on almost forever.

In reply to mine, I received this telegram from Ambassador Harriman:

> September 6, 1968—Following message to you relayed from Paris: Dear Mrs. Stockdale. I appreciate your sharing with me your concern regarding the recent Copley News Service article on our prisoners of war in North Vietnam. I can tell you that we have no information to substantiate the assertion in the article that our prisoners will be exploited in connection with future negotiations on a settlement in

South Vietnam. In fact, North Vietnamese representatives here have indicated to me that the release last month of three pilots was a gesture of good will. I have urged them to give serious consideration to further releases, including those pilots that have been held the longest time, and those that have been injured. I am sure you realize that the welfare and early release of our men held prisoner continues to be uppermost in my mind. Sincerely W. Averell Harriman

No, Ambassador Harriman, I thought when I finished reading this message, I'm not sure I do realize the welfare of the men is uppermost in your mind; nor do I think you, of all people in this world, should be advocating early releases, which are a violation of the Code of Conduct.

While I searched for a way to take my story to the press, I was reminded that I'd met a man from the Copley News Service at the Mendel Rivers luncheon. He'd given me his card and urged me to contact him if ever he could help in any way. That was how I would go about it. I would write out my story, get it cleared with Bob Boroughs, and then send it to this Copley News Service fellow and tell him I wanted to have it printed.

After I had written out my story, however, I began to have second thoughts about sending it in for publication. When I had first proposed publicizing my personal story, Bob Boroughs had opposed the idea. He was in favor of publicity about the prisoners' plight in general, but was apprehensive about *my* doing it, because of my covert communication with Jim. I had worked on him for some weeks before convincing him it was important for me to take the lead in going public to give other wives the courage to do so. I could hardly encourage them to publicize their stories while I refrained from telling my own.

But what if my publicity did somehow backfire and cause Jim further harm? There was no assurance that my going to the newspaper would accomplish anything positive. Maybe I should just forget the whole thing. But, my God, I hadn't had a letter now from Jim since that one in March. Things seemed to be getting worse rather than better. And Bob Boroughs would never have acquiesced if he didn't honestly believe it would be okay.

After clearing my written story with Bob, I finally sent my piece to the Copley News Service. I prayed it was the right thing to do. It was a chance I felt I had to take.

I was shocked when a few days later my Copley News friend telephoned to ask me if I wanted to sell the story.

"Heavens, no," I replied, "I just want to tell the world the truth about what's happening to Jim."

He decided to send a reporter to interview me. I was nervous about talking to her, but she put me at ease right away, and on Sunday, October 27, 1968, the *San Diego Union Tribune* published my story.

I really had a twofold purpose in making my statement: I hoped the publicity might put some pressure on our government and motivate them to demand that the North Vietnamese abide by the Geneva Convention. In part the article said:

> By terms of the Geneva Convention Relating to Treatment of Prisoners of War, North Vietnam was morally bound to notify the U.S. government of Stockdale's capture, to send a photograph of the prisoner and to allow him to communicate with his family through channels established by a neutral intermediary, or by the International Committee of the Red Cross. By terms of the convention, the North Vietnamese agreed to let a neutral intermediary inspect their prison camps. They have not abided by either agreement. . . .
>
> Last fall the prisoners' wives here organized formally as the League of Wives of American Prisoners in Vietnam.
>
> "The main purpose of the organization," says Mrs. Stockdale, "is to try to help the men in any way we can, by writing letters to Congressmen, by trying to bring pressure on Hanoi.
>
> "The North Vietnamese," she says, "have shown me the only thing they respond to is world opinion. The world does not know of their negligences and they should know!"

Most of the text of Jim's first letters was quoted and pictures of him and me were included. I felt greatly satisfied with this effort. I sat up against the pillows in our antique spool bed on a cool, foggy Sunday morning reading and rereading the article. I was glad I'd gone ahead and taken this step. Now I'd try to get some of the other wives in my situation to do the same. I wondered if I'd hear any reaction from Washington about my having violated the "keep quiet" policy, but during the following weeks there wasn't a sound. It was as if they were waiting to see what consequences I might suffer from having taken this bold, unadvised step.

❖

That October, I wrote two letters to Jim, one long and one short. Following the example of the last letters to come out of North Vietnam, written on seven-line forms, the U.S. government advised that using a similar short form might increase chances of mail being delivered to our men. Bob Boroughs said to write one of each. Both were encoded. I drew a light pencil line between each line printed on the form, writing on thirteen lines altogether. After all, the instructions printed on the form sent by the government said, "Write only on the lines." It didn't say I couldn't draw more lines if I wanted to. Bob laughed when I explained my rationale to him. This way we could work with twice as many words for encoding.

It had been a year since Jim's mother had died. I had let him know about her death in every letter I'd written, but there was no evidence he knew she had died. There was still only that one letter received from him in March 1968. In the long version of my October letter, I told him about the family: Jimmy was a freshman at Ohio Wesleyan; Sid a freshman at Coronado High School after a bout with Osgood-Schlatter disease; Stanford was in the third grade; Taylor in the first.

A couple of weeks later, on the November evening of Election Day, I sat glued to the television reports about election results. Never before had I felt the outcome would greatly affect my personal life, but I was convinced that this election would have everything to do with my future and Jim's. Nixon had to win. He had to beat the Democratic candidate, Hubert Humphrey. Otherwise, the future was bleak and hopeless. We had to have a change of political party and a fresh approach to this quagmire we'd gotten ourselves into. I began to smile with satisfaction as Nixon pulled ahead. Before I went to bed that night, I was sure his election was official. Surely now things would begin to get better. I was tremendously relieved.

During my drives to and from school in the days following the election, I began to try to figure out some way to reach President-elect Nixon directly. While he was planning his administrative strategy, we needed to impress him with the dire circumstances our American prisoners were in. I read that he would be attending a governors' conference; our own governor, Ronald Reagan, would be there also. I tried to get through to Governor Reagan by phone but was told I could neither talk to him nor make an appointment to do so. No amount of pleading changed the scalding response of the underling handling my call. I settled for firing off an irate telegram to Governor Reagan, deploring the fact that I'd not been permitted to talk to him and imploring him to impart my message to the president-elect. Then I promptly put the entire exchange out of my mind as I prepared to celebrate Stanford's ninth birthday.

When the telephone rang one evening the following week, I was puzzled and fascinated by the marvelous resonance of the masculine voice asking to speak to Mrs. Stockdale. Whom did I know with such a magnificent voice? It sounded familiar, but I couldn't place it.

"This is Ronald Reagan speaking," he said. My mind went into overdrive. I had any number of practical-joker friends who might be partying and trying to raise my morale this way. I almost quipped, "And this is Sophia Loren. What do you have in mind?" But that voice stopped me. It did sound like Ronald Reagan. And it was.

He assured me he'd given President-elect Nixon my message. Also, he wanted me to know I could talk to him by phone or in person whenever I wanted to, and he made sure I had numbers where I could reach him. This was the first time any public official had made an extra effort to help me or gone out of his way to be kind; usually they replied with obviously insincere form letters. My morale was genuinely bolstered by the governor's taking the time to telephone. I thought things really might begin to get better now that the Republicans had been elected.

Our League of Wives meetings now were becoming planning sessions about things we could do to publicize the plight of our men. Five other wives had published their stories in the press. We'd made a beginning. At our January session, just a few days before the Inauguration, we decided to organize a last-minute telegraph-in to the president. In the next two or three days, we telephoned and telegraphed everyone we knew who might help us, making a special effort to contact as many prisoner-of-war and missing-in-action wives as possible. The local newspaper helped with an appeal, and everyone who participated received a telegraphed reply from President Nixon. We were thrilled to hear that over 2,000 of our telegrams reached him on his first day in office. It felt so much better to be able to do something that might help in some small way. Now we had to persuade the new administration to change the "keep quiet" policy. We needed to have our government leaders denounce North Vietnamese violations of the Geneva Convention.

At the end of January, I made a quick trip east to attend a family wedding. Hoping I might have a personal visit with President Nixon, I scheduled my flights with a Washington stopover and sent him an appointment request by telegram. One of Jim's close friends was now assistant to the secretary of the navy and he was hopeful an appointment could be arranged. I waited in Washington an extra two days, but was told the president was too busy to see me.

"Confidentially," my friend said as I was getting ready to leave, "the military aide to the president is an air-force general and he's not about to have a navy wife see the president unless an air-force wife is there, too."

Soon after I returned home, our League submitted a formal request for a meeting with the president. We hoped it wouldn't be too long before we heard he would see some of us. During these early months of 1969 and President Nixon's new administration, I urged our San Diego League members to rack their brains for any ways we could bring pressure for change in government policy. I dreamed of seeing the president, as commander in chief of all the armed forces, publicly condemn the North Vietnamese for their mistreatment of our men. I hoped, too, that the massive bombing program I thought he planned would start soon. I was not too worried that our prisoners would be bombed; I knew the big bombers could hit their targets selectively, and I felt sure the locations of the POWs were known from the encoded messages our government had received.

In my February 1969 letter to Jim, I told him Sid had had another long siege with his legs in casts; Stan was being treated for a mirror-vision problem but was doing fine in school; and Taylor had lost his first tooth. My letter had a confident tone that didn't really reflect my feelings about Sid and Stan. This was Sid's third six-week session in casts for that school year, and he desperately missed being able to participate in the sports he dearly loved. Stan was having school problems. The doctor thought it was emotional blindness, but began testing him for a possible brain tumor. Blessedly, he found no evidence of any kind of tumor. I didn't tell Jim any of this.

Meanwhile, word of our organization had spread, and I was getting mail from all over the country from more and more wives and mothers of our captured and missing men. Throughout the spring of 1969, I was working on another way to pressure Hanoi. The North Vietnamese now had an embassy in Paris. Their representative at the peace talks was Minister Xuan Thuy. We figured we might get some response about who was dead and who was alive if we bombarded Xuan Thuy with telegrams.

Our new U.S. ambassador at the peace talks was Henry Cabot Lodge. After contacting him—partly to make sure he had no objection to such a plan and partly to let him know our San Diego organization was going to take action (thereby possibly putting more pressure on him to do something)—I sent out a mimeographed letter to the more than sixty wives I knew of throughout the country. I told them to contact me for details if they wanted to join our telegram campaign, and to pass the letter along to any others they might know in our situation.

Replies began to pour in, and from the tenth of March on, a new batch of telegraph inquiries clacked into Xuan Thuy's office in Paris. I was sure our efforts were having some beneficial side effects, whatever the outcome might be. Shortly after sending out my letter, I received a phone call from a young wife in Anniston, Alabama. Someone had passed my letter along to her. She told me her husband had been missing for three years and I was the first person in the same boat she'd ever talked to. She sobbed out her gratitude and pleaded with me to think of something else she and others could do to help.

This evidence that others around the country wanted to take unified action bound our San Diego League more closely together. We began to meet every other week. We so thoroughly enjoyed each other's company and so appreciated the release afforded by freedom of communication and mutual understanding that we felt the need to be together frequently.

About this time I began getting evening phone calls from a POW wife in Minneapolis named Mary Winn. She had heard about my form letter but hadn't seen it. Her husband, Air Force Colonel David Winn, had been shot down a few months before and she'd heard I knew more about the prisoner situation than anyone in the country. We became close telephone friends and seemed to have a lot in common. She had four children about the ages of mine and I could tell she was a very intelligent and persistent lady. I would ask her what she thought of my ideas and encouraged her to let me know any ideas she might have to pressure both the United States and North Vietnamese governments. She agreed that we now needed a truly powerful way to reach millions of people with the truth about our story. I remembered the Editorial Writers' Conference I'd read about late last fall and felt I'd found my powerful medium. If we could enlist their help, they could put pressure on both Hanoi and Washington at the same time.

After school on the very day I thought of it, I drove straight to the editorial offices of the *San Diego Union.* In answer to my questions about how to get a list of the world's most prominent editorial writers, I was given an out-of-date copy of the *Editor and Publisher Year Book.* I hugged it close to me as I hurried back to my car. I was excited about this newest idea and raced home to type out another form letter to mimeograph and send out to POW and MIA families. I selected about twenty editorial writers of newspapers with the largest circulations and included their names and addresses in my letter. Soon hundreds of letters from the families could begin reaching the editorial writers. Even though I went to the post office every few days to buy envelopes and stamps, I was more than happy to be spending my recreation money this way. The other wives in the San Diego League helped write and send out letters, and I got Mary Winn started on the same project in the Midwest.

I was encouraged to be notified that a group from the Nixon administration in Washington was coming to San Diego on March 26 to talk to us about the prisoners and missing. What a change— they were actually coming to talk to us without our having browbeaten them! A representative from the State Department and Defense Department and a former POW from Korea would address our group after dinner at the Officers' Club. Air-force and marine wives from the Los Angeles area would join us. Bob Boroughs wanted me to wear my hidden tape recorder, and again I would dress in my flowing costume to conceal its bulk.

If this group from Washington, which some of us flippantly referred to as the "Washington Road Show," expected a quiet, subdued audience, they were surprised indeed. The air-force wives had been particularly neglected. One wife unveiled a painting that she said depicted the lack of compassion by the air-force brass, contrary to the motto "The air force takes care of its own." She slammed this painting onto the floor, telling the speakers to take it back to the Washington generals to let them know how she felt. There was a quiet hush in the room after her outburst. Then wife after wife got up and voiced her disgust with the government's performance. I pleaded for a government change of the "keep quiet" policy, pointing out that no one had had any mail since October; it seemed that things were getting worse instead of better.

There was no question about our feelings by the end of the meeting. The three men from Washington were somewhat wide-eyed. I couldn't help but feel a little sorry for them; they had walked right into a hornet's nest. It felt good, though, to tell them how I felt and to know I was not alone. I couldn't write Jim any of this, of course, but he was probably not getting my mail anyway. I had not been among those receiving mail the previous October, so it had been a year since I'd heard anything. I felt sure that if Jim wasn't being allowed to write, he wasn't being given any mail from me, either. The two usually went together.

In my letter to Jim at the end of April, I told him Sid and I had agreed he'd apply to South Kent School in Connecticut for the fall. It was a good prep school where Sid had a close friend from the shore. Sid would repeat freshman year.

While getting ready for my own school on Monday morning, May 19, 1969, I was irritated by the ringing telephone. A secretary asked me to wait on the line to talk to Mr. Capen from the Defense Department and Mr. Sieverts from the State Department. I frowned, wondering what these two, who'd been part of the "Washington Road Show" at the chaotic Miramar meeting, wanted to say. They both greeted me somewhat excitedly. Mr. Capen, Secretary of Defense Laird's assistant, did most of the talking.

"Before you leave for school this morning, we wanted you to know that here in Washington, in just a few minutes, the secretary of defense is going to do the thing you've been wanting him to do for so long. He's going to publicly denounce the North Vietnamese for their treatment of our American prisoners and for their violation of the Geneva Convention. We know you've been working long and hard for this day, and we wanted you to be the first to know."

That was a real switch. A high official in the Nixon administration was going on the record. The administration was publicly abandoning the "keep quiet" policy, as its predecessors should have done years before.

My heart sang during the drive to school, and I smiled that evening as I watched the news. I slipped into a peaceful sleep that night, thinking things surely would get better for Jim. I wondered if it was a coincidence that today was Ho Chi Minh's birthday.

Less than a month after the public denouncement of the North Vietnamese, I received my first letter from Jim in 1969. It was only a seven-line form letter, but I knew even from these few lines that Jim hadn't had any mail from me since before autumn of 1967—almost two years ago. If he'd had even one short form from me, he would have known about his mother's death. Instead, the letter said:

> Syb, My thoughts included you all again this Christmas. The teaching you do must be good for all, influencing our four sons to study well. They all have my unlimited concern and adoration. Give them and the three grandparents my hugs, love and kisses. Tell the whole family about my being in good health. I love you completely, Syb.   Jim

I didn't let the awkwardness of some of his expressions worry me—I knew the entire thing was in code for Naval Intelligence. Bob Boroughs wouldn't give me a clue as to what it contained, but I suspected on my own that it may have involved prison locations and the setting up of pickup boats and airplanes in case any escape plans were successful. I also thought they had been telling Jim about counteragents safe for communication within the North Vietnamese prison system.

I asked Bob if he thought it would be safe to have Jim's letter reprinted in the newspaper. I felt that personalizing the story for the public in this way would involve them emotionally and thus motivate them to demand action for better treatment for our American POWs. I was relieved when he gave his okay. Indeed, we both took secret satisfaction in publicizing this encoded letter. It pleased me particularly because I felt this was the best of all ways to dispel any notion the Communists might have that Jim and I were sending coded messages. At the same time, it seemed crystal clear to me that anyone reading Jim's letter could detect from his guarded statement about his good health that the life he was leading was far from the calm, civilized existence the Communists hoped would be interpreted.

After Jim's letter had appeared in the paper, the local TV station, KOGO, sent a reporter to our house to do a story. The interviewer and I sat on the sofa chatting about Jim. My voice was quavery and my palms sweaty; I'd never been on TV before. That evening, as I listened to my nasal-sounding comments and saw my less-than-perfect image on the screen, I winced and groaned. I'd have to swallow my vanity if I wanted to personalize the prisoner issue for the public, I thought. But at least I'd had the courage to make a beginning in the media to educate the public. Only a couple of years ago, I wouldn't have dreamed of doing such a thing. It felt good to be taking action I felt was constructive.

Some developments on the home front made me feel less optimistic, however. Stan had been seeing a variety of doctors all spring, and since none of their tests had been very conclusive, we were left with the original diagnosis of emotional blindness. I took him out of school for the final three weeks of the third grade and handed in my own resignation, reluctantly, in June. I had concluded that part of his trouble might be that I was away from home too much, and when I *was* home, I was too tired or too busy to give him the love and attention he needed. I hated having to give up my teaching—I was head of my team-teaching department, had made good friends among the faculty, and derived strength and moral support from them. I would miss the stimulus of being away from home each day; I would miss my students, who were loads of fun; and I'd miss the daily conversations with other adults. My morale drooped at the thought of it, but I knew my first responsibility was to Stanford. My principal asked me to reconsider, but I told him I couldn't; I didn't really have a choice. I just had to hope things would be better for Stan in the fall when he had a new teacher and I'd be at home all day.

✧

While I was in the middle of packing to go east that summer, Karen Butler telephoned to say a West Coast editor of *Look* magazine would see us in Los Angeles on Friday, June 20. She and I flew to Los Angeles that morning and spent more than an hour pleading with him to publish a story about our husbands. He said he'd tell the New York editor but doubted they'd be interested. Sitting there in that plush office looking out over Los Angeles, I thought to myself, I'm crazy to try to tell the world the truth about all this. These people don't care and I'm never going to be able to get through to them.

As we got up to leave, we asked him to contact our League of Wives secretary if he had a change of heart.

"You have an organization?" he asked, suddenly perking up.

We answered his many questions about the League, pleased to have him interested in us in some way.

"We might be interested in doing an article about your organization," he said as we said farewell.

On our way home, Karen and I reviewed our visit. "You know, Karen," I said, "his only interest was in our organization. What we need is a *national* organization to attract national publicity. We already have a national group with our people all over the country writing to editorial writers and sending telegrams to the North Vietnamese. Why don't we call ourselves the National League of Families of American Prisoners in Southeast Asia? I'll offer to be the national coordinator, and I'll call some of the others to get their okay. We could get a post-office box and have stationery printed and we'd be in business. Maybe the fact that we had a countrywide national organization would help get more publicity for our men."

During the spring, while organizing our efforts to contact editorial writers, I'd talked to a few wives in other parts of the country who had started local groups. I'd talked to Mary Winn frequently, and when I got home from Los Angeles I called several others: Louise Mulligan in Virginia Beach, Bonnie Singleton in Texas, Emma Hagarmann in Washington State, and Jill Lockhart in Louisiana. I'd never met them, but we shared the same goal. They all agreed it might be helpful to give our national effort a name and that I should act as national coordinator.

By July we were going strong, with 350 on our mailing list and twenty-four area coordinators all over the country. My first official letter to our group read in part:

> As you can see by the letterhead, we have somewhat formalized our efforts and have set up an arrangement which will allow us to communicate more efficiently. We are hoping and praying that many of the MIA are prisoners and thus the singularity in our name. . . . We have 24 area coordinators who have volunteered to forward information to you which is a wonderful help for me. . . . Enclosed is one editorial which should warm your hearts. As one person said, "When the *Washington Post* writes like this, it is really something!"

I enclosed the following editorial from the May 23, 1969, *Washington Post*:

HANOI AND THE AMERICAN PRISONERS

Secretary Laird's plea in behalf of American prisoners in North Vietnam deserves much better than it initially got from the chief Hanoi delegate in Paris. Mr. Laird urged North Vietnam to make public the names of the prisoners, to release the sick and wounded among them, and to allow visits, proper treatment and mail for the rest. To this eminently reasonable and legitimate request, Xuan Thuy replied that Mr. Laird would "never have the list" (of prisoners) until the United States ended the war and withdrew.

It is hard to see how so retrograde a response advances the interests of any government that seeks to present itself to the world as fair and humane. The bombing which led to the capture of most of the prisoners—their number is put between 300 and 800—was halted more than six months ago. The Paris peace talks have reached a stage where expectations of movement have been widely stirred. The prisoner issue is strictly humanitarian and has no proper place on the table at Paris. It is obvious that a generous North Vietnamese attitude to the prisoners could have a measurable effect on the American and world publics. Surely Hanoi ought to be able to see the many advantages to itself of a compassionate approach.

Never was a national organization launched more efficiently. The fact that I was already in communication with the membership and that each of us paid her own expenses simplified the organizing process. Few if any of us realized there were established procedures for formalizing an organization; we just did it the way we'd always done it when we set up a wives' club. It was a very straightforward procedure. Our own simple objective was to educate the world about the Geneva Convention.

As I stepped out of the car at Sunset Beach that summer, I took a deep breath, savoring the salty smell and taste of the air. It was a misty June evening and I heard the foghorn blowing off Branford Reef and the bell buoy ringing near Johnson's Point. I could tell it was low tide from the sharp mud-flat odor coming from the lagoon at Summer Island. The wind must be from the east. I knew I was back in the land of my childhood when I was surrounded by these familiar sounds and smells. It was good to come back here each summer. The boys were already in the neighbors' houses, renewing friendships, and I was glad to sit with my parents once more and watch the ever-changing patterns of the sea and sky.

On my first night each year in Connecticut, I would usually think over what had happened in my life since I'd left the year before. This year I'd had a letter from Jim, and he seemed to be holding his own. Up to the time he wrote his note in January, he seemed safe from being apprehended in his covert communication. Thank God.

As for the children, Jimmy had had a successful freshman year at Ohio Wesleyan and had a summer job at a local foundry here in Branford. Sid's knees were all well again and he'd been accepted at South Kent School in the fall. I knew he'd have good male leadership and teachers there and it would be better for him, even though we'd miss him dreadfully at home. I had my fingers crossed that Stan would be okay with me at home each day and with a fresh start in the new school year. The doctors all seemed to think it would make the difference and that his emotional blindness would disappear. Taylor was his happy-go-lucky little-boy self, so I had no worries there.

I felt good about our national organization. I was hearing from more and more family members all the time, and I thought as an organized group we really might be able to accomplish something. It made a world of difference to have the U.S. government on our

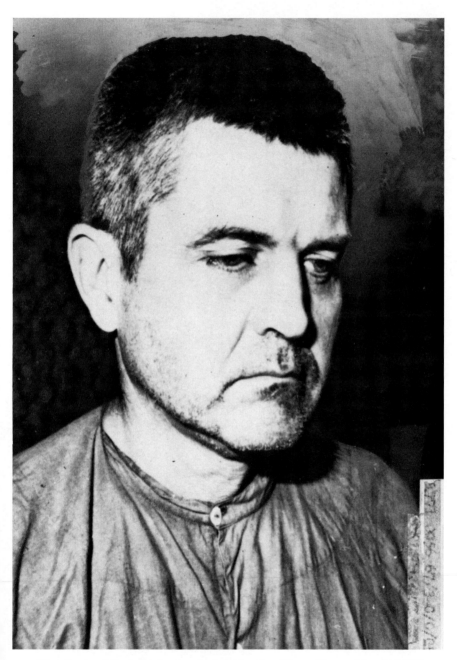

The photo of Jim which appeared in the San Diego *Union*, May 2, 1966.

Commander Bob Boroughs, Sybil's contact at the Pentagon, who became a crucial ally in the government.

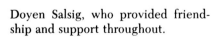

Doyen Salsig, who provided friendship and support throughout.

Christmas 1966—one of the first pictures Jim received in prison.

Sybil and the boys at Sunset Beach, August 1966. Jim received this photo during his second winter in prison.

Sybil's parents, Lucretia and Sidney Bailey, on the porch at Sunset Beach.

The neighbor's rose garden came in handy for photos to send Jim.

Sybil with Mother's Day roses bought as "seconds" for the photo.

Rabbit threatened Jim with this photo of Jimmy in January 1969: "If you
want to see this boy again, you'd better start cooperating with us."

Miami Beach, 1972. Sybil and a blind Vietnam veteran accepting the petition for President Nixon.

Sybil, founder of the National League of Families of American Prisoners and Missing in Southeast Asia, meeting with President Nixon, May 1972.

Summer 1972. Sybil with Taylor and Stanford in a front page photo in the New Haven *Register*.

side and some of its officials speaking out in the media. I'd given my first few speeches at service clubs before we left California, and felt we'd be able to get a lot of support there in the future. We had yet to see President Nixon, although our request from San Diego had been in for six months. Still, there had been some good changes this year, and I felt the most important of all was having a new party and administration in office.

Toward the end of July, I, along with several other wives and parents of MIAs and POWs, was invited to attend a meeting in Secretary of Defense Laird's office in Washington. I decided to stop in New York City on the way down from the shore and try to generate publicity for our cause. My hopes were high as I checked into the Biltmore Hotel. Happy memories of college-day visits in this hotel carried me to my room in bright spirits.

I'd written ahead to *Life, Time, Parade,* the *New York Times,* and the "Today" show. But as I made my phone calls from my tiny room and a sleek-sounding secretary turned me down in each location, my spirits spiraled downward. Then, blessedly, a Mr. Rogers at *Parade* said, "Sure, we'll be glad to help you. Come on over." What a lifesaver. I raced to his office as fast as I could make it. He was just as nice in person, taking down the essentials of my story, making a date to call me after the Laird meeting and an appointment for a photographer to come to the shore in Branford to take a picture of me and the boys.

I was so elated by this success, I decided to walk into the *New York Times* "cold" on my way back to the hotel. The man at the desk smiled when I announced I'd like to see the editor, Mr. Reston. I wanted to ask him to run a front-page letter asking the North Vietnamese to treat our prisoners humanely. I was told if I would wait a few minutes, I could visit with Mr. Palmer, who was Mr. Reston's assistant. A tall, soft-spoken man soon invited me into his office, and I told him my story as succinctly as I could.

"We've been getting a lot of mail on this subject," he said thoughtfully, "and we're wondering if somehow the government is responsible."

"The government is most certainly *not* responsible," I replied, raising my voice. "Right here I have the original of my letter to our group suggesting they write to editorial writers and giving them the names and addresses of several."

Smiling, he replied, "This may explain why we seem to be

getting mail for writers no longer at this address. Where did you get your editorial writer's list?''

"From an out-of-date *Editor and Publisher Year Book,*" I replied.

Taking up his pen, he began writing out a list of newspapers he felt were influential even though they had a small circulation. He gave me new addresses in place of my out-of-date ones, and he gave me the name of a *New York Times* reporter I was to call in Washington both before and after the Laird meeting. It was late when I got up to leave his office and he walked me out to the elevator. "Don't give up, Mrs. Stockdale," he said as the elevator door opened. "You're really on the right track."

What a lift those words gave my morale.

The next morning in Washington, I talked to the *New York Times* reporter before going to the Pentagon. He made a date for a follow-up visit and photograph afterward. I concentrated as hard as I could on Secretary Laird's message about President Nixon's plans for "Vietnamization." It sounded kind of complicated to me. The secretary assured us that the bulk of U.S. forces would remain in Vietnam until after the prisoners had been released. He told us his main purpose that day was to reassure us of the depth of concern about our men on the part of President Nixon, Secretary of State Rogers, and himself.

As I sat there in the secretary's handsomely decorated, spacious dining room, I felt we were beginning to make some progress. This was the first time I'd heard any talk about specific plans for the end of the war. There'd been no indication in the press that the end was anywhere near, but the secretary of defense certainly knew far more than the rest of us, and it was good to hear that detailed plans were on the drawing boards. I had to conclude that this "Vietnamization" I was hearing about for the first time was President Nixon's secret plan to end the war. I thought it was a pretty weak plan, myself, but I couldn't help liking Secretary Laird. He'd ended the "keep-quiet" policy and had the guts to talk about the truth of the prisoners' treatment in public. I secretly felt that the organizational efforts of us wives and families on a national level had been influential in forcing our government to join us in speaking out publicly. One official in the Defense Department told me they knew they'd

better join us or we were going to mop up the floor with them. That
was exactly how I wanted them to feel.

The *New York Times* article, published on July 31, 1969, covered almost a full page. It included a large picture of me on the U.S.
Capitol steps and as much information as I'd hoped it would. I felt
sure the North Vietnamese in Paris would read it.

In early August, I was invited to be interviewed in New York
on CBS-TV's morning news program. It was exciting having the
professional makeup applied, but scary wondering what questions
the host, Joseph Benti, would ask. He was considerate, however,
not pressing me with the political aspects of the war. I slipped easily through my replies and in a few minutes it was all over. Millions
more would now know the truth about prisoner treatment in Hanoi.

Good luck—and I suspect some help from behind the scenes in
Washington—had gotten me an appointment to see a Mr. Gottlieb
at the "Today" show about a possible future appearance on that
program, too. The appointment with Mr. Gottlieb was for 2:00 P.M.
and my train left at 4:00. Since his office at Rockefeller Center was
on the way to the station, I checked out of the hotel, taking my
suitcase with me. I was sure I could find a place to check it on the
main floor of Rockefeller Center, and left myself plenty of time to
do so.

When I got there, the doorman said he thought there were
some lockers "down the escalator at the end of this hall." The hall
turned out to be about a half-mile long and it seemed like twenty to
me with my suitcase. Finally, I saw the lockers—but every single
one of them was taken. I couldn't believe it. I asked a man if there
were any more nearby, and he replied, "Down around the corner,
almost to the subway."

Off to the subway I went—but no luck there, either. What was
I going to do? Maybe somebody would watch it for me just a little
while in one of the shops along the hallway. My shoulder ached
now and I stopped once in a while to rest. I'd make it. There were
some nice-looking shops up ahead. Jewelry, no. Drugstore, no. Ah,
there it was—a little travel shop with posters of New England summers in the window. That meant home and comfort to me.

The lady was busy giving folders and information to a young

couple, and then to a young girl. I waited until everyone had left the shop. I explained about the appointment and the suitcase and the lockers, and asked her if I could leave the suitcase behind her desk for about thirty minutes. Her face just froze solid and she said, "No, I never do anything like that. I can't be responsible." I couldn't believe it. I pleaded with her to help me. She was cold and adamant. "Absolutely not."

I sort of stumbled out into the hallway again and looked for the door at the end where I came in. But the door wasn't there, only a wall, and I realized that somehow I was lost. I didn't even know where I'd made my mistake.

Oh, God, what have I done to deserve this on top of everything else? I was trying so hard to do everything I could to help Jim. The Joseph Benti show was a beginning, and the "Today" show might make the difference. But these people were smooth and sophisticated, and I had to make the right appearance. I couldn't just go clumping in there like a hick, carrying a big heavy suitcase. I couldn't go there at all, in fact, if I didn't find the elevator.

I felt myself beginning to lose control. Oh, no, I thought. Dear God, I can't cry now. But there was no controlling it. My eyes filled up and my face began to twist and I looked frantically around for a ladies' room. There was none, no place to go, but I had to get out of this hall because by now I knew I was going to have a hard cry, which would have to run its course. Frantically, I looked around for anyplace to take refuge. I saw a room with soft green carpets and just a few people inside. It looked peaceful. I walked in with tears streaming down my face and asked a man if there was someplace I could be by myself for a few minutes. He gave me a hard look and rushed up some stairs. I sat down in his chair by his desk and turned it to the wall and sobbed and sobbed and sobbed.

When it eased a little, I groped around in my purse for a handkerchief, finding only a piece of dirty Kleenex. I mopped at my face, and the sobs took over again. I knew people behind me were staring, horrified. I knew I was making a fool of myself, but I couldn't help it.

Finally, my crying began to ease a little again, and it passed. I found a mirror and began to dab at my face, still half-crouched and facing the wall. My eye makeup was all smeared and running down my cheeks, and I thought, Can't I have anything for myself, even

the fun of showing the children the professional eye makeup? I
powdered my nose and traced on lipstick, squared my shoulders,
and turned to face those staring at me. I realized I was in a bank. I
couldn't blame anyone for staring at my performance. I summoned
every inch of dignity I could find and said, "Can you tell me how to
get to the seventh floor, please?" One lady gave me simple directions. I picked up my suitcase and tried to smile as I went out the
door.

Mr. Gottlieb's secretary assured me she'd watch my suitcase
while I visited with him. Mr. Gottlieb stared at my puffy eyes, and I
explained that I'd had a little trouble in his basement. It crossed my
mind that maybe my appearance would make him more sympathetic
about an invitation to be on the program. I was almost a bit surprised myself when I told him I was seriously considering going to
Paris soon to see the North Vietnamese in person. I told him we'd
been sending telegrams for months and no one had had a reply. We
wanted to know who was held alive, and we wanted the International Committee of the Red Cross to inspect the camps to assure
our men humane treatment.

Mr. Gottlieb seemed genuinely interested in the prospect of
my having a personal confrontation with the enemy in Paris. Little
did he know how I cringed at the idea of their confronting me with
questions about intelligence communications.

On my way back to Branford, I decided I would have to make
the trip to Paris. It was the one thing that had interested the "Today" show producer.

The last day before we left for California that September, I
drove Sid up to begin his freshman year at South Kent in northwest-
ern Connecticut. Stan and Taylor were with us. Jimmy had already
left for college. It was hot and humid up in those Connecticut hills,
and when we went up to the top floor of the dormitory where all
the freshmen lived, the heat seemed to press in all around us. We
found Sid's iron cot and battered bureau. We looked at the communal closet and bath at the end of the big room. Then it was time to
say goodbye. Sid had trouble keeping back the tears, so I kissed him

quickly and said we'd talk by phone soon. From the car, I could see him standing at the dorm window trying to smile. I pushed my emotions down inside me and smiled and waved as Stan and Taylor called out "'Bye, Sid!" I knew I had to get out of Sid's sight quickly. I drove about a block and began to shake with sobs, so I stopped the car. I sobbed and sobbed while Stan and Taylor told me it would be okay. Seeing me so upset frightened them, and I hugged them and said it was all right. I knew Sid would be happier at the school, but I was going to miss him so. Leaving Sid, I felt as if another seam of my soul had been ripped apart.

On the plane the next day, I began to think about my plans to go to Paris to see the North Vietnamese in person. I had been making inquiries about what the government's reaction might be to such an idea. Bob Boroughs had liked the idea but sympathized with my fears about intelligence questions. When I asked him what I should say if such a thing happened, he said he knew I'd think of something. I wasn't so sure. But I was pretty sure I was going to make the trip. I thought a group of us should go as representatives of our National League of Families. And by the time we landed in San Diego, I had decided whom I'd ask to go with me.

A few days after we'd unpacked in the Coronado house, we were joined by a writer from *Good Housekeeping* magazine who was doing a story about me and the organization. He stayed in a nearby hotel and interviewed me morning, noon, and evening. The phone rang frequently with calls from throughout the country. I was making final arrangements for a group of six of us to represent our National League in Paris, taking along hundreds of letters of inquiry from our membership. We represented all the armed services—army, navy, marines, and air force—with officers and enlisted men serving in North Vietnam, South Vietnam, and Laos. We were five wives and one father, and one of us was black. We bought our own airline tickets but would be reimbursed by *Reader's Digest* and Fairchild Hiller Aircraft Company. This financial help was a real sign that we were making progress in our campaign. I felt the government was quietly helping us accomplish our objectives.

Every so often during the frenzy of this planning, the calm, cool, and collected professional writer from *Good Housekeeping* would look up at me and say, "You know, Mrs. Stockdale, you have to remember to pace yourself. You have to conserve your energy for whatever may lie ahead." I laughed and assured him I had an overabundance of energy and I'd always be able to do whatever needed to be done, as long as it was something that might help Jim.

Knowing our trip to Paris would be publicized, I arranged to have Stanford and Taylor stay with friends in northern California. I realize now I was extra sensitive, overwrought, and full of fears at that point. I didn't want reporters frightening the children with questions while I was away, and I also worried about Communists kidnapping them. I'd had a dreadful fright once in 1966 when Stanford fell asleep under an easy chair and we couldn't find him for about an hour. I didn't know to what lengths the enemy might go to bring further pressure on Jim. Stanford and Taylor knew I was going to see the North Vietnamese, but they didn't know any of the details about their dad's torturous treatment. I didn't want them frightened by either rumors or the truth. I felt much more comfortable having them away from Coronado with close friends while I was gone.

At Kennedy Airport in New York on September 28, I met the others making the trip. Although, in order to have a better chance of seeing the North Vietnamese, we were going without government sponsorship of any kind, an air-force colonel briefed us privately, showing us pictures of Communists whose whereabouts our government was particularly curious to know. We were advised not to make contact with the U.S. Embassy in Paris unless we had an emergency, and were wished good luck. We had a press conference before boarding our TWA flight, and another in Paris when we arrived. At both, the reporters' questions had a hard, critical edge. They didn't seem to like the idea that we were spotlighting the shortcomings of the North Vietnamese. Did we disturb the perception some reporters seemed to have that the United States was all wrong in this war and the North Vietnamese were all right? That was the only reason I could think of for this group's hostility toward us.

It was a relief to check into the Intercontinental Hotel, which we'd chosen for its good telephone service. It seemed wonderfully luxurious to me, and I slept peacefully without any sleeping pills the first night. We'd telegraphed ahead for an appointment with the North Vietnamese, and the next day I dialed their number. When I identified myself, an ice-cold, clipped foreign voice came on the wire, saying he was Xuan Oanh, head of the delegation. (Actually, he was temporarily head of the delegation while Xuan Thuy was in Hanoi.) With a leering tone he said, "Yes, Mrs. Stockdale, we've heard about you and the government man with you." I calmly explained that the man with us was the father of a missing marine pilot and was in no way associated with the government. Silently, I prayed he had heard about me only in the context of organizing the League. He told me we'd have to wait to hear whether we could have an appointment. Three times I repeated my room number and hotel phone number. He hung up abruptly. I was left holding the dead receiver in my hand.

Day after day we waited. Each morning we gathered to review our plans for presenting our case and answering questions. Two of the wives were young enough to be my daughters. I took the telephone-listening duty each afternoon so they could go shopping and explore the city. Minor bickering erupted among us after the initial excitement had worn off. Our nerves were on edge and we had to work hard to stay on an even keel. I was taking a Seconal tablet each night to help me sleep. I'd never used it before and it was like magic; the doctor had given me enough for the trip.

Each afternoon I sat in my room, waiting for the phone to ring and staring into the mirror as I practiced what I wanted to say to the North Vietnamese. I telephoned Xuan Oanh every other day to remind him we were waiting. I left the hotel only one day, to have my hair done. I knew he wouldn't call that day because the Paris peace talks were in session. It was just as well our men didn't know they met only once a week. It wasn't a very convincing demonstration that either side was anxious for progress.

We had been told they would not see us on the weekend, either, but on Saturday morning, October 4, at 10:00 A.M., my phone rang and Xuan Oanh was calling. He instructed me to come with my group to the North Vietnamese Embassy at 4:00 that afternoon for tea. I was both elated and terrified that we were actually going to see the enemy face-to-face. After a final conference with the others, I closed myself in my room for a final rehearsal of my remarks. I hadn't come to any firm conclusion about what I would say if they confronted me about the intelligence communications. I'd just have to play it by ear as Bob Boroughs had advised. As the time to leave drew closer, I made three trips into the bathroom, retching hideously with the dry heaves. I prayed God would see me safely through this ordeal with no harm to Jim.

Exhaustion from tension calmed me as I went through the door into the North Vietnamese Embassy. Four North Vietnamese men stood inside and greeted us but didn't tell their names. I asked which was Xuan Oanh. He was a stereotypical short, slender, enigmatic-looking Oriental. He directed me to sit opposite him while the others sat on both sides of a long, low table. I silently nicknamed the other three men Brown Suit, Mr. X, and Glasses. They never did reveal their names and I needed some way to remember each so he could be described to the Intelligence people later.

To help break the pall of gloom that enveloped the room, I asked Glasses if I could borrow his spectacles to read my remarks. Xuan Oanh had nodded permission for me to read rather than speak extemporaneously. Passing the glasses from one side to the other lightened the atmosphere as each of us in turn presented our requests. They were similar in nature and not very complex. Each woman clearly identified her husband, and the father his son, and described the known circumstances of his capture or disappearance. Each wanted the information required by the Geneva Convention furnished in the case of her/his loved one.

I spoke for myself, as Jim's wife, saying I knew he was injured but that I had no evidence his injuries had been given proper treatment. I also spoke for all the other members of our organization who had sent the letters I gave Xuan Oanh, telling each man's circumstance and asking for information about him. I asked if each member of our League had to come to Paris in person to make this inquiry.

The only absolutely clear response we generated from the enemy during our visit was that it was not necessary for any more wives or parents to come to see them in Paris. Xuan Oanh said that our written inquiries would be answered, but his phraseology was so cleverly evasive that it was difficult to tell exactly how this would be done. I tried repeatedly to pin him down to promising a response before Thanksgiving, but each time he would slither around a direct answer.

I had begun to feel somewhat more relaxed when suddenly

Xuan Oanh stood up and pulled the *New York Times* picture of me from his pocket. Holding it up, he said, "We know all about you, Mrs. Stockdale." I could almost feel my blood congealing. He had a leering look as he continued. "We know you are the founder of this movement in your country and we want to tell you we think you should direct your questions to your own government."

Giddy swirls of relief went spinning through my head. Is that all? I thought. I began to relate the many government offices we'd visited in our own country.

The North Vietnamese representatives took our letters of inquiry for our men in North Vietnam, but insisted we'd have to see Madame Binh about anyone in the South. The North Vietnamese still preserved the facade that they had no troops in the South. It was a disgrace that our own government allowed such a travesty. Our hosts insisted they'd answer these inquiries by mail, and once again they emphasized that no more relatives need come to Paris. I insisted I also wanted some evidence that my husband was no longer in solitary confinement. They answered with silence and ushered us into a room where we were shown a propaganda atrocity film. Afterward they served us tea and Vietnamese candies. I wondered if possibly they were similar to those Jim referred to in his first letter almost four years ago.

In retrospect, I realize that our visit was more for the publicity than the substance of our meeting. We knew the North Vietnamese were not reliable about keeping their word anyway. The central purpose of our visit was to spotlight in the world press the situation our men were enduring.

Emerging from the North Vietnamese Embassy into the sharp October air, I saw darkness had fallen while we were inside. A somewhat impatient and bored-looking cluster of press closed in on our group. Sarcasm salted their questions. I was thankful our marine father was our spokesman. Why were they so angry with us? I wondered as I stood in the lineup facing their glaring camera lights. Because you are living, breathing proof that the North Vietnamese are inhumane barbarians rather than the warmhearted, innocent, loving humanitarians some of the press preferred to believe, I answered myself.

"What will you do now that you've had your visit here?" one reporter asked me sharply.

"Go back to the hotel and get some rest. We're so tired," I replied with a sigh.

Ever so faintly from the cluster of questioners I heard a male voice drenched with sarcasm say, "Ohhh, yes." The way he sneered those two words conveyed his complete disdain for the truth of our circumstance.

The following day, October 5, 1969, this article appeared in the *San Diego Union:*

PARIS VISITS UNNEEDED, HANOI SAYS

Choisy-Le-Roi, France (A)—A North Vietnamese spokesman told a group of Americans yesterday that the families of US servicemen missing in Vietnam no longer need to come to Paris to inquire about them and that Hanoi would answer questions by letter.

This was reported by a spokesman for a group of six Americans seeking information about missing servicemen (including Mrs. Sybil Stockdale of San Diego), who met with North Vietnamese representatives at their headquarters in this Paris suburb.

Thomas Swain of St. Paul, Minn., the spokesman for the group, said the North Vietnamese promised to "investigate and notify families about the status of their missing relatives."

Xuan Oanh had said we would receive replies to our inquiries, and it didn't take the North Vietnamese long to figure out how to get credit for being true to their word about giving us information and at the same time put us into a situation completely repulsive to anyone with a sense of honor. My telegram to Xuan Oanh of October 27 made our contempt of their plan for us clear.

Mr. Xuan Oanh
Delegation of the Democratic Republic of Vietnam
8 Avenue General Leclerc
94 Choisy-le-Roi
Paris, France

Dear Mr. Oanh,

During our recent visit with you, you promised that the wives and families of the men missing and captured in North Vietnam would receive replies to their inquiries about their loved ones from the government of North Vietnam. Mr. Kunstler now says that this information will be available only from the New Mobilization Committee, who plan to open an office in Washington for this purpose. To force the prisoners' families to apply to such a political organization is an unnecessary exploitation of their helplessness. It only diminishes the humanitarianism of the gesture your country is making in releasing the list of the prisoners. The world will see no logic, only vindictiveness, in such an arrangement. I entreat you to use your good offices to hasten the release of the information which you have promised and which Mr. Kunstler says is available. Your government will win the world's respect by showing consideration and compassion for the anguish of the men's families.

> Sincerely,
> Mrs. James Bond Stockdale,
> National Coordinator for the
> National League of Families
> of American Prisoners in
> Southeast Asia

William Kunstler was an attorney who represented David Dellinger, Rennard Davis, and Tom Hayden, who were members of the New Mobilization Committee. I felt strongly that these antiwar activists were spreading enemy propaganda in the United States and prolonging the war. If they hadn't kept shouting in the media that the poor innocent North Vietnamese were the victims of United States imperialists, our own population would have been more inclined to support our forces trying to prevent the Communist takeover of South Vietnam.

I was not the originator of the idea to send that telegram to Xuan Oanh. Frank Sieverts from the State Department had called to ask if I was considering sending Xuan Oanh a telegram in response to the announcement about the formation of the New Mobilization Committee. Whether he wanted us to reject or accept their plan was never clear, but I concluded that if the U.S. government wanted me to send a telegram rather than do it themselves, there must be a good reason. I did think they could offer to reimburse me for the $25 cost of the message, however.

Doyen helped me phrase the telegram, and someone from the government must have notified the media about it—because at about 9:45 the morning after I sent it, a local TV studio called to ask if I could be there by 11:00 A.M. to do an interview about it for the national news programs. It was about a forty-minute drive to the studio, so there was no time for grooming. I shuddered when I saw the condition of my hair while I quickly dabbed on lipstick. But I either had to go "as is" or miss this chance to get the word out on the national news.

That night, after I'd watched my interview on the evening national news, another POW wife telephoned and scolded me for not having my hair done before such an appearance. She said I was not to represent her on TV again looking that way. That really burned me up. Here I was working eighteen hours a day to get the truth out to the world and this woman thought I went on TV looking like a frump by choice. Damn some of these picky women anyway, I thought.

The following morning, however, I forgot all about my crankiness when a telegram arrived for me from the parents of another POW:

> Your appearance on TV and message to North Vietnamese magnificent. Thank you. We love and appreciate you and will continue to work and pray with you for our loved ones.

Chapter 11

Fighting Hard

On the twenty-fifth day of January 1969, all three of us were right back where we had been three years before: Pigeye, Rabbit, and I in room 18, Hoa Lo Prison, the ropes and the iron bar with the leg lugs laid out before us. I had just screamed "I submit" after my first roping following my removal from Alcatraz. And Rabbit was true to his word: He did not follow the usual line of questioning—reconstructing the past, setting up cross-ruffs in the story of the Alcatraz riot by which he could pit my answers against those of Jenkins or Denton. He had asked me only one question before Pigeye was turned loose on me: "Will you be my slave or not?" And the statement they were now extracting from me said, in effect, yes. I wrote something like this:

> I understand that I am a criminal who has bombed churches, schools and pagodas of the Democratic Republic of Vietnam. I have opposed the Camp Authority and incited others to oppose the Camp Authority. I know the nature of my sins, and I now submit to you to do whatever you tell me to write, say, or tape.

It was midmorning when Rabbit took the paper, Pigeye slammed and locked the double doors with his improvised traveling-iron lash-up, and I took my place at the room's only peephole, in the corner of one of the glass panes in the French doors. I saw Cat walk out of what had to be his office (now located diagonally opposite room 18 across Heartbreak courtyard), meet Rabbit, and stroll back in with him in thoughtful conversation. They were reading my capitulation statement. It was my guess that my fate would be decided in the strategy session that would ensue.

Room 18 had been stripped of everything but the long quiz table with blue cloth, and a rusted-out slop bucket. I had stood at that table to write the statement. I had not seen or felt my blanket roll since I had been braced up against the wall outside my Alcatraz cell in the darkness and had my arms wired behind me. Heartbreak courtyard showed no signs of any Americans or Vietnamese Army red-tab guards who were in charge of us. (Army men were about, but they wore green tabs on their collars, which meant they sat in the machine-gun towers that commanded the dry moats and provided general security for the civilian operations of the prison.)

That there would be little American-prisoner activity here in the headquarters area of the Vietnamese prison system made sense. On March 31 of the previous year, LBJ had ceased all U.S. bombing north of twenty degrees north, then backed it off to nineteen degrees, and since November 1 had shut it off altogether. It stood to reason that all Americans except those in special punishment categories would be either up in Las Vegas within these walls or at one of the outlying camps.

In the buildings surrounding Heartbreak courtyard, about fifty civil-service clerks were employed to maintain the records of the civilian prison system of the country. In my previous stays in room 18, I had learned that they were periodically required to attend lectures in an assembly room just around the corner from 18, toward Heartbreak Hotel. They were holding serious lectures in that room on this January 25, just five days after Richard Nixon had been inaugurated president. I could hear the Vietnamese voice of the speaker. The name Nixon (Nick-sohn) came up in every second or third sentence.

The lectures went on and on that day. There would be breaks, and quiet conversational groups would sometimes cluster just in front of my French doors. Again, the name Nixon could be recognized. There was no hostility; the conversations were very serious and calm. I said to myself, Could it be that these people think Nixon is a dove? That he will let them push him around? The more I listened and watched, the more I believed they *did* think he was a dove; that their speakers, their Communist party cadres, were putting out ideas about a possible American capitulation in those early 1969 days. It would stand to reason for the run-of-the-mill Party hack to come to that conclusion. The Communists so personalize international affairs, and "Johnsohn" and "MachNamarah" had so dominated the news broadcasts as the only enemies of the North Vietnamese state for the previous five years, that any man who replaced Johnson *had* to be of an antiwar persuasion. I shook my head in disbelief. I snickered to myself and thought, What a surprise *they're* in for!

Late afternoon—here come Rabbit and Pigeye. Pigeye is carrying a chair! Cat has given them the game plan.

Rabbit walked in and I bowed. "Show me respect; sit on the floor." He towered over me as Pigeye situated the chair for him at the end of the long table. Rabbit continued: "You have never submitted a complete report of your military activities in the months preceding your capture. We need to know the number of people and the names of everybody in your units. Take this paper and sit in that chair and list the titles of your units, the number of people normally assigned, and their names."

I thought to myself, Same old crap; every time they need an excuse to hammer you, they dredge up the old "incomplete biography" story. But there may be a second purpose here: they've asked me to include personnel rosters. They may know navy unit manning lists are "classified," just like Eagle's in-flight refueling tracks. They certainly have no use for the information five years after the fact; I smell a "blackmail package" already. They obviously have something big in mind up the road and they need me on the hook to get me to do it. This would fit Cat's mentality; thinking bureaucratically, he would expect my Achilles' heel to be my willingness to do anything to keep my navy record spotless. Probably his idea of leverage is holding documentary evidence of something he thinks would ruin it. Well, I'm sure of one thing: the one way to really get on his hook is to do this free of charge.

"No!" I shouted.

Pigeye was out in a flash, back in with bar and ropes, right up to me, standing astride my legs, popping me on alternate jaws with soft fists, Rabbit shouting, "You will bow down!" The ropes on, cinched up, jerking, jerking, then sandals fly past my eye. Pigeye is down, speaking a few words of newly learned pidgin English in my ear. "Don, do not scream. Do not scream, Don." (They don't want Vietnamese civilians to hear it.) Now he's standing on my back, head down, down. I am suffocating! "Yes! Yes! I submit."

"Put at the top of the paper: secret personnel report. Now, how many men were on your ship?"

"I once read in a newspaper that there were over three thousand people on a carrier of that size."

"Okay, put that down. Now write down the names of all the officers and enlisted men who were assigned . . . now identify which were pilots in which squadron . . ." And so it went for over an hour, I listing some of the dwindling number of shipmates I remembered, and listing more that I made up.

As he got ready to go, paper in hand, Rabbit said, "You will learn your lesson."

"I have had no food today."

"You are to get no food until you learn your lesson. The guard will bring you water."

Out he went, the door slammed. Pigeye came back in with a jug of water, clamped the traveling irons around the twin doors' knobs, grabbed the blue cloth off the table, and walked away into the early darkness with it. I lay down on the floor, cold with no blankets or gear of any kind, and dozed fitfully, thinking of my old Alcatraz Gang. I put them on a three-day fast; that means they've got another day to go. I have no right to complain about hunger. This is going to be one tough pull, and in any sort of reasonable ordering of priorities, food has to be put down as a trivial consideration. What is the old formula? A person can go four minutes without air, four days without water, and forty days without food, and I suppose forty years without company. I was feeling so secure with those Alcatraz guys and now I'm on my own again—isolated. With Cat bearing down on me. With nothing but trouble ahead. . . .

Early the next morning Rabbit and Pigeye were back to commence three more days, two on one, of much the same: I filled out My Secret Report on the Defenses of My Ship. ("We have fighter planes and antiaircraft guns, but I don't know the caliber." . . . "It doesn't matter, just say guns.") Then there was My Secret Report on Aircraft Tactics over the Target. When I took a hard stand on this one, Rabbit got mad enough to disappear and come back with my photograph of my son Jimmy, the Ohio Wesleyan freshman. He held it up and said, "If you ever want to see this boy again, you must change your attitude."

So it was the ropes again. ("We go to the beach with fighters and bombers; when we get near the beach, the fighters deploy to the north to guard against the attack of MIGs, the bombers bomb targets, and when they get finished we all get together and go home. . . ." "Okay, that'll do it." I could tell even Rabbit was becoming embarrassed at the foolishness Cat was imposing on him.) My Secret Report on All the Targets I've Struck followed, and so on and so on.

By the fourth night, Chihuahua started coming in with Rabbit and putting in his two bits. "Tell us of every conference you attended at high headquarters on this trip to Vietnam, and every detail of what was said at each conference. . . . Is it not true that you attended a conference in Honolulu on the way out here?"

By that time I was really getting pissed off at this rigmarole. Oddly, this anger relaxed me and allowed me to come as close as I ever did to beating the ropes. I was so mad at that Chihuahua that when it came down to the claustrophobia phase, I was able to really practice what they preached at Survival School. Only my mind didn't take me to Washington Primary School in Abingdon; it took me back to Alcatraz, where I circled the cellblock, and paused at the cell door of each member of the Gang and made myself remember his identification song. Mulligan—"When Irish Eyes Are Smiling"; Rutledge—"Oklahoma"; Jenkins—"Maryland, My Maryland"; Sam Johnson—"The Eyes of Texas"; Shumaker—"The Pennsylvania Polka.". . .

I was coming up on Ron Storz, just getting "The Sidewalks of New York" into my mind, when I realized Rabbit and Chihuahua were leaning over me, shouting at me frantically to "submit." I guess I must have submitted; the ropes were loosened. But I got up boiling mad and shouted at Chihuahua: "What in the hell is going on around here? Yes, I went to a conference in Honolulu; we commanders were told what the venereal-disease rate in Manila was, what the venereal-disease rate in Japan was, what time the Seventh Fleet curfew took effect. There were so many U.S. Navy ships in the Philippines, so many in Yokosuka, so many in Sasebo, and so on!"

"Just write all that down in your Secret Report."

My most credible answer that week came in response to the following, which Rabbit read from his list: "Give the subject matter of all secret conferences you attended on your ship."

I said that early in the cruise I had told my captain, Bart Connolly, "If you know anything you don't want exposed in a Communist prison camp, don't tell it to me; I'm going to fly over the beach every day and you can expect me to get shot down and captured." I said Bart never invited me to any secret conferences.

Rabbit liked that one; he wrote it down in his own book. He frankly admitted that what we were putting together was a blackmail package. (He had never heard the word until I used it. After a break he came back and said: "I looked that word up in my dictionary and you are right—this is blackmail.") The final humiliation came after yet another rope session when he dictated, and I wrote, something like this:

> To the General Staff Officer, Dear Sir:
> Here is a summary of the military information that you requested. I would like to present this and would be willing to do so at your office if you so desire. This material should be of value to you, and it is the first installment of more to follow upon your request.
> James Bond Stockdale

After that, my blanket roll was brought in, and I set up a sleeping area on the floor with my mosquito net above it. A bowl of soup and some French bread was set before me, but by this time I had decided that two could play this fasting game: I commenced my own hunger strike and refused all food. I was just plain mad about that blackmail package. I guess I should have felt good. The bottom line was that I didn't give up anything I felt guilty about—and that, of course, defeated the purpose of Cat's whole drill.

On the sixth day, Rabbit came and (I think painfully) delivered the following message: "I come from the general staff officer. He thanks you very much for your secret information and says it will be very helpful. He realizes that according to your Code of Conduct you can be put in prison in America for giving him that valuable information. He says, however, that your being the source of it will be kept in strict confidence as long as you are cooperative. And now he has suggested that you be permitted to take a bath and become more comfortable."

Pigeye was at the door with a bar of soap and a razor, and I knew the jig was up. A razor to me was starting to mean "Get ready to go downtown."

It was midafternoon on a cool but sunny January day when Pigeye escorted me across the main courtyard of Hoa Lo Prison toward Heartbreak Hotel. In the days I had been living in room 18, I had not seen any Americans in the courtyard and presumed I was the only one in custody on this side of Las Vegas. We passed many civilian workers I was beginning to recognize.

We wheeled in through the green door of Heartbreak, and I was steered left into cell 8, the old bath-and-dump room. Pigeye gave me the razor and soap, said "Queekly," and left to attend to some other duties. (He popped a couple of peepholes. Could Americans be in here?)

I had lived enough years close to Cat's horns to realize that this was no free shave. He had pushed all the buttons to intimidate me, and the stage was set for my imminent personal exploitation in public. I had to use my initiative to do something to derail it. My only hope was to disfigure myself.

Already I had the plan. To hell with washing—work fast! Pigeye will be back in a minute! To look authentic, I stripped. Faucet on, wet the soap and get it sudsing, blade into the razor, now stoop forward over the faucet, direct your bare ass to the peephole. Head under the faucet for a splash, now lather your hair and cut a swath right down the middle of your head, from way back right down to your forehead. Make it a "reverse Cherokee," cut it right down to the skin. *Pop!* goes the peephole. "Queek!" yells Pigeye, then it pops closed. I'm up to the count of two and the bolt has not been thrown. Good! Pigeye is going about more chores. Cut, cut, cut. God, my old hair is matted and tough from a week of sweat and tears. What's this? Blood! I must be tearing up my scalp trying to rip this hair out! Cut, cut, cut. *Pop!* goes the peephole. "Don!" screams Pigeye. *Clunk* goes the bolt, and he swings the door open. By this time, there is blood all over my hands and the floor, and in my soapy hair. Pigeye grabs me by the arm, screaming, *"Eeoow!"* Out we rush into the central court, I totally naked, blood running down my shoulders now, civilians all over the courtyard, men and women, standing aghast.

By no means expecting us back so soon, Rabbit had left the door of room 18 ajar. We entered the room at a half-run. Pigeye jabbered Vietnamese to his superior, making excuses, I supposed. But the view of what was going on in there just as we entered was more interesting than Pigeye's sound effects. I had caught Rabbit and Chihuahua both on their knees, trying to tie a tape recorder up under the table with regular old farm binder twine. They were trying to get it up under where I was to sit when I came back, using the "Ho Chi Minh" cloth to cover any evidence of it. So much for the electronic-bugging sophistication of North Vietnam!

Rabbit looked at me, wheeled, and nearly expired of shock. I was slow to realize that, seeing all the blood, he thought I had tried to kill myself. I felt good, felt that I was on the track. I figured I had the ropes coming, so I sat down in position for Pigeye to put on the straps and get it over with. Rabbit and Chihuahua both started yelling "No! No! Get on your feet!" Typical Vietnamese face-savers, I thought. It was my idea to take the ropes, so they say, "No! You are not entitled to the ropes!"

I stood up as Chihuahua was shouting, "Why are you taking your own life? I know you want to kill yourself, but you must not do it. You have things to do. You have an appointment to keep tonight. The general staff officer wants to see you downtown tonight."

A strange guard came in from Heartbreak and threw my prison clothes on the floor as Rabbit was babbling about what I was to have done downtown that night—wear civilian clothes, have a strong guard who would have made sure I obeyed, and so forth. My script for the night was to have been rehearsed there at the blue-draped table with Rabbit and Chihuahua as soon as I'd had my bath and shave. And as I just observed, I was to have been secretly recorded at that rehearsal in case I clammed up tonight before the movie camera.

Rabbit and Chihuahua knew they had to work fast. Cat would be furious. What to do? Send Pigeye for the hair clippers! When he came back, he sat me in a chair, wiped my soapy head with a towel, and worked away with the clippers while the two Vietnamese officers scowled. This would never do—the hair was irreparable for tonight. Rabbit had an inspiration: "You *will* make the movie tonight! We will get a *hat*!" All three of them—Pigeye and the two officers—strode out of room 18 into that late-afternoon sun, locking the door behind them.

Now the ball is in *my* court again. What can I do to counter the hat move? I had already considered self-destruction with everything in the room. There was the crap bucket with its rusted-out jaggedness. Cut myself up? I don't like the infection risk. The windows in the French doors can be broken (those are just about the *only* glass panes in Hanoi accessible to prisoners). But why go that far? They've brought in the quiz furniture for the afternoon's work around the hidden tape recorder. Why not this heavy mahogany quiz stool I've sat on so many times?

That's it! Get going! Close those eyes! You bruise easily! Mash those cheekbones! You *know* how swollen-eyed you used to be after playing in the center of that line all game.

I picked up the fifty-pound stool and *thump! thump! thump! thump! thump!*—left cheekbone. Now right—*thump! thump! thump! thump! thump!* Now left again . . .

I wasn't any more conscious of pain than if I had been running up my imaginary hill evading capture with a leg full of morphine. I kept thumping, and then the French doors started to shake. There was a crowd outside trying to look in! I could see the faint outlines of their faces against the painted panes in the doors. Now they were starting to talk loudly and to shout. No time to worry about that bunch of civil servants. *Thump! thump! thump! thump!* These eyes aren't quite closed yet. In the background, I can hear Rabbit's voice above the crowd. Now the key is in the door. The crowd is pushed back by Pigeye at the doorway as Rabbit and Chihuahua stride in with a silly-looking hat. I can hardly see it; my eyes are mere slits. Blood is running down the front of my pajama shirt from cheekbone cuts.

Chihuahua steps forward and shouts, "Now look what you've done. What are we going to do? What are we to do? You tell me what we are going to tell the general staff officer about the trip downtown after the way you have behaved."

"You tell the major that the commander decided not to go."

They then sent Pigeye for traveling irons and handcuffs. He locked both on (cuffs in front), and the three of them went over to see Cat while I waddled to the back wall and banged my face against the bricks some more, just in case.

In half an hour they were back, all business. Chihuahua had a sheet of stationery and I was summoned to waddle over to the blue-clothed table. Pigeye took off my cuffs, the binder twine was taken off the tape recorder, and the machine was put on top of the table. This was to be a recording session. Chihuahua laid out his single sheet of paper done with fine penmanship (probably his). "You are going to read what is on this paper, we are going to tape-record it." A session then started that lasted till about two in the morning. I stood most of the time, Pigeye behind me, hands on my wrist so he could twist my arm on signal.

Chihuahua's paper was weird, almost humorous. It started out like this:

> You don't know me, and I don't know you. It is not necessary that you know my identity nor that I know yours. I am a businessman from the United States, recently arrived in the Democratic Republic of Vietnam, and I want to tell you that big things are happening at home. We have a new president, and he has a secret plan for ending the war. We hope that this conflict will end. A delicate situation is in the making. Take hope, but act with caution. Observe all the regulations that are naturally required of any group. Take this advice from me as a man who knows that the best way for you to act is to do what you're told, and things will work to your advantage. . . .

This was sort of a screw-loose document, and I won't say I had it all figured out that night, but certain things were obvious. This was not Rabbit's work. It was too delicate and tricky. He was not given to this European indirectness. It had to be Chihuahua's work. The document went out of its way not to be antiwar in a way that would trigger enmity from the likes of me. I had trouble with the screwball fact situation on which it appeared to be based. Cat thought Nixon might invoke some "secret plan to end the war," and being an archetypal forehanded military bureaucrat, he was preparing a contingency plan for a propaganda extravaganza on the chance that an order would come down from his superiors on the general staff for a sudden release for us all. Could there be any real truth to the idea that Nixon would take over the presidency and immediately cop out? Surely not.

I spent the rest of the night avoiding uttering anything they could pass off as a conscientious reading. What with my experience, I had a whole battery of "spoiler" voices I could use singly or in combination—seldom quite in a way that would justify immediate ropes, but never in a way that would allow anybody to think I was not trying to screw up a tape: guttural, singsong, mumbly, wrong-syllable accent, etc. Rabbit and Chihuahua had counterplays: "Read softer," "Read louder," "Read faster," "Read slower." The pointless game finally ended. They locked me in the heavy "jumbo" irons with leg lugs and all marched out mad.

It was easy to tell that Rabbit and Chihuahua had gone over to Cat's office; I could hear my just-recorded voice booming out of his recorder through the early-morning darkness of the courtyard. Then I started realizing that I had stumbled into winning! I had all the trends going in my direction: I was well into a hunger strike, I was unpresentable in public and would take pains to reblacken my cheeks every day. Rabbit and even Chihuahua were getting fed up with me, and fed up with Cat's pretentious ambitions.

I put my good right arm back and worked my way onto my blanket where it lay on the floor and thought of the picture of Jimmy that Rabbit had brought in and taunted me with and just started to sob—sob for joy! I had learned how to make these sons of bitches work every step of the way! I had finally learned to *not* be reasonable. The only thing they had going for them was to try to get a person to take options, *their* options, which were dressed up as "the only sensible way to go." I was finally learning what Dostoevsky's "underground man" knew: "What a man craves is not a rationally desirable choice, but an *independent* choice!" I pray I can pull it out, with honor. And that I will make Syb and those boys of ours proud in the process.

By now it was mid-February. I was still being harassed by day, kept in jumbo irons at night. Also, I noticed that I was now being checked by a roving red-tab military guard every hour all night. He looked me over through the four-inch gap between the French doors, which opened up when they were pulled out as far as Pig-eye's traveling-iron "lock" would allow. This had started right after I had cut my head open, and was to continue for months, inconvenient as it must have been since the guard had to interrupt his rounds way over in Las Vegas. I had to conclude that they were never sure I wasn't suicide-prone. Rabbit had pronounced the all-night-session tapes "no good," and there were more "no good" sessions. I was not eating, was losing weight daily, and was keeping my eyes swollen almost shut with surreptitious early-morning bashings of my face with the stool and with my fists.

I had the idea the clock was ticking in my favor. The sounds of the courtyard were indicating a reversion of political mood, frequent huzzahs for Ho Chi Minh from the political lecture room, very few Nick-sohns. Was my assigned material getting out of date? One day late in February, after a desultory try at tape refinement, Rabbit just sat back and talked disgustedly. "You see, this is not to be a monologue, but a dialogue. A young criminal is being filmed, too. Lots of both films will be cut out. You come on and say something like 'I want to tell you that big things are happening at home.' Then the other film is spliced in and the youth says, 'Oh, yeah? What's going on?' You say, 'President Nixon has a plan for ending the war. . . . It's a very delicate situation for us. . . . I advise you to do exactly what the Vietnamese tell you to do if you want to be released as part of our president's plan.' And so on. Don't you get it? Now, let's get those important parts right."

That was Cat's and Chihuahua's idea of show business. And it figured. I had saturated their camp system with my orders and name. If I was the big leader, who better to lead the prisoners out in accordance with the DRV propaganda plan? This was to even the score on the "two-year setback" of their program.

And not a foot of that film got shot.

Bashing my face with my fists eventually made both hands and face so sore that it really became a test of self-discipline. So also was the hunger strike that was wearing on so long. At Alcatraz I had once gone ten full days without a scrap of food, but that was an "all off" and then an "all on" type of drill. Here in 18, I had been on a self-imposed "self-destruct" low-calorie intake for nearly six weeks. I would save some bread and treat myself to a couple of gulps in the middle of the night. I remember literally feeling my stomach grabbing those two or three bites and flooding them with digestive fluids. This would bring an aftershot of mental exhilaration almost like a shot of whiskey. And then I would dream, always the same dream: I would be let out of prison, and after walking a couple of blocks I would come upon Syb and all of our sons, all situated comfortably in a Western house. They would want so much to get me to relax and be loved by them, but I was always nervous for fear I would be late getting back to prison. It seemed that I had a commitment to be back in my cell before sunset, and this would destabilize my whole day with them.

Of course, I had to stage an act every day that shielded all growing anxiety and self-doubt. I built my act around an invention of mine, the "puke ball." Puke balls were little scraps of laundry soap that I kept concealed in my pajama pocket. When alone in the daylight, I was seldom away from the peephole, and the approach of a guard or interrogator with a key meant a quick gulp of soap and a brisk walk to the slop bucket in the corner. By the time the door was open, I was retching. When asked what was wrong with me, I said I had a disease known as "nervous stomach." They took this information to the old doc several times, and apparently he was puzzled, but he was not permitted to call on me because a Camp Authority rule denied his access to those in punishment. (That was to my advantage; I knew their rules well enough to use them as protective cover.)

Rabbit, of course, was the least confused by all this. One day when we were about a week into March, I saw him coming out of Cat's office with his ever-present tape recorder, heading for my door. He came in calmly, saw me through my dry heaves, then laid out pencil and paper and declared that I must let Sybil know that I was desperately ill.

After three and a half years of one-on-one with Rabbit, I had learned that he never did anything straight. So working against the grain, I grabbed the tablet and wrote, "Dear Sybil, I am sick. Your friend, Jim," and handed it to him.

"No, you don't get it," he said. "You have black malaria. You might die at any time, and she must know that. Now I want you to know I'm through with you. I hate you. All we have been doing is just furnishing you a stage on which to perform. You are the world's greatest actor. And you love it! I have been granted permission by the general staff officer to leave this case. This is the final document I intend to get from you. Shall I call the guard?"

Something was different about this. Rabbit was right. I had become a good actor. That was the only way to stay even with these bastards, and I *was* loving it. Maybe I was going to get to dump Rabbit and become a regular prisoner after all. All he wanted was an undated letter in the file that he thought I thought would explain my disappearance should they elect to give me the ax. It was supposed to scare me, make me think I could be killed on a whim. I was not scared; I was weak. I decided to hassle him over the wording and save my strength rather than take another stand.

It came out like this on about the fifth draft: "Dear Sybil, sorry to inform you that I'm very ill. I'm told I have malaria. It's a very serious illness and I'm weak. I want you to know I send you my best regards, Jim."

Now it was time for the tape recording of the above. They loved to play taped letters of sadness from American prisoners in Hanoi to their families in America over the "Voice of Vietnam." These were seen as helping to demoralize our soldiers in South Vietnam. Like the written version, the tape was to be kept locked up until I died. It was to be the facile explanation of my death to the world. (As a precaution, in addition to the "best regards" of the letter, I left the "phony" mark on the tape's identification code simply by exaggeratedly pronouncing my state of birth as Illi-*noise*. No intelligence agent would miss that.)

With that, Rabbit walked out of my life for keeps.

I was occasionally checked by other interrogators, but talk of the tape, the film, the "secret plan to end the war" dropped immediately to zero. I let my face heal and started to eat less sparingly. I could see Cat checking my plates for the amount eaten after Pigeye brought them out. They started to bring me a special sweet rice soup that apparently was for them a treat. On two occasions I watched Cat himself bring the steaming bowls right out of his quarters across the courtyard and hand them to Pigeye. Cat had not written me off.

But the jumbo irons continued and I was kept in room 18 until mid-March 1969. Then Pigeye came in one morning and gave me the "roll up" signal. We went directly across the Heartbreak courtyard to another isolated room surrounded by central prison administration offices. The number on the door was 5. It was dirty and had used bandages strewn all over it, with a pile of them in a square hole in the corner. A board bed on sawhorses had been improvised. I hung my mosquito net over it while Pigeye got a box of crude tools and went to work on taking the heavy door off its hinges to patch its holes and strengthen it. I started helping him fix the door. We worked all day and I got caught up in the exhilaration of actually being functional—sawing, driving nails. We were a good team;

we communicated by grunts and nods, he calling me Don. Pigeye was a good, reliable worker who had common sense, the sort of guy you would like to share heavy work on the farm with. He was even that way as a torture guard, seldom erratic. I always thought he felt sorry about breaking my leg.

He wound up his job by fashioning a guard's peephole with a cover activated from the outside, right in the center of the big, strong door. (Meanwhile, while Pigeye was preoccupied, I had also found time to secretly stuff lint into a nail hole right in the middle of the door, below the new peephole. I was able to camouflage this with smudges of grease.) We finished the day with pride in a door that a bull couldn't butt his way out of. And of course, I was left with a perfect peephole from which I could remove my plug and enjoy the action throughout the courtyard. Pigeye sensed my relief at being moved. He gave me a kind of salute when he left. He was never assigned to lay a hand on me again.

I had probably bottomed out at a little under 120 pounds during that last hunger strike, but now I was very slowly coming back up to the 140 at which my metabolism comfortably kept me with full prison rations. Being absolutely alone and underweight that spring put me into a state of great high-mindedness. I had many mental adventures, and my memory had never worked so well; I could bring up details from my childhood that were inaccessible in the clutter of conversational life. One of the greatest gifts I ever received in prison was sent over to my cell in Alcatraz by Bob Shumaker (via Nels Tanner's finger signals) about a month before the Alcatraz riot. Bob had sent: "If you get stuck alone, remember that e to the x is equal to the sum, from n equals one to n equals infinity, of the expression x to the n minus one, over n minus one, factorially."

I had memorized that, in the way we all filled up our dried-out minds with memory data in solitary. There alone in room 5, I realized Bob had given me a precious instrument. It was the "Taylor" expansion for exponential function, and with it I had the key to natural logarithms that could be calculated to two decimal places in four or five iterations with a stick in the dust. Over the weeks I reconstructed, by gently tickling my memory, the logic of the whole exponential system of numbers. That made it possible for me to change bases from *e* to 10. For the first time I brought into my mind's eye and understood *all* the scales on that log-log duplex deci-trig slide rule dad had bought me when I went away to Monmouth College. I became the world's greatest authority on the exponential curve and answered to my satisfaction such questions as: Why must *any* number to the zero power necessarily equal one? How can zero factorially be equal to one?

I spent a month thinking about the physics of the musical scales, and concluded that what sounded like a symmetrical scale to our ears was not mathematically symmetrical and thus must be a cultural adaptation. To conclude that, I first had to deduce that the frequencies of the tones of adjacent keys (blacks or whites) on the piano keyboard were related by a single proportionality constant. That being so, it seemed reasonable (after a couple of weeks of almost uninterrupted thought) that this proportionality constant had to be the twelfth root of 2—which I quickly calculated, in the dust with my stick, to be 1.0595.

I also spent a lot of time thinking about the wonders of the human body. I still had pain in my left leg after standing on it twenty minutes or so, but I had a daily ritual of "going" from cell to cell around Alcatraz cellblock, doing a little barefoot clog dance to the identification song of each member of the Gang. That became a kind of leg exercise as well as a period of tribute to those wonderful guys to whom I prayed I had not brought harm. In that spring of 1969 in room 5, I had no quizzes. Every day was exactly the same: I was given a standard ration of rice that I ate on a fixed schedule, and a fixed amount of water that I drank on a fixed schedule. I found out that this repetitive regularity had transformed me into a human clock. With all that fluid intake (rice is mostly water), I was having to get up once every night to pee in my toilet bucket. I would be groggy and sometimes curious about the time of night. I discovered a fixed conversion factor between the number of seconds I had to pee to empty my bladder ("one thousand one, one thousand two, one thousand three . . ." and so on) and clock time: Twelve seconds and it would be 11:00 P.M.; nineteen seconds, 4:00 A.M.; and so on. I calibrated this by waiting for the next striking of the twin Hanoi clocks; that done, I could pee, count, know full well I had the correct time in my head, and go right back to sleep.

In those late-night hours, I could hear the roving guard from Las Vegas pop my peephole open every hour. The idea of my suicide was evidently institutionalized in their system.

By day, I became an expert on the physical layout of the courtyard, on the habits of the people who strolled it, on all the guards' routines. Cat was an interesting subject. Everybody who had an office on the courtyard came on a bike and parked it outside his door. In general, the more important the person, the better the bike. Not so with Cat. In terms of social prestige, he was second only to the head man of the civilian side of the prison, but he practiced a kind of reverse snobbism by having the junkiest bike. He always came to work about 7:00 A.M., and went home most nights about dark. Some nights he stayed over in his office. He had the best uniforms I ever saw in North Vietnam. His favorite was a winter tunic-style suit of heavy wool. It had a unique color, somewhere between dark green and chocolate. He was always self-consciously erect, pleasant to people, and they liked him. It was not uncommon for civilian guards to salute him. All that winter and spring, Cat and I never had a face-to-face. He had no idea I watched him.

And Cat surely had no idea that I watched the almost daily noon-hour aimless courtyard strolling of an insane American POW outside rooms 24 and the ceremonial room. He was kept alone in Heartbreak. A red-tab guard, usually Pigeye, would always supervise him. His mental state was reflected not only in his vacant stare and shuffling gait but in the diverted eyes of the Vietnamese civil servants who pointedly ignored him. My heart would go out to this poor lost soul, not much younger than I, who later died there in prison. The Camp Authority was literally driving him to his grave.

The green-tab military guards were interesting to watch. From my room 5 vantage point, I observed that they were quartered above the civilians' political lecture room, just a little way toward Heartbreak Hotel from room 18. The green tabs' duties included accompanying convict working gangs who left the main gate every morning. Maybe three soldiers would go with twenty convicts. The soldiers would carry rifles. The convicts came out of the tunnel on which Heartbreak Hotel's green door was located. The tunnel was the link between the main courtyard and that half of the prison behind Heartbreak (which we later nicknamed "Camp Unity").

Some of the convicts were lifers, some were only short-timers (three or four months). No matter which category they were in, each had to sit at a little table before an interrogator once or twice a week and write after he talked. Nobody got out of there without a confession, an apology, and an atonement. For everybody, Communist prisons are "re-education" centers and the inmate bears somewhat the same relationship to his interrogator that an American bears to his psychiatrist. The interrogator understands you better than you understand yourself. You have to be made to understand that you must overcome antisocial tendencies.

Every morning the police would arrive at the main gate with their nightly haul of antisocial derelicts and street hoodlums—maybe a dozen, in some cases twenty-five or thirty. (I sometimes saw them bring them all in in a bunch, with a big chain locked around the whole body of them, the whole organism then being steered up the walk and into the tunnel and into "Unity," some individuals walking forward, some having to walk sideways or backward to stay within the chain.) Within twenty minutes these same antisocial people would come marching out of Unity in prison pajamas, heads shaved, walking to the cadence called by the tan-uniformed civilian guards. They marched out the front gate, across Hoa Lo Street, into the Ministry of Justice, picked up their sentences, and back down the sidewalk into Unity. The trip to court and back might take fifteen minutes.

The sultry May heat was upon Hanoi when in the late afternoon on the fifteenth, my door was thrust open and I was told to "roll up." There was a big crowd of assorted interrogators and guards out front; there was a sense of urgency among them. I could see a crowd of Vietnamese over around room 18, also. I said goodbye to my bed in the corner of this place of happy solitude as I put all my belongings in the roll and tied it with my second pair of pajama pants.

The prisoner about to replace me, Ed Atterberry, was to be killed in that bed within three days.*

I was blindfolded, given my roll to lug along in front, and was walked over through the kitchen area toward Las Vegas. Right after

*See Appendix 5.

I left the cooking smells, I felt myself being guided to the right and then straight. I had to be going along the narrow path behind Riviera. Then the gate. Then right. Could I be going to Stardust? No, right again, through a gate, out of Las Vegas, and straight to Cat's quiz room. My God, I thought, this is crazy. I don't think Cat even uses this place anymore. I'm not going to be taken before him; that would have happened off Heartbreak courtyard.

Blindfold off, and I'm standing in familiar territory, but it's now rigged as a bedroom. There in the corner was a bed board on sawhorses, much like the one they had improvised for me in room 5. The geometry of the overall shed had been changed. Two years before, we used to enter this room from a hallway that ran east and west through the center of the building. Now we came directly in through French doors facing the wall, facing Stardust. There was no door into the old "hallway," but there was a long, high, barred window where it had been. And, my God, it was hot! There was no ventilation. At a glance, it was easy to tell that I was the first permanent tenant with this new setup, and that the idea of fresh air after they had locked the doors had been forgotten.

I was relieved after a few weeks had passed and I had figured out that they had no program for me; I was just on a stash, like I had been in room 5. This had obviously been a hurried and improvised move brought on by their urgent need for an isolated place to torture Atterberry. They wanted to keep me in Hoa Lo Prison. New Guy Village was full of Vietnamese prisoners, and they didn't dare put me back in Las Vegas where I had caused all the trouble two years before. So here I was in Vietnamese "officers' country," cooped up like a chicken.

I washed twice a week, and for me the "Ted Williams shift" was still standard Las Vegas procedure. In the silence of the noon siesta, I would be taken with my bucket, in through the gate of Vegas, past Stardust, on down to the sewer hole between the Desert Inn and the Mint for a dump and bucket scrub, then to the bath shed for a wash, and back to CQR (Cat's quiz room). I was watched continually; not a chance for communication.

There was lots of pacing room in my quarters, and I could look through the bars into what had been the hallway at my leisure while I was alone. The hallway was now a tiny room full of radio receivers and recording equipment, none of which I could reach, nor did I normally hear them. Several times a day, a senior Vietnamese guard would come into this radio room, put on earphones, pull the curtains behind the iron bars, and go to work silently recording introductory American music from broadcasts of the "Voice of America" onto a tape on which the American prisoners would record their daily readings, which were played on the Las Vegas cell speaker system.

This "camp radio" (squawk box) thing was the really irritating part of my new life. I had not heard any cell squawk boxes since being in Las Vegas two years before, when in the spirit of "Unity over Self," they had been kept clear of any American prisoner voices. Now twice a day we heard fifteen minutes of recorded voices of American prisoners in Las Vegas reading propaganda articles or news of the world as translated from the North Vietnamese government press. In the passing years the propaganda had become more skillfully written, the news worse (now it was all about some "National Front for Liberation" in South Vietnam), and the idea of Americans reading it even more depressing.

The real shocker came in an hour-long dialogue between two self-acknowledged American senior officers, "Bob" and "Ed." They talked freely, and obviously without prior torture, about the illegality of the war. I shuddered as I thought how that self-serving tape by that pair of misfits was guaranteed to destroy the morale of any young aviator who heard it. Hearing things like that, which *nobody* in Alcatraz would have tolerated for a minute, was dismaying. I spoke aloud to myself: "What the hell has happened to American spirit in this place? What American is running this camp? It seems like we are going backward; our hard-won gains, our unity, our sense of responsibility for each other, are slipping away in a vacuum of zero leadership."

Life in Las Vegas was clearly without central American authority—although, to be sure, less frantic than it had been two years before during the BACK US purge. Most guards were new. The prominent ones in my life seemed to be two older men, neither of whom spoke English, but both obviously having had ten or fifteen years in the army. They were not nasty, and seemed to be leaders among their peers. One was tall and gaunt, with prominent cheekbones. I called him "Chink." The other, short, with a hook nose and quick of motion, I called "Hawk." I had a peephole into the little court-yard on my side of the wall between CQR and Stardust, and watched the officers eat at their mess area outside their headquar-ters shed just beyond my adjacent radio room. Bug was occasionally there, but never came near me. The senior officer, the commander of Las Vegas Camp, was a rotund professional army man, perhaps forty years old—"Buddha." His second-in-command (whom I called the "executive officer," or "XO") was tall, English-speaking, a political commissar type. Cat would often walk over from his of-fice on Heartbreak court and have noon meal with them; they would all show him great deference, with simpering smiles. He clearly had complete control of their futures.

The XO was new; in fact, I think he was just being briefed on the camp activities the week I got there. He would be closeted in headquarters, behind the far wall of the radio room, one-on-one with various camp authorities for hours at a time, and I could hear their serious-sounding conversation in Vietnamese. All whom he consulted were officers except for Chink and Hawk. I tabbed them as Party members. The XO's wife was around, too. I think they were moving into the apartment upstairs across from Stardust, from which the Lenin portrait stared down on the walkway toward the Desert Inn. They had two little children, a boy and a girl, who would play with simple pull-toys outside my bolted door while their mother attended the briefings in headquarters with her hus-band. I could hear her asking many questions during the briefings. She looked and sounded smart, and I judged her to be a Party member, too. Their little kids seemed quite restless and indulged, more like bourgeoisie than peasants. They were an upwardly mo-bile family.

The XO asked that my door be opened one morning, and came in and looked around. I bowed on his entrance, and he took it with grace, not surliness. He was clearly new with Americans, though his English was fair. He wanted to know how my health was. I said it was getting bad because I had no fresh air; I needed ventilation in the summer heat. He nodded and left.

At noon, Hawk came in the door of the radio room, pulled the blue curtains back, and motioned that he would leave the door open to give me air. This became a noon-hour ritual—and sometimes, if there was no recording to be done, the door would be left open in the evening.

Off-duty guards typically met right after dark in the guard room just inside the pedestrian gate, down the alleyway by Stardust (the one Harry and I were led up, blindfolded, after we got out of the truck those years ago). They would sing a few patriotic songs and then conduct what sounded like a nightly criticism/self-criticism session. One hot night in late June, while such a session was in progress, I heard a frantic American coughing signal. I had a quick look out of my peephole (risking loss of it, you could be so well seen in your lighted room from outside at night), and couldn't believe my eyes. Over the top of the wall, I could see an American prisoner in plain view, boosted up to the ceiling and waving a fan from my old cell, Stardust 3. (He also was a sitting duck in his room light.) He was waving his fan, motioning me to move from my French doors down toward the (then-open) radio room door. Sure enough, as I leaned up against the bars, I could see him through that open door, even after he was let down to stand on a top bunk.

Quickly the silent flash code started—he with his fan, me with my arm extended through the bars into the light of the recording room. It was Will Forby, still with Tom Curtis and still in Las Vegas since they had been left across from Sam and me in Thunderbird 3 when Rabbit was trying to set us up for a communication pinch in 1967. Hallelujah! My first contact with an American in six months! Yes, I would come up in this same manner in the safer dim shadows of the noon lights-out period tomorrow. Dangerous now, CUL ("see you later").

I could hardly sleep a wink that night. As I lay there under my bare bulb, I thought, Good old Forby and Curtis, wouldn't you know it? They took a long chance tonight to get me on the wire. They had my situation all figured out: what hours my visual-access door was left open for ventilation, who I was— the whole thing. I'd thought I heard a little cough when Chink walked me under their window to dump last week. They'd remembered the "signature" of my crippled gait from Thunderbird days.

Every noon we took a twenty-minute chance and exchanged some words. Being old hands at this, we first concocted a cover story we would use if we were detected in our communicating positions. Then we agreed on danger signals, and finally Will gave me the fallback communication plan to be used if this net was destroyed.

Will Forby and Dave Hatcher (who was also in Stardust) had already established a backup note-drop communication system, on which Will then briefed me: "Behind the cement skirt under the sink on the right side of bath 6—the one nearest Thunderbird—is an old bottle in which we would pass notes. To get it, you must reach to the right and down into the spider webs. Our signal device for note drop is a vertical wire high above the right sink. Wire bent south means there is note in bottle for you. Wire bent north means there is note in bottle for me. Wire straight up and down means note picked up and no trouble. Wire bent back against wall means danger, system compromised."

During our session the next noon, I sent the message: "Tell me about American leadership in Las Vegas."

Forby told me there was no camp-wide American organization in Las Vegas, that the senior man, a bird colonel, had arrived there soon after we left for Alcatraz and would not answer communication attempts. He was in the Desert Inn, had the place bottled up, and they couldn't even get the total lineup out of there.

Will also informed me that for my background information, we had a psycho man in camp, John Doe in the Mint. He said he was not violent, talked little, but told our dishwashers crazy things.

Throughout the next two weeks, Will gave me the camp lineup—name, rank, service, and approximate date of shootdown for every man in every cellblock in Las Vegas except for Desert Inn. I told him the Alcatraz story and all that had happened since I had seen him. It took Will three of those noon-hour sessions to brief me on the "Cuban Experiment" that had been going on at the Zoo since the summer of '67. Two Cubans were out there working over Americans on a carrot-and-stick basis, evidently trying to figure out whether prisoners who had been tortured could ever be made safe bets for good Vietnamese propaganda agents in America if talked into fink releases. In the process these Cubans had driven an American out of his mind to the extent that he had to be force-fed and then "burped" by his cellmates. (The poor guy later died in prison.)

All this communication with Will Forby was a wonderful reprieve from six months of total isolation for me. Then one afternoon

I was suddenly moved out of Cat's quiz room and back down to my tiny old cell in the Mint, number 1 in the corner. As I walked in, a maintenance man was disconnecting the squawk boxes in all three cells.

Mint 3 had been emptied; Mint 2 was occupied by a Thai Special Forces sergeant, Chaicharn Harnnavee. At that time Chaicharn spoke very little English (the Vietnamese thought he spoke none). He spent most of the day outside as a yard laborer, doing odd jobs for the Vietnamese, whose language he did speak. We talked little, but I could tell he considered me a pal; we exchanged winks whenever we found ourselves in unobserved circumstances outside, and he once said, "You pilot? Me ladio [aircraft radio operator]."

Thank goodness Will had positioned that note-drop procedure with me. I would have been stranded without it. I had no means of accumulating writing materials, watched as I was, and taken into the yard only when the Ted Williams shift was on. I spent my nights unraveling threads from my pajamas and then composing what I called "braille" messages by tying tiny knots in a spacing that could be read like the tap code as a person ran the thread between his fingers at a uniform rate. Will and sometimes Dave Hatcher were getting these and were able to figure out how to get an intelligible message from those old knotted threads they found in the dirty medicine bottle among the cobwebs under the sink of bath 6. At least I was getting notes in answer to what I had been telling them, notes written in toothpaste on the dark paper towels we were then using for toilet paper.

How to carry notes was a problem I had to work on. I was almost always taken to the bath by that squared-away guard called "Hawk," and he had evidently been instructed to frisk me coming and going each time. But Hawk was a peasant boy, and like peasant boys the world over, he had an innate sense of modesty that I felt justified in taking advantage of. I devised a way of carrying notes in a secure place by what I dubbed "the scrotum suspension method," and he never laid a hand on a one of them.

I began getting a note every couple of weeks. There was the news about Atterberry's death. And one time the guys from Stardust just sent me the poem "Invictus," by Henley. Lots of meaning there.

My luck on notes in cell 1 of the Mint ran out on an afternoon in late August 1969. I had just successfully brought in a note from Hatcher. He knew they had taken the squawk boxes out of the Mint when they moved me in, and he had written me a long note giving the bad news that soon after I had left Cat's quiz room, the Vietnamese had played on all squawk boxes the taped "farewell" statements of two more fink prisoners who had accepted parole release. (This made a total of five so far to illegally fly the coop; the first set of three had left the year before.) Dave had signed his note "McKinlay Knowland," his joke code name, the same as that of an American soldier who had defected in South Vietnam and who continually supplied Hanoi Hannah with tapes about "crossing over to the people's side." My "braille" answers were taking too long to prepare, so I decided to answer Dave by way of his toothpaste-on-brown-paper method.

The door of cell 1 of the Mint was hinged on the left, as seen from inside, and the middle hinge had a piece missing that afforded the inmate, if standing by the leg-iron lugs, enough of a view of the narrow passageway outside to detect the shadows of an approaching guard. In preparing to write the note, I repeated the elaborate precautions I had used for years. I waited for the roving patrol guard to take his hourly peek at me through his peephole, and then I quickly set about making the area around where I was to work look like a session of rereading the few old letters I had. Then I reread Dave's note, tore it into tiny pieces, rolled them in a little piece of paper towel, and stuck them in my toilet bucket.

Ready to reply to Dave, I stood where I could see the passageway floor through the broken hinge. I had more or less covered up my toothpaste tube with old letters and pictures, and had positioned toilet paper and a tooth from a comb I was to use as a stylus. I started to print on the paper: "Dear McKinlay . . ." I thanked him for the note, discussed the Fink Release Program, and mentioned my appreciation for all his help in keeping me in touch with the camp. I was just about ready to sign it "Chester," a code name Dave had given me and also distributed to all of Las Vegas should they hear from me, when a voice quietly said over my right shoulder, "What are you doing?"

It was the roving patrol, an English-speaker we called "the Kid." He had doubled back and I had missed his approaching shadow—and he had opened the peephole so quietly I missed that, too. But I didn't come unglued; I moved things around rather deliberately and deftly, and said, "Just looking at these old letters from my wife the Camp Authority lets me keep in my cell."

"No, I mean what are you writing? I was watching your arm move."

I repeated my denial as the Kid started shouting for the turnkey, who was waiting in the Mint vestibule. I flung the toothpaste tube into the corner and followed the Kid's order to "wall." He was watching the turnkey (Hawk) approaching, and keeping me in sight through the peephole. Abruptly, I walked over to where I had been working and, appearing to be putting my old letters in a stack, palmed my all-but-finished fresh note. As I walked back toward the rear wall, I plunged my hand into the top of my pajama pants and got the note locked near my crotch before it was time to swing my hands overhead again. By now the cell door was open and Hawk was in the room with me. He frisked me hurriedly. The cell was too small to search with me inside so he sent me to the wall at the far end of the little passageway, by Mint 3, while he and the Kid ransacked my belongings.

Hawk—the decent, patriotic fellow—was methodically doing his job. There was no evidence left in Mint 1, and he came out, frisked me again, and motioned for me to go back into the ransacked cell. The damned note had been slipping every time I moved, and was down between my thighs when I began my six or eight steps back down the passageway to the safety of my cell. My leg action was always peculiar because of my stiff knee, but I really looked funny when I tried to walk holding my upper legs together. I'll never forget Hawk's half-laughing/half-agonized expression as he watched my contortions. Then the note fell out of my pant leg right in front of him. He picked it up and ran, and the Kid locked me in my cell and followed.

I was devastated as I waited alone in the empty cellblock. (Chaicharn was working in the yard.) I was in the worst sort of trouble. Ever since I had left Alcatraz, the Camp Authority had spent untold energy and manpower trying to keep me "sterilized," away from any form of prisoner contact. They had put me in special cells, they had laid on special guards. I felt sure that before this afternoon they'd been convinced that there was no way I could have been conversant with names, events, or anything to do with the prisoner community in Las Vegas.

But that note was written proof that I had been in communication with so-and-so and so-and-so for some time, and was involved in discussions of fink releases they had kept from me by removing squawk boxes. Even the note-drop procedures were so intricate that they implied an articulate and precise transfer of words over a long period.

That note was *full* of leads they could exploit in the ropes. There were, literally, long lists of things that logically they now could know that I knew. And so, I was now to be roped and tormented for weeks while we worked back through all the intricacies and details of how the note drop worked, how I learned about it, from whom, when, how he had flashed me the instructions in CQR, what I knew about the man who had been in Mint 3—on and on. They had the drawstrings of a web that would suck dozens of my old friends and many I had never directly communicated with into complicity. All my friends would first go into the ropes. In turn, third parties would be involved, and then *they* would be put in the ropes. I was about to be the cause of another Las Vegas purge, with all the grief and death that this was likely to entail.

About dark, Hawk came to get me. Buddha stood outside. I was blindfolded and walked out toward Stardust, then turned right. I could smell food; I knew this kitchen route now. I was turned left. Then out in the clear again, a *right* turn. That meant I was in totally new territory. As we stopped, I could hear a lock being banged against a wooden door. Now, up two big steps, and I was inside. Off came the blindfold. I was standing in two or three inches of dust in a cobweb-infested cell that appeared to have been locked up for years. It was tiny, the ceiling was very low (just above my head— very unusual for Hoa Lo Prison), and I saw a little slit window on my right as I faced the back wall. I was sat down in the dust, traveling irons were put on, and Hawk locked the door and departed.

I lay back in the dust, despondent. This stuffy old hut in the stinking scullery area of this stinking prison *has* to be the pits themselves. It's like the Black Hole of Calcutta. I have the honor of being the first American resident here. I name it Calcutta.

As the evening shadows fell (before that damned bare bulb

hanging overhead came on and made the place seem like a tomb), I got an eerie feeling. I was studying the mishmash of old brickwork fashioned over the years to plug what was once a barred window on the wall straight ahead. It looked like the back of a man's head, a head I'd seen before. It was bald except for a big, chunky pigtail flowing back from the crown, intersecting strands at the top of the head, each hanging down toward his ears. Maybe I was having a flight of irrational fancy, but, so help me, it was Tecumseh! To me in that hour of hopelessness, it looked like the back of the bronze head of Tecumseh, the old Indian chief, as seen looking up the sidewalk toward the front steps of Bancroft Hall at the Naval Academy.

Why now? I wondered. Is it because of dad and me and how we studied that old bronze figurehead while watching the evening parade "as evening shadows fell" the night before I was sworn in over a quarter-century ago? Maybe, but that Tecumseh brickwork rings a more fundamental bell than even that. I'm looking at the back of that statue as a seven-year-old little boy from a hick town in Illinois, staring through it, watching the same parade while standing between my mother and dad, as the drums roll and the bugles blare. I'm remembering how it was to accumulate obligations, all that precious emotional baggage, that self-doubt, that conscience, all those debts to pay.

Bang! The door is being unbolted again. It's the big, slow-moving, older guard, Chink, from Las Vegas, and Bug!—from God knows where. Now they've got Bug in this mess! Bug is handing Chink another pair of traveling irons—*squeeze* irons, this time. Chink takes off the regular pair I have on and pushes my ankles into those squeeze irons that keep constant pressure on the anklebones. It doesn't seem so bad right now, but wait till about 3:00 A.M., after you've moved around a little and there's been time for friction and swelling. You'll be ready to blow your brains out.

Not a word is said. Something weird about the mood around here—even weirder than the usual slow burn that is generated by having caught me pulling the rug out from under them again.

In a day or two I got the picture on the weird mood. Ho Chi Minh was on his deathbed, or dead. It was odd to think of him over there in his house, a mile or less away. I could almost yell over

there. What would I say? "You old son of a bitch"? No, I'd probably say something like "Goodbye, you old bastard. You know how
this game is played. You didn't snivel—*and neither will I!*"

And then the dirge music started being played all over town.
The Communists use art as a national resource just like bullets.
Good music can become state property and be classified, just like a
secret document. I remember the night back in Thunderbird 6E
when Sam heard a guard going down the free-fire zone outside in
the moat, bellowing a new tune. He said, "That's about the Paul
Daumer Bridge; we must have dropped a span today." Sam was
right—they have songs all made up and in the safe, ready to
cushion any disaster. A target is destroyed in midafternoon; the
songs avenging it are on the radio that night, and a week later
they're faded out. Tonight the funeral songs of Ho Chi Minh are on
the radio. They're overpowering in their calculated discordance,
more special than the Paul Daumer Bridge song. But these songs,
too, are state property. They will be faded out in a few weeks and
saved for future situations when all the emotional stops need to be
pulled out.

It's early morning. The guards are coming to get me. They've
been up most of the night crying about Ho Chi Minh. What a rotten
time to go to the Star Chamber, room 18. I miss those last-minute
pep talks Jim Mulligan used to tap to me at Alcatraz just before I
went into torture. I feel so alone, so in need of advice from an
experienced friend.

No blindfold; out and down the walk to the left, straight
through the building on the north side of the main courtyard, right
by the side of my old room 5 where they killed Ed Atterberry just
after I left, out into Heartbreak courtyard and over to room 18. Bug
is there waiting, face all screwed up. No Pigeye! Just Chink and
Hawk—but I also trust those two guards not to lose their cool.

The courtyard is desolate today. The country is in mourning. It
looks like they're going to work me over in broad daylight. Anyway, with Ho Chi Minh's body lying in state, who's going to give a
damn about a little screaming in room 18? Bug is behind the single
big table, over there where it was the day I caught Rabbit and
Chihuahua trying to tie the tape recorder under it. No stool. I am

summoned over, a guard on either side of me, and charged with grave crimes of an unspecified nature. "Get on your knees!"

"I only have one knee; I'll do the best I can."

And that's how we spent the day—me on my right knee, left leg out straight to the side, Bug after information. Very inept operation; no ropes. It clearly develops as a second-team operation; is the varsity tied up with Ho Chi Minh? Bug just stands or sits before me, fires abstract questions about the chain of events that got me into communication with the camp at Las Vegas, and lashes me across the face with a two-foot-long strip of rubber from a truck tire (we prisoners named them "fan belts") whenever he feels like it.

Bug had my note before him. "Who is McKinlay? We have no McKinlay in this place."

"That's a joke. I was writing about McKinlay Knowland, the black American soldier who deserted the American army and lives in the jungle with a Vietnamese woman and sends those tapes to the 'Voice of Vietnam' all the time. Don't you know who I mean? Don't you laugh at those tapes like we do?"

The whole subject seemed new to Bug. He would get up and leave. My right knee was about to kill me after about three hours; it was bearing all my weight. Later in the afternoon, when Bug left, I would roll over on my side and Chink and Hawk would act like they weren't noticing and one would keep a lookout for Bug. When he approached, they would suddenly get tough and brace me up.

By late afternoon I was worn to a frazzle, but was somewhat mystified. Bug had worked all day, slapped the hell out of me with that fan belt, cut my face, but he didn't seem to be closing in on the subject like Rabbit would. We had spent hours arguing about what different words in the note meant. I had not pulled any great coups, but here it was evening and Bug hadn't even got the name of Dave Hatcher out of me. Rabbit and Pigeye would have had that in fifteen minutes.

About dusk, a guard came in with my blanket roll and threw it down by the north wall, opposite the table. Chink came in with traveling irons, put them on me, and bound me with "loose ropes," which partially constrained my arms but did not induce steady pain. Bug had left for the time being. I was being motioned away from the table area when I suddenly saw Buddha looking in the door. I was soaked with sweat and hadn't had a drink of water all day.

"*Nook! Nook!* [water]," I shouted to him. The fat little camp commander nodded, left, and came back with a drink for me. Odd happenings. Maybe I had beaten the rap! Maybe Ho's death was destabilizing the whole setup!

I waddled over to my blanket roll, got myself down onto the floor, and put my head up on the roll, prayerfully counting my blessings. How had I been so lucky? Maybe it was over, after all!

"Don! Don!" A suddenly enraged Bug was standing in the doorway with a guard beside him. "Get on your feet. You are not to rest!" He motioned for the guard to bring his chair from behind the table and put it right in the middle of the floor. "You will sit in that chair all night. You will contemplate your crimes against the Vietnamese people. These are bad days for us. Our beloved president is dead. You have seen nothing yet. Tomorrow you will give me details. You will see. Tomorrow is when we start; you will be brought down!"

I worked myself to my feet, waddled to the chair, and sat facing the table as the French doors were locked with the old traveling iron, Pigeye style, and pulled out, leaving the four-inch crack so the roving patrol guard could check my activities.

Darkness fell. A guard from Las Vegas we called "the Engineer" (because he wore a shoulder patch with the image of a tractor on it) had the roving patrol duty, making hourly checks on me. But I was hardly noticing such details. I was thinking, Tomorrow is the day. Another purge, more deaths. My fault again. I don't have a hint about what happened at Alcatraz after I left. How many of them died in the ropes trying to protect me? Why is it I who cause all the trouble? Maybe it's better just to sit on your ass and keep quiet. Lie low in your cell like Colonel Kingpin over there in the Desert Inn and let Americans—misfits, psychos, and all—fend for themselves.

But I've got to go on the offensive; I can't just wait for the ax to fall and then be sorry about it. I'm right where I was last winter when Rabbit and Chihuahua went for the hat; I've got to *do* something. I have to stop that interrogation; I have to stop the *flow*. If it costs, it costs.

No stool here tonight. That rusty toilet can is still a loser, but those windows . . . I didn't have the guts to break one when Cat was gearing me up for the release movie, but now I do. This is the only cell with an inside light switch in Hanoi. I'll douse it while I do it! These loose ropes can be worked even looser to give me enough arm action. The Engineer left a few minutes ago; he'll be back in maybe half an hour. It's now or never!

I'm in automatic—I know the motions without thinking. The courtyard is abandoned; all are on a mourning holiday. I waddle to the light switch. Light off! Pop the glass with the heel of my hand; nobody to hear the shattering and tinkle. Dig out those long shards—get ones with sharp points—don't think—move quickly—light back on—waddle to chair in the traveling irons—sit down and *go* for it—the *artery!* No use messing around now.

Chop chop chop chop chop on the left wrist. Blood! Running all down my hand and onto the floor! God, it's *blue;* is that right? Go at it again . . . and again . . . and again. This is tough, even in these loose ropes; get a good sharp piece in your left hand. Chop chop chop chop chop on the right wrist. Now again . . . and again. How do you get more blood? Squeeze your hand, wring it out . . . it out . . . wring it out. . . . My God, the floor is coming up to meet me. . . . The blood . . . I'm lying in it . . . is this right? . . .

"*Eeoow!*" I seem to have heard it in the distance; maybe the Engineer is back. Lots of talk and footsteps all around me. Somebody is waking me up and taking my arm ropes off. The room is full of people! All the green-tab guards are in here from upstairs next door! The old doc with the spectacles who checked my eyes in Riviera 1 is bandaging my arms, very carefully. He's not supposed to see people in "punishment." Bug is here now, shouting alternately, "How *dare* you do this!" and "*Why* did you do this?" Chink and Hawk, silent as always, are stripping my clothes off; then they are wringing blood out of my sweaty pajamas. They wipe the bloody floor with them and disappear with them. A pair of shorts is brought in; I am moved while buckets of water slosh across the floor. Some is sloshed over me.

It's now quiet. The leg irons are back on. My blanket has been spread out on the damp floor and I'm lying on it. Hawk is back and sitting at the table with a rifle in his hand. My pajamas are laid out on the floor; he has washed them. The smell! Sweet! Like fresh alfalfa hay. It's some sort of disinfectant. I'll bet embalmers clean up their table with something like that. I watched the geckos all over the walls. They seem to me to be biting each other in two.

It's daylight. Bug enters with two steaming cups! Chink is with him, and Bug instructs him to take off my irons. "Will you have some tea?" Bug asks sweetly. I am agreeable. I sit at the table with him. "What made you do that terrible thing?" he finally asks.

I say something like "I'm tired of being treated like an animal, being followed, questioned, hounded. I'm a prisoner of war and I'm tired of being nagged to death."

Bug comes in with the line about my being a criminal, but then announces, "This morning you will be moved." Not a word about my being a communicator. Not a word about the note. Not a word about continuing the interrogation. "I have stopped the flow," I say prayerfully to myself.

I was taken back to Calcutta and left to myself for about six weeks while my arm wounds healed. They were dressed every few days by the old doc who didn't speak a word of English. I found my spirits coming up. I really had stopped the flow! I paced the floor behind Tecumseh and thought of dad and how he might have thought that his trips to Annapolis were worth it after all.

After my arm bandages were permanently removed, I was called to my first quiz since leaving room 18. It was short, and with Bug. The message was that I was going to be moved and that Bug hoped I had learned my lesson and would cease to communicate. Then he said, "The Camp Authority is investigating the possibility of improving living conditions. The senior officer is no longer in charge." Wow! The glacier is starting to move, thought I.

I was taken right back to the Mint, cell 1. Everything was the same there, camp radio speakers still removed, Chaicharn still in cell 2, and cell 3 still vacant. Chaicharn and I now exchanged a word or two under the door from time to time. I got the idea that he knew exactly what I had been through. It had been he who had brought me my meals in Calcutta the last few weeks. He had always been escorted by a guard, of course, but we had been able to exchange cautious winks and gestures of friendship. Chai was to become a very close friend of mine in the later years in prison. (I was to learn he had been captured in May 1965 as the back-seat radio operator of an American civilian contract pilot operating in northern Laos.)

I sat up the first night in the Mint "writing" a braille "note," tying knots in a piece of thread for Forby, Curtis, Hatcher, and all in Stardust, telling them the story of my latest episode from the time my note to Hatcher was grabbed by Hawk. Like as not they knew I had been hauled out. I had to get the word out that I had protected all names, that there was no danger of purge; those in the communication link needed to know that—standard operating procedure. I was glad to find that the wire in bath 6 was *not* smashed up against the wall; the system was still "go." I put my thread in the bottle and set the signal for a Stardust pickup. A week later the wire was straight up and down: message delivered.

One day, who should pop my peephole open but the Cat! I couldn't believe my eyes. He smiled and said, "Hello, Staw-dale. I am the camp commander here now! I will be talking to you soon." He left quickly.

I could have been knocked over with a feather! For Cat to announce that he was camp commander was like a four-star admiral mentioning at a cocktail party that he was now the skipper of a destroyer!

Sure enough, I was called in—to Cat's quiz room, no less. I bowed, then sat on the stool in the usual fashion. His first words were "Well, I am glad you are well again!" It was not a friendly remark, just a heavy, sardonic sort of enigmatic double-meaning statement. Then he gave me *five* letters from Syb! And following that, he said, "Staw-dale, you have been alone a long time. You are an old man. I am going to arrange that you will have a cellmate. He has been alone, too. And, Staw-dale, please take care of him."

My head was spinning as I went back to the Mint with Syb's five letters.

Jimmy had finished his first year at Ohio Wesleyan in good fashion, and was working stripped to the waist as an ironworker in a plant in Branford. Syb was thinking of sending Sid to prep school in Connecticut this year. I so hoped it worked out for sweet little Sid.

Taylor had finished the first grade and Stan the third in Coronado. Stan was having a little eye trouble and wearing glasses. Syb had been teaching school at Southwest Junior High for over two years, but had just resigned to spend more time with Stan and Taylor. Dear Syb was devoting her life to raising four wonderful boys all by herself. But in addition, there was a new, easy familiarity with the Washington, D.C., scene in her writing that gave me the idea she was working very hard on other things, too.[1]

So I was to get a cellmate. The last American I had talked to, the last hand I had shaken, was Sam Johnson's two years and three months ago. Lord, would I be glad to be with a fellow human being again! "I must never forget," I told myself, "that a human being is the most precious thing on earth. I must, as even Cat says, take care of this cellmate and never be mean to him or lose my temper, no matter how small the cell seems to get." In the cool days of November 1969, in the Mint, I was thinking of those grand prospects of human friendship when I suddenly realized that I could stand on my bad leg indefinitely without pain. The leg had permanently fused itself stiff at last! It had taken just over four years. This had to be a sign that good things were coming!

Just after noon on November 17, 1969, Hawk came by and said to "roll up." I joyously put everything together and followed him out of the Mint, into Thunderbird, past Sam's and my old TB6E, around the corner and into the alcove where Rabbit stationed his entrapment guard, and into Thunderbird 3. Hawk opened the door and I stepped in, grinning. On the bunk to the left sat a man all bundled up, arms clasped around flexed knees, face long and soulful. He seemed irritated by my arrival. I stuck out my hand and gave him my name. He said, "I know. I'm Lieutenant Colonel John Doe."

Chapter 12

Washington Episode

Not long after my return from seeing the North Vietnamese in Paris in the fall of 1969—and after my TV interview about the telegram I'd sent Xuan Oanh voicing my dissatisfaction with using the antiwar New Mobilization Committee as a channel of communication—the North Vietnamese dropped their plan of forcing us to work through that committee. Instead, a group from Women's Strike for Peace announced the formation of their Committee of Liaison with the Families of Prisoners and the Missing. From then on, we were to send our mail through them. I disliked this idea as well. "Why doesn't the State Department insist on a more proper channel?" I asked Bob Boroughs on the phone.

"I'm not sure someone over there at State didn't suggest this idea you object to," said Bob wryly. "Some of those fellows are pretty cozy with some of these women on the Committee of Liaison. As much as you and I hate it, though, you've got to send your letters through them. It may improve chances of getting our stuff through to your husband."

I didn't have time to dwell on these concerns for long. The White House announced that President Nixon would give a prime-time TV talk on Monday evening, November 3, 1969. I had high hopes he'd include the plight of American prisoners of war in his television message. Not a word was said about them, however, and shortly thereafter I wrote:

Dear Mr. President,

For many months and years, the wives and families of Missing and Captured American Servicemen have been very patient hoping that some development would effect relief and release for their loved ones. Particularly during the past few months, our hopes have run high but many are exceedingly discouraged as the months and years pass and all our hopes and efforts bear no fruition. Ten months ago, by telegram, I personally requested a visit with you. I could understand that your busy schedule did not permit such a visit at that time. I have been under the impression since that time that a standing request had been made through your representatives in the Executive Department for a meeting with a representative group of the wives and families in my circumstance. Many of the families were deeply disappointed that you did not mention the plight of the prisoners in your message to the nation on November 3rd. . . . We are at a point where we feel that we must meet with you personally so that we may be reassured about your own personal interest and thoughts pertaining to the most desperate straits in which our husbands and sons find themselves. If you can find time to see a representative group from our number, we would be deeply grateful. We have been and remain your loyal supporters.

> Very respectfully,
> Mrs. James B. Stockdale
> National Coordinator for the
> National League of Families
> of American Prisoners in
> Southeast Asia

Others were beginning to join our campaign to educate the world, however. The Junior Chamber of Commerce launched a program called "The World Is Watching," aimed at focusing attention on Hanoi's treatment of our POWs. And the Longshoremen's Union announced that they wouldn't unload Russian ships in U.S. harbors unless the Russians influenced Hanoi on the POW issue. God bless the longshoremen, I thought. They were real people who understood about real life.

Mail was pouring into my mailbox from more and more organizations becoming interested in the problem, and I was receiving more and more invitations to speak before groups and appear on TV talk shows. I was scheduled to do a local San Diego TV talk show the day before Thanksgiving. It seemed to me this was a good chance to make those in the White House state their position on the prisoner issue. After all, the president is the commander in chief of all the armed forces.

Very early on the morning of the talk show, I telephoned the White House and asked to talk to Mr. Harry Dent. Somewhere I'd heard that he was an assistant to the president. A White House voice reported he was out of the building. Then I asked for someone else I'd heard was a presidential assistant. I'd probably read about him in *Time* magazine. I was told he was out of the building, too. Then I remembered Mary Winn had mentioned a friend of hers, a retired air-force officer named Alexander Butterfield, who worked at the White House as a presidential aide. I asked to talk to him. He was out of the building, too. I left a message for him to please call me back before noon.

Not a sound from the White House, and it was almost time to go to the studio. I tried Alexander Butterfield again. He was still out of the building, I was told.

"For crying out loud," I shouted at the White House voice, "what are you doing around there, having a fire drill? I have to go on ABC-TV in thirty minutes and I want some assurance the White House is even aware of the POW issue."

Instantly, a male voice broke in saying, "This is Alex Butterfield, Mrs. Stockdale. I can assure you the president is very concerned about the prisoner issue."

"Well, how close are you to him so you know that?" I said sharply.

"I sit fifteen feet from his desk," said he, "and I give you my word he is doing everything he can about the situation."

"Well, he needs to do something publicly," I fired back at him. "We aren't going to wait forever. I have to go now or I'll be late for the program. You tell him what I said."

You know, I thought to myself as I drove to the TV studio, that guy must have been right there on the line all the time. I wonder how often they do that.

As I arrived home from the talk show that day before Thanksgiving (and the day after my forty-fifth birthday) and nudged the little green Volkswagen close to the curb in front of the house, I saw little Stan waving to me from the sidewalk. His slender, almost ten-year-old body quivered with excitement. When I came around the car, smiling at him, he clasped me around the waist and said reverently, "Oh, mom, dad is coming home." I stiffened and for just that one flash of a second wondered if it might be true. Could the war have somehow miraculously ended while I was on my way home? I hadn't had the car radio on. Stan was continuing with great excitement.

"A man called on the telephone and he said the prisoners had been released."

"No, Stan," I interjected as fast as I could. "I'm sure there's a mistake, sweetheart. Don't get your hopes up. I'm sure it's not true, but I'll call somebody right away."

Stan's face turned from ecstatic to crestfallen as I talked to Washington on the phone. Some of the antiwar activists just back from Hanoi had released a list of names of Americans being held prisoner. None of the information was new. A reporter had called our house and Stan had misunderstood. Damn this rotten, rotten business, I thought as I hugged Stan close and consoled him.

"Someday it will be true, Stan, but never get your hopes up by what some outsider says."

Thirteen days later, on December 8, a young man from the Navy Department in Washington telephoned to say that I and a few other wives and parents, a representative group from all the services, were invited to meet with President Nixon at the White House on December 12. At last, eleven months after asking for a meeting, we were going to see the president in person. Mary Winn telephoned that evening saying she was invited, too, and had asked that she and I be allowed to stay together in Washington in the same room. She laughed when she told me about the air-force response to her request: They were shocked to have an air-force wife and navy wife ask to share the same room.

Plans for us all to stay in separate locations around Washington were revised, and while unpacking our hastily assembled wardrobes, Mary and I chattered happily together in our room at the visiting officers' quarters at Bolling Air Force Base. "Don't let me forget to call Jimmy for his birthday before we go to the reception at the club tonight," I said to Mary as I shook the wrinkles from my party dress. "I get so distracted sometimes, I'm afraid I'll forget my own kids' birthdays. He's nineteen today. We were stationed in Norfolk when he was due, but he was born across the bay in Newport News because that was the only place nearby I could find a doctor who'd practice natural childbirth. He arrived with the dawn on December 11 of 1950. I'll never forget the look of pure joy on Jim's face when he came to the hospital that afternoon carrying about a hundred red roses. I'm glad we can't look into a crystal ball and see the future, aren't you?"

Mary was nodding and I saw she already had a note on the phone to remind me to make my call.

All the bigwigs were at the reception and dinner at the Officers' Club that evening. The heads of the army, navy, air force, and marines were there, as well as the secretaries of all these services. The secretaries of defense and state were there, and slews of assistants. Some formula had been used to select twenty-six relatives (wives and mothers) of captured and missing Americans.

"I'm glad I made the list," I said to Mary as we hung up our coats.

"I don't think you have to worry about that," said Mary, flashing a smile. "They know you can influence the other families, and the administration wants our support. They want to stay in your good graces if they can."

A few minutes later, at the reception, I saw Secretary of State Rogers standing tentatively in the doorway of the big, noisy reception room. He reminded me so much of my father in younger years, and he looked very shy and apprehensive standing there alone. Poor man, I thought. It's not his fault we're all in this mess. Boldly, I introduced myself to him and said, "Come on, Mr. Secretary. Don't be nervous. I'll introduce you to the wives."

"I'd really be glad if you would," he replied.

Taking his hand, I led him from group to group, making introductions.

After dinner, one of the defense secretary's assistants pulled me aside, saying, "Sybil, after the meeting with the president tomorrow, there's going to be a press conference with President Nixon and just a few of you wives. We'd like it if you'd act as spokesman for that press conference. The president will go in with you and make a statement for the press, and then you'll take over when he leaves."

I was honored to be asked to do this, but apprehensive, too,

about what might take place. Before sleep that night, I said to
Mary, "I've heard that the Washington press corps is a brutal,
mean, and ruthless crowd. I'm not sure I'm ready to face their grill-
ing about the history of this war. I know too much about it."

"You'll be fine," said Mary soothingly. "Just be yourself and
everything will come out fine."

"You sound like my mother and I hope you're right," I said
before starting my prayers.

The next morning, dressed in our Sunday best, we boarded
official-looking buses for the ride to the White House. I had on the
same bright pink wool suit I had worn for Jim's change of command
in 1965 and to see the North Vietnamese in Paris. As guilty as I had
felt spending $89 for it, I really felt now I was getting my money's
worth. Mary confided she'd spent $200 for the dress she had worn
the night before.

On our way to the White House, I thought how good it felt to
be here with people who were in the same boat. As we left the bus
to go into the White House, our ID cards were checked and re-
checked. We assembled in the library, a room warmed by a sparkling fire and filled with exquisite treasures. I kept looking around,
trying to take in and remember everything at once. One of our
group was in a wheelchair, and she reminded me we'd corresponded by mail as she introduced herself as Iris Powers, mother of
Army Sergeant Lowell Powers, missing in action in South Vietnam.

Suddenly Mrs. Nixon was there in the room with us, shaking
hands and greeting each of us individually. She is tiny as a tooth-
pick, I thought as she looked straight into my eyes. A male voice
announced the arrival of the president, and in he came, taking his
place in front of the fire. He was not as tall as I'd thought he would
be, and he was so tanned that he looked as if he had makeup on. He
was better-looking than his pictures made him seem. I tried hard to
listen to what he was saying so I'd be better prepared for the press
conference shortly afterward. He told us he would try to separate
the prisoner issue out from the war. That didn't make any sense to
me. How could you separate one from the other when one was an
integral part of the other? How could I ever explain his idea of
separating them to the press? Now he was saying the behavior of

the North Vietnamese toward American prisoners was unconscionable. My God, I wasn't even positive I knew the meaning of *unconscionable.*

My heart was pounding and my ears seemed kind of plugged up. Now I and four other wives were just outside the Oval Office on our way to the press room. My insides were jumping around like one of those pachinko machines Jim used to bring the kids from Japan, and I heard myself saying, "Mr. President, I wish you'd go over those points you want to make for the press once more. I'm so excited just being here, it's taking me longer than usual to function."

"Oh, sure," he replied. "Come on into my office and we'll go over them again."

Inside the Oval Office, my eyes were bulging once again, trying to take in everything as well as pay attention to him at the same time. He seemed glad to go over the points again himself, as if he were practicing for the press, too.

Suddenly someone said, "It's time to go," and we all walked into the press room. It was packed with press people, and we walked up onto a little stage. The president made his speech and then left us with the press for further questions. I stepped to the microphone and said we would begin by each describing her husband's circumstances and what details she knew. It was an easy question-and-answer session after that. The press people were nice as pie. They asked only simple questions about our letters from our husbands and so on. When the questions ended and we walked out of the room, there was an uncomfortable silence, so I turned back to them and said, "Merry Christmas!" Most of the networks that evening showed that part on television, as well as some of the rest of the press conference. The commentators said how great they thought it was for me, who was in so much trouble, to wish them a Merry Christmas.

As we left the White House, a handsome fellow congratulated me. "I wanted to meet you in person," he said, shaking my hand. "I'm Alex Butterfield. We've talked on the phone. Give my regards to Coronado when you go home—I went to school there."

I wanted to ask him if that phone conversation had had anything to do with our finally seeing President Nixon in person. But I knew I'd get a noncommittal answer, so I just exchanged pleasantries and tried to look my most determined self. I wanted him to see that I'd never give up my fight for Jim's rights.

That Friday night of December 12, 1969, I slept soundly. For the first time since Jim was shot down more than four years ago, his commander in chief had gone on record in support of the Geneva Convention Relative to the Treatment of Prisoners of War.

The day before Christmas, the mail brought a picture postcard from Jim. The front of the card showed bright red roses against a garishly bright blue background. The message side read:

> Syb, I send much true love to each one in the family. Best wishes for the new year. I'm quite healthy. Your adoring husband, Jim.

Quite a difference from his letter written four years ago this Christmas, I thought as I arranged the packages under the tree. His letters don't really have anything to do with us anymore anyway. I wondered if he'd be home by next Christmas.

By January 6 of the new year, 1970, everyone was back in school and I'd finished vacuuming up the last of the Christmas-tree needles. I spent most of that Tuesday sitting in front of my typewriter writing to Congress. I was laying the groundwork for my next visit to Washington and New York. The article about me to be published in *Good Housekeeping* would appear in the February issue, and I was astonished to learn the magazine would pay my expenses for a trip to New York and had arranged for me to be interviewed on the "Today" show. All this just to plug one article.

I was reluctant to leave Stanford and Taylor again, so I decided to take them with me, paying their expenses myself. In addition to the New York stop, we'd go to Washington and to Connecticut to see my parents and to visit Sid at prep school, and then visit Jimmy at college in Ohio on the way home.

At the top of my list of members of Congress who could help the most by their public endorsement of humane treatment for our POWs were the five most vocal antiwar senators: Fulbright, McGovern, Kennedy, McCarthy, and Goodell. During my December trip to Washington, I had suddenly found myself standing next to

Fulbright in a congressional elevator. As I wrote to him now, I remembered clenching my fists so I wouldn't grab him by the lapels and scream at him. What had stopped me was the certainty that the powers that be would have loved it—they could have just written me off as one more irrational, hysterical female.

I began to type:

January 6, 1970

Dear Senator Fulbright,

My husband is a Prisoner of War in North Vietnam and has been there since September 9, 1965. Last summer, I wrote to you asking for an appointment with you and expressing the idea that the most vociferous critics of the war had very probably lengthened the war and thus had a detrimental effect on the possibility of release for the Prisoners. At that time, you refused to see me on the grounds that my idea was so "preposterous" that visiting with me would serve no purpose.

I, and many other Americans, still believe that the critics of the war have strengthened the will of the Hanoi regime not to negotiate. I am going to be in Washington again on the 15th and 16th of January. I will be en route to the "Today" show where I have been invited to appear. When I visited with the staff at "Today" last summer, they asked me if I had talked with you and I told them you had refused to see me. I am sure they will ask me about it again. I would like to see you now to make a request that the members of our organization have asked me to see you about personally.

I hope that you may have time to visit with me on one of those two days and will wait to hear from you.

Yours Sincerely,
Mrs. James B. Stockdale

Senator Fulbright was no dummy. He granted me an audience this time and promised to preface his televised antiwar speeches with an appeal for humane treatment for our men. On occasion he buried his position in favor of humane treatment cleverly in some of the endless writings Congress regularly spewed out to cover themselves in every possible direction. He used this medium, which practically nobody read, to prove he was true to his word. I never heard him say a word on TV about humane treatment.

I visited with Secretary of State Rogers that same January day. As I sat facing him amid the exquisite furnishings of the State Department's seventh floor, I was surprised as both our voices rose in our verbal exchange and I heard myself saying, "Why doesn't the United States pressure Russia to cut off war supplies to Hanoi? That would bring North Vietnam to its knees. It can't hold out alone against the U.S. if we really want to end this war. I think you're going easy on Russia so they'll go ahead with the SALT talks. At the same time, you tell us you're doing everything you can to help our men. It doesn't add up."

Raising his arms and stabbing the air to emphasize his point, he almost shouted, "You have got to believe we are doing everything we can to bring the war to an end and get our prisoners home."

I shouted back, "I'd like to believe it, but I don't! I just can't believe a country as big as ours can't win this war if they want to!"

On my way down in the elevator, I felt pleased to have been sharply frank with him even though I liked him quite well. I thought to myself, President Nixon put him in charge of this place only to keep these State Department types from botching up the peace efforts the president and Dr. Kissinger are working on.

At South Kent during the weekend, I found Sid a contented, popular fifteen-year-old. My parents, Stan, Taylor, and I all cheered him on during his hockey game. He was on the tripod team—a team for new skaters who depended on the hockey stick to keep them upright as well as to hit the puck. After the game I knelt on the cold bare boards of the South Kent chapel floor and thanked God for the love that surrounded Sid.

On Tuesday, January 20, I arrived at the "Today" show studio a few minutes before seven. I was to be on the 7:30–7:45 A.M. segment. I wore a new heather-blue knitted dress I thought would look well on the color sets, and I probed the makeup crew for hints about how Barbara Walters might act. I'd heard she was abrasive and antagonistic. The makeup people didn't say anything sympathetic about her. I hoped she wouldn't prevent me from making my points. I was relieved during the interview to find the opposite was the truth: Both Barbara Walters and Hugh Downs were as sympathetic and cooperative as could be. She asked good questions to help me explain my point of view. It was all over in a flash, and I felt both relieved and satisfied. I was just as glad I didn't have to watch myself on the screen later. That was one advantage of a "live" show.

During the next couple of days, while Stanford and Taylor were sightseeing with a friend from Connecticut, I did a radio interview with Arlene Francis. On my way out of the studio I met the former baseball player Joe Garagiola. Mr. Garagiola said something that made me feel hopeful about the future.

"Don't you feel the antiwar people are prolonging the war?"

"Yes, I surely do" was my reply.

"I've always thought so," he answered, "but I wondered how you felt."

I was fascinated by the dramatic antics of Barry Farber during my interview on his radio program. First he whispered and then he shouted into the microphone. Mine was a long interview and he knew just how to emphasize all the drama in my story. I closed by softly saying the prayer I sent Jim at the end of my letters to him:

> God keep you, dearest, all this lonely night;
> The winds are still,
> The moon drops down behind the western hill;
> God keep you, dearest, 'til the light.

A pile of mail was waiting when we returned to Coronado. The Navy Bureau of Personnel had sent instructions about the Committee of Liaison's seven-line form on which all my letters to Jim must now be written. "Via Moscow" was stamped on the front of the form. I flinched when I opened my December telephone bill—$497. God Almighty. I had to get some financial help from somewhere.

Later that week I began my search for financial support by writing to the same fellow at the Copley News Service who had helped me before. I explained I had been paying all the business expenses for the National League of Families out of my own pocketbook. The twenty-four coordinators paid their own expenses, but the major phone, telegraph, and mailing expenses were mine, and the costs were outdistancing my ability to pay them. I could go out and beg the world for help for Jim and his buddies, but I just wouldn't beg for money. Could he think of any way to help me? I felt sure he would do everything he could. I told him I felt we were making some progress and hoped his newspaper would be able to write about the homecoming of the POWs in 1970.

On that same day, I also answered a typical perfunctory letter I'd received from Congressman Allard Lowenstein. He had been at Stanford University teaching international law when Jim did his graduate work there, and the two had become good friends. He was a leader in the antiwar movement now. If I could get him to protest inhumane treatment in the same loud howls he bellowed about the war, it couldn't help but advance the cause of truth. So I wrote him a blistering letter, making Jim's torture a vivid picture for him to contemplate.

He telephoned while I was frosting the cupcakes I'd baked for Taylor's Valentine party at school. Lowenstein frantically wanted to help, had a plan he felt was truly worthwhile, and asked me to meet him in Los Angeles for dinner on February 24. I thought this might be the breakthrough we needed in Congress. With a hopeful heart, I made my airline reservations and baby-sitting arrangements.

When I emerged from my PSA flight in the Los Angeles airport, a fat, black-haired woman grabbed my arm. "The congressman's waiting for you," she said. "He doesn't have much time. He has a speech to make and can't spend more than fifteen minutes with you."

I was in a state of semishock as a small, slightly balding, darkhaired fellow introduced himself, saying, "Just call me Al." He walked me to a stand-up bar and ordered drinks. I'd be hearing more from him later, said he. He'd probably be wanting me to come to Washington soon to meet with a bipartisan congressional committee he planned to form. His office would be in touch with me. Sorry he had to run. "Duty calls" was his parting phrase as the fat woman pulled him away.

I stood alone at the bar and finished my drink. I was not really hungry anyway. I'd see if I could change my ticket for an earlier plane home. I was glad Jim didn't know how his great friend had just behaved.

During the spring of 1970, public awareness about the treatment of our men in North Vietnamese prisons increased dramatically. Two other Coronado POW wives came to my house daily to help with the mail and phone calls. Our big oak dining-room table was piled high with bumper-sticker designs, newspaper ads we were constructing, billboard-cost quotations, responses to the *Good Housekeeping* article, and unsolicited checks from family members and concerned citizens. From dawn until long after dark, I raced from one civic-club speech to another, to radio and TV stations, to the hairdresser, to Instant Print, to the boys' schools for conferences, to the washer and dryer, to the commissary, and to doctors' appointments. If I could just run fast enough, maybe I could accomplish my goal more quickly. I wasn't sure I had enough energy to keep up this pace forever. I didn't feel my usual energetic self much of the time, but I didn't have time for a physical exam—and, anyway, if anything was wrong, I didn't really want to know it. I had to keep going, no matter what. But I was feeling a level of exhaustion I'd never experienced before.

One of my late-night calls that spring was from Senator Robert Dole. He told me he had attended a tribute for POWs in Constitution Hall in January. I'd heard it was a pathetic affair, poorly advertised and poorly attended. Senator Dole, who has a crippled arm due to World War II wounds and was, I felt, particularly sympathetic, had vowed to fill Constitution Hall with a tribute for the prisoners before the end of May. Now he was not sure he could pull this off. If he helped me arrange government transportation, could I deliver 1,000 family members? The tribute would take place on May 1, International Law day, and would be called "An Appeal for International Justice." As much of society as possible would be represented on the stage of Constitution Hall: Vice-President Spiro Agnew; Senator Barry Goldwater; assorted congressmen; an astronaut; a mayor; movie actor Bob Cummings; the DAR's president general; entrepreneur Ross Perot; assorted POW and MIA wives; et cetera. I, along with others, would testify before Congressman Clement Zablocki's congressional committee the day before the tribute.

I stepped up the pace of my days at home. I encoded my letters to Jim early in the morning to be as sure as possible I wouldn't make an error that could cause his execution. Bob Boroughs had arranged a safety check on my encoding now, which took away some of the terror. I wrote fewer letters to Jimmy and Sid away at school. I shortchanged Stanford and Taylor on bedtime stories and whizzed through their prayers:

"Now I lay me down to sleep, I pray the Lord my soul to keep.

If I should die before I wake, I pray the Lord my soul to take. God bless teddy bear, Santa Claus, grandma, grandpa, daddy, momma, Jimmy, Sidney, Stanford, Taylor, Brownie, Tick-Tock, and a special prayer for dad. Amen."

In April, when arrangements for Senator Dole's extravaganza were going into their final phase, Bob Boroughs telephoned with some unsettling news. A group of retired military officers in Washington had heard my doubts about whether I could continue to carry the expense and pressure of the National League of Families on my own much longer. Boroughs said these retired types were eager to gain control of the National League. They would set themselves up as its paid officers in downtown Washington offices. We wives would be allowed to come in and lick envelopes or open mail. Membership would be open to the general public, and our organization would lose the one thing that made it unique and gave it public appeal: the fact that only relatives of POWs and MIAs could be members of our group. I had learned that lesson well from Mr. Palmer that day at the *New York Times*. The slightest taint of Washington slickness was the surest turn-off for the media, who were our strongest allies.

Boroughs continued: "These guys are well organized, already funded by government contractors, and hope to present their plan to the families at your meeting the day after the tribute. If they get on that stage, they'll convince the families this is the way to go. You've got to prevent them from ever getting on that stage."

"My God, how can I do that, Bob, if they're on the agenda?"

"You'll think of a way," he replied somberly. "You have to. This is important."

Sure enough, a few days later, one of the Washington men Bob had named telephoned. He'd be in Los Angeles on business and could he come to Coronado and take me to lunch? He had a proposal he wanted to talk over with me.

I wore one of the new dresses I'd splurged on for the Washington trip to the tribute. Thank God for Bob Boroughs, I thought as the man told me about the marvels of his plan. It certainly sounded interesting, I replied. I'd look forward to hearing more about it during the family meeting in Washington.

Before cooking the boys' supper that night, I changed out of my new dress—and saw the price tag still hanging from the back of the belt. Doyen laughed when I told her about it later. "He'll think I'm a real scatterbrain," I said, to which Doyen replied, "Boy, is he in for a surprise at that meeting!"

Even though I knew this retired-officers scheme was not the way to go, I realized that somehow I had to arrange to have others help carry on the work of the League. Bob Boroughs suggested I ask Charlie Havens what he thought I should do. Charlie was a Washington attorney now in private practice, but I had come to know him when he was in the Office of International Security Affairs in the Pentagon. He was there during both the Johnson and Nixon administrations, and he was one of only a few in Washington whose opinion I still respected. Havens, Boroughs, and I planned the strategy I carried out during the Washington tribute trip.

I invited four other gals to meet me in Washington before the formal events began. We visited Under Secretary of State Richardson, Secretary of Defense Laird, Attorney General John Mitchell, and White House assistants General Hughes and Mr. Holdrege. We had specific requests and suggestions for each of these men. Iris Powers was recovered and out of her wheelchair now; she seemed a powerhouse of charm and intelligence. Mary Winn scared the daylights out of Secretary Richardson when she asked him about special State Department permission to set up an American colony in Hanoi. He even paused in his doodling as she described her idea. She had a marvelously imaginative mind.

Two evenings before the tribute, we had a planning meeting in my crowded hotel room for several League members I'd asked to attend from around the country. Charlie Havens was present, and between us we engineered the establishment of an ad hoc committee to incorporate our National League of Families in the District of Columbia. Charlie's voice of legal authority rolled over the opposition. The tenor of our meeting was much like that of the city around us and of the country in general. The Communists' Cambodian sanctuaries had just been bombed for the first time. Much of the population was incensed, and we had warring factions among our wives and families as well. The turmoil of conflict pervaded every facet of our lives. When I completed my testimony before the congressional committee the next day, one congressman admonished me to pray. I could hardly believe my ears. Did he think I hadn't thought of that before? Were my tax dollars paying him to make such brilliant comments?

After the tribute itself—for which Senator Dole did fill Constitution Hall to overflowing—Mary Winn laughed softly and said, "It truly warmed the cockles of my heart when all one thousand family members rose as a body applauding when you were introduced."

At the family meeting the next day, I managed to prevent the retired officers from presenting their take-over plan. As I strung out the agenda and allowed confusion to overwhelm order, the pitchman for the take-over plan glared at me from backstage where he waited to be introduced. Shortly before I announced that time had run out, he realized he'd been had.

The take-over group still persisted, however. Three weeks later I was back in Washington for the meeting of our ad hoc committee to incorporate the League as a nonprofit organization in the District of Columbia. Charlie and I had selected about twenty representative volunteers for this committee. Minutes after we'd voted to incorporate as an exclusive "family" organization, the heavy oak door of Charlie's office burst open and my luncheon host of five weeks earlier entered the room with one of our wives. There was complete silence as they circled our table, jerked out chairs, and sat down with conviction. The rudeness of their entrance stunned us all. Charlie was the first to regain his composure, asking their business. With relief, we reported we had just completed our vote to remain the National League of Families. Our visitor exited as abruptly as he had entered.

During the next month I made two more trips to Washington from San Diego to complete the business of the incorporation of the National League of Families and to get our office organized. On June 30, 1970, I presided over the formal opening of our office at 1 Constitution Avenue, Washington, D.C. I had talked Iris into moving from Florida to set up the office. Our Internal Revenue Service number as a nonprofit corporation came through in three weeks. "I think somebody important behind the scenes is pulling some strings for us, don't you, Charlie?" I said with a twinkle in my eye when he told me this news. He smiled broadly in reply, not saying a single word.

✧

I'd decided to move to Washington myself before the school year began in September. Stanford needed vision therapy, and I was convinced that the best doctor in the country for this was in Washington. I thought, too, that perhaps if I lived closer to Congress, I could do more to pressure them into helping Jim. And maybe the naval hospital at Bethesda would be a better place for treating Jim if he ever did come home. The navy would pay for our move, and maybe a change of scene would bring me good luck. As chairman of the board for the League, I wouldn't have to make any more cross-country trips. I'd never felt as tired as I did that summer. I had a college girl living with us to be with the boys when I was gone and to help on the domestic front. Even so, I was so exhausted that I felt like a stranger to myself.

I rented the Coronado house to navy friends and rented a big brick colonial house on Western Avenue in northwest Washington for me and the boys. The house needed fresh paint inside, and I reasoned that as soon as I moved in, I'd be inspired to paint and decorate it the way I had all our homes in the past. Inspiration deserted me, however. Once in the Western Avenue house, I felt more exhausted than ever. The thought of coping with the complexities of city life, big business, and all the tenseness and haggling of the League members overwhelmed me. Furthermore, the fifth anniversary of Jim's shootdown had passed. Each morning I forced myself to get up and have breakfast with Stan and Tay before they left for school. I tried to be my natural self as I packed their lunch boxes and chattered about their school activities. I had dropped each of them back a grade as this school was more advanced than theirs in Coronado.

As soon as they were safely on their way, I climbed the stairs and sank gratefully back into bed. I pulled the covers over my head and silently began my litany of worry for the umpteenth time. Over and over and over again. What have I done? I've made a terrible mistake. How am I ever going to get out of here? Things aren't as I thought they would be at all. The boys don't have anyone to play with. I've used up my one free navy move and I hate this place. My God, what am I going to do? The expenses here are staggering. What if I run out of money? Do I dare use the boys' college money to move us back to Coronado next year? I try to figure up my assets, but give it up. My heart pounds. I flop over onto my back and stare at the ceiling. Morning traffic churns by in front of the house. The traffic here is unbelievable. How will I ever learn my way around? I've got to get a prescription for Stan's medicine. How am I going to find a doctor? I've got to do that today or tomorrow. I can't put it off any longer.

Stan—definitely diagnosed last spring as emotionally blind, with 20/400 vision—was taking a prescription drug to relieve his hypertension and was doing fine in his new class. But I had to get a new prescription for that drug now that I was in a new location. If only I could go to the naval hospital in Bethesda and just get a new prescription. But, no, that was hopeless; Stan would have to be subjected to batteries of tests all over again. The poor kid had been scared enough when they wired him up for encephalograms and every other thing they could think of in San Diego. I had to get out of this bed and call somebody and find a civilian doctor.

Instead, I turned on my side facing the wall. My God, what have I done? How am I ever going to get out of this place? I began my balance-sheet conjecturing once again. And on and on it went into the afternoon. The boys would be home at 3:00 P.M. At 2:45 I dragged myself onto my feet. I wandered from bedroom to bathroom naked. I couldn't decide what to wear. Two strangers inside of me began a conversation. What difference does it make? You're not going anywhere. I know, but I can't decide. Well, for God's sake, get something on. You don't want the boys to know you've been in bed all day. Oh, my God. What am I going to do? I hear Kitty (our college-girl helper) saying, "Hi, guys. Did you have a good day? Your mom's upstairs. She'll be right down." I throw a dark blue wool dress over my head and tie a red and blue scarf around my neck. I stare hard at myself as I powder my nose. I am losing weight. I am not even hungry all the time the way I used to be. I look like a hag. I paste on my smile and start down the stairs.

"Okay, everybody. Today's the day we go looking for new shoes!"

As I continued to feel worse instead of better, I decided I must have some obscure disease. I asked Iris—who was by now like an older sister I never had—if she knew a good gynecologist in Washington. Dr. William Cooper on New Hampshire Avenue was her immediate reply.

"When you see him, Syb," said Iris in her throaty, confidential, I'm-giving-you-good-advice voice, "ask him what he thinks about your having a little psychotherapy."

My body stiffened. Every fiber of my New England-trained body reverberated with the shock of such a suggestion. All my mother's maxims marched through my mind on the double.

"If at first you don't succeed, try, try again."

"God helps those who help themselves."

"Practice what you preach."

"You teach your children by your own example."

How in the name of God could I justify being such a weakling that I needed psychiatric help? Only those who caved in to self-pity and self-indulgence went to psychiatrists. It was not my mind that was exhausted, it was my body. My body wouldn't do what my mind told it to do. My body wouldn't get out of bed and start hanging curtains at the windows. It stayed in bed hiding its head under the pillow, trying to shut the world out.

I asked Dr. Cooper what he thought about my having psychotherapy. Ever so gently, this kind and thoughtful man softly replied, "Sybil, I don't think a little psychotherapy would do any harm."

By now I felt so dreadful, I'd have done anything to get better. Karen Butler, who was still in San Diego, had heard all was not well with me. In early October she arrived at my front door, and before she left I had an appointment with a psychotherapist at Bethesda Naval Hospital. I never used the word *psychiatrist*, even to myself. That was too close to an admission of total failure. I was due in the navy psychotherapist's office at 9:30 A.M. on Tuesday, October 13. He was in Building 7, floor F.

There was no place to park at Bethesda. The nearest place seemed miles from Building 7. I arrived at the doctor's office a half-hour late in tears of frustration and anger. As we sat down, he took out a notebook. I ordered him to put it away. "You're not to write one word about me," I shouted at him. "As far as I'm concerned, the navy is so screwed up, they probably will give that report to my husband before anything else when he returns."

The doctor asked me some background questions and asked that I come back the next day. I'd spent most of his scheduled time looking for a place to park, of course.

When I returned the next day, he said he wanted me to see a civilian doctor in town. I told him the navy was certainly going to pay for it, because it was their fault I was in this mess. He told me that a military health-insurance program would pay most of the bill.

On Friday, October 23, I saw the civilian psychotherapist. It was one of the spookiest encounters I'd been in. This doctor's office was positively tiny; you could hardly stretch your legs out in the waiting room. Also, it was in a residential apartment building. What kind of a second-rate doctor was this, I wondered, who couldn't afford a regular office? His inner office featured the proverbial couch, no less. The doctor himself hid behind a fuzzy beard, a real symbol for me of antiwar politics. He just sat there and waited for me to talk. I sat there and waited for him to ask questions. Dead silence. After a while I thought, Am I going to have to pay to sit here and look at this spook? Finally we exchanged a few words. Just as I was leaving, I asked him how old he was. He said his age didn't have much to do with the problem at hand. He made another appointment for me, but I canceled it and called Dr. Cooper, asking him to recommend someone. He said, "Go see Robert Moran on 'K' Street."

I had my first appointment with Dr. Moran in November. I was relieved to see he had a good-size office in a real office building, no couch, and no beard. He talked a steady streak, hardly letting me get a word in edgewise. Most of what he said was about topics far from my problems, but I liked hearing his stories about his family and friends. Afterward, I tried to figure out what points he was trying to make to me. After two or three visits, every so often with a twinkle in his eye so I knew he was joking, he'd say, "Come on, Stockdale, let's make love." I told him I thought he was the crazy one in the room. I was sure he knew me well enough by now to count on my refusal and probably he felt that the invitation would boost my morale. At first I saw him twice a week. My visits to him became the high point in my life.

Everyone was being extra nice to me. Iris kept me filled in on what was going on at League headquarters. I congratulated myself on its incorporation in Washington in the nick of time. I attended the board meetings but left the rest to others. Admiral Moorer was chairman of the Joint Chiefs of Staff now. I received a handsomely engraved invitation to attend a formal dinner at his quarters on December 17. That would be a lovely Christmas treat for me.

After my next visit with Dr. Moran, I splurged on an elegant red velvet dress. It was hanging in the closet beside my bedroom phone when Admiral Moorer telephoned on Saturday morning, November 21. He wanted to know what I thought about the Son Tay raid. The night before, the TV news had been full of the U.S. government's effort to rescue prisoners from a North Vietnamese camp near Son Tay. The rescue party had found the camp deserted, however. All the Americans who'd been there had already been moved to another location. The media speculated that the U.S. government had staged the entire scenario to make the Nixon administration look better.

I told Admiral Moorer that I thought the raid was absolutely great and that I hoped they wouldn't wait too long before they tried another rescue. I told him it was a real shot in the arm to know our government was trying to do something to help our men. He said he'd heard some of the POW wives didn't think we should expose their husbands to the danger of attempted rescues. I told him it was my bet their husbands didn't feel that way. I added that anybody who thought playing it safe was best at this point in time didn't understand the problem.

Shortly after Thanksgiving, Dr. Cooper announced that he had scheduled a hospital stay for me to have some tests. He had reserved a bed at Sibley Memorial Hospital for December 17. When I'd first gone to him for a checkup, he had given me the routine test for cervical cancer. A few weeks later he had repeated that test—and he was concerned about the results. He'd detected some cellular changes, which are the way cancer begins, and he wanted to investigate more thoroughly.

I hung a plastic cover over the elegant red velvet gown and sent my regrets to Admiral and Mrs. Moorer for their dinner party. I vividly remembered my mother telling about her mother's painful death from uterine cancer. I was certain Dr. Cooper would not have me in the hospital the week before Christmas without good reason. Dr. Moran helped me face up to this new fear that I might have cancer.

Before I left for the hospital, I placed a note for Jimmy in my top drawer with instructions in case I died. It would help him with my funeral plans if I gave him some guidelines:

1.   I want to be buried in the national cemetery on Point Loma in San Diego. I prefer the hillside facing the Pacific Ocean. Call Admiral Moorer for help with the site.

2.   Include the Navy hymn and the Mount Holyoke Alma Mater in the music. You choose the rest. Call Mount Holyoke College music director, Miss Ruth Douglas, for Alma Mater.

3.   Give all my clothes to Doyen.

4.   Put my Naval Academy miniature and wedding ring in a safety deposit box in case dad comes home someday. Tell dad I love him.

5.   Don't worry about me. I'm with God.

Fortunately, I returned home from the hospital two days later and Jimmy didn't have to use my instructions. My hospital tests showed I needed some surgery, of a "female nature," as my mother would say. I needed to have a hysterectomy to be on the safe side of the cancer threat. After Christmas I began to make plans to be in the hospital about ten days beginning February 17. I was glad I wouldn't have to miss our National League of Families board meeting with Dr. Henry Kissinger on Saturday, January 23. We'd been given an appointment to see him instead of President Nixon. Dr. Kissinger was so knowledgeable about U.S. foreign policy, we had high hopes he would give us a sense of optimism for 1971. We'd been wanting to see President Nixon again ever since our meeting on December 12, 1969. Repeatedly we'd been told that no useful purpose would be served for us to see the president if he didn't have anything new to report to us. Our meeting with Dr. Kissinger would take place on Saturday afternoon, January 23, at 4:00 P.M. in the White House. We were excited at the prospect of hearing what he had to say. Several of our more dedicated members were flying in at their own expense just to attend this meeting.

On Saturday morning, while we were formulating our questions for Dr. Kissinger during our regular board meeting, a phone call from the White House announced that Dr. Kissinger couldn't see us—he'd be attending Senator Russell's funeral—but we could see his assistant, General Alexander Haig. We'd never heard of him. It was too late to notify the people flying across the country just to see Dr. Kissinger. We were stunned with disappointment, which rapidly turned to anger. We were tired of seeing assistants to assistants. Weren't our men important enough for the White House to have given us more notice? Senator Russell had died on Thursday. They could have given us more notice if they cared. We discussed calling the White House and telling them that we weren't coming at all. Instead, we decided to go and let our rage register with this General Haig, whoever he was. None of us knew anything about him. We decided to go over there at 4:00 and let the general have it.

We began our journey in an antiquated air-force bus. The noisy gears hauled us through the city to the west gate of the White House. There a guard boarded the bus to tell us to have our identification ready for inspection as we entered the grounds. Some of us pulled on our white gloves. Our breath blew frosty clouds as we stepped down from the bus. For most, this was a first visit inside these hallowed portals. We were carefully checked through both the outer and the inner gates, with the police guards cross-checking with their lists. A marine held the door open for us at the west wing and we entered the reception room.

Inside the White House, I felt transported into another world. The floors were highly polished and covered with handsome Persian rugs. Lovely artwork covered the walls; there was an elegant flower arrangement on every table. A model-like receptionist sat behind a finely carved antique desk, and various White House assistants bustled around greeting us. I knew our faces were a little stiff with our displeasure.

After all the coats were hung, we were invited into the Roosevelt Room. It had deeply piled wall-to-wall carpeting. In the center there was a long table that seated about eighteen in leather chairs with wooden arms. There were sofas and easy chairs along the walls. Our board sat at the table and the other guests in the outer ring. Before each place at the table, there was a perfectly sharpened yellow pencil and small pad of notepaper inscribed "The White House." I sat next to the head of the table and an assistant's assistant told us the general would be with us in a few minutes. A few chatted quietly, but most of us just sat and waited. What would Jim think if he could suddenly see a picture of me sitting in this room in the White House waiting to reprimand a general? He'd smile, I thought. But when I tried to picture how he looked when he smiled, I couldn't remember.

The general walked into the room. With his trim haircut, deep tan, dark blue blazer and flannel trousers, General Haig was a strikingly handsome man. His eyes were almost as blue as Jim's, but not as large. I reminded myself not to let looks deter me from my mission.

He started in a soft voice, standing at the head of the table. After his apologies for Dr. Kissinger's absence, he started a long, familiar line about how concerned everyone was about our situation and complimented us on our courage, patience, and bravery. As he started to relax a little, he put his hand into his left trouser pocket. He paused and was about to continue speaking when one of our more vocal members from the other end of the table interrupted to say she was tired of hearing the same old line; that we'd heard all this many, many times before in offices all over Washington; that we had come to see Dr. Kissinger and we felt he could have arranged his schedule so as to see us if indeed he was so deeply concerned.

The general started to reply, but was again interrupted, and so it went around the table as all of us had our say. When one wife, standing herself now, pointing her finger at the general and stamping her foot, said she had come 2,000 miles to talk to someone on a policymaking level, the general replied that he believed he qualified as a policymaker. His brow wrinkled. I saw a light film of perspiration just below his hairline. I interjected that possibly he did not understand that we were just plain sick and tired of seeing assistants to assistants and being shuttled around at the convenience of the policymakers. We had come to see Dr. Kissinger, and expected him to keep his appointment with us. We had wanted to see President Nixon for more than a year now, we hadn't seen him since December of 1969, and had settled for second best by agreeing to meet with his assistant.

General Haig's hand dug deeper into his pocket. He told us he was sure Dr. Kissinger would be glad to meet with us when we had our next meeting in Washington in two months.

My voice shook with rage as I replied, looking him straight in the eye, "We don't want to wait two months to see Dr. Kissinger, General Haig. We want to see him in two days. We'll still be here on Monday, and if he cares about our men, he'll somehow make the time to see us. We're tired of being put off. Do you understand what we're saying? Are we communicating with you?"

He wrinkled his brow and looked troubled. "Yes, Mrs. Stockdale, I can assure you that you are communicating with me very well—so well, in fact, that I have worked a hole in the pocket of my pants and my change has all fallen out on the floor."

With that we looked down and saw his money on the carpet. That broke the tension. The meeting came to a close with his assurance that he would be in touch with us the next day. We all shook hands and were our ladylike selves again. We felt we'd made our point.

By Sunday afternoon we received a message that Dr. Kissinger would meet with us at 5:00 P.M. on Monday. I was relieved he had the good sense to see us. If he had put us off, it would have meant a declaration of war between us and the White House. I knew that would be a battle we could never win, and I hoped it would never begin.

On Monday we presented ourselves once again at the west wing outer gate. The general's assistant, who had been present at the Saturday meeting and whom I had seen hiding a smile while we were railing at his boss, was at the gate waiting for us. "We meet again soon," I said, shaking his hand. "Evidently we communicated on Saturday."

"Yes, I thought you communicated very well." His beaming look told me he had thoroughly enjoyed Saturday's proceedings.

The guards carefully checked us through to the marine doorman, and there again was the model-like receptionist, every hair in place. This time we were ushered into a small room with machines lining the walls. It seemed a strange place to meet. We were told this was the Situation Room. Appropriate name, I thought as Dr. Kissinger entered. He shook hands and looked straight into our eyes as we introduced ourselves. Then he sat down at the head of the table. There was no sign of General Haig. I sat next to Dr. Kissinger. I wondered on what note he'd begin.

Kissinger spoke with an exceedingly soft voice. I had to strain to hear every word, and it took me a few seconds to adjust to his German accent. I studied him carefully at close range. I couldn't detect a glimmer of the physical sex appeal we read about in the news. His receding hair was bumpy and his physique was pudgy. I settled down to listen carefully as I watched him closely.

He told us he didn't know what we had done to General Haig. He had never seen the general so shaken as after our meeting with him, and he thought Haig had left the building when he heard we were coming again. This relieved the tension and made us feel good. Then he told us he wasn't going to try to fool us with any false assurances or promises. Above all, he was going to be as honest with us as he could be. He had agreed to see us because he felt that we had suffered the most as civilians as a result of the war. He explained the president's hopes for his Vietnamization program, but cautioned us not to expect any results in the near future. He explained in detail the difficulty of negotiating with the North Vietnamese; how much harder it was to negotiate with them than any other power in the world.

For an hour and a half, he answered our questions, always reminding us that he would not discuss secrets. He painted the blackest possible picture for us. We were quiet, subdued, and sick at heart. There wasn't a ray of hope for the near future. He didn't pretend that there was. We sat there and faced it. Dr. Kissinger agreed to meet with us again in two months because he felt we deserved to know as much as he could tell us, but he did not want to raise false hopes in our hearts. We thanked him and walked single file back through the now empty offices, up to the main floor.

"Well, we saw him anyway," someone said as we shrugged into our heavy coats.

"I almost wish now we hadn't," someone else replied.

I turned up the collar on my camel-hair coat as I walked toward the parking garage alone. Oh, my God, my God, my God, I thought. If I can feel this down, how must Jim feel? I'm glad he can't know about this meeting today.

My surgery took place as scheduled on February 17. I stayed in the hospital ten days and spent the next six weeks home in our

Washington house recovering. I wrote to Jim in April on my seven-line form I'd converted to thirteen lines. I told him all four of our sons were doing well in school (which was true) and that I hoped the Easter season gave him the strength and courage he would need until we were reunited. I told him I felt more confident about the future. What I meant was that I felt sure it would be a while yet before we were reunited.

I began to count off the days until we could go back to the shore in Branford for the summer, and then from there back to Coronado. I had asked the navy if they would sponsor my move, and their ready agreement made a warm place for them in my heart. I had my last visit with Dr. Moran in early April. During that visit, I told him it was hard to know how to proceed with plans for the future. "I don't know whether to count on Jim's coming home or not."

He answered, "Plan on his not coming home. That way, if he doesn't, you'll have your life planned in that direction; and if he does, so much the better."

I was relieved to have some guideline for the future. Dr. Moran knew I was not about to become emotionally involved with anyone else, so he was safe with his advice.

I knew that if I ended up living the rest of my life alone, I would want to travel. So I decided to make an experimental trip. Our college helper would be leaving us in June to go back to her own family, and this was a last chance to leave her in charge while I was away. I had never been to Hawaii. Jim wasn't too crazy about the commercialism that had developed out there, so I didn't think he'd want to make it a vacation spot if he did come home. I had close friends stationed at Pearl Harbor, and I made plans to go out and see them.

The government had given POW/MIA wives permission to ride on government aircraft within the limits of the continental United States if space was available. Someone had told me to check the White House planes, too, as they were on a separate schedule and often went back and forth to President Nixon's western White House in San Clemente. Sure enough, they had one going in the middle of May, and it was even going to land at North Island Naval Air Station right in my own Coronado on the way. It was Mrs. Nixon's plane, I was told, and was going out empty. They had to pick something up at North Island before going on to El Toro, near San Clemente.

I drove out to Andrews Air Force Base in a torrential down-pour and boarded the nifty little jet. I was the only passenger and I was treated like a royal highness all the way. I smiled, remembering my childhood daydreams about being a princess. The greatest fun was sitting in the cockpit with pilot and copilot as we came in for the landing at North Island. Doyen was there to meet me. We laughed and cried and hugged each other wildly all at once. We giggled as we watched my suitcases being carried by a smartly uni-formed marine from the jet, and placed gingerly in the back of her old gray pickup truck.

I spent only one night in Coronado before going on to Hono-lulu on Western Airlines. It felt strange being in my own town with someone else living in our beloved old house. I didn't go into our house at all. I knew it wouldn't be long now before we'd be back living here. It was enough now to look at it and blow it a kiss as I walked by.

After three or four days at Pearl Harbor with my friends, I was off to the other islands for a five-day trip with a tour group. This would be the acid test of my ability to travel alone. I got along fine, learning a little more each day about how to enjoy being alone and how to handle being a single female in a group. Sometimes I had dinner sent up to my room and ate while reading a book, or I took a long walk wherever we were spending the night and found some informal place where I was comfortable eating by myself. I was disappointed not to hear any real Hawaiian music; there were no hula dancers in grass skirts, either. It was a long way from the heady romance of my holiday in Japan with Jim six years before, but I figured I'd be able to cope with life alone if I had to. I think that subconsciously I believed Jim really would come home someday.

After my Hawaiian vacation, I felt completely refreshed. My psychotherapy had made me feel strong mentally, and I had com-pletely recovered from my surgery. The enforced rest during my convalescence was exactly what I'd needed, and I also had the pleasant prospect of leaving Washington when I returned from my trip. I got back to Western Avenue just before Memorial Day and began getting ready for the moving van, which was due on June 17.

✧

The summer of 1971 was the first one since Jim's shootdown in which I didn't make any trips from the Branford shore to Washington. I left the seaside only once, to travel to Abingdon, Illinois. That little town of only 3,200 people had organized a spectacular personal tribute to Jim. It took place in the football stadium and brought out the entire population as well as Jim's representative in Congress and Illinois Governor Ogilvie. Prickly chills tingled up and down my spine as I sat on the platform looking out at all Jim's grade-school teachers lined up in the front row, his athletic coaches and music instructors behind them, and a veritable sea of friends filling the stadium behind them. If only Jim could have seen this sight. I had to be satisfied with my encoded message dated August 29, 1971:

> Jim Dearest,
>
> Summer's highlight was Abingdon's tribute to your courage, attended by hundreds. We are going to Calif., driving, in two days, but the older boys are going back to college and studying as usual. Sid is going to help drive to Calif. and then fly back to South Kent. Jim of course will have another year to study before getting his degree. Soon you'll be safely home. Future looks brighter. I love you completely.
>
> Syb

I really did feel that the future looked brighter, maybe because I was so happy to be going back to Coronado. I tried to protect myself from future devastation by constantly reminding myself that Jim might not return. Whenever Stanford or Taylor questioned me about whether or not I thought their dad would come home, I would reply with a cautious "I just don't know. We have to be prepared for the worst, but hope for the best." A little silence always followed that answer, but I felt it important to protect the boys as well as myself from too much optimism.

Back in Coronado in September, I wanted to hug everyone I met on the streets. By the end of the month, I was off to Washington once again to attend the League's second annual meeting. Again, I testified before Congressman Zablocki's congressional committee and reams of verbiage were cranked out in the *Congressional Record*.

There was a seething unrest among the POW/MIA families at

the meeting. Some felt we should become a political rather than a humanitarian organization. We decided to establish a political-action committee within the League itself, and I carefully impressed on Dr. Kissinger at each of our subsequent meetings that revolution against the administration was brewing within our organization. President Nixon paid a surprise visit to our final banquet, reassuring us about his personal concern and pledging his wholehearted support for our future objectives. As I watched the evening's events unfold, I wondered if he would have come if we hadn't formed a political-action committee. I doubted it. The 1972 election was only a year away.

It didn't do any harm at all to have a radical fringe group as part of our organization. When some of the activist wives asked me what I thought about their picketing the White House, I told them to follow their own best judgment. It didn't hurt to let the White House know our loyalty was wearing thin.

The day before Christmas, the mailbox was stuffed with Christmas cards. Among them I found three notes from Jim. The first was dated 9 October 1971. Five years to the day, I thought, from that morning in 1966 when I dropped my first Naval Intelligence special letter into the big box in front of the Coronado post office. There were no postmarks on any of these notes. They had all been brought in by the peaceniks and undoubtedly read and photographed and tested in every imaginable way before being sent along to me. My eyes fell lovingly on Jim's handwriting. It was now different from any I ever knew before he was shot down, but here and there some letter formations looked somewhat familiar.

9 October 1971

Syb, I am sure you know all of my very true love is constantly with you. Put much confidence in that, old girl. Kiss and hug the boys as always. I hope the old Coronado beach sun and tennis are unusually good at this time of year. Sure hope our grand big boys are getting ready for this season's football. Syb, always know I truly adore our four kids, but you are the one for me.

Jim

This message was addressed to 547 "A" Avenue here in Coronado; apparently, when Jim wrote those words, he had no idea we'd moved to Washington, spent a year there, and moved back home again. Reading these notes, I realized once more, as I had during the past year, how little Jim's and my letters had to do with our own communication. They were primarily the product of the covert communication with Naval Intelligence. This fact gave them an impersonal aspect that seemed almost unworthy of our love. And yet I knew it was this very covert communication that sustained our morale. It was as if our personal lives were on hold.

The next note, dated 3 November 1971, was addressed to our Western Avenue number in Washington, D.C. When he wrote this, he'd learned we had moved, so sometime between October 9 and November 3 he'd been given a letter from me. Tingles of excitement went through me when I saw the opening words—Bob Boroughs would be delighted, and he'd be amused as well to hear that they'd given Jim a photo, too. Jim began by referring to a picture taken in the front yard on Western Avenue.

> Syb, your photo with Stan out of doors near his swing looks great and I think you have a superb figure. Much news in your letter. The surgery you had to undergo surprised me of course. . . . Tell my dear Jimmy I put full confidence and trust in his success as a clean cut new Ohio Wesleyan graduate next June. [He'd obviously heard about the hippies and the student revolutionaries.] Syb, to both Jimmy, and you too, I send birthday greetings. I think of each member of the family on his birthday, and of course on all holidays, especially Xmas. I don't expect to be home for this Xmas, or for the next, but my thoughts are with you always.

I read that last sentence again and then again, and again, and again. And, yes, it said what I'd thought the first time: He didn't expect to be home for Christmas this year *or* next year. Oh, my God. I can't think about that now. I'll have to think about that later. I pushed the thought into a dark closet in the back of my mind and slammed the door shut. Maybe that had only to do with his covert message, but I doubted it. I went on to Jim's next note, dated 10 November 1971. In this one his handwriting was small and cramped. He wrote on only five of the seven lines allotted.

> Syb: Thank you for the very nice gifts you have been so thoughtfully sending me from time to time. All I need is just coffee of the freeze-dry variety and pipe tobacco. Just send a large supply of this and I'll be fully contented Syb. Syb I love you. I pray daily that you and Jimmy, Sid, Stan and Taylor are all in good health and doing well. I'm OK.   Jim

Chapter 13

Alcatraz Gang

It had been two years and three months since I had been in a room with an American. On that day Sam Johnson and I had said goodbye in that cell right across the Thunderbird hallway from this one in which I was now meeting John Doe. It was now midafternoon on November 17, 1969.

It was true that I had been officially tipped off by my American friends that John Doe often acted like he was off his rocker; they'd told me this when I'd checked in with Stardust from Cat's quiz room last summer. But when this soulful, seemingly shy man first said his name, I thought to myself, Help this poor man. In those years in solitary, I had repeated to myself a thousand times, "Never undersell the infinite goodness of any human being; cherish him as the most precious object in the universe."

After an hour or so of civil conversation that first afternoon, I grew anxious to have a go at the wall on my side of the cell. On the other side of it was another American full of information. I hadn't been by a wall with an American behind it for a year. So I went and got my cup and walked back to the wall to plug us into the Thunderbird communication system and get the lineup, the news, and so on. I asked Doe to please keep a watch under the door for the guard.

I'll never forget my shock at his sudden terrified rage. "Listen, you son of a bitch, don't you realize that half the Americans in these cells are working for the Vietnamese? The Vietnamese have told them that you, the big shot, would be coming in here with me, and to be ready to copy what you said and turn us both in. I've been had by people like you in this place before. I don't want you in this cell. I always prefer to live alone so I can control my own destiny."

Throughout the two and a half years of his imprisonment, Doe had apparently taken pains to avoid firsthand experience with prisoner tap-code communication, and he scoffed at my pleas about how the Vietnamese did not have the ability (what with abbreviations and early tap-offs) to monitor what was said. Within two hours after my arrival, he had explained how it was people like me who had brought him nothing but grief since his capture. "The only way to keep these Communist bastards away from you is to live like a totally silent mouse. They like to have people like you around because you stir things up and get everybody illuminated and make us all vulnerable."

Score one for the Cat, I thought to myself. As 1970 approached and Cat had found himself demoted, stripped of general-staff status, and forced to participate as a mere camp commander in the step-by-step liberalization of our prison regime, he had filled in the square of getting me out of solitary by locking me out of command from the inside. He did this with the master stroke of locking me up with this Doe, who he must have guessed would place the insidious and flat demand on me that as long as we lived together I was not to communicate with any other Americans.

In no way could anyone who had ever met Doe think of him as a collaborator. There was none of that in him. He hadn't placed his "no communication" demand on me because he liked the Vietnamese, or because he thought "reasonableness" on our part would incur their good favor. He was neither that opportunistic nor that naïve. He did not want me to communicate because he had it in his head that the Vietnamese were omniscient, that they had listening posts and informants on every hand and wanted us to communicate so they could gain information on his personal life and then close in on us in the trip-wire style with which we were both familiar.

❖

As the weeks wore on, my association with Doe went from bad to impossible. He not only thought the Vietnamese were omniscient, he considered them omnipotent. He had decided that with physical power they could make people do anything they wanted them to do. He as much as told me, either as a fact or as a bluff, that it was dangerous for me to communicate in his presence because he could not offer worthy physical resistance to giving up secrets. And then there was another thing he said more than once: "If you communicate, I guarantee you I'll screw you in the end." I didn't know what he meant by that, but it scared me.

Doe's personal political line was all the way to the right—right up against the wall. From what he said, it appeared to me that just sullen, nasty hatefulness was his main weapon in the torture room. He pressed his obsession with destroying communism to the point that I got the idea he thought "having it way down here" for ultra-right causes could somehow make up for his revulsion to being slapped around when one-on-one with a tough commissar.

There was no doubt that he hated the North Vietnamese. "But hate," I told him one day, "is a hell of a debilitating emotion. You're a big Las Vegas gambler—when you go up to that crap table, do you set about to *hate* the croupier? No, you've got to mousetrap him, and keep your mind clear, free of hate, if you're to win. Same thing here with Communists. Think of ways to skin those sons of bitches alive, but don't hobble yourself emotionally by going around all choked up in a seething ideological rage all the time."

I eventually came to believe that Doe should not have been flying combat missions over North Vietnam in the first place. He told me he had not wanted to leave his engineering duties and come here. He was not by nature a physically competitive person (he said he had always abhorred body-contact sports), and he had been very badly injured in a jet crash, a training accident in the United States, as a young pilot. I remembered his description of the terrible pain he'd lived through during prolonged hospitalization, following the accident. Seeing him made me think of Ernest Hemingway's description of one of his characters as a man who had run out of tolerance for pain: "A man is born into this life with a capability of accepting a fixed amount of pain, and when it's all used up he can't take any more." I told Doe that story in a moment of sympathy. He scoffed in a rage.

In early 1970 we were moved into Golden Nugget 1. I was glad to get out there because my inability to relay messages had been jamming up the communication flow in Thunderbird. The fact that I was in enforced silence was really beginning to get to me. We were missing out on communication-link intelligence about obvious and big changes that were going on in prisoner treatment. On our rare trips around to the east-side bath stalls, Doe and I started seeing old picnic tables outside the Desert Inn. Were some prisoners in the Desert Inn now having communal meals in the yard? Was torture off? Could we expand our operations with immunity? All bath-house doors were being cut in two, made into Dutch doors for better ventilation. This made bath-to-bath communication a piece of cake. "Hey, guys in bath four, all clear, speak up!" would come the pleas from around the corner. God, what I wouldn't have given to have some of my operational questions answered. I would look at Doe as he clenched his teeth and glared a warning dare at me: *If you communicate, I will screw you.*

The insidiousness of this fix was that Doe and I both knew that if either of us made our mutual incompatibility known to the Vietnamese, the spotlight he hated would have been on him. In his mind, that would have given them a perfect opening to call him in, tie him in knots of argumentation logic, and make propaganda demands on him.

As always, Doe's logic had a certain factor of truth in it. A political prison is not like a college, where you can request a new roommate and get him and assume the matter will rest there. A clever commissar *can* manipulate known personality frictions between inmates to his own advantage.

I had a quiz with Cat early in 1970. I was shocked at how thin and drawn he was. His purpose that winter's day was to tell me that Alcatraz had been closed and that "your friends are back." He said this while waving his hand pointedly toward Stardust, toward the wall outside his door over which I had flashed with Forby the year before. I should have known that torture was off from that quiz alone. It was really strange for Cat to tell me where Denton was! As a matter of fact, we then chatted about Denton. Cat said he'd told Denton that I was here and that I was *"tranquille,"* mouthing the French pronunciation "trong-keel'" with relish. (And why in the hell wouldn't I be "trong-keel'," thought I, cooped up with that loony bastard he put me with.) Cat then asked me how Doe was. I said he was okay, and then he brought up the idea of putting Mulli-

gan and Denton together—what did I think of that? I couldn't believe my ears. I said I thought it would be good, that they would
make very compatible cellmates.

When I got back to the Golden Nugget, I told Doe about that
quiz and he was enraged. To him it was more evidence that the
Vietnamese had in mind my communicating so they could close in
on him—that Cat was trying to goad me into trying to get in
contact with Denton. When I told him that Cat had asked about
him, Doe felt that was the clincher—it was all a plot to get him in
trouble.

But then Doe thought for a minute and thanked me for telling
him his name had come up in Cat's quiz, like I had exhibited a rare
bit of candidness. Never having been in a regular prisoner communication net, Doe didn't know that "telling everybody all that
happened at quiz" had for years been not only standard operating
procedure, but a matter of moral obligation for all of us.

A few days later, Doe was called to quiz. We were in the bath
at the time and he dressed and left with the guard. This was my first
and only opportunity to get a message out without going to war
with him, and I was on the wall in an instant. I told Bill Lawrence in
the next stall to get the message to Denton in Stardust that I could
not communicate, that I was locked up with a psycho. I didn't like
to put the word *psycho* into the communication system, but there
was no other quick, clear, truthful way to say it. I knew Denton had
probably sensed my predicament and had taken charge of the camp
already, but I felt good to make it official and let him know I knew
the Gang was back and in Stardust.

The pressure built up and up in that shed-room of ours in the
Golden Nugget. I would lie awake all night in torment. During my
imprisonment I had spent time in cells cooped up singly with Dan
Glenn, Jim Lamar, and Sam Johnson. Later I was to spend a whole
hot summer with Jerry Denton, Harry Jenkins, and Howie Rutledge
in a cell too small for a single person. The constant closeness of such
periods of uninterrupted contact gets on everybody's nerves to
some extent, but in no case save with Doe did I ever find myself
thinking really angry thoughts about a person in with me. I just
could not hold to the prayers I had said before being put in with

Doe. I found myself gritting my teeth constantly in agony. We were at opposite philosophical poles, and his thought processes disgusted me.

Finally we were moved back into Thunderbird and I just told Doe, "Go ahead and screw me," and got on the wall with my old friends Fred Crow and Al Brady next door. My first wall conversation had to be conducted while an enraged Doe stormed about our tiny cell, stripped his gear from the bed under me, threw mine on the floor, and moved himself to the dead-wall side of the room. The valuable news from next door was that torture was indeed dead and that few prisoners were without cellmates, but that in order to bring pressure to close that gap, Jerry Denton was instigating a campwide hunger strike.

I must admit that Doe's and my cell had been under heavier surveillance than I had suspected. Soon after I opened up tap communication, Hawk unlocked and opened our door, nodded to me and took pointed note of my bed gear now being on the live-wall side, and left immediately. Denton's hunger strike took effect the next day. We (Doe included, in order not to illuminate himself) refused food, were immediately split up, and moved out of Thunderbird and into the Mint—I into my old cell 1, and Doe next door into 2.

We had done it! We had gotten separated! It was like Spook finding my phony note to Denton under the grille in my Alcatraz cell all over again! Aha! Caught in the act! Or was it that way? Maybe Cat had me covered all along and was just taking advantage of my softheartedness. Maybe I had been too nice to Doe. Should I have just forced myself to ignore him and joined the covert communication system the first week? In hindsight, we would have been split up immediately and both been better off. But what about Unity over Self? For years I'd been telling everybody that your highest value should be attached to the guy next to you. This Doe case was a quagmire of moral dilemmas and I never felt comfortable with it.

On the second day in the Mint, I was called to quiz. I practically whistled a merry tune as I limped along, I was so happy to have a wall between me and Doe. I was led to Cat's quiz room, where I bowed on entering and then worked my way over to sit down on the stool. Cat was thinner than ever. His hands were even shaking. He announced with what seemed like regret that with the hunger strike I had forced him to punish me. I would be sent back to "the small room"—he gestured toward the kitchen area, toward Calcutta. But as with the Cat of old, he had a counterdeal to propose: If I would make a public appearance with him, all would be forgotten. He almost pleaded: "I have an obligation to get someone to talk to an American college professor who is visiting Hanoi. As a military man you know what these obligations entail. I assure you there will be no propaganda. The old days are gone; no longer do we dictate. All I want you to do is see him."

"No, you know I won't do that."

Cat continued in a pathetic way about his past ("You know, Staw-dale, that I *did* sit with the general staff"), about how much we had in common ("You and I are the same age. . . . We have some college, and I just hoped you would do this"), and about his problems ("You know I have pressures on me, just as any military man does").

When I refused again, Cat called for a guard. It was time for me to go to Calcutta. To my astonishment, Cat walked me to the door, chatting amiably like an old and troubled friend. For a moment I thought he was actually going to put his arm around my shoulder.

"How long has it been, Staw-dale?" he asked.

"It's been nearly five years."

Cat stood pondering, and then said, "I am afraid it's going to be a few more."

Neither I nor any other American prisoner ever saw Cat again.

I stayed in Calcutta until mid-July 1970, and it was hot as hell under that low roof in the tropical sun. I had been its first American occupant nearly a year before, but I could tell by the absence of floor dust, by stains of hand sweat here and there, and a hundred other clues that long-time prisoners get good at picking up, that there had been others here since I'd left.

Chaicharn Harnnavee, with guard escort as before, would bring my meals and take my toilet bucket back for dumping at Las Vegas. I would wait for Chai's footsteps coming up the walk and take up my position in the crack of my door. As he came in sight, his eyes would be focusing right where he knew mine were, and through the expression in those eyes of his, he was able to give me intelligible signals as to whether the guard was close behind or if we might have a minute for hand signals as soon as he popped open the latched door.

I made use of Chaicharn's good offices by marking my toilet bucket with an intentionally sloppy but clearly readable big *S* with a piece of whitewash I snitched while outside by a faucet they now sometimes let me use. In one of those rare private moments Chai and I had together, I was able, with motions and pidgin English, to make him understand that this *S* was my mark and that he should carry it so my "friends" in Las Vegas would see it. Chai seemed to know who my friends were, and I later found out that he made sure he walked the bucket past the place where the Gang from Alcatraz was washing, the *S* outboard and clearly showing. The Gang knew Chaicharn was in contact with me, and that I was stashed alone but okay.

I somehow knew I just had to stay stashed there in the Calcutta hotbox until somebody else acted up to an extent that the Las Vegas camp commander felt compelled to stick him out here and bring me back. That could be tomorrow, or a year from tomorrow. I was lonesome, hot, demoralized by the Doe experience, and coming to the end of my string again. I was starting to get these spells of depression more and more frequently. I ate little, to show my despondency, and was starting to have little crying jags. My nerves seemed worn out. That Doe interlude had been such an unexpected, crazy thing—worse than another winter in isolation.

It was a hot afternoon when I got the "roll up" signal from Hawk. Somebody had finally pulled the Vietnamese's chain far enough! I was blindfolded and led with my blanket roll through the kitchen, to a right turn that I knew would take me down the narrow path behind Riviera, to the gate leading onto the Desert Inn-Stardust walk, where I waited while Hawk opened it. Surely I would go left to the Mint. They could put me no place else.

What's this? Hawk had taken my elbow and nudged me to the *right*. My God! I'm going to Stardust! This hit me like a ton of bricks. I had never dreamed I would actually be back with the Gang. I was stunned, like I had just unexpectedly been handed a precious gift.

Left turn, up the steps I had trod that January night nearly four years before, past my old cell, and a right turn, to cell 4, the one Jerry Denton had been in the night this place opened. My door was slammed and bolted, and there I was at last with those guys I had remembered every day for a year and a half, each with a special clog dance and personal song.

Cup out and onto the wall, waiting, waiting, maybe ninety seconds, and then it came, the shave-and-a-haircut: tick tick—ta tick tick. It was from cell 3, my old cell. Bob Shumaker and Nels Tanner. Yes, the Alcatraz Gang was all there—except Storz. He had become very very emaciated and weak during their last days at Alcatraz. When the Vietnamese were closing up the camp, some of the Gang had heard them trying to get Storz to move into one of the interrogation rooms where he would have more room in his terrible state. He refused to move away from the Gang. As they finally left, to the best of their belief, Storz was about to be put in the first Ministry of Defense quiz room. Nobody thought he could have lived through the past winter. There was no doubt in anybody's mind that Ron Storz was dead.[1]

The emotion of it all—the reunion, Storz—was too much for me. I was out of gas, and just sat there on the cool floor of Stardust 4 and cried in remorse and joy all afternoon.

The next morning I told Jerry Denton to keep the lead until I got myself together. We had been passing it back and forth for most of five years, in fact throughout the whole period from the time torture was instituted in Hanoi until it was stopped. We were now to see the trends toward "easy street" continue. Within months, certainly by April Fools' Day, 1971, in the manner of Oriental theater's swift and subtle scene changes, the Camp Authority would have receded into the mist, and a regime of simple straightforward detention have taken its place.

The Stardust lineup for that fall of 1970 was Sam Johnson across from me in 5; Jerry Denton and Jim Mulligan in the back row center cell (6); and in the back corner divided cell, Jenkins in 7, with Rutledge against the far wall in 8. On the front, Shumaker and Tanner were in my old cell (3), where Forby and Curtis had lived when they got me on the line from Cat's quiz room over the wall.

On the other front corner opposite me, in 2, were escapees Coker and McKnight. With them was John Dramesi, the other living Hoa Lo Prison escapee. That fall I passed the "four years' solo" mark and joined the very small club of only two other American prisoners who already held that distinction: Howie Rutledge and Jerry Denton.

The whole camp routine was being liberalized; by October there were very few of us left alone. Then one day Hawk opened my cell door wide and there in the hall stood Sam Johnson with a big grin on his face. The big Texan with the terribly crippled right hand and two deformed and broken shoulders strode in, picked me up, and whirled me around, hugging me. We had last been face-to-face the night I threw Rabbit out of Thunderbird 6E, three years and three months before.

Sam and I just got to "visit" in my cell during the day at first. Like his, mine was a one-bunk cubbyhole, and Sam would be locked up across the hall after evening dishes were done. Later, we got to spend some days with Shumaker and Tanner—we would have a regular four-man gabfest in there.

Of course, the Alcatraz Gang used the wall tap like a telephone between cells, and lived like a single organism as we had during the years we'd spent in those little cells in leg irons. As soon as I awakened on the morning of November 21, I had a call from Tanner. "Did you hear bombing last night?" (Tanner was quite excited; we hadn't had any of that up here for two and a half years.)

"No, I slept like a log right straight through."

"Well, about midnight I heard a lot of airplane racket, sort of far off."

In a few days, we started seeing new guards in camp—more guards than Las Vegas could use. Then we heard the sounds of hammering and sawing within Hoa Lo, here and there in the distance. Something was up. What it was became clear when Hanoi Hannah closed one of her programs with the sarcastic comment ". . . and how dare Mendel Rivers say that America could land airplanes on the streets of Hanoi and pick up prisoners?" A yelp of joy went up all over Las Vegas. The racket the other night, the sounds of construction, the new guards—all of it started to fit together. America had raided a POW camp someplace near Hanoi!

Of course, that was the Son Tay raid. The American prisoners had been moved from the camp at the little town of Son Tay before the helicopters got there, but all prisoners of war in North Vietnam were to reap great morale benefits, and even more concrete living-condition benefits, from that daring Son Tay maneuver. During those late November days of 1970, unbeknown to us, the Vietnamese were starting to move their large population of civilian convicts out of Hoa Lo and preparing to put all the American prisoners into what we would call Camp Unity, the western half of the prison. Their apparent thinking was that no future helicopter rescue missions would dare penetrate downtown Hanoi.

In our renewed face-to-face comradeship, Nels, Bob, Sam, and I were meanwhile having a happy December. We were together about five hours a day, and spent a little time each day bringing each other up to speed on our respective experiences since I had left Alcatraz. Christmas was a particularly happy day; we made a small design for the wall, and everybody brought all his family pictures over to Stardust 3, where the four of us got better acquainted with each other's family. I got no letter that Christmas, but Bug came to the Stardust 3 door in midafternoon, called me out front, and handed me two pictures of a big house I didn't recognize. I said, "Where's the letter these came in?" Bug replied, "You do not deserve a letter," and locked me back in with my three pals.

On the bottom of the pictures, in Sybil's handwriting, was the address 6345 Western Avenue, Washington, D.C. It was a lovely big brick house with a nice yard, and in the few remaining minutes of visiting, the four of us examined and animatedly discussed the house's layout as only those with starved eyes and minds can do. The thing that caught our imagination was the big screened porch. We decided that we would all meet on that porch on some soft summer evening and have a party, we four couples. We thought it might even be a bridge party; Sam was sure there was ample room for two tables.

About 7:00 P.M. on that Christmas night, 1970, Las Vegas was invaded by a horde of guards, and a mass extraction of prisoners was started. Cell by cell we were all blindfolded and marched into

Camp Unity, behind Heartbreak. Most of the people I had known over the years wound up in a cellblock building we later knew as "Rawhide." Four men were assigned to a cell. We couldn't understand what was going on at first, but then we were invaded by a large number of experienced Vietnamese police detectives. Cell by cell, they ordered us stripped for search. These were not the modest peasant boys who had been our guards. These men knew their stuff and checked every crevice in our bodies for contraband. We were going to be put into big cellblocks, and this was their preparatory check.

The next day, December 26, we all remained in our Rawhide cells, but just after dark we were marched over and put into what we later called "Building 7," one of seven big cellblocks that ringed all but the south side of Unity courtyard. There we were joined by enough men from other holding points to fill every sleeping space. But few of us in Building 7 got any sleep that night as we embraced one another, shook hands, and tried to put the past together. All the Alcatraz Gang (except poor Storz) were there to see all the others face-on for the first time. As Jerry Denton and I embraced young George Coker, our "Jimmy Cagney," our escape artist, we bracketed the Gang's age spread. Jerry and I had been plebes at the Naval Academy on the day little George had been born.

It was not age, or school background, or geography, or roots that welded the ten of us together. It was not even our common experience in prison so much as our mutual respect, our pride in knowing that our experiences, our bond of comradeship, did not come about by any process of random selection. You had to be a threat to the North Vietnamese prison system to get to Alcatraz. We had learned to be very effective at making trouble for our adversaries, and at taking care of our own. And we loved it. It made life make sense to us. We were not here to cope, or languish, or sit out the war, or "be reasonable." And we pledged to "stick it in their ear," to keep it up, no matter how long we stayed.

And on that night, there was no reason to believe that peace was in sight. True, my anxieties about personal exploitation had all but disappeared with the disengagement of Rabbit, Pigeye, and now even Cat. But there were no bombs falling, and nobody who lived in North Vietnam in those years could envision the United States bringing about the end of this saga with just the power of her maxims. We owed the great reunion of this night to a president who had the guts to give the go-ahead to the Son Tay raid. Even so, that event also betrayed a kind of national desperation that gave us an insight into the true hopelessness of our predicament.

December 26, 1970, marked the fifth anniversary of my writing that first letter to Syb. The cell where I'd written it in Heartbreak Hotel was just five feet behind the wall adjacent to my bunk here in the southeast corner of Building 7 where I now stood with my Gang. Five feet in five years was not much, and the full sadness that went into that letter was every bit with me on this night. God bless Syb and all our sons in whatever she's doing on Western Avenue, Washington, D.C. She's there to help us guys over here. That *has* to be it. I *know* it.

Chapter 14

Premonitions of Jim's Return

All during the 1971 holiday season, I realized I was functioning almost like a robot. I had perfected my ability to prevent the sentimentality of the season from destabilizing me emotionally. On New Year's Day of 1972, I removed my invisible protective coat of armor and sank back into my familiar life-style. It was inevitable, however, as I hung the new calendar, that I would wonder if this would be *the* year.

On Sunday, January 2, 1972, I savored the luxury of sipping fresh, strong coffee while lolling in bed and reading the *San Diego Union*. I saw in the television schedule that that night Dan Rather would interview President Nixon on CBS-TV. As I listened that evening, I was thrilled to hear parts of the interview go something like this:

Dan Rather began by telling President Nixon he wanted to clearly understand a quote from the president in *Time* magazine. The issue of Vietnam, the president was quoted as saying, would not be an issue in the campaign as far as the present administration was concerned because the administration would by then have brought American involvement to an end. Dan Rather asked President Nixon if, by this, one could properly assume that by Election Day there would be no Americans—land, sea, or air—and no residual force fighting in support of Laotians, Cambodians, or South Vietnamese. President Nixon replied that that depended on the situation with regard to our POWs.

My gosh, I thought, pulling my robe more closely around me, they're getting right into it at the beginning. This is more like it.

President Nixon went on to say that we were still pursuing the negotiating track and that he hadn't given up on that possibly succeeding. He said we were continually reducing our numbers in Vietnam, and that if we continued at the same rate, the number of Americans in Vietnam would be down to a very low level by election time. But, he said, the president of the United States could not withdraw all our forces as long as the enemy held one American prisoner of war. He said we would have to keep a residual force in Vietnam and continue the possibility of air strikes as long as Americans were held in Hanoi.

Well, thank God for that, I thought as I continued to watch and listen.

Dan Rather said he didn't see how the president could campaign saying all Americans would be out of Vietnam by Election Day and at the same time say some of our forces would remain as long as our POWs were held.

President Nixon replied that the important thing was whether or not the American people felt their president had done everything he could to bring the war to an end, as well as everything possible to protect Americans being held. He said we were dealing with international outlaws.

Oh, good, I thought, *that's* more like it, too.

He said he wanted to give some hope to our POW people and continued that he didn't think the enemy would choose to continue to hold our men at the cost of having our residual force stay in Vietnam.

The interview continued for some time, but as far as I was concerned, the important part was over. I felt greatly elated. President Nixon himself had introduced the subject of the POWs into the interview. Before millions of American television viewers, he had just made a strong statement against sacrificing the POWs in order to get all of our troops out of Vietnam before the election in November. He was on record now with a strong commitment to our men. That night I thanked God that, for the first time since the tremendous troop-withdrawal program had started, Jim's commander in chief had committed himself, one hundred percent, to the release of the prisoners.

The next day, however, my confidence was shattered. Someone from the League called with the news that in a follow-up conference the president's commitment to American prisoners had been watered down—"clarified," as the White House phrased it. The president, I was told, might have misunderstood some of Dan Rather's questions—thus the need for this "clarification." Would I consider sending Dan Rather a telegram? He had been cleverly used by the White House to give millions the impression of total dedication to the prisoners. Almost no one would read about the follow-up "clarification."

Angrily, I scratched out a telegram to Dan Rather. I decided to address it to him care of the White House Press Corps, Washington, D.C. That way the White House staff would have a copy, too. Most of all, I wanted them to know we weren't going to sit quietly while they kicked us in the teeth. I dialed Western Union's number in San Diego and read the following message to the operator:

> To Mr. Dan Rather, CBS News, The White House Press
> Corps, Washington, D.C.
>
> Last night I was extremely pleased to hear President Nixon's strong commitment to our POWs in North Vietnam. Today I was outraged to learn that the White House had "clarified" the president's commitment to our men. A reading of the transcript of your conversation with the president will clearly show he did not misunderstand your questions. I believe the American people were grossly misled. The majority will never be aware of the retraction. Since you were the vehicle for this misunderstanding, I feel you should make your audience aware of the White House "clarification" and its implications for our American POWs.
>
>
> Mrs. James B. Stockdale
> Founder, National League
> of Families
> 547 A Avenue
> Coronado, California
> 714-435-0506
>

If, as I suspected, the White House staff thought they had most of our present League officers in their pocket, that message would show them that all of us weren't fooled by their double-talk.

The White House could react fast when it wanted to. On Wednesday, January 5, a secretary's silky voice on the telephone asked me to hold for a call from General Hughes at the western

White House in San Clemente. He was President Nixon's military assistant and, I'd been told, was the person who vetoed my seeing President Nixon in January 1969, because the air force wouldn't be represented at the same time. General Hughes was air force.

He was boiling mad when he came on the wire. He bawled me out in no uncertain terms for sending that telegram to Dan Rather. He bellowed at me that there was no clarification, that Gerry Warren (Nixon's press secretary) was only responding to press questions. I thought to myself, He must think I haven't learned by now that lots of press questions are planted. He raged at me for having officially gone on record with the press and for signing my name as founder of the National League of Families. As I listened, I thought to myself, This man is out of control. I thought I knew where his real concern lay when he yelled that he had only twenty-seven more days in his job (as the president's military assistant) and then this would no longer be his concern. I replied that, unfortunately, some of us couldn't walk away from our situation in twenty-seven days. He concluded by denouncing me as having done the president of the United States a grave injustice.

My mother, who was visiting for the winter, looked up from her crocheting after I hung up. "Who was that?" she asked. "I could hear him all the way over here."

"That was an air force general at the western White House who thinks he's God Almighty," I replied. "He was incredibly rude. I'm glad I didn't lose my temper in return. I'm surprised I didn't. I'm really kind of proud of myself."

"He should be ashamed of himself," my mother concluded.

With that, the phone rang again and General Hughes came on with an apology for losing his temper. He wanted to assure me he meant everything he said, but should not have lost his temper. A few days later, his secretary telephoned again and invited me to ride to Washington with General Hughes on his White House airplane for the League's board meeting.

"You tell General Hughes," I said calmly to the secretary, "that Mrs. Stockdale does not care to ride anywhere with General Hughes." I could afford to be choosy now. It wouldn't be as plush, but the League would reimburse my expense for a commercial airline ticket. I preferred to ride in steerage than in luxury with General Hughes.

Hanoi's Gia Lam airport, February 12, 1973. Jim being escorted from Rabbit's release gate to a waiting Air Force jet for the flight to Manila and home. (Wendell B. Rivers on left, Jim on right.)

547 A Avenue, Coronado, ready for Jim's return, February 15, 1973.

Jim with Alan Shepard, shortly after his release.

Spring 1973, after Jim's return. Left to right: Taylor, Jimmy, Sybil, Jim, Sid, Stan.

A family chat with President Ford before the Medal of Honor ceremony at the White House, March 4, 1976. Left to right: Sid, Taylor, Stan, Sybil, Jim, President Ford, Jimmy's wife Marina, and Jimmy.

Sybil receiving the Navy's Distinguished Public Service Award—she is the
only wife of an active duty naval officer to receive the award.

Jim and Sybil en route to Abingdon, Illinois, March 9, 1978.

Jim and Sybil en route to the U.S. Naval Academy, October 1982.

Hawaii vacation, November 1981.

Six of ten living Alcatraz Gang members aboard aircraft carrier USS *Yorktown* at a reunion, October 1982. Left to right: Jerry Denton, Jim Stockdale, Jim Mulligan, Sam Johnson, George McKnight, George Coker.

Dr. Kissinger postponed his January 21 meeting with us for one week. On January 25, President Nixon announced that Kissinger had been having secret peace negotiations with the North Vietnamese since August 4, 1969. Since before I saw the North Vietnamese in Paris, I thought, listening to his announcement. Maybe this was the beginning of the end.

I was in Washington on January 25 for our board meeting when this news broke. The next morning, January 26, Bernard Kalb interviewed me on the CBS morning news. As I waited for the interview to begin, I thought back to my 1969 interview with Joseph Benti on this same program. I'd been much more nervous then than I was now.

Bernard Kalb was cross with me because I wouldn't say I would happily sacrifice Saigon to save my husband. I told him I didn't feel I could make a decision like that in view of all those who had died in the war. He really tried to box me in, but I didn't knuckle under to him. After we were off the air, he scolded me, saying we wives had to either make policy or demand our men back. I wished I had thought to say to him, "What we are demanding is an honorable policy." I rarely thought of the answers I wanted until it was too late.

✧

We weren't going to see Dr. Kissinger until Friday of this last week in January, and so I decided to use Thursday to go to New York City and see the Chinese. The Chinese had now been accepted into the United Nations and had taken up residence in the Roosevelt Hotel. Charlie Havens and I wanted to let them know about our League so they could contact us directly if they had any suggestions about ways to advance their own self-interests while at the same time helping the prisoners. This was Budd Salsig's idea, and Charlie and I thought it was worth a try.

I flew to New York City on the shuttle and went to the Roosevelt Hotel. I was told the Chinese delegation was on the fourteenth floor. I made a run up and down in the elevator, pushing the button for floor fourteen but not getting off there—just surveying the situation as the door opened and closed. Sure enough, there was a big, burly, Russian-looking guard stationed right outside the elevator. I went back to the lobby and telephoned the delegation, saying I wanted to come up and see them. They kept asking how many were with me, and I kept repeating that I was all alone. Finally they let me come up.

The fourteenth floor was like being back in the North Vietnamese Embassy again. I was led down a long, seedy-looking hallway to a bedroom converted into a sitting room. My escort left me sitting there alone. If they stuffed me down the laundry chute, I hoped Charlie Havens would remember where I was. After some time, a cold-looking Oriental man entered and asked me my business. I suggested the Chinese might want to intercede on behalf of the American prisoners. He gave me a long speech about the Chinese not having anything to do with the war in Vietnam and told me I'd have to go to my own government.

A man appeared with tea in chipped cups, the tea slopping over into the saucers. I thought my interviewer might now warm up a little, but he never did. We went through the same conversation three or four times, and I ended by telling him where he could contact us if he changed his mind. I thanked him for my tea and was glad to make my way back to the lobby. It seemed pretty clear the Chinese weren't going to cooperate.

When we met with Dr. Kissinger on January 28, he was more relaxed than I'd ever seen him. A good crowd was present, including our most strident anti-U.S. government members. Dr. Kissinger described in detail how the North Vietnamese negotiated. He told us how they held and we gave; they held and we gave some more; they held and we continued to give. He was convinced that when the end came, it would come quickly, and it would be when the North Vietnamese were absolutely convinced they had wrung every last drop of blood out of us. He did not want to give us the impression he thought that time was imminent. Again, he did not want to give us any false hope. He was glad the secret peace negotiations had been revealed, but there was still no evidence the North Vietnamese were ready to settle.

We didn't see him again until Monday, April 10. By then he had been to Peking and back with President Nixon. He was deeply tanned and in the best of spirits. I told him the League would have a special meeting in May to consider becoming a political organization. I told him I hoped this course could be avoided but there was increasing unrest within our group. He said he could understand our feelings but hoped we would give the administration our support.

That special May meeting of our National League of Families was a storm of controversy. The sad part was we didn't really have any choice at all. President Nixon was running for a second term against superdove George McGovern. Nothing would please the Communists more than to have McGovern elected president. They would react by keeping our men prisoners forever while they nickeled-and-dimed us to death with their demands. Our only hope was to get President Nixon on record with commitments to the POWs—commitments the American people would demand be honored. The League elected three of us members to fulfill the following resolution hammered out amid the controversy:

> BE IT RESOLVED THAT: The National League of Families of American Prisoners and Missing in Southeast Asia at the National Meeting May 5–7, 1972, shall elect three of its members in whom the majority has complete confidence who shall arrange a meeting with President Nixon (within the next 10 days) to question the President as to what arrangements he has made or is making for the release of prisoners-of-war and an accounting of those missing-in-action; and that this committee shall report back to the League membership, in writing, within 5 days of such meeting.

On Monday, May 8, the White House announced that Haiphong Harbor had been mined and a blockade of the port was in effect. During that week the League office had trouble trying to get an appointment for our delegation to meet with the president. I called the new military assistant to the president, General Brent Scowcroft, and persuaded him to let me plead for an appointment in person. He was a slightly balding, sandy-haired, mild-mannered fellow, almost my height, and his air-force uniform hung loosely on his birdlike figure. He was afraid if our delegation met with the president, we might denounce him politically in a press conference afterward. I promised him I would personally support the president politically if he would give us the meeting. The next day, the White House notified our League office that our delegation could see the president on May 15.

Before the meeting that day, on our way to the Oval Office,

General Scowcroft was visibly nervous. My maternal instinct took over. Walking down the hall, I took hold of his arm, which was thin as a stick in his uniform sleeve, and said, "Don't be nervous. It's going to be okay," just as I'd reassured Secretary of State Rogers, two and a half years earlier. By now, I was no longer afraid of generals.

Dr. Kissinger, who seemed like an old friend, greeted us outside the Oval Office. We proceeded inside to shake hands with the president, who indicated I was to sit next to him in one of the chairs in front of the fireplace. We were no more than seated when, by some signal, a herd of photographers stampeded into the room. They really moved at high speed, some literally running. President Nixon said, "We'll have a couple of pictures first and then we'll visit."

After about two minutes, at a signal from Dr. Kissinger, all the photographers raced out of the room again. There must have been a dreadful penalty if you were a laggard in these circumstances. One photographer seemed to have permission to cover parts of the room where others weren't allowed. He got way over on the side and took pictures of the president and me alone. I was glad I had splurged on a shampoo and set at Elizabeth Arden.

Finally, we settled down to the business at hand. The president assured us the blockade and mining of Haiphong Harbor would cut off the supplies the North Vietnamese needed to continue the war. Their oil supplies would last only about four months, and without the oil and other supplies, he felt the North Vietnamese would be forced to negotiate. He told us this timetable was confidential, but for the record he assured us the blockade and mines would be left in place until all the prisoners were released, and that he would do everything he could to follow through on accounting for the missing. He said frankly that he couldn't promise the accounting would be complete, because there were other countries involved, but that he would do everything in his power. His manner was natural and breezy all during our visit. When referring to the North Vietnamese, he said such things as "I mean business with these clowns. I've listened to enough of their malarkey," and "We aren't going to put up with any more of their nonsense."

As we left the Oval Office, Press Secretary Ron Ziegler told us several press people would like to talk to us in the Rose Garden, but, he added, we didn't have to see them unless we wanted to. I smiled and told him we most certainly did want to. I had learned that much at least: Unless you document it in the press, what official Washington tells you might as well never happen. Before I went home to California, I double-checked with a Defense Department official about how long the North Vietnamese could hold out without fresh oil supplies. Four months was his reply. That confirmed it, and I concluded that the war had to be over by September.

At home in Coronado, the boys had a big Happy Mother's Day sign spread across the fireplace. Their homemade gifts were on the mantel. Secretly I celebrated with a new joy in my heart.

I began to make long-range plans for our family life in California. I started a massive remodeling of our house on "A" Avenue. Also, during the past few months, Karen Butler had talked about wanting to buy a ski condominium at Mammoth Mountain, about an eight-hour drive north of San Diego. In my exuberance, I decided we should pool our money and buy a condo together. Over Memorial Day weekend, we headed for Mammoth with our young children singing and romping in the back of the station wagon. Once there, I succumbed to the spell of aromatic pine trees, crisp mountain air, alpine chalets, and a persuasive real-estate agent. By the time we rolled back down the mountain toward home, I owned not one condominium at Mammoth, but two. My problem in life would be finding enough time to count all the money I'd make renting my property when not vacationing in it. The fact that no one in the family was a ski enthusiast and that Jim had been reported as crippled didn't bother me at all. I was on a high the likes of which I'd never known before. I was convinced there was no physical problem Jim could have that modern medicine couldn't mend. He'd be home by September, and from then on life would be one constant state of absolutely happy perfection.

I had to remind myself that I mustn't diminish my efforts to educate and involve the public in my mission to maintain pressure on the governments in both Washington and Hanoi. In my most recent eastern visit, I'd seen an executive at ABC-TV, Mr. Martin Pompadour. He'd suggested "The Dick Cavett Show" as a good forum for my message, and promised that someone from that program would contact me. The Dick Cavett audience was a segment of the population I really wanted to reach. They were the young, stay-up-late, idealistic voters most easily taken in by McGovern's impossible-to-fulfill promises.

In June, a Miss Potter from the Cavett show telephoned me in Coronado. She had probably been required to make the call by her superior. She was extremely reluctant to acknowledge that my message was appropriate for the program. I told her I would be in New York City in a few days and got her permission to come by and visit with her in person. I felt I could talk her into having me on if I could see her in person. I was not exactly going to be in New York City as I'd said, but I *was* going to Ohio for Jimmy's graduation from Ohio Wesleyan. A chance to talk to the Dick Cavett audience was worth the price of a ticket from Ohio and back.

Miss Potter was not easy to convince when we met, but finally the arrangements for my trip to be on the show were made: If I'd fly to New York at my own expense, they'd let me appear on the Fourth of July.

During the Ohio Wesleyan graduation, I thanked God for Jimmy's loyalty to his dad. It hadn't been easy for him to walk the fine line between the influences of his antiwar peer group and loyalty to his military father. It was good, too, to have Sid here beside me for this event. He'd be a South Kent senior next year and had been so successful as a member of the crew that he'd be off to Milan, Italy, this summer to row in the Junior Olympics. Jim would be pleased, I thought, if he could look through a window at this moment and see these two fine young men who were his sons.

Every time I review my experiences during the next few days, I laugh and cry at the same time. Changing planes in the Los Angeles airport on my way back from Jimmy's graduation, I saw a headline proclaiming a two- or three-day bombing halt in Hanoi. Only in Hanoi, I thought, not in the rest of Vietnam. That oversized headline stuck in my tired but excessively optimistic mind and slowly it jelled into the idea that the bombing had really been halted to allow the POWs in Hanoi secret, safe transport to Hong Kong, where they would be released!

On June 14, the morning after I returned from Ohio Wesleyan, I called a commander at Air Pacific Headquarters. I wanted to ask him a routine question about a future sea voyage for POW/MIA children, but I was told by a secretary that the commander had gone on temporary duty to the Western Pacific until October. I was flabbergasted—I had talked with that commander just a few days before, and he had said nothing about leaving. I then called a captain in Washington to ask him my question and was told that he, too, was on temporary duty at sea. Putting all my pieces of information together, I decided that the USS *Constellation* was going into Hong Kong to pick up the POWs. I was thrilled by the brilliance of making it all happen on Flag Day.

I felt that I had stumbled into the innermost chambers of world diplomacy. I had to share it with someone, but couldn't talk about it with just anyone. I couldn't call Bob Boroughs, because I felt I shouldn't talk about it on the phone. Then I remembered that Bob had said some time back that if I ever needed to talk to an official somebody about intelligence stuff, I could go to a Captain Zembrowski over at the Air-Pac Headquarters in Coronado. I'd never met the man, but I drove straight over there. On my way in, I looked at the officer at the outer desk and thought, If you only knew what I know, you wouldn't be so casual.

I felt pretty seedy walking down the blue-carpeted hallway to Captain Zembrowski's office in my pant-dress with a scarf tied around my hair. But my talk with him couldn't wait an instant—I *had* to see him and tell him what I was convinced was the truth. He had on his "whites" and was ever so friendly. He was obviously curious about what had brought me plummeting into his office. I poured out my revelation to him as he listened carefully. Then he said, "You know, that may explain a message that went through here a couple of weeks ago that I couldn't make any sense of at the time." He told me the message was for the USS *Constellation*, asking what its capacity was for handling a large number of recuperation cases. Together we concluded that the *Constellation* was not really on its way to Japan as it was supposed to be, but that that was a cover for her trip into Hong Kong to pick up the POWs.

The fact that he didn't dismiss me as foolish and just full of super-wishful thinking was the final switch I needed to turn me on about my grandiose discovery. I drove home convinced that I was one of about ten people in the whole wide world who knew the glorious truth. On that Friday, June 16, 1972, I wrote in my diary:

> 5:00 P.M. Went and saw Capt. Zembrowski (Intelligence officer at Naval Air Station, North Island) and told him I felt in my heart, Jim knew his ordeal was over on June 14—*Flag Day*. Believe war's end will be announced next week and POW's will already be at sea on "Connie" when announcement comes. Bought gold wings with diamonds today to celebrate. Feel all cold chills and light headed.

I hid the diary in the folds of the quilt in the blanket box under my bed.

The mind is a marvelous machine, and once the imagination takes hold, it can really work up a head of steam. In my case, all sorts of things from then on became "clues" that further confirmed my discovery. On Saturday, June 17, I decided that the island of Coronado was going to be the place to which the POWs would be returned. The USS *Constellation* was home-ported here at North Island Air Station right on Coronado. I could see signs of preparations for cordoning off the island of Coronado to all who wouldn't be allowed to participate when the ship returned. I even imagined that some of the people involved in this preparation smiled at me knowingly as I went through town. Oh, la! I was on a happy plane!

I decided I had to get a message to Jim, but of course I had to be most cautious and not give away the secret at the same time. Ideas raced through my mind about what and how to send. I called Bob Boroughs; I was sure he was in on the secret, and, in cloaked double-talk phrases, I let him know I knew. I told him about the various preparations going on in Coronado. He seemed elated that I knew. I told him I wanted to send a message to the skipper of the *Constellation*, and that I wanted to say, "All here happily await your return. Dearest love to my *roommate*." To my delight, Bob said he thought it was a fine message. That clinched it, to my way of thinking: If he thought it was a fine message, he also must think I should *send* the message, so I must have come to the right conclusion about the release of the POWs.

I called Captain Zembrowski, and he was obviously excited about the message. His voice shook with emotion when he read it back to me on the phone. He said they'd send it "through the back door," meaning by secret navy channels—another small thing that made me even more sure.

I had to think of something to explain my air of exuberance to people in general and let off a little of my accumulated elation. I decided to say that I had dreamed that Jim was safely back on his ship. I told my parents that when I talked to them on the phone on Father's Day. To add further fuel to my fire, the CNO, Admiral Zumwalt, and his wife called on Sunday afternoon to tell me they were thinking about me on Father's Day. I thought their call was a cover to share their jubilation also, and I told them about my dream. The CNO said, "Sybil, I think your dream may be prophetic in a way," and now I was surer than ever. It was a good Father's Day, indeed. I bought a case of champagne to be ready to celebrate, and Sunday evening I had supper with Karen and told her the wonderful news about my discovery. We drank a bottle of champagne, and I could tell Karen wasn't sure whether to kiss me or commit me. We laughed and hugged each other and cried a little at the wonder of it all.

I thought the news announcement would come on Monday morning, June 19, and when nothing happened, it didn't faze me a bit. I was positive I was on the inside track and that soon the whole world would know the truth, too. I saw new red carpeting being carried into the house where no one ever lived across the street on "A" Avenue, and decided that house would be some sort of a headquarters for the return of the POWs. Bob Boroughs had said years before, when we had talked about the men coming home, that he thought the best place for Jim to rejoin his family was right in our own living room. I thought the whole rehabilitation center was being set up right around me. What a perfect idea—to use Coronado Island, which they could block off so easily and which no one would ever suspect, because it was so close to home!

During the following week, I worked full-time trying to speed up the house remodeling. On Thursday I drove to San Diego to get the light fixture for the new bathroom. As I started up over the bridge from Coronado, I suddenly wondered if Jim was really in the navy or if he was working for the CIA and his being in the navy was a cover! And then right at the top of the bridge, I thought, Dear God, maybe he volunteered to parachute into Vietnam to be a CIA man on the inside, thinking he would be there only a few months, as his early letters indicated. Maybe that was why in one of his last letters to me before he was shot down he said that he had been over to Thailand talking to the CIA people and was thinking about "Air America." Maybe that was his way of giving me a clue way back in the very beginning, and it had taken me until now to catch on.

All of this was racing through my mind as I walked into Sunlight Electric to buy the bathroom light fixture. The lady who waited on me seemed too kind and understanding. Maybe she worked for the Agency, too. Maybe many people knew the truth and were just waiting and feeding me clues until I caught on. If that was the case and Jim did work for the CIA, then there was an extra bank account someplace with money in it I didn't know about.

I was in a sea of confusion surrounded by blinking electrical fixtures, and when the money part occurred to me, I found myself ordering a light fixture that cost twice as much as I'd planned to spend. By this time I knew I was going to fall apart. I tried to think what to do. I drove straight to Air-Pac and, at Captain Zembrowski's office, talked to Bob Boroughs on the SAFE telephone that couldn't be tapped. I poured out the gist of my thinking and asked him if he thought I was crazy. He said, "I think you're doing fine." A very noncommittal answer—unless you wanted it to mean something special.

As the days went by, I finally gave up the whole idea about the men having been released. Strangely enough, it didn't depress me too much. I concluded I had made some sort of a miscalculation, but never mind, a few days more or less were not critical now that the end was so near. Adding to my confusion was the house remodeling still in progress. Mobs of workmen were pounding and smashing in every room. The electricity and gas were turned off while the kitchen was gutted.

I was relieved in early July to leave the chaos of remodeling and fly to New York and Dick Cavett. Miss Potter had warned me the show was not political and I was not to make any political statements. As the show unfolded, it became clear that Dick Cavett would make the political statements and I was to be Mrs. Dumb Dumb Navy Wife who could only sit and wring her hands. When his remarks seemed to me critical of the present administration, I reminded him that Johnson, Rusk, and McNamara had gotten us into this war. I was relieved when the show was over. I was glad to have told his audience where they could order POW bracelets and not too sorry later to hear that the program had been canceled.

The remodeling chaos was coming to a conclusion by the time I arrived back on "A" Avenue. On July 11, I wrote in my diary: "Scratch entry for June 16!" I then recorded that I now had some reason to believe the POWs would be released on August 21. It couldn't be too much longer. The four months from the date when the North Vietnamese supply of oil was cut off would be up in mid-September. As we settled in at the Connecticut cottage in mid-July, I wondered what we'd be doing during the summer months a year from then.

Shortly after we arrived, the *New Haven Register* carried a picture of me with Stanford and Taylor, as well as our dachshund, Herman, on the front page of the July 25 edition. I was pleased with the informal picture and found the article pleasantly flattering.

POW WIFE, VACATIONING HERE, THINKS NIXON WILL BRING MATE HOME SOON

Branford—A Navy wife who meets on a bi-monthly basis with President Nixon's special adviser, Henry Kissinger, and who has had several 45-minute meetings with Nixon, said today the outcome of the next presidential election will make a tremendous difference as to whether North Vietnamese officials will release American prisoners of war.

Mrs. James Stockdale, of Coronado, Calif., is the wife of Capt. James Stockdale, who was taken prisoner by the Vietnamese on Sept. 9, 1965. It is believed that he has spent most of the past seven years in solitary confinement.

While at a vacation cottage here, Mrs. Stockdale expressed confidence that President Nixon will effect the release of POWs and that the men will be home by Christmas.

Her confidence is based, she said, on lengthy conversations she has had with Nixon and Kissinger. "Much of what was discussed during those sessions cannot be revealed," she said, adding that she "can't believe that President Nixon would lie to me."

When questioned about the statement, Mrs. Stockdale said at a May 15 meeting with Nixon (at which two other Navy wives were present), he promised that the mines placed in Hanoi's Haiphong Harbor on May 8 would remain there until POWs are released.

"A war cannot be run without supplies; tanks without oil, machinery without electricity, all of which are now cut off from Haiphong," Mrs. Stockdale said.

Speaking of the presidential campaign, she said she thinks Sen. George McGovern's pledge about obtaining the release of prisoners of war 90 days after his election is "incredibly irresponsible."

"It is not the President of the United States who releases the POWs," she stated, "but the Communists. If we don't have a President who understands how the Communists operate I think the POWs will stay there indefinitely."

"Strength is the only thing Communists respect," she added. She credits Nixon with having that quality and says the Communists know it. Mrs. Stockdale said she doesn't think Nixon wants to be President of this country if the country wants to just "throw in the towel and turn its back on 50,000 servicemen who have died."

Instead of going to Washington, that summer I took a few days away from the home front alone in New York City. Returning to my room at the Gotham Hotel on Tuesday afternoon, August 22, after lunch with a friend, I found an urgent message to call a Mr. Van Shumway at the Committee to Re-elect the President, in Miami Beach, Florida. I'd never heard of him, but the Republican National Convention was going on in Miami Beach, so I called him right back. He wanted me to come down there that very night to accept a petition the next morning to be presented at the Doral Hotel (the convention headquarters) by the Vietnam Veterans Against the War. He explained that they needed someone with credibility about the war to accept the petition for President Nixon. It would be presented in the street in front of the hotel, but he didn't think it would be dangerous. I would be reimbursed for my trip and he would have a room for me at the Doral Hotel.

I told him I'd call him back in an hour or so. After checking with General Scowcroft, I called Mr. Shumway back and told him when I'd arrive and that I reserved the right not to make my final decision about accepting the petition until after arrival. That was okay with him, he said, adding that he appreciated my making the trip on short notice. He said to take a cab to the hotel.

On the plane ride south, I was somewhat nervous about the

confrontation with these Vietnam Veterans Against the War. I'd been told they could get pretty nasty, and I didn't relish the thought of being knocked down and trampled in the street. The hot, humid, sticky air closed in around me as I searched for a cab at the Miami airport. At the desk of the Doral, they couldn't seem to locate a reservation for me. I began to feel better when, after much searching, they came up with a room. By now it was after 1:00 A.M. Before getting into the elevator, I was told I had to have a security badge. In a big room where badges of different colors were being issued, a nice young lady made me welcome and helped me get the right badge. I was amazed at the security precautions, even here in the hotel, none of which allayed my fears about the next day's meeting. I was given staff-dining-room privileges, which meant I could eat among some of the high and mighty on the committee.

At breakfast the next morning, I was asked to attend a meeting in one of the rooms at 9:00 A.M. A blind Vietnam war veteran named John Todd was to accept the petition with me. No one thought there would be any physical danger, because there would be Secret Service men right behind us and the street would be roped off so only representatives of the Veterans Against the War could get to us to present the petition. We were to stick to the one theme: that we would get the petition to the president.

While our meeting was still going on, the time of the presentation was changed from 10:30 to 11:00 A.M. Too much chaos was still going on in the streets; the police didn't have everything under control. At 10:45 we went to the lobby and saw a milling crowd outside. They were being moved back behind a roped-off area. At 10:58 we moved out into the cleared street. About fifteen very dissimilar-looking people approached us. None looked like veterans to me. A spokesman explained that theirs was a group with representatives from the war, the poor, and the senior citizens. I introduced myself and the blind veteran to them. His arm was firmly linked in mine. The press closed in, almost ramming their microphones right up my nose. I announced that we had come to accept the petition and deliver it to the president.

Immediately, a fat, boisterous, older man from that other group hollered that it was a dirty trick to send us out to accept their petition. He then read their petition, which was just a mixed-up mess about the poor and the senior citizens and how the war had made their lot so dismal. At one point while he was reading on and on, I said quietly to a young man standing next to me, "Are you one of the Veterans Against the War?" He replied, "Yeah, they got me to come down here, but I'm not too sure about this crowd. Are you really a POW wife?" I said yes, and he said he felt sorry for my husband. "Where is he from?" he asked. I said, "Illinois," and he said he was from Illinois, too. "Well, some funny way to meet, isn't it?" he commented. "I wish you good luck." He seemed like a nice young fellow.

By then the petition reading had ended, and I reached out to accept it. But the leader wouldn't give it to me. He demanded to know whether or not I was a member of the Republican National Committee. I told him the Republican National Committee's headquarters were at another hotel, and if he wanted them, he'd have to go there, but I could deliver the petition to the president if that was what he wanted. He kept balking about giving it to me as I tried to accept it. We were getting pushed and shoved and jammed in tighter and tighter in a knot in the middle of the street. A few onlookers were beginning to come across the ropes. I almost lost my footing while holding on to the blind veteran. One of the security men behind me said, "Tell him you're going back into the hotel and this is his last chance to give you the petition." As we started to leave, the grubby paper was passed to me and we safely returned to the hotel lobby.

The officials seemed pleased when we got back inside. One asked me if I'd like to stay that night and attend the final session of the convention. I was glad to be asked. I'd never been to a convention before and wanted to see what it was like. That night I wrote in my diary:

> Charlton Heston gave Invocation—very strong about POW's. They turned off lights for this—Thank Heaven—for I cried and cried and didn't know whether I could get a handle on crying or not— (Waiting in lobby to take bus to Convention Hall, band at party played "Hello, Dolly" and all of sudden I felt the tears coming up.) By time lights came on I had just gotten eyes mopped. *So* glad I had Kleenex. Man next to me wondered what my problem was, I'm sure. After that, I was OK.

After we left the convention hall that night, the antiwar agitators set off tear-gas bombs in the parking lot. My escort was a young woman who had obviously been told to stay with me. She was stunning-looking—very sleek, slim, and sophisticated in a bright green dress that showed off her tan beautifully. I felt frumpy in my orange and white cotton. With everything else going on, she couldn't have been too pleased to drag me along with her, but she didn't duck out on me, which I halfway expected.

We waited in the convention hall for an extra hour or more until it was reported safe to leave for our bus. But when we got into the parking lot, the buses had moved and we milled through the crowd, first trying to locate the buses and then searching from bus to bus to find one going to the Doral Hotel. Clouds of tear-gas fumes mingled with the exhaust from the buses getting warmed up. At last my escort darted into a bus, with me behind her. Seconds later a man looking like a taller, more slender President Nixon came aboard with two men behind him. We were all standing jammed in the aisle. The driver slammed the door shut, gunned the engine, and we were off. The driver announced that no matter what happened en route, he was going to keep driving—that he wasn't taking any chances with the president's brother aboard.

We all hung on as we careened through the streets. Outside our hotel some offenders were being frisked and cuffed by police. Squad cars surrounded the hotel doorway. We made our way into the lobby, showing our passes every ten steps. At the victory party, I saw Alex Butterfield across the room. Some nasty man promptly blew a big cloud of cigar smoke into my face and, eyeing my name badge, said, "Well, and who are you, Sybil Stockdale?" I didn't stay long after that.

Back in Coronado in early September, Bob Boroughs telephoned and told me some Hanoi travelers were leaving shortly. There was no time to prepare a coded message, so with Bob's permission, for the first time in six years, I wrote Jim a straight letter.

My Very Dearest Jim,

     I have just heard that three family members [misguided people influenced by the North Vietnamese sympathizers] of American prisoners of war will travel to Hanoi and have offered to deliver mail. Thus, I hasten to write a long letter which I pray the authorities will allow you to receive. My thoughts continue to be with you every hour of every day and night. I am optimistic about the future and feel in my

heart that the end of our long separation is near. My love for you is
constant as is that of our fine sons and your hundreds of loyal and
devoted friends.

We have just returned from Connecticut where we once again
spent the summer near my parents. They are well but elderly now as
you can imagine. They continue to be completely devoted to you and
your family. My mother's eyesight is very limited but my father still
drives and together they are able to live the same life they have for so
many years, spending the winter in East Haven and the summers in
Branford. They were here for two months last year and I hope will be
able to come again this winter.

Jimmy graduated from Ohio Wesleyan in June. Sid and I attended
his graduation. You would have been very proud of him, Jim, as he
read a poem during the baccalaureate service and sang with a quartet
as part of the graduation ceremony. He has a certificate to teach elementary school but in his words "wanted to let some of his learning
settle a bit" before continuing in the academic atmosphere. He has an
apartment near Yale University. He has a Volkswagen convertible and
enjoys a life of contrasts between concerts and lectures and work at
the steel mill. His apartment has a small fireplace and on free days he
plans to cut some wood on the land my father has given us near the
winter house. Jimmy has your superb sense of humor and story telling
ability. He combines this with great common sense and a fine ability
to sort out the important from the trivial in life. He has the complete
approval of his grandparents and is both kind and understanding with
them. In my mind's eye, I see you warming to long intellectual conversations with him about philosophy which you love so well.

Sid drove the car we used this summer across the country for me.
One of his friends from South Kent came with him and they looked at
some colleges along the way. Sid is a very mature eighteen and ever
so much like his Grandfather Bailey in every way. He will be a senior
at South Kent this year as I dropped him back a year when he started
there, after a year at Coronado High. He is a superb athlete. He will
play tight end for the first football team this fall, is one of the stars of
the first hockey team and will be captain of the crew next spring. He
went to Milan, Italy, this summer to take part in the Junior World
Rowing Championships and was there for his eighteenth birthday. He
had a manual labor job in Branford after he returned and earned over
$200.00 in two weeks. He and Jimmy are genuine friends and Sid
continues to be devoted to his younger brothers. As I write on this
Sunday afternoon, he and his friend have Stan and Tay out at the
beach teaching them about surfing. I gave everyone haircuts just be-

fore they left! Both Jimmy and Sid have a healthy interest in girls but neither has yet become really attached to anyone in particular. A situation I am sure you would approve of.

Stanford is just beginning to like girls, unlike his brother Taylor who still finds them generally repulsive! Stan is extremely handsome with his dark brown hair and your beautiful eyes. He will be in the sixth grade this year as I kept both him and Tay back a year when we were in Washington. Stanford has both athletic and musical ability and excels in both. He is still taking piano lessons although they are not his favorite. He plays the alto saxophone in the band and won a scholarship to summer music camp for being the best musical boy in his school. He didn't attend because we were in Connecticut but someone else was able to go in his place. He was selected for the All Star Little League team last spring. He does well in his classroom work and no longer wears glasses at all. We discovered at one time that he had a muscular vision problem and that has been completely corrected through therapy . . . part of the reason I moved to Washington for that one year . . . well worth it, although I did not enjoy living there at all. Stan looks forward to being a teenager and accepts responsibility well. He is our dishwasher now and tends to his lawn work conscientiously. He has his own set of drums which he plays well having had instruction from Sid. Sid is a superb drummer and has his set of drums at school. Both Sid and Stan have a real flair for dramatics also and thoroughly enjoy those activities at school.

Taylor continues to remind me in many ways of your Uncle George. (Uncle George is not with us anymore, Jim, having passed on six months before your mother joined him.) Taylor will be in the fourth grade and looks forward to going back to school tomorrow. He combines a very easy going approach to life with a maturity beyond his years. He was thrilled to have been selected for a major Little League team his first year out. He stands up at the plate with great confidence, combining it with doing a little jig to please the crowd! He is a very appealing little boy to everyone he meets and very serious about wanting to do the right thing. He adores his older brothers and longs for the day when he can know you and play with you. He is all boy with his pockets jammed with treasures and his shoes most often untied! He begins his piano lessons seriously this year having taken a few in Washington and showing that he has your natural musical talent. Both he and Stanford are trying out for the swimming team this fall. Tay looks more like you than any of the other boys.

I am completely back to battery, Jim, after my operation of more than a year ago. I attend the Episcopal Church now and feel a real

communion with God there. I have had our house remodeled so that
it is a truly comfortable family home. I added a study for you where
the porch used to be behind the dining room. There is a bath next to it
with a deck all across the back of the house. I finally got that wall out
of the kitchen leaving only the one pantry (dad's pantry) and have a
lovely big kitchen with a built in dishwasher. I had all the bathrooms
modernized but otherwise the house is exactly the same. There is a
Benjamin Franklin fireplace in your study and I feel confident that
soon, my dearest, you will be able to enjoy its fire as well as the deep
and enduring love we all have for you.

The Salsigs have moved to Flagstaff as Budd is in partnership with
a man there making educational films. They just left in June and I will
miss Doyen dreadfully as we have been so close for so long. When you
return, she will come at once however, to help me, as she has done so
many times in the past. I am still in close contact with all of your
friends and when you are ready, they long to see you.

Your courage has sustained me, Jim, and will continue to do so
until you return. Our love is a true gift from God . . . the kind few are
given. I just live for the day when I can devote myself completely to
you.

I *love* you always,

Your Own Syb

During the days and weeks following the four-month period
when the North Vietnamese were to have become desperate for
supplies, the newspapers carried the same daily reports about the
prosecution of the war. They were hardly distinguishable from
those of a year, or two years, or five years before. I felt myself
slipping into the same catatonic lethargy I had experienced in the
fall of 1970. I recognized the symptoms more readily now and
wished Dr. Moran were not a continent away.

None of my plans about the Mammoth condominiums was
working out. As soon as I'd completed the initial payments, the
development company that was to handle the rentals could not be
reached by telephone. I was going to be paying out $400 a month
with nothing to show for it. I went over and over the finances in my
mind, hoping to see some solution I'd overlooked the time before.
It seemed to me the payments would eventually eat up all our savings and we'd go broke. I felt trapped because if Jim didn't come
home, I'd be miserable forever; and if he did, he'd hate me for
losing our money, so I'd be miserable forever. I was terrified by the

situation I found myself in. I considered moving to Mammoth, but that would take me too far from the naval hospital if Jim did come home.

I knew I had to have professional help. I located a civilian therapist (I still couldn't come right out and call him a psychiatrist) in San Diego, and even though he had a beard, I faithfully talked and cried my way through three sessions a week in his office. An absolute saint of an attorney, named Bob Sullivan, made numerous trips all over California and finally located the real-estate-and-development people who'd gone into hiding. Somehow Bob convinced them to buy back my condominiums. I was more than glad to sell at a loss.

Day by day I slogged my way through the months of autumn. The days seemed to last forever. By two in the afternoon, I felt I'd been up at least forty-eight hours. My doctor told me to take one day at a time. As the Christmas holidays approached and I heard on the news that President Nixon had sent the B-52s to bomb Hanoi, my spirits began to lift just a shade. Maybe my president hadn't abandoned his men after all. Maybe 1973 would be the year.

By January 23, 1973, I was feeling strong enough to take a Red Cross course to become a hospital volunteer. At the end of class that day, someone told me that Dr. Kissinger was returning home from the current session of the Paris peace talks earlier than expected. On my way home, I heard on the car radio that tonight President Nixon would address the nation on TV. My heart skipped a flutter, but I immediately reminded myself not to get my hopes up. He was probably just going to announce again that Hanoi wouldn't negotiate. That evening, I could hardly believe what I heard President Nixon saying.

"The Peace Treaty will be signed on January 27 and the POWs will begin coming home two weeks later. They'll come out in three groups, each about two weeks apart."

No shouts of joy. No tears of elation on my part. I warned myself again to be careful, not to get my hopes too high.

The next day the clock hands began to move more quickly. On Saturday, January 27, the cease-fire agreement really was signed. The first group of POWs would be home in two weeks. After that information had been confirmed and reconfirmed, I allowed myself to believe it was true. For the first time in years, I unlocked the heavy metal boxes containing all Jim's personal effects sent home from the ship in 1965. One by one I lovingly lifted out and hung in the closet his navy blue uniforms. The long passage of time showed only too clearly on the darkly tarnished gold braid. Each day I added a few touches that I hoped might make him feel a little more at home when he arrived.

Early on Saturday, February 10, Bob Boroughs telephoned and said, "Syb, Jim is coming out with the first group. He's going to be released tomorrow."

"Are you sure?" I gasped, hardly able to believe it was really happening.

"I'm sure," he replied in his gravelly voice. "It's really going to happen."

I stared at myself in the mirror near the telephone after hanging up. So much to think about and do so quickly. It was going to happen almost too fast. These were the moments I wanted to mull over and savor. As I dialed the long-distance operator to call Jimmy and Sid, my parents, and Doyen, I thought how lucky I was to be calling them with this kind of news. I remembered yet again the verse that for so long I'd written at the close of each of my letters to Jim:

> God keep you, dearest, all this lonely night;
> The winds are still,
> The moon drops down behind the western hill;
> God keep you, dearest, 'til the light.

Out the window, I saw the water in San Diego Bay sparkling in the sunshine.

Chapter 15

Release

The American Son Tay helicopter rescue attempt of late 1970 had prompted the North Vietnamese to crowd all of us 350 American prisoners into the back half of Hoa Lo Prison in downtown Hanoi. Their instructions were simply to keep us subdued and quiet, to let up on the propaganda push, just to keep the lid on. That lid was quickly blown off; it was blown off by the pressure of pure exuberance of strong-willed, resentful American prisoners who suddenly had enough maneuvering room after years of frustrating constraint and humiliating silence.

The explosion was triggered by Vietnamese insistence that within those large cellblocks in which we were housed, no American was to stand up and address all his roommates at once. North Vietnamese Communists opposed organized opposition above all else and would divert all resources to its immediate destruction—if necessary, to the detriment of other priorities, other ongoing projects. The idea of a public speech by one American to a group of Americans drove the Vietnamese leadership right up the wall.

Even in that relatively benevolent atmosphere in which we were permitted conversation (though not between cellblocks), improvised games (with playing cards we made of toilet paper), and outside group bathing and exercise (isolated by cellblock), the single suggestion of prisoner unity, self-governance, came to be a dynamite issue. And the issue came to a head over a point that got universal prisoner support—the holding of Sunday church services. The Communists could accept our milling around a cellblock and talking to each other in private conversations, but for a single

American to stand before a group and lead a prayer, or for a trio to stand before the group and sing a hymn—was a provocative act.

To us as Americans, that Communist view of life would never work. They had thrown down the gauntlet; we would pick it up. Even if our new life of ease was at stake, so be it. We were tired of that carrot-and-stick crap; like Dostoevsky's "underground man," we were tired of the tyranny of reason.

So we staged the provocative act in Building 7 on a Sunday in mid-February 1971, about six weeks after we had been put together. On that afternoon, we quietly assembled for religious services. Even those among us who would normally never have gone to church gladly took seats up front in the interest of unity. The prayer was led, and the trio assembled, and then in burst the waiting Vietnamese guards, rifles drawn. Those churchmen who had addressed the group were quickly dragged off to solitary confinement in Heartbreak Hotel next door.

That triggered what became known as "the church riot of 1971." Building 7 burst into a standing, shouting rendition of "The Star-Spangled Banner" that could be heard over much of downtown Hanoi. Each of the big cellblock buildings around the circle picked up after us in turn, and then they all vied for militancy and loudness in a one-after-another rendition of American patriotic songs. The Vietnamese appeared with machine guns and tear-gas canisters, but contented themselves with taking perches in our high windows and glaring down at us, rifles drawn, bayonets fixed.

The next day, as in an old French Foreign Legion movie, the top half-dozen or so of us known leaders of Building 7 were taken out one at a time, jerked and bound into tight ropes, and then paraded individually through a cordon of armed soldiers en route to small cells and leg irons in Rawhide. But it was very clear to us that this was merely a pageant for the benefit of a watching gallery of downtown Hanoi officials and citizens who had heard the ruckus the day before and were being shown "the iron fist of righteous Vietnamese vengeance."

To us, the whole exercise was in the category of a lark; men who have spent years in a political prison can sense the lifting of the canopy of fear and guilt, the removal of the commissar's extortionistic fangs. Now we were beginning to feel like we were just in a normal POW prison. And all we had to do was act like normal prisoners and take a little crap like leg irons once in a while. The difference was overwhelming; our minds were now free, and we knew it. Jerry Denton and I were put side by side in irons in a cell. We could talk! There was no more "repentance"! We dropped off to sleep laughing every night.

After about a month, the turnkey came in and let us each remove one leg from the stocks. We decided that if we had a secret radio and could send three words to the Oval Office as a "Hanoi situation report," they would be *One leg out* (not to worry). And by April Fools' Day we were clear of the stocks.

In late 1971 we began to hear air-raid sirens again, and a new generation of prisoners started to trickle in to join us. Off and on for the next year, we had somewhat the same tactical raid situation we had known five and six years before.

But a totally different atmosphere finally swept Hanoi about an hour after dark on that momentous night of December 18, 1972. At first we thought it was a regular tactical raid of the sort that were then coming in two or three times a week. The bombs were hitting out where they usually hit—in the railroad yard, power plant, and airfield areas. Some of the prisoners did detect higher-level explosions early in the bombardment, but it wasn't until these explosions were still being heard twenty minutes later that the cheers started to go up all over the cellblocks of that downtown prison. This was a new reality for Hanoi. These were big explosions—and the bombs kept coming! Though landing thousands of yards away (and we knew they would continue to land out there; those bomber pilots knew where *we* were), they shook the ground under us and plaster fell from all the ceilings. The days of Mickey Mouse were over! Our wonderful America was here to deliver a message, not a self-conscious stammer of apology. "Let's hear it for President Nixon!" went the cry from cellblock to cellblock, all around the courtyard.

The bombers kept coming, and we kept cheering. Guards who were normally enraged by loud talk, guards who normally thrust their bayoneted rifles through the bars and screamed at us if we dared shout during air raids, could be seen silently cowering in the lee of the prison walls, their faces ashen in the light reflected from the fiery skies above.

So it went, hour after hour, night after night, with frequent tactical raids in the daytime. Once in a while, prisoners with good vantage points identified a particularly brilliant torch among the array of bursting antiaircraft shells and surface-to-air missiles. Some claimed they could then make out a tumbling, burning B-52. But if they could see one, all Hanoi could see it, too. For the North Vietnamese to see that and the bomber stream continuing to roll right on like old man river was a message in itself—proof that all that separated Hanoi from doomsday was American forbearance, an American national order to keep the bombs out on the hard military targets. We prisoners knew this was the end of North Vietnamese resistance, and the North Vietnamese knew it, too.

At dawn the streets of Hanoi were absolutely silent. The usual patriotic wake-up music was missing, the familiar street sounds, the horns, all gone. Our interrogators and guards would inquire about our needs solicitously. Unprecedented morning coffee was delivered to our cellblocks. One look at any Vietnamese officer's face (Bug, Chihuahua, et al.) told the whole story. It telegraphed accommodation, hopelessness, remorse, fear. The shock was there; our enemy's will was broken. I *knew* I was going to be home right away. I knew it as surely as a person in a sickbed knows his fever has broken and that he will get well.

By December 29, 1972, Hanoi was almost out of ammunition (the overdue mining of Haiphong Harbor had worked, too). There was no need to continue the bombing. The word around the American cellblocks was "Pack to go home." It was all over; there was no question about it. Within two weeks, Henry Kissinger had it on paper, and in accordance with a clause that he insisted be in the articles of surrender, each of us was given a personal copy of the complete document and prisoner-release schedule by the Vietnamese turnkeys.*

As preparations for our release were being made, I was called to quiz by Chihuahua. Sitting behind him were a couple of senior-looking Vietnamese I had never seen before. Chihuahua got right to the point: "The former general staff officer has asked me to warn you against saying anything bad about the camp authorities or about the Vietnamese people when you get home. He reminds you

---

*See Appendix 6.

that in the course of your stay here he has had you write many documents that he can acquire."

"That sounds to me like some more of Major Bui's blackmail bullshit," I replied, daring to use the Cat's real name, which had been given to us by a South Vietnamese prisoner.

"Major Bui no longer speaks for the Vietnamese government" was Chihuahua's enigmatic reply. I was immediately sent back to my cellblock.

The first third of the prisoners shot down were lined up on February 12, 1973, in our release order ("first in, first out"), and marched out the main gate of Hoa Lo Prison and into buses. I took a good look at the Ministry of Justice and Hoa Lo Street, a better look than I'd had the sense to take on that rainy Sunday morning in 1965 when I rolled up to the curb in the back of that old truck. I thought about that day, and how worried I had been about my knowledge of and connection with the Tonkin Gulf events of the year before.

> For man also knoweth not his time: as the fishes that are taken in an evil net, and as the birds that are caught in the snare; so are the sons of men snared in an evil time, when it falleth suddenly upon them.[1]

I was in a dream as up I went over the bomb-damaged Paul Daumer Bridge, to Gia Lam airfield. Out on the distant parking ramp, we saw a couple of big transport jets of a type I had never seen before. They had USAF markings on them; we learned they were called C-141s.

There were to be delays in our release while more planes arrived, and while arrangements at an official turnover gate were completed. We were put in a kind of screened-in dining area a mile from the gate to wait. We were under guard, but not harassed; little groups of us stood around chatting. Then it came time to get into the bus and sit in order of shootdown. We drove down and parked before a big tent. Beneath it were long tables at which both Vietnamese and American military officers were sitting. We saw the first plane take off as we were told to get out of our bus. All in our group had been shot down in late 1965 to early 1966; we were to be the second planeload. According to plan, we marched smartly in ranks toward the tent, two abreast, in the right plane-loading order.

Each captive was to march through the tent and out the gate when his name was called. I was one of the first. I heard a familiar voice call, "James Bond Stockdale."

I went into the tent, headed for the gate at its other end, and then I saw him standing at the side with his clipboard: Rabbit. I looked at him, and I think I smiled faintly as he dared glance up at me with a knowing eye. Then his deep voice enunciated the next name: "Wendell B. Rivers."

Clear of the gate, there he was—the USAF colonel who was the official greeter, arms out for a hug as we saluted each other. It was really happening! A big sergeant grabbed Wendy Rivers and me around our shoulders and steered us up the dropped-back ramp of that beautiful plane. Loaded and ramp up, we were soon on the runway with takeoff power. We cheered when we felt the familiar acceleration, and shouted with glee as we felt ourselves break ground for our destination—Clark Air Force Base in the Philippines.

After we had been airborne awhile, all in animated chatter, an orderly came to me and said that I was wanted up in the cockpit. When I got there, the pilot said I had had a call on the radio from Vice Admiral Hutch Cooper. He said Admiral Cooper was commander of Task Force Seventy-seven, the American aircraft-carrier force in the Western Pacific. But by now we seemed to be out of Hutch's radio range and couldn't raise him.

I went back to my seat thinking of my times with Hutch Cooper right down there in those waters below, now nine years ago. So old Hutch was the big cheese of all American naval aviation out here now. That told me something right there. In those days of 1964 when the plot in the Tonkin Gulf got thick, Hutch Cooper was one senior officer in the Western Pacific who I knew would always level with me. Afterward, he had let me go to my dying dad's bedside when it wasn't exactly in accordance with regulations, and backed me up in a million other ways, sometimes when I might not have deserved it. Hutch was a diamond in the rough, the salt of the earth—nothing like those flashy Washington-oriented bastards who always seemed to be looking over the heads of mere fighter pilots, trying to see something way up ahead of us all. But old human Hutch had wound up with the stars after all. It made you feel good about your navy.

But how, I marveled, did he know I was coming out today? And how did he even know I would be in the second airplane? Before I had time to figure that out, we got to Clark. And what are these thousands of Americans—military and civilian husbands, wives, little kids—doing out here, lining fences, waving flags? And then down the ramp, and a handshake with Noel Gayler at the bottom, four stars now.

Did I know I had just been on live TV, worldwide by satellite? No, I didn't know anything about satellite transmission of TV. And soon after I got into the hospital, more miracles of communication—good mainly because of the miracles of love they brought:

> To Clark Air Force Base, Philippine Islands, Pass to Captain James Bond Stockdale, U.S. Navy: My dearest Jim: Overwhelming joy filled my heart as I watched you step off the plane. No words can express how much I love you and long to be with you again. All our boys are fine and will be here waiting for you. Messages pouring in from your friends everywhere. I am counting the hours now and loving you always. Syb

Unstated in this wonderful message was a truth that I'm sure Syb knew would come through to me: She was not being allowed to come out to meet me along my way home. I knew she would come if she were allowed, just as she came to Japan when I needed her eight years ago. One can't be married and in love with a bright person for over a quarter-century and not read her signals.

We ex-prisoners each spent about three to five days in the isolation ward of the military hospital at Clark Air Force Base. Although we did take some medical tests, it was soon apparent that all the authorities were trying to do was decide whether we were nuts or not before they put us on other airplanes heading east.

It was at the hospital that each of us was met by an intelligence "debriefer," the military intelligence officer who would piece together the story of each individual's imprisonment and write an official narrative report. I leveled with my guy about that Tonkin Gulf thing that had been eating at me all those years. What had happened to the Tonkin Gulf Resolution? Why didn't the Vietnamese close in on me? This subject caught my debriefer cold; he said he would look into this through his intelligence channels and try to give me some answers.

On our second night at Clark, my name appeared as one of those scheduled to board the plane for points east the next day. We took off the next afternoon on schedule, and were due to make our first stop, for fuel, at Honolulu after midnight. The C-141s were rigged as medical evacuation planes, with choice of seats or bunks, and there were few enough of us aboard for all to have one of each. The flight nurse told me that I should get some rest; that as senior prisoner on the plane, I would be expected to say a few words when we got off the airplane in Honolulu. "An outdoor speech at one o'clock in the morning?" I asked as I went back to my bunk.

"I don't believe you understand the importance and size of the happenings you're involved in," she said.

I was starting to get the picture that I had been swept up in an unprogrammed road show, but even that realization didn't prepare me for Honolulu-after-midnight. I stepped out of the airplane into a sea of flashbulbs, was greeted by the commander in chief of the U.S. Pacific Fleet, and was led to a microphone where I faced thousands of townspeople lined up on the ramp. I said some pleasant things, but they didn't reflect my true astonishment at the reception. I was too shocked to acknowledge the great big banner being held up by high poles in the middle of the crowd, saying, "Welcome Home Jim Stockdale." That was carried by my many old Navy and Marine Corps friends on Oahu.

As soon as we lifted off from Honolulu, my intelligence debriefer sat down beside me. "I've been working on your Tonkin Gulf question, and I just got my final answers there in Honolulu.

"First of all, on that AP release of 12 August 1964, based on the press conference on the *Ticonderoga*, your story was in the European edition of *Stars and Stripes* just like it had been in the American papers. You saw the copy your friend had sent you from Germany before you were shot down. Now, you aren't going to believe this, but for some unknown reason the paragraph about you and *only* the paragraph about you had been deleted from the AP script as it appeared in the *Pacific* edition of *Stars and Stripes* of the same day. I'll get a copy of both the Frankfurt and Tokyo editions so you can see exactly how they differed.

"And on that resolution—and I was still in high school when it was enacted, and so didn't actually follow it too closely—the whole issue became a political football while you were in prison. Fulbright's committee in the Senate had big hearings about it, everybody became disillusioned with it, and finally sick of it, and it was Nixon who finally declared the thing null and void, repealed it. But by then it was 1971 and most people wanted to forget about it. In summary, the old thing petered out in a slow and undramatic way."

My God, thought I, "I returned and saw that time and chance happeneth to them all."

We were heading for Travis Air Force Base, just north of San Francisco. There I would be expected to give another planeside talk. After we landed, I headed for the cabin door, my mind peaked up for the dramatic challenge. I'm getting good at this now, I think as I stride toward the mike. Eric Sevareid repeated my words on national television news that night:

> For the past seven or eight years, I doubt that there was a prisoner of war in Hanoi who did not occasionally hum that old refrain, "California Here We Come." Well, California, we have come. I'm proud to be the representative of this group of wonderful warriors right behind me, and to express to you people here our thanks for your loyalty to us. The men who followed me down that ramp know what loyalty means, because they have been living with loyalty, living off loyalty, for the past several years. I mean loyalty to our military ethic, loyalty to our commander in chief, loyalty to each other. And now we're home to rest and regain our strength to continue productive lives. As that Athenian warrior and poet Sophocles wrote over 2400 years ago, "Nothing is so sweet as to return from sea and listen to the raindrops on the rooftops of home." We're home. America, America, God shed His grace on thee.

Then we got turned over to some reporters before we could get back on the airplane for San Diego. One wanted to know if I knew we had put a man on the moon. No, I did not. No, I had not heard it in Vietnam, or in the Philippines, or in Honolulu. No, I was not surprised. And, no, I did not think getting a man to the moon was the greatest news I had ever heard.

As we neared San Diego, I went up to the cockpit and the pilot let me twist myself into the copilot's seat. I felt awkward; my left shoe had had to come off to get my stiff leg into place. Looking down on the familiar terrain as we approached the Miramar break, I thought of the thousands of times I had made the circuit of this landing pattern. I was always getting ready to head back to Vietnam. For ten years I had been operating "well outside my envelope," just as we operated those Crusaders well outside theirs on Yankee Team in Laos.

As I contemplated the significance of this moment, I grew kind of scared. What will they think of me down there, Syb and the boys? My hair is totally white now. I can't see to read (too many months in the dark, too many weeks in the blindfold)—I couldn't read that message on the back of that picture now, and where would we have been without that? I'm forty-nine years old and crippled and can't raise my left arm. And there will be Jimmy, out of college now and, from his pictures, much taller than I; and Sid, a schoolboy athletic marvel who can throw right-handed or left-handed and do all the physical things his dad could never do very well; and Stan, who has had such a tough time with his loneliness for a father, and with his emotions, and with his eyes. And then there will be eleven-year-old Taylor, who probably really can't remember anything about me. Can we put it all back together after all these years?

Well, if we can, if this family will survive, it will be Syb who will pull us together, as she always has. Syb always goes that extra mile, always gives up that personal pleasure to meet our needs, always meets us all—and especially me—more than halfway. I have a hunch she's been at it ever since I left, straightening out the family, maybe even straightening out the country. She's been carrying enough responsibility to crush a normal person. God, let me help her properly now. Help me to let her know how much I love her.

We're in the final stages of taxiing in now; I've got to work my way out of this cockpit seat and get ready to make another speech. I swear I think I can see Syb waving from the ramp. "Stand up straight now," I tell myself. "You've got to make her proud."

Chapter 16

Homecoming

Once I knew Jim would be coming home in less than two weeks, I was overwhelmed by all I wished I could do to get ready. Flowers and phone calls began to pour into 547 "A" Avenue. I had hoped to have time to shop for a really special outfit to wear for Jim's arrival, but when I didn't, I realized that almost everything I owned would be new to him anyway. Besides, clothing would probably be the least of our concerns. In a recent briefing about what to expect when our husbands returned, we wives had been told the men would probably be sexually impotent and might be hostile toward those they loved. Their first stop on the way home after release would be Clark Air Force Base in the Philippine Islands. No wives were to try to go out to meet their men. Our first reunion would take place at Miramar Naval Air Station in San Diego. Just how soon after arriving at Clark a man would be able to proceed home depended on his physical and psychological condition.

According to my clock and calendar, Jim actually left Hanoi on February 12, 1973. I liked the touch of having Jim regain his freedom on Lincoln's birthday. In the middle of that night, the boys and I, along with a few close friends, sat in our den breathlessly watching the POWs arrive at Clark Air Force Base and walk from the huge airplanes that brought them from Hanoi. Jim was in the second plane to land. He hesitated in the door of the plane, seeming to estimate whether or not he could descend the steep steps successfully. I thought I could see him shrug off the proffered help of a young escort. That was a good sign and I took a tiny breath of air. Then—thinner than I'd ever seen him, and snow-white-haired—

Jim, all alone and holding on to the railings with both hands, slowly descended toward the senior officer awaiting his salute at the foot of the steps. Jim squared his shoulders, faced his senior, and saluted.

Tears of love and pride spilled down my cheeks. The TV camera followed Jim for a minute as he walked away with his stiff-legged gait. He looked far more natural than I had imagined he might and I found his walking style most appealing. It seemed too good to be true that he was actually back in United States territory.

At our homecoming-preparedness briefing, we'd been told our first contact with our men would be a phone call from the hospital at Clark Air Force Base. I was apprehensive about this and wondered just how to begin a phone conversation with a possibly hostile husband after eight years. A beginning such as "How have you been?" didn't seem to strike quite the right note! I just hoped for the best.

The next day when the call came through I relaxed when I heard the familiar midwestern tone in Jim's voice. Young Stanford attached a recording device to the telephone so we would have our words recorded for posterity. Most of them sounded like a fairly ordinary conversation. The part I liked the best was when Jim said, "I have a stiff leg, but I think it gives my walk a little style." He didn't seem the least bit hostile, which was reassuring.

The next day I was told he'd return to Miramar on February 15. Sid had to make the difficult decision about whether to stay at South Kent and play in the championship hockey game (which his coach felt sure the team would lose without him) or be present the minute his dad arrived. If he played in the hockey game, he could arrive in San Diego in time for dinner. He stayed and played in the game. I felt sure his dad would approve of his decision.

On Valentine's Day, gorgeous American Beauty roses arrived from Jim with a card saying, "God Bless You, Syb. All my love, Jim." The "God Bless You" was a little out of character, but I knew I must be prepared for changes.

On the morning of February 15, we hung a tremendous Welcome Home banner across the front of our house. Then Jimmy, Stanford, Taylor, and I were driven in a navy car to Miramar. All of us wives who knew each other so well were unusually quiet as we sipped coffee in the air-operations waiting room. This was the big day. We couldn't help but wonder what the future held.

The plane is on final. It's time to go out on the ramp. The airplane door opens and there he is. He's escorted to a microphone where he makes appropriate remarks. He's still referring to his beloved Greek philosophers, so I know he's in fairly good shape. He has on a khaki uniform they've outfitted him with somewhere along the way. I know he'd despise the cap if he saw it from the back. It's rigid and stiff instead of pummeled and slouched into a proper fighter pilot's shape. His shoulder boards have the four gold stripes of a navy captain. I've never seen him as a captain before. Now he turns toward us and begins to walk in our direction. I feel Jimmy squeeze my shoulders as he stands behind me. I grip Stanford's and Taylor's hands firmly. Jim and I exchange one quick, loving, all-knowing look before we embrace. We come together with so much force and emotion that for a split second I think we might topple over. What a horrendous scene that would make for the TV cameras.

I don't remember one single word we said until we were seated in the car to go to the hospital. The boys were driven there in another car. Still, we were incredibly cramped in the back seat with Jim's stiff leg stretching across the back of the car. A driver and escort were in the front seat. Not much privacy. I remember Jim somewhat apologetically said something like "I don't really have much news about anything." I couldn't imagine why he would think I'd been expecting him to bring me news. I think I explained about Sid and the hockey game, although I believe I had already sent him a message about that. We had a pleasant conversation during the thirty-minute ride to Balboa Naval Hospital. I remember thinking how normal and natural it seemed to be riding along with him, talking about our children.

A real comic-relief scene took place as we got off the hospital elevator. Just before he'd left, Jim had sold his old clunker car to another fighter pilot. He was among those on official escort duty and was waiting when we arrived on the sixth floor. With a twinkle in his eye and a jocular tone in his voice, he welcomed Jim home, said he was the fellow who'd bought Jim's car for $125, and that he'd been waiting to tell Jim the car had blown up the week after he'd bought it.

Laughing about that, we were escorted to Jim's private suite, no less. The bedroom had a narrow, high, old-fashioned hospital bed, but the sitting room was carpeted and had a sofa, easy chairs, and round dining table. Our dinner that evening would be served there. The rest of the afternoon was spent greeting visitors and milling around, going from room to room to visit with other couples and families. It was fascinating to meet for the first time the husbands of the wives I knew so well.

Jim stayed close by my side and every once in a while said, "You won't leave me here alone, will you? You'll stay here with me tonight, won't you?" I assured him I would stay right with him every minute, having no idea whether or not the hospital rules would allow it. I doubted the authorities would physically eject me if I held my ground. That single high, narrow bed didn't look as if they were counting on wives staying. I wondered what had happened to the double beds we'd heard had days ago been installed in the POW rooms at Portsmouth Naval Hospital in Virginia.

We were told dinner was on the way. Sid had arrived by now and we all sat around the table. We looked at each other as if to say "I can hardly believe we are all sitting here at this same table together." I asked Jim if he wanted to say Grace and he nodded his head yes, but after a moment of silence, in a quiet sobbing sort of way he said, "Syb, I just can't do it. I'm so happy." For a moment we were all very quiet, and then I said, "Let's all say our old family Grace together." In unison we said, "God is great, God is good, And we thank Him for our food. Amen."

With perfect timing, dinner arrived and we ooohed and aahhhed about the thick, juicy steaks. Most of our conversation was about Sid's hockey game, which his team had won. After dinner, Jimmy drove the boys home and Jim and I chatted with a few more visitors before locking our doors to the hall. We opened a fresh bottle of champagne and decided to sleep on the soft plush carpeting on the floor of his sitting room. We made a sort of love nest with the sheets, blankets, and pillow from the bed and turned out the lights. Before drifting off to sleep with Jim's arms holding me closely, I remember thinking how completely wrong our briefers had been about the sexual impotence.

The next morning an early phone call from the Chief of Naval Operations in Washington welcomed Jim home once again. We laughed afterward about Jim's response. He'd said, "Yes, sir, everything is just fine here at the hospital and Sybil is right here in bed with me."

Jim first returned to 547 "A" Avenue on Sunday afternoon. When we pulled up in front of the house, we marveled at the fact that the little green VW we now used as our second car was the same one in which Jim had had his last ride to the ship in Japan a month before he'd been shot down. Our good friend Roger Netherland had loaned me the car before he deployed in 1966; he had been shot down and listed as missing on the cruise, and Gloria later sold me the car. Jim felt sure Roger had been killed at the time of his shootdown. Jim and I both sat quietly for a moment looking lovingly at the little green car and remembering all the good times we'd had with Roger and Gloria.

Jim had planned to return to the hospital Sunday night, but felt so comfortable at home, he stayed all night. Sometime in the middle of the night he switched from the bed to the floor because the bed was too soft. I switched with him, wondering if this was to become a way of life. At breakfast Monday morning, he began to tell us about some of his prison experiences. He seemed to have a strong need to share this information with us. We listened and asked questions and talked about some of his most dreadful treatment in an astonishingly natural way. Later in the morning, I drove Jim back over to Balboa Hospital so his debriefing and medical assessments could begin.

This schedule of being home at night and in the hospital by day continued for a couple of weeks. About a week after his return, he sprang from our bed early one morning (floor sleeping was becoming less and less frequent) and announced in a loud and hostile voice that he guessed now it was his turn to go places and do things—that I'd had my turn, and everybody else had had a turn around here, and now it was his turn. I immediately recognized the hostility the briefers had talked about and was thankful they had done so; otherwise I would have reacted quite differently. Now I remained unusually quiet, agreeing with Jim from time to time, and as his tirade came to a close, I slipped down to the kitchen to make coffee. That was the first and last of Jim's hostility being directed toward me.

We now lived with a pattern in which Jim's navy debriefer came to our house every morning and sat on the new sun deck with him while the tape recorder made a fifty-two-hour record of Jim's experiences in Vietnam. Jimmy stayed at home for several months to help his dad with his writing and public speaking—indeed, to serve as his dad's assistant in every department. The closeness I had envisioned became a reality between them. Sid had returned to South Kent, but he and Jim were fast friends already. It was to take longer for Stanford and Taylor to learn to know their dad. There were no real problems there—it was just that they didn't know him. It takes more than a few weeks to begin to know and love someone.

Before Jim returned, I predicted we'd be fully readjusted when he'd been home as long as he'd been away. To this day I feel that was an accurate prediction. And compared with many others, our readjustment was relatively easy. We had a strong and loving marriage before Jim left and were dedicated to the idea of keeping it that way.

One morning shortly after his return, Jim joined me in the kitchen saying he was afraid he might lose my love. I assured him there was no way he could possibly do that, and he seemed relieved. I marveled that he could be concerned about it after we'd been through so much. But the pressures on him during his first year home were becoming horrendous. While his debriefing still continued, he learned the government had not tolled the statute of limitations for the few POWs who had illegally accepted parole and come home early. His broad and loyal constituency was enraged by this. They were even more enraged when the government announced that it would not prosecute the two senior naval-service officers against whom that constituency had methodically preserved evidence of collaboration. As the senior POW in the naval service, since the government had shirked its duty, Jim was the man who had to charge the guilty men. For Jim not to have done this would have been a violation of the loyalty and trust all his men had shown him throughout their imprisonment.

The navy provided massive investigative and legal support, even prepared charges that the judge advocate general declared were amply supported by evidence, but the service insisted he sign them as a private citizen. All that pressure and stress, and sometimes hate mail, became a routine part of Jim's first year at home. While the rest of the POW couples were taking free trips and enjoying leisurely vacations, Jim worked in our den with various naval officers until long after dark.

One Friday evening at about 6:30, some six weeks after Jim's return, while he and yet another naval officer continued their conferences in the den, I sat in the kitchen crying and blubbering to Jimmy that this was not the way I'd thought it would be at all. We hadn't had any time to ourselves since his return, and Jim predicted that completion of the charges would take about a year.

This wasn't my first cry since his return. That had come about two weeks after he came home. While I was soaking in the bathtub, Jim had said that most of all he wanted command of an aircraft carrier as soon as possible. That would take him to sea for many more months, I reminded him, and was dismayed and dissolved into tears at his calm acceptance of this possibility. In April I was saved from this prospect when Admiral Zumwalt, who had been CNO since 1971, telephoned early one morning to tell Jim he had been selected for the rank of rear admiral. As I held my breath in the next room, I heard Jim say, "I believe this is one of the greatest moments of my life." Later that month we went to Washington, where Jim wore his admiral's uniform for the first time while visiting with President Nixon alone in the Oval Office.

Jim was assigned to head an aviation-warfare command, with an office at North Island Naval Air Station. At his insistence, he had to fly out to the carriers and make landings, stiff leg and all. We were offered a lovely big home for our quarters on the base, but declined so we could stay in our family home on "A" Avenue. After Jim's return, one by one, our sons had said to him, "You won't sell our house, will you, dad?" He'd assured them he most certainly would not do that.

On March 4, 1976, Jim was awarded the Congressional Medal of Honor by President Ford. I knew that was one of the truly greatest moments of both of our lives. His citation reads as follows:

For conspicuous gallantry and intrepidity at the risk of his life above and beyond the call of duty while senior naval officer in the Prisoner of War camps of North Vietnam. Recognized by his captors as the leader in the Prisoners of War resistance to interrogation and in their refusal to participate in propaganda exploitation, Rear Admiral Stockdale was singled out for interrogation and attendant torture after he was detected in a covert communications attempt. Sensing the start of another purge, and aware that his earlier efforts at self-disfiguration to dissuade his captors from exploiting him for propaganda purposes had resulted in cruel and agonizing punishment, Rear Admiral Stockdale resolved to make himself a symbol of resistance regardless of personal sacrifice. He deliberately inflicted a near-mortal wound to his person in order to convince his captors of his willingness to give up his life rather than capitulate. He was subsequently discovered and revived by the North Vietnamese who, convinced of his indomitable spirit, abated in their employment of excessive harassment and torture toward all of the Prisoners of War. By his heroic action, at great peril to himself, he earned the everlasting gratitude of his fellow prisoners and of his country. Rear Admiral Stockdale's valiant leadership and extraordinary courage in a hostile environment sustain and enhance the finest traditions of the U.S. Naval Service.

Epilogue

In April 1976, Jim Stockdale was transferred to duty at the Pentagon. He and Sybil rented their home in Coronado. In August 1977,
Jim became a vice admiral and president of the Naval War College
in Newport, Rhode Island. From there he retired from the navy to
become president of the Citadel in Charleston, South Carolina. At
Jim's retirement ceremony, the chief of naval operations presented
Sybil with the U.S. Navy Department's Distinguished Public Service Award. She is the only wife of an active-duty naval officer ever
to be so honored. Her citation reads as follows:

> For distinguished public service to the United States Navy as the or-
> ganizer and first Chairperson of the National League of Families of
> American Prisoners and Missing in Southeast Asia. By her courageous
> and determined actions, Mrs. Stockdale performed an outstanding
> public and humanitarian service for captured and missing military
> members of all services, their families and for the American people.
> Her actions and her indomitable spirit in the face of many adversities
> contributed immeasurably to the successful safe return of American
> prisoners, gave hope, support and solace to their families in a time of
> need and reflected the finest traditions of the Naval service and of the
> United States of America. In recognition and appreciation of her out-
> standing service, Mrs. Stockdale is eminently deserving of the Navy
> Distinguished Public Service Award.

At this writing, Jim is a senior research fellow at the Hoover
Institution on War, Revolution, and Peace, and a lecturer in the
philosophy department at Stanford University. Jim and Sybil live on

the campus at Stanford but return to their permanent home on "A" Avenue as often as possible.

Jimmy Stockdale has a doctorate in education from Auburn University and is headmaster of a private school in Chicago. He and his wife, Marina, have one child, Elizabeth, born in January 1984.

Sid Stockdale teaches history and coaches football, hockey, and crew at South Kent School, where he was a student during part of this story.

Stanford Stockdale teaches at a private boys' school for dyslexic students, located in northern New York State, and Taylor Stockdale is a senior at the Colorado College in Colorado Springs.

Each year the Navy Department presents the James Bond Stockdale Trophy for Inspirational Leadership to an outstanding command naval officer in the Atlantic and Pacific Fleets. On the occasion of Jim and Sybil's thirty-fifth wedding anniversary, Jim presented Sybil with the original trophy, on which he had had engraved, "To Syb, The Love of my Life, from Jim."

Appendix 1

Aviators' Immediate Accounts of the Gulf of Tonkin Action of the Afternoon of August 2, 1964

General Résumé, 3 August 1964

On the afternoon of Sunday, August 2, 1964, the USS *Ticonderoga* was conducting flight operations in the South China Sea. One scheduled evolution was an exercise in which Air Wing airplanes of various types were to expend their ordnance on smokelights near the ship in a practice coordinated strike. Four F8E airplanes, flown by the officers submitting this account, were to have participated. The airplanes were catapulted from the *Ticonderoga*'s deck at about 2:15 P.M. . . . At about 2:55 P.M., the F8s were directed by the *Ticonderoga*'s air controller to cease the drill and to switch radio frequency. In response to *Ticonderoga*'s instructions, the four airplanes, now led by Cdr Stockdale (senior of the group), immediately headed northward toward the USS *Maddox*, some 300 miles distant. The flight climbed to 32,000 feet and set a speed of .86M (to maximize nautical miles covered per pound of fuel used), and assumed a "combat spread" disposition (for maximum mutual protection if attacked). *Ticonderoga* informed the flight immediately that *Maddox* was being threatened with surface attack. At the distance where radio communications with *Ticonderoga* commenced to decay, a frequency shift was ordered to that of *Maddox*. When within 125 miles of *Maddox*, two-way transmissions between flight and ship were loud and clear. *Maddox* supplied the flight with a running commentary of her situation; the flight leader supplied *Maddox* with estimated "minutes out" on request. All aviators remember receiving such key *Maddox* reports as "Under attack by three PT boats," "Torpedoes in the water," "Am engaging the enemy with my main battery."

About ten minutes after the latter transmission was received, the flight commenced a descent in order to be at approximately 10,000 altitude at the ship's estimated position. The aircraft's ADF Homers indicated the ship's bearing in the descent when "short counts" were given on request. Lcdr Southwick picked up the *Maddox* on the mapping mode of his AI radar when the flight was fifty miles out. At about the time the *Maddox* was sighted, she transmitted to the flight, "Your mission is now to attack and destroy the PT boats" (or words to that effect).

The following array was sighted by the aviators as they approached in descent (time approximately 3:30 P.M.): The most prominent feature was an incongruous long "cloud," probably smoke, low on the water, extending roughly east and west for perhaps a half-mile. *Maddox* was perhaps two miles south of the eastern part of the smoke. Three PT boats were about three miles north of the smoke's eastern extremity, heading north. The high speed of the PT boats was indicated by their long wakes. When first sighted, two boats were together, with the third boat about a mile astern of the first two. At the time of the first firing run (Cdr Stockdale's), the boats had closed their relative positions to two approximately abreast, with the third somewhat less than a mile in trail. The disposition did not strike one as a practice tactical formation, but rather as a fleeing trio who preferred to stay together if none had to sacrifice speed to do so.

As the flight passed *Maddox* in descent at about 400 knots, Cdr Stockdale assigned "Firefighter aircraft" (VF-53s) the rear boat, and called "in" on a left-hand arcing approach toward the lead boats with the "Batterups" (VF-51s). From this point onward, accounts are individually composed.

J. B. STOCKDALE
R. F. MOHRHARDT
C. E. SOUTHWICK
R. W. HASTINGS

(Excerpts of) *Individual Account of Commander Stockdale, 3 August 1964*

My initial run was made on the westernmost boat of the two in the van, from his starboard to port across his quarter, my wingman, Ltjg Hastings, almost simultaneously attacking the running mate to the east. A single Zuni was selected and fired, and during my pullout, shortly after I had seen the rocket splash close aboard the boat's port beam, I heard Ltjg Hastings announce that he had "been hit," and that part of his port wing droop was gone.

I immediately picked him up in my right-hand rearview mirror, at my altitude, on a parallel track, also climbing. I told him to cut back toward *Maddox*, and as we both turned left, joined him after he passed behind me. *Maddox* was perhaps ten miles from the lead PT boats at this time, and I examined Ltjg Hastings's airplane while en route and during a circle of that ship at 15,000 feet. By visual check and through radio communication with him, four important facts were established: (1) His damage was flagrant (the inboard three feet of the port outer wing panel leading edge droop was missing and his port wing aileron was punctured and cracked), but at our reasonable cruise airspeed no further damage was being caused by aerodynamic forces. (2) There was no evidence of fire. (3) He was having no particular difficulty in controlling the airplane. (4) There was no evidence of fluid leaks (hydraulic or fuel) from external observation or cockpit-gauge indication. He had adequate fuel to wait for me, was located over the safest ejection site within 250 miles, and there was possibly some merit in his waiting for a few minutes to verify his fluid-system integrity. I therefore told Ltjg Hastings to wait over the destroyer for the homeward-bound flight, told *Maddox* what I was doing, and returned to the action.

. . . As I crossed *Maddox* (departing), I gave the ship the final situation as I left it: "All boats hit, two still under way toward the coast, one dead in the water and burning." *Maddox* replied with "Well done and good luck" (or words to that effect).

. . . While passing about 10,000 feet in descent toward the field I gave Ltjg Hastings the signal to raise his wing, and to be ready to drop his nose and lower it quickly if uncontrollable roll commenced. The aileron held together, and he was able to find a workable approach speed regime. He proceeded straight in to the field, and executed a good landing. I exchanged a few words with him on the radio and then returned to *Ticonderoga*. I came aboard three and a half hours after I had been catapulted for the routine training flight.

J. B. STOCKDALE

(Excerpts of) *Individual Account of Commander Mohrhardt, 3 August 1964*

On my first run I made a Zuni rocket attack on one trailing PT boat and observed both rockets to hit within twenty-five feet in his wake. As I pulled off I heard Ltjg Hastings say he was hit but his aircraft was under control.

I then made 20mm strafing runs from abeam across both lead boats and observed hits on each. After pulling off I saw that the trailing boat was almost stopped and observed Lcdr Southwick make an excellent strafing run on the trailing boat, scoring many hits.

I then made a strafing run on the trailing boat and observed him to be dead in the water and burning on the stern. I also saw someone on the boat throw a smoke bomb in the water as I pulled off. At this time my fuel state was such that I was forced to leave. . . .

R. F. MOHRHARDT

(Excerpts of) *Individual Account of Lieutenant Commander Southwick, 3 August 1964*

I remained at approximately 8,000 feet until Cdr Mohrhardt completed his Zuni run on the trailing boat. I observed his, and the other sections', Zuni impacts, all occurring within approximately thirty feet off his port bow. I also observed the boat perform an S-type evasive turn around the impact marks on the water. I pulled up to the left and after 270 degrees of turn, initiated a 20mm strafing run 90 degrees to his course from stbd to port. I began firing at 4,000–5,000 feet slant range and observed the first rounds impacting at his bow, slightly short. I held the lead I had and the rounds began impacting over the entire boat. Prior to recovery at an estimated 1,000 feet slant range, the entire boat was obscured by spray resulting from projectile impacts on the surrounding water. After recovering from the run, I observed that the boat appeared dead in the water emitting black smoke from the afterdeck area, and that a smoke generating device had been thrown into the water. . . .

C. E. SOUTHWICK

(Excerpts of) *Individual Account of Lieutenant Junior Grade Hastings, 3 August 1964*

. . . As Cdr Stockdale started his run I tried to establish lateral separation to the right to avoid starting my firing run from a trail position. Also I tried to stay as high as possible so I would be able to make a 30-degree dive on the PT boat. This maneuver put me above, behind and to the right of Cdr Stockdale. This way I believe I managed to establish a 30- to 45-degree difference in-run in heading.

My roll in altitude was approximately 6,000 feet and I fired 2 Zunis at about 3,000 feet. Almost immediately after firing my Zunis I noticed flashes on the boat I was shooting at. I distinctly remember thinking, "That is too early for the Zunis to hit." After firing I started a 5 to 6 "G" pullout. During the pullout I felt a sharp jolt and immediately checked my rearview mirrors. I immediately saw that I had lost part of the leading edge droop on my left wing outer section. I then broadcast, "This is Batter-Up 102, I've been hit." I continued my climbing left turn to get back to the *Maddox* and checked my "PC" pressure gauges and my transfer fuel gauges. I was very relieved to note all instruments reading normal. . . .

R. W. HASTINGS

Appendix 2

McNamara's Use of Radio Intercepts
to maintain his claim that North Vietnamese naval units
attacked American destroyers in the Tonkin Gulf
on the night of August 4, 1964

Three and a half years after August 4, 1964, during his last days in office as Secretary of Defense, Robert Strange McNamara was called before the Committee on Foreign Relations of the United States Senate to give testimony about the events in the Tonkin Gulf on the night of August 4, 1964, and the legitimacy of their being used as justification for American reprisal air raids against North Vietnam the next day. The day-long proceedings of that February 20, 1968, are reported in *The Gulf of Tonkin, the 1964 Incidents* (U.S. Government Printing Office, 1968) and all page citations below refer to this document.

At the hearing, McNamara placed special emphasis on four intercepts of North Vietnamese military radio transmissions. The first two were the ones I knew about before I took off at 8:46 P.M. that Tuesday night of August 4th to fly to the aid of the destroyers. The first was the intercept I was told about at the dinner table after I got back from my Tuesday afternoon flight. *Maddox* and *Joy* were identified and located earlier in the day when they had been close to the shore of North Vietnam in broad daylight (see my page 11). McNamara described this simple message as "indicating there were two objectives, enemy attack vessels, located at a point at which the *Maddox* and the *Turner Joy* were located, or located within 3,000 yards of them" (p. 92). The second intercept was the one my friend told me about in the passageway just before I manned my plane for the flight Tuesday night, the one he said made the destroyers suspect they were about to be attacked (see my page 14). During McNamara's testimony on February 20, 1968, it came to light that this intercept number 2 consisted merely of some orders to two Swatow boats (which are not capable of carrying torpedoes) to "make ready for military operations" (p. 92), "with one PT boat if the PT could be made ready in time" (p. 17). It contained nothing about the nature of the operations, nor did it mention *Maddox* or *Joy*.

Nothing in either intercept number 1 or number 2 made them incompatible with the fact situation in the Gulf on August 4, 1964. But neither do they add weight to the idea that any attack took place. To me they sound like normal everyday military chitchat.

But McNamara then introduced two more intercepts, numbers 3 and 4, which were unique in two ways: (1) both described events that in no way resembled the fact situation in the vicinity of the *Maddox* or *Joy* in the Tonkin Gulf on August 4, 1964, but (2) both numbers 3 and 4 resembled what a Vietnamese observer standing on the deck of one of the PT boats which attacked the *Maddox* on Sunday, August 2, 1964, *might* have decided was the fact situation of *that* day. As the only person in the world who had a good first-hand look at both the episode of the 2nd and the episode of the 4th, I cannot avoid the conclusion that McNamara wound up using August 2nd material when analyzing events of the 4th. I know this sounds like a simple and tragic way to commit a nation to war, but that's the way I read it. Recorded replays of action reports of the August 2nd fracas, or after-action summaries of that actual PT boat-destroyer confrontation transmitted later, got into the August 4th file in the Pentagon. Now for more explanation.

McNamara said the third intercept was received "twelve minutes after our ships reported that they were being attacked" (p. 92). Since he said that he received a flash report of this attack "about 11 A.M." in Washington (p. 10) [11:00 A.M. Washington time was 10:00 P.M. on my cockpit clock in the Gulf that night], McNamara would have had it being transmitted by the North Vietnamese out there right in the middle of my hour-and-a-half stay over the destroyers. Its text "reported an enemy aircraft falling and enemy vessel wounded" (p. 92). Nobody was shooting at our destroyers or our airplanes that night. No aircraft "fell" and no ships were hit.

His fourth intercept reportedly came into Washington right after the "battle." McNamara said it reported " . . . that they had shot down two planes and sacrificed two ships" (p. 92). In addition he said that that night Washington received the name, squadron number, and boat number of the commanding officer of the PT attacking group (pp. 18, 75).

First off, McNamara himself admitted that a Vietnamese naval officer captured in 1967 had given the *same* name, squadron number and boat number as above as the commanding officer of the PT attack group that carried out the *Maddox* raid on August 2, 1964 (p. 75). That's a strong clue right there that the Pentagon was reading August 2nd material to analyze events of the 4th. Moreover, one of the senior subordinates of this officer on that raid against *Maddox* of the 2nd (and who, incidentally, was taken prisoner by Americans after his boat was sunk in 1966 by the plane of U.S. Navy Lieutenant [jg] George Coker, who wound up as one of my cohorts in a Hanoi prison later) testified as a willing American collaborator on many subjects and yet said he had never heard of a North Vietnamese PT boat attack on the night of August 4th, and that he was positive no North Vietnamese PT boats could have been involved in such an operation and he not know it (pp. 18, 74).

With regard to the content of McNamara's intercept number 3 reporting an enemy aircraft falling and an enemy vessel wounded, and number 4 reporting that the Vietnamese had shot down two planes and sacrificed two ships, one has only to study my Appendix 1 (above) to sense their connection with the events of August 2nd. As the last American to leave the scene of action on the 2nd, it was clear to me that the Vietnamese had sacrificed one boat for sure, with a 50-50 chance of each of the other two sinking before they reached port. And the *Maddox* was wounded (however slightly) that day.

How about the claims of damage to our airplanes—one reported "falling" in the first message, and finally two lost altogether? Here is the way the North Vietnamese press described my flight's August 2nd action (copied from *Daily Report*, Thursday, 13 August 1964, Foreign Radio Broadcast, FBIS (CIA), North Vietnam, p. jjj 7.):

> Five jet aircraft from a U.S. aircraft carrier rushed to the spot to give aid . . . The U.S. aircraft swiftly attacked our boats from all directions. Our combatants closely observed the paths of the enemy, maneuvering the boats to avoid the enemy, and fired back violently.
>
> The first jet aircraft was hit. It tried to climb, but it was too late. The U.S. jet burst into flames in the skies. Then the second U.S. jet was hit. It hurriedly fled, leaving behind a stream of black smoke. When the third jet aircraft was hit, the two others were panic-stricken, fired innumerable bullets into the sea (several words indistinct) and finally flew away.

On pages 7 and 8 of my text and in Appendix 1 are descriptions of my four jets coming in fast, immediately rolling in on firing runs on the boats, seeing their guns firing back, Hastings' plane pulling off as though hit, mine duplicating his actions and paralleling his track as we stayed close to the water, spewing black smoke, disappearing into the peculiar east-west "cloud" on our way to the *Maddox* which was by then at least ten miles distant. To the Vietnamese on the PT boat deck, we "fled, leaving behind a stream of black smoke." Within three minutes, I had deposited Hastings over the receding *Maddox*, a ship probably out of sight of the Vietnamese by then, and sped back into the fray as the "fifth" plane.

At least a linkage between what happened on August 2nd and what the intercepts said happened is not infeasible. But to try to establish a connection between what the intercepts said and real life happenings on the night of August 4, 1964, is ridiculous. And I find it difficult to believe that McNamara didn't know that.

Appendix 3

The Fate of Critical Prisoner-Gathered Intelligence

By the time I and my fellow prisoners were returned to Hoa Lo Prison on the night of January 26, 1967, my first two coded letters had completed their processing in the Washington chemical labs and their messages had been read. But Uncle Sam failed to do his part for two more years and four months, during which time torture was rampant and Americans were killed in the North Vietnam camps. It was Averell Harriman who insisted on keeping the torture evidence under wraps in the interest of furthering his "delicate" negotiations on the prisoners' behalf, all of which ultimately came to nothing. Even after the Johnson administration was out of office, Harriman tried to prevail upon the new secretary of defense, Melvin Laird, to continue the "keep quiet" policy. On May 19, 1969, Laird, convinced of the stupidity of keeping quiet about the mistreatment of American POWs, lifted the wraps Harriman had imposed. American headlines then delivered the message, and within six months a politically sensitive North Vietnam had made a scapegoat of their overall prison commissar, Major Bui (the Cat), and relieved him of command. Five months after that he was permanently sent packing, away from all prison camps. Soon the prisons of North Vietnam were operating more or less in accordance with the dictates of international law.

Appendix 4

International Press Coverage of Stockdale's Appearance in Downtown Hanoi

On July 7, 1967, Hanoi radio broadcast a description of my appearance downtown on that night in late June 1967. It was composed by an eyewitness, Polish correspondent Wojciech Zukrowski, and was entitled "Hanoi at Night." (This was a rebroadcast of a Warsaw radio broadcast of July 2.) The following transcript was taken from the FBIS *Daily Report*, 7 July 1967, North Vietnam, p. jjj 6.

> Sultry darkness stared at us through open windows. We sat quietly waiting for soldiers to bring in one by one American pilots who had been shot down. Indirectly I was to put questions to them which were agreed on in advance with a Vietnamese officer who was to translate them from French into English. Although I know English, the Vietnamese did not want me to address the prisoners directly. They wanted to avoid an irritable tension which might make the prisoners withdraw behind a barrier of offended silence. Our television crew was allowed to shoot the first few minutes of the talk. The spotlight was irritating, hot and attracted big moths, which kept brushing noisily against the whitewashed walls of the room.
>
> A small covered table, a teapot, a mug, and a plate of biscuits created the illusion that our talks would be almost a social conversation. It is true that the prisoners did not know whom they were going to meet, but they knew the questions and eagerly agreed to answer them. I knew what they hoped for: they had an opportunity, through our publications, of informing their families, their colleagues, and the world that, although their planes had been shot down and burned in a ricefield, they were safe and alive; alive— the only thing that mattered to them.
>
> Among the trees I saw a lantern. I heard the bells of cyclists and the prolonged and impatient clamor of truck horns demanding free passage. A stale and damp stench came in through the windows. I wiped my sweaty hands and fanned myself with my notebook. A drop of sweat trickled behind my ear.
>
> They are here, the officer sitting beside me whispered. I saw the dark rings under his eyes and his haggard face. Bring them in one by one, he gave the order to the sentry.

The first prisoner was a strapping fellow dressed in loose pajamas. In comparison his guard looked like a boy playing soldier. The prisoner's features were full of rancor and irascible obstinacy. He looked like a black character from American movies and, indeed, tried to pass for one. James Bond . . . For us he acted like a hero from the adventure movie serials. He knit his eyebrows and stuck out his chin. It was a pose, nothing but a pose, because his eyes darted to and fro, trying to guess what awaited him.

James Stockdale, born 23 December 1923 in Illinois, flew the A4E aircraft from the American fleet. . . . USS *Oriskany* was his ship. Has four children. Like his father, the eldest son is James.

Take him away, an order rang out.

The second American was a big, big child with chubby . . .

Appendix 5

The Fate of Escapees

Atterberry–Dramesi

In 1968, USAF Captains Ed Atterberry and John Dramesi had planned an escape from a cell they shared with seven other prisoners in an area of the Zoo opened after I left it. Americans came to know it as the Zoo Annex. The two officers' preparations were elaborate. They were going to climb up into an attic in their cell on a dark, rainy night and get out on the roof by removing, and then replacing, the red roof tiles. They would take things with them that made them look like Vietnamese peasants in case they were seen by casual passersby in that very densely populated part of southwest Hanoi and environs.

They made camouflage nets from stolen blankets, complete with grass clumps (which they got from rice straw collected from old brooms) affixed to them. They made food bags and stashed such high-energy items as raw sugar to take along. They acquired some iodine pills for water purification. They also found out that these pills could be ground up and mixed with red brick dust to make a skin-coloring cream that matched the shade of most Vietnamese faces. They improvised hunting knives; surgical masks of the sort peasants wore on the street to prevent the spread of disease; black peasant-type clothes; straw conical hats (made from the rice-straw mats we used as "mattresses"); and even a long bamboo carrying pole and two big bread baskets of the sort one saw everywhere in Vietnamese cities and towns. The two men got into physical shape by running in tight circles, a mile and a half each day in their cell.

Dramesi and Atterberry had hoped to go earlier, but were delayed. Finally, when one of their sought-after dark rainy nights occurred on Saturday, May 10, 1969, they got all their gear together and went up through the roof. Their disguises worked well and saved them in many close calls with unexpected confrontations, both in getting down from the roof and across the prison yard, and later. As they suspected, the wires atop the wall were electrified. They shorted them together, blew the fuses, and got away. Feeling that search parties were forming in the suburbs, they were trying to work their way through the open countryside. Before daylight they hid in a thicket in a churchyard.

After sunrise they were discovered when, as an afterthought, after his party had conducted a futile search of the churchyard, a young soldier decided to crawl into their thicket.

They were taken back to the Zoo, separated into two different locations, whipped unmercifully, manacled, and given the ropes until late afternoon on May 15. As I was led over to Cat's quiz room that afternoon, the Vietnamese from the Zoo were putting Dramesi into room 18 and Atterberry into room 5, which I had just left. Bug interrogated Dramesi and seemed to want organizational information—e.g., "Who ordered you to escape?" Dramesi was worked over heavily and cried out, and he could hear Atterberry over in cell 5 doing the same. Said Dramesi later in his book *Code of Honor* (New York: Norton, 1975):

> On the night of the eighteenth of May, I could hear them beating Ed. Suddenly the hush of death seemed to fall over the whole prison. I could not hear any noise anywhere. I held my breath, afraid I would miss a sound. I leaned toward the door, and I heard them patting Ed's face and talking to him in low voices as though they were trying to revive him. They knocked him out, I thought.

That was the last anybody ever heard of Atterberry until his body was returned to the United States after we were released.

Dramesi was brutalized for a long period and kept in room 18 until I was brought back there for torture for the note they found in my possession in the Mint in late summer 1969.

At the time the Dramesi–Atterberry escape took place, the United States had been in a state of total bombing cessation throughout all of North Vietnam for over six months.

Coker–McKnight

Contrast the above Vietnamese reaction to that after the Coker–McKnight escape of nearly two years before.

USAF Captain George McKnight and Navy Lieutenant junior grade George Coker were removed from Las Vegas to an improvised prison in the north part of Hanoi we Americans called "Dirty Bird Annex" on September 14, 1967, as part of the "BACK US" purge of that fall. They were kept there in handcuffs. After about two weeks, they were assigned solitary cells, two doors apart. They learned how to pick their handcuffs and cautiously spent time without them being latched. McKnight had had an opportunity to see much of the area around their prison, and told Coker they were just over a rise from the Red River. Out of their handcuffs, they devised a method of jimmying the locks of their rickety cells and set about planning an escape on an appropriate night.

Their preparations were not as elaborate as those of Dramesi and Atterberry. They just decided to fill up on water before they left, make it to the river, swim down it by night, and bury themselves in its muddy bank by day.

They figured on a two-knot current and, both being good swimmers and having a knowledge of the local geography, thought they would be at the river's mouth after three or four nights of swimming. There they would overpower the crew of a sailboat and head for the U.S. Navy's Seventh Fleet. All in all, they figured on an eight-day trip to the navy ships. They would drink polluted river water as necessary and live off the land for food, and figured they wouldn't get really sick till they got where they were going.

On October 12, 1967, they put dummies in their beds and got out. They had some near-misses—almost being sighted by the guards as they crawled over a wall—then made for the river in the late hours of the night. They raced through Hanoi, lurking in shadows in between sprints, got to the river's edge, stripped down to their underpants, and buried their pajamas. Each tied a wrist to an extended piece of tied-together pajama drawstrings they had stolen from a prison clothesline; then they went into the water, right near the Paul Daumer Bridge.

The current was more like five knots, and they silently swam downstream, through the riverboat traffic, throughout the night. Just before dawn, they made for shore. They had trouble finding a satisfactory place to bury themselves, and had to settle for a crevice halfway up the bank, into which they further dug themselves. They were able to whisper in seclusion for a couple of hours, and felt all was going okay until about 9:00 A.M., when an old woman and a younger man who were fishing along the bank appeared overhead and looked down at them in bewilderment. Soon they were surrounded and recaptured. They were fifteen miles downriver from the Paul Daumer Bridge.

On that morning of October 13, 1967, they were taken back to Hoa Lo Prison, separated, and each put in jumbo irons in New Guy Village, arms tied behind them, and blindfolded. Their line of response to questioning (agreed upon before) was "we were both badly tortured in August as a part of the Las Vegas purge, so what had we to lose by trying to break away?" On the second day, their blindfolds were taken off and they got regular meals. After four or five days of just jumbo irons, they were taken back to Dirty Bird Annex and paraded before the guards there. Then they were brought back and put in the Mint in irons until the night of October 25, when we all went to Alcatraz. They got no worse treatment at Alcatraz than anybody else there.

At the time of their escape, we Americans were bombing throughout North Vietnam, Hanoi included.

Appendix 6

North Vietnam Casualties During the B-52 Raids
of December 1972

The Vietnamese total military and civilian casualty figure over the ten-day bombing period—a figure that for twelve years they have insisted is correct—was 1,318 killed. (That was the lowest figure to come from any significant bombing of an industrial complex in half a century; there were numerous cases of 50,000 and 60,000 killed in raids in a single night in World War II.) The sad thing about watching all this from the ground in downtown Hanoi was the realization that such a collapse of Vietnamese will could have been brought about in a like manner in any ten-day period in the previous seven years and saved the lives of thousands, including most of those 58,012 Americans who died in Vietnam.

Notes

Chapter 1: Three Days in August

1.   Of the four of us, only Mohrhardt fought through that war unscathed. Southwick and I spent most of it in a North Vietnamese prison camp; and Hastings, barely twenty-four years old at the time of this flight, died two years later aboard the hospital ship USS *Repose* in these waters after having been struck by fragments of a crashing Crusader that hit a carrier's ramp on landing. Hastings had been the landing-signal officer, standing on the flight deck and giving lineup signals to the landing pilot, a job I had recommended him for.

2.   Years later when I came home from prison, I found that my wife, Sybil, had collected several books that had been written about this night. Stuck between the pages of one that had been written a couple of years before I was released was a letter from its author, Eugene Windchy:

> Dear Mrs. Stockdale . . . I just saw your letter in *Time* magazine of December 27, 1971. You have my deepest sympathy on the extended imprisonment of your husband. . . . You might have noticed that a number of references to your husband appear in my recently published book, *Tonkin Gulf*. I did not use his name, however, because the book might go to North Vietnam, and I supposed that the reaction there would not improve his circumstances.

Two Eugene G. Windchy references (*Tonkin Gulf* [New York: Doubleday, 1971]) to the F-8 during this hour:

> . . . Captain Barnhart [commanding officer of the USS *Joy*] saw rockets or tracers leave the plane. Yelling for everybody to hit the deck, Barnhart grabbed the man next to him and pulled him down. Fortunately, nothing hit the destroyer. Possibly the jet was diving on a knuckle in the wake. (p. 205)
>
> The airmen, unable to find good targets, were really baffled. As they risked their lives darting around "on the deck," the pilots gritted their

teeth, fuming at the weather, darkness, and air control. Commander Jackson [executive officer of the USS *Maddox*], who had been an air show parachutist in his 'teens, marveled at how the F-8 ... came down at a tremendous speed, just a hundred feet above the water. He was either insane or one of the best pilots I ever saw. (p. 206)

3.   The *Maddox* sent flash precedence messages in plain language to save time. See Samuel E. Halpern, M.D. [medical officer of the *Maddox*], *West Pac '64* (Boston: Branden Press, 1975), p. 184.

4.   Immediately after the flight of the night of August 4, 1964, while I was still in the ready room, I was assured that my report of no boats would be put on the wire immediately. This message went out. See Anthony Austin, *The President's War* (New York: Lippincott, 1971), p. 305. See also Windchy, *Tonkin Gulf*, p. 206.

Chapter 5: Shootdown

1.   The city we were near was Thanh Hoa, where the Dragon's Jaw Bridge crossed the river. This was the morning of September 10. In November my wife, Sybil, got a phone call at our home in Coronado, California, from a personal friend in the Navy Department in Washington with the first hint that I might be alive. A short item had just appeared in the Soviet newspaper *Pravda*. It was translated as saying that their reporter had seen a "tall blond American Air Force Captain sitting on a bench outside a hospital near Thanh Hoa" and that his name was reported to be "James B. Stakdael." In reality I was five feet, nine inches tall and my hair was gray. I don't recall talking to anybody or seeing any non-Vietnamese, but I was rather groggy.

Chapter 7: Learning the Ropes

1.   Eccles. 9:11.

Chapter 9: Strength in Unity

1.   John Colvin was consul general at the British Mission at Hanoi during 1966 and 1967. He had grown very skeptical of the prospects of America's breaking the will of the North Vietnamese by tactical bombing through 1966 and up until midsummer 1967. He has written of the collapse of North Vietnam in late August as the summer 1967 sustained tactical bombing campaign turned the tide, and of the almost immediate shutdown of our successful offensive in late September by timid defense intellectuals who couldn't bear the thought of victory. *The Washington Quarterly*, Spring 1981:

And every morning since I reached Hanoi [in 1966], the streets of the quarter had been lined with war materiel brought in overnight from China across the Paul Daumer Bridge, amphibious vehicles, artillery, ar-

mored fighting vehicles, Sergeant surface-to-air missiles on flatbeds, sau-
cily parked even outside the British and Canadian missions. By the time
that I returned from London in June [1967], their numbers had somewhat
decreased. By August and September [1967] there were none at all, and
early-morning constitutionals in other districts and to the main railway
station itself showed that the explanation did not lie in diversification
elsewhere. (pp. 150–51)

The D.R.V. in late September [1967], when I left that unhappy
country for England, was no longer capable of maintaining itself as an
economic unit nor of mounting aggressive war against its neighbor. . . .
But although some spasmodic bombing in the northeast quadrant took
place after September, it was on a greatly reduced scale and frequently
interrupted by long periods of inactivity during "peace initiatives," all
illusory if not contrived, and anyway occasions when the campaign should
have maintained, even increased, momentum. Above all, that factor—the
persistence of the campaign—which had sapped North Vietnamese en-
durance was discarded. . . . Victory—by September 1967 in American
hands—was not so much thrown away as shunned with prim, averted
eyes. . . . A war directed by men who believed that it should not be
waged at all was not one likely to be prosecuted with vigor nor one in
which the military command—whom the "intellectuals" in their arro-
gance despised anyway—would be permitted military decision. (p. 153)

2.   Joseph Conrad, *Lord Jim* (New York: Doubleday, 1899), p. 88.

Chapter 11: Fighting Hard

1.   I'll always believe that Sybil saved my life in that September 1969 incident when the Vietnamese discovered me in a pool of blood on the floor of
room 18. She was by then, unknown to me, a national figure in America and
well known to the North Vietnamese diplomatic corps as the organizer and
chairman of the National League of Families of American Prisoners and Missing in Southeast Asia. (See page 322 above.) It was that League which was
positioning itself between American public opinion and the well-planned
North Vietnamese propaganda program. My picture had been widely publicized in the world press, and for me, the husband of the founder of the League,
to suddenly die in Hanoi would have presented North Vietnam with a major
public relations problem.

Chapter 13: Alcatraz Gang

1.   Ron Storz's remains were sent back to America after we returned. He
had died in that winter of 1970.

Chapter 15: Release

1.   Eccles. 9:12.

Index